USER INTERFACE DESIGN
A STRUCTURED APPROACH

LANGUAGES AND INFORMATION SYSTEMS*

Series Editor: Shi-Kuo Chang
University of Pittsburgh
Pittsburgh, Pennsylvania
and Knowledge Systems Institute
Skokie, Illinois

*Series was formerly entitled:
MANAGEMENT AND INFORMATION SYSTEMS

HUMAN–MACHINE INTERACTIVE SYSTEMS
Edited by Allen Klinger

LANGUAGES FOR AUTOMATION
Edited by Shi-Kuo Chang

MANAGEMENT AND OFFICE INFORMATION SYSTEMS
Edited by Shi-Kuo Chang

USER INTERFACE DESIGN: A Structured Approach
Siegfried Treu

USER INTERFACE EVALUATION: A Structured Approach
Siegfried Treu

VISUAL LANGUAGES
Edited by Shi-Kuo Chang, Tadao Ichikawa, and Panos A. Ligomenides

VISUAL LANGUAGES AND APPLICATIONS
Edited by Tadao Ichikawa, Erland Jungert, and Robert R. Korfhage

VISUAL LANGUAGES AND VISUAL PROGRAMMING
Edited by Shi-Kuo Chang

USER INTERFACE DESIGN
A STRUCTURED APPROACH

Siegfried Treu

University of Pittsburgh
Pittsburgh, Pennsylvania

SPRINGER SCIENCE+BUSINESS MEDIA, LLC

Library of Congress Cataloging-in-Publication Data

Treu, Siegfried.
    User interface design : a structured approach / Siegfried Treu.
        p.   cm. -- (Languages and information systems)
    Includes bibliographical references and index.
    ISBN 0-306-44681-2
    1. User interfaces (Computer systems).   I. Title.   II. Series.
QA76.9.U83T74   1994
005.4'2--dc20   94-19149
                                                                CIP

PUBLISHER CREDITS

A number of figures and tables have been reprinted herein, mostly in revised form, from published papers. In such cases, written permission from the publishers is acknowledged in the corresponding figure captions and table footnotes. In addition, various portions of text from published papers have been extracted and usually updated and revised extensively. Publisher permission for such usage is more conveniently summarized at this point. Kind permission was granted by each of the following:

- *Academic Press Ltd.*, London, UK: for selections of text from each of: Tyler and Treu (1989), used in Chapter 13; Bournique and Treu (1985), used in Chapter 7
- *Butterworth-Heineman Ltd.*, Oxford, UK: for selections of text from Treu *et al.* (1991), used in Chapters 10 and 11
- *Pergamon Press Ltd.*, Oxford, UK: for selections of text from Treu *et al.* (1989), used in Chapter 12
- *ACM Press*, New York: for selections of text from each of: Treu *et al.* (1990), used in Chapter 10; Tyler and Treu (1986), used in Chapter 13
- *North-Holland Elsevier Science Publishers B. V.*, Amsterdam, The Netherlands: for selections of text from Sanderson and Treu (1993), used in Chapter 13

ISBN 978-1-4613-6031-5   ISBN 978-1-4615-2429-8 (eBook)
DOI 10.1007/978-1-4615-2429-8
©*1994 Springer Science+Business Media New York*
Originally published by Plenum Press,New York in 1994
Softcover reprint of the hardcover 1st edition 1994

To Erika and our family:

Kevin and Julie, with

Zachary and Emily;

Ramona and Steven;

Marvin and Kristine;

Steven;

and Lexie

PREFACE

Some researchers and developers may consider it a craft (e.g., Wroblewski, 1991); others may advocate an eclectic approach to its design (e.g., Dayton, 1991); most probably agree that it cannot or should not only be based on science and engineering (e.g., Karat, 1991). Nevertheless, the ever-increasing and diversified uses of computers by different people in our society should compel us to address the design of human–computer interfaces or of human–computer interaction (HCI) in a deliberately *systematic* manner. We need to develop methodology that is analogous to what exists in various engineering fields. That does not mean that the result will be based purely on science and engineering. Indeed, the methodology itself should enable the introjection of craftsmanship and of various alternative design techniques at appropriate stages of the decision.

Because HCI is inherently dependent on multiple disciplines and also multiple specialties in computer science, any methodology for its design and evaluation must be multifaceted accordingly. This means that it must be *comprehensive*, taking all major facets and sources into account. This book is an attempt to present a comprehensive, methodological framework. However, comprehensiveness here does not imply that all relevant materials are included. That is simply not feasible. A book on HCI, with the intended scope, obviously cannot cover all relevant techniques from computer graphics, computer interaction languages, and other specialties in computer science; nor can it detail the wealth of pertinent knowledge available in psychology and cognitive science. But, such material can be presented selectively within an organized framework, and suitable references to important resources (publications) can be given.

The left half of Fig. P1 (see page xiv) depicts the organization of this four-part book. The right half identifies the topical contents of the companion book on interface *evaluation* (Treu, 1994). Because of limits in book length, the combination of all materials on design *and* evaluation in one volume was not feasible. Instead, it was determined that dichotomizing the study of HCI into two separate but very much interrelated resources was the way to go. As one consequence of this decision, the reader will find a number of cross-references between the two books.

Part I of this book contains two introductory chapters. Included is a high-level model of the human–computer relationship, as it has evolved over the years. Part II develops the major, preparatory topics for HCI design. Its six chapters are stratified according to the following topics:

- Types of users and what they need, want, can or cannot do (Chapter 3)
- User-oriented analysis of computer applications and tasks (Chapter 4)
- The computer capabilities that affect the user in HCI (Chapter 5)
- Interaction techniques and styles, their bases and compositions (Chapter 6)
- Models and methods for representing all of the above (Chapter 7)
- Special models and tools to support HCI design (Chapter 8)

The material in Part II is considered to be prerequisite to HCI design. That is, the knowledge that it characterizes is essential to being able to utilize fully the methodologies for design in Part III. Much of the material is also important to interface evaluation (Treu, 1994). Minimally, a good designer and/or evaluator must be sensitized to the knowledge areas described and have access to corresponding expertise.

The three chapters of Part III first formalize the definitions of design terms, in Chapter 9, followed by their direct application in the development of design methods in Chapter 10. The latter provides a step-by-step prescription on how to conduct design studies and leads to a special focus on methods for designing interface objects (Chapter 11).

The last part of the book gives two examples of special-purpose designs. In each case, one selected design principle takes a very prominent, all-encompassing role. Chapter 12 deals with those design features that promote or reinforce a network-oriented perspective for the user. Finally, Chapter 13 describes models and techniques for rendering the interface adaptive to its users, with the help of expert systems from artificial intelligence.

So, how can this book (and also the companion book) be characterized? Quite naturally, it (they) reflect(s) the priorities, preferences, and biases that I developed over nearly a quarter century of research and teaching. My graduate-level courses have been in the areas of "Interactive Computer Graphics," "Computer Networks," "Modeling and Simulation," and "Interface Design and Evaluation." As a result of these experiences, together with the products of my research in HCI, the following are important elements:

1. *Definitions*: There are many of these, perhaps more than the reader will deem necessary. But they were chosen with the objective of clarifying relevant terminology and with the hope of being better able to articulate and communicate the methodology.

2. *Models*: There are lots of these as well, ranging from models of any objects included in the interface system, at whatever level of representation, to models of specific methods and processes representing (all or parts of) the overall methodology.

3. *Categorizations and taxonomies*: Whenever the HCI designer is faced with options and, hence, choices, with regard to the factors, features, principles, methods, etc., to be identified and applied, efforts are made to categorize, enumerate, and describe them. The results may not be exhaustive—any particular option may require more details, perhaps available in the literature cited—but the enumerated types or groups should at least provide a reasonably complete picture of the possibilities that are open.

4. *Structures*: Consistent with the book's title, a large variety of structural patterns and paradigms are intertwined in the material presented. In some places they are implicit; in others they are explicitly defined and justified. Indeed, the entire book exhibits an inherent structure, as evidenced by Fig. P1.

5. *Methods and techniques*: These encompass all of the above, and result in composite *methodologies*, with the objectives of providing well-organized overviews of the prerequisite knowledge areas and of presenting clearly defined steps for utilizing them in creating HCI designs. The coverage is in terms of *abstract specifications* of what is required and what is to be done, *not* in terms of the details for *practical implementation* of those specifications. This distinction is analogous to teaching abstract data structures (e.g., stacks, queues, trees) and abstract software designs (e.g., algorithms) as distinct from the details of their programmed implementations.

6. *References to the literature*: There are many of these, to supplement the necessarily limited size and coverage of this book, in its current form, and to enable the reader to pursue selected topics in greater depth.

7. *Conceptual framework*: All of the above are constituents of a framework to be used for teaching HCI. The development of such a framework was identified as one of the visions and themes resulting from a recent workshop on the topic (Gasen and Aiken, 1993). Another workshop theme was an emphasis on "multidisciplinary integration." This book's framework is definitely intended to reflect such integration.

I have attempted to create the above-profiled framework in a matter-of-fact manner. That is, after introducing the subject and its historical problems, in Part I, an interdisciplinary but pragmatic approach is simply adopted and taken for granted. Using that perspective, the book is about ways for achieving in practice what has been discussed and debated, in theory, for years. There is no more need to question the importance of HCI, or of creating HCI designs that will be beneficial to humans.

Accordingly, the book is *not* about editorializing and philosophizing on the desirability and consequences of human interaction with computers. Computers are here to stay. Yet they can cause stress, as discussed in the companion book; we want to minimize such stress. Yes, the human and the computer entities are modeled as a unified system. But that model is to serve the type of methodology to be developed; no mythical or mystical union of the two entities is to be attributed to their combination. Nor is it to detract in any way from the status of the human being and from what it means to be and remain human in the face of computer technology. Essays on such topics are intriguing (e.g., Sheehan and Sosna, 1991). The nature of human existence and the fact that technology may cause us to design new "ways of being" (e.g., Winograd and Flores, 1986) are certainly important considerations. But these are not addressed in this book. Yet the methodology developed is consistently oriented to giving the benefits— including the ability to control (or override)—to the human side of the HCI partnership.

This book is also *not* an implementation document as such. It presents the major elements that must be understood and used in making HCI design decisions and the corresponding specifications of required design features. However, once those decisions are made and the requirements are specified, the actual implementation of the interface software on a target hardware platform is left up to skilled developers and programmers. Some recommendations are made on effective tools and high-level software architecture, but the choice of programming language, choice of widget support, etc., are not in the scope of this book.

While undoubtedly conveying my preferences on desired design features, especially when describing several illustrative prototype interfaces, this book is also *not* intended to present "the best and only" interface designs. Indeed, that would be contrary to the major point of this book: comprehensive methodology, if carefully and systematically employed, should enable the designer to arrive at what is good (if not the best) design under his/her particular circumstances. Thus, emphasis is on design *process* (how to achieve a design that is good for you), not on proving or proclaiming that certain (existing) design *products* are just the right thing for you.

Further, the book is *not* oriented to a show-and-tell approach. I deliberately avoided illustrations and other uses of any particular computer manufacturer's or software supplier's interface. Except in several descriptions of prototype interface case studies, I even refrained from naming and citing any computer and software products. In years past, we often resorted to using someone else's product as the currently best available. The objective then became simply to acquire or emulate it. But the HCI field is progressing significantly. The time seems right for it to move beyond the mode of copying and enhancing already existing interfaces. At least for teaching purposes, we should be able to abstract and extract from the experiences of successful design efforts and incorporate the results in methodology that is *independent of particular, named products.* The reader may well ask: why reinvent the wheel? That's not the point here. A knowledgeable HCI designer and evaluator should know about everything that goes into the design and evaluation, i.e., how to construct the wheel. And a student aspiring to become knowledgeable should learn these things. We have an increasingly diverse and rich assortment of hardware and software devices and tools now available. At the same time, there are numerous computer applications out there that are awaiting better interface solutions. Much room for ingenuity and creativity remains. It would be sad indeed if we felt that the ultimate interface designs have already been achieved. In looking to the future, the HCI designer should *ideally* be able to employ a methodology toward achieving a successful, original design, for whatever new and novel application and by targeting whatever hardware platform and software environment is found to be most appropriate.

Consistent with that view, the book is primarily oriented to teaching and guiding its reader in the creation of new and original interface designs, using structured and comprehensive methodology for doing so. This does *not* mean that a partial design (in cases of certain parameters already being fixed) is not possible; it also does not mean that a design cannot be based on specific imported modules (e.g., for windowing) if deemed most appropriate. It does mean, however, that the book is basically not oriented to "do-it-like-so-and-so-did" approaches in the design stage.

Lastly, what are the intended purposes in the utilization of this book? It can be used either as a reference or as a text. For reference purposes, its modular organization, subject index, and numerous literature citations should be helpful. Its use as a text is implied by the exercises located at the end of each chapter. In addition, students should also find the bibliography and subject index useful. The exercises are designed to cause the student (1) to read selected publications listed in the bibliography, (2) to be critical of both the text and the cited literature, and (3) to exhibit a substantial amount of individual judgment and insight.

As a text, the book is intended to serve either undergraduate or graduate students. A one-semester, graduate-level HCI course can cover all, or nearly all, of the text. But that depends on how extensive the laboratory component might be, e.g., requiring students to design, implement, and possibly evaluate some substantial interface objects and features. Graduate-level homework and project assignments can include the pursuit of selected topics, in depth, via readings in the cited literature. An undergraduate version of a one-semester HCI course can concentrate mainly on Parts I through III. Some chapters (e.g., Chapter 6) can be elaborated extensively, both for graduate- and undergraduate-level purposes, subject to the preferences and backgrounds of professor and students.

SIEGFRIED TREU

Pittsburgh, Pennsylvania

ACKNOWLEDGMENTS

Special appreciation is due to the (former) graduate students in computer science at the University of Pittsburgh whose work is described and cited at various places in this book. They are: Pete Sanderson, Paul Mullins, Sherman Tyler, Rick Bournique, Roman Rozin, Ravi Sharma, and Joel Adams. Particularly significant contributions were made by Pete, Paul, Sherman, and Rick. The prototype interface systems that they developed and utilized as platforms for completing their Ph.D. dissertations are portrayed individually in later chapters. It was a genuine privilege and pleasure for me to work with such an outstanding group of graduate students.

Also, the research support provided since the mid-1980s by the National Science Foundation (NSF Grant DCR-850562) and by the NCR Corporation, Cambridge, Ohio, is gratefully acknowledged. Much of the resulting research, including the development of several prototype interfaces (SAUCI, NUIS, N-CHIME), is reflected in the coverage of this book.

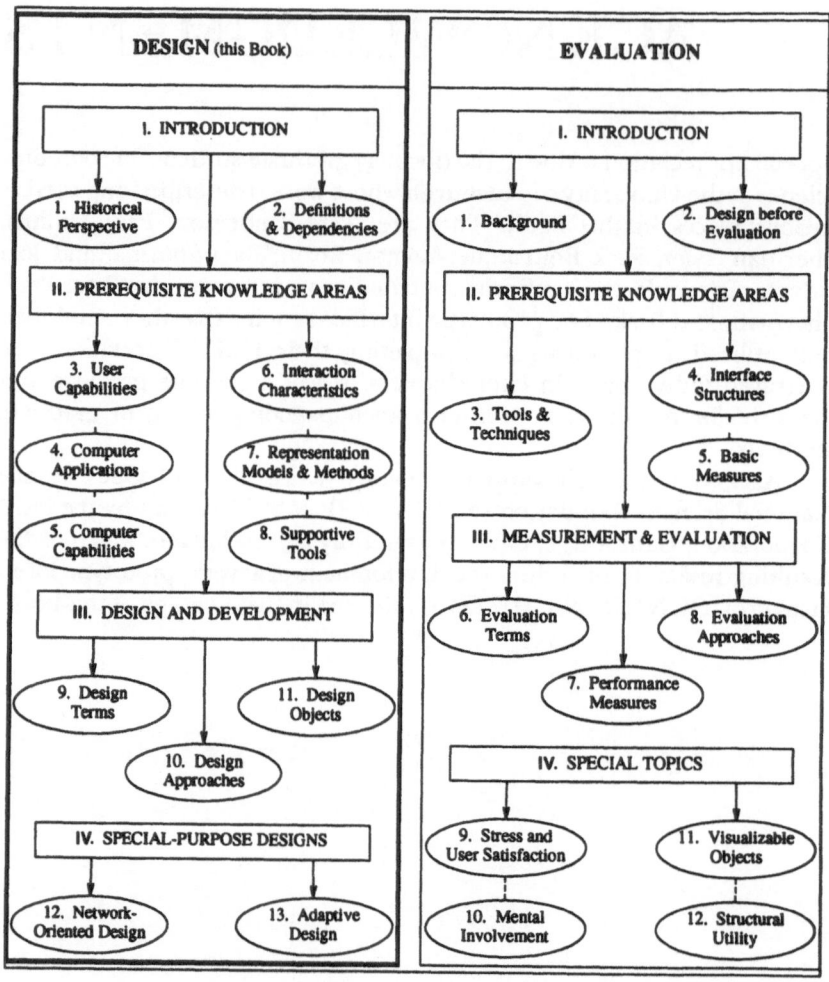

FIGURE P1. Organizations of Design and Evaluation books.

CONTENTS

PART IV
SPECIAL-PURPOSE DESIGNS

INTRODUCTION

This two-chapter part provides background for the study of human–computer interface (HCI) design and evaluation. A brief historical perspective, in Chapter 1, focuses on selected individual and organizational contributors to the area. The HCI literature is also characterized. Chapter 2 presents and traces a high-level, binary model of the human–computer relationship, as it has evolved. It defines the major terms relevant to HCI and identifies disciplines and specialties on which the study of HCI is dependent. That chapter also distinguishes the significant attributes of "methodology" and introduces a symbolic functional view of the design decision-making process for thematic use in subsequent chapters.

HISTORICAL PERSPECTIVE

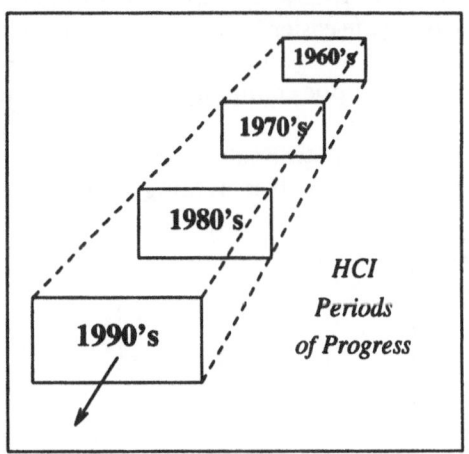

HCI Periods of Progress

1.1. Overview

To gain a better understanding of present-day human–computer interaction (HCI) and the prospects of continuing its improvement in the future, we should look at its past. Every generation is urged to "learn from history." Of course, such advice is typically motivated by wanting to know the causes of major human events, such as war and peace. Does the human adventure, over the last half century, of creating and using ever more complex computer and communication technologies for increasingly sophisticated applications also rate as a major human event? If not already today, then historians will surely consider it as such in the future. It certainly has had revolutionary impact on humankind.

The evolving human relationship with computer technology has produced amazing levels of dependence on that technology. Included are increasingly direct, or "intimate," forms of interaction with those computers. Can we learn anything from the history of that relationship? We can at least make observations about how both the human side and the technology side of the human–computer partnership influenced progress toward more effective HCI.

These observations can be portrayed by identifying several overlapping time periods, as shown in Fig. 1.1:

- *Period 1:* Technology dominated while the user was secondary. With "mainframe" computers, operated in batch mode, the design focus was primarily on how to get the most computing out of the hardware and software. Interactive use of computers was only beginning, and making life easier for the user was not a high priority. The fortunate user had access to a typewriterlike terminal but had to tolerate whatever cryptic commands and procedures were required by the technology.
- *Period 2:* Advances in technology enabled and stimulated more attention to the user. With increasing availability of time-sharing

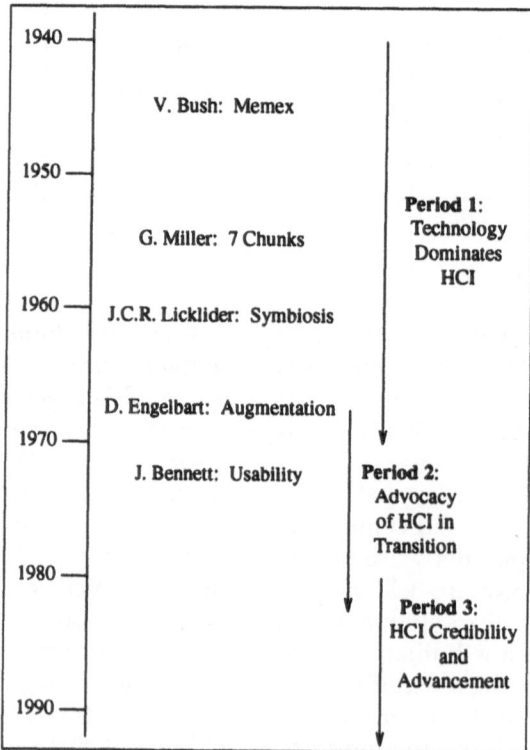

FIGURE 1.1. Historical periods in HCI.

systems, minicomputers, computer networking, and CRT terminals, the user became a natural beneficiary. That is, as more users gained more convenient access to networked resources, they became more knowledgeable and also more demanding. As a result, this period exhibited slowly growing advocacy of user-oriented design. Limited numbers of HCI researchers became increasingly vocal about the need to design computers primarily to serve the capabilities of the user, rather than to maximize computing capability (as in Period 1).

- *Period 3:* The user gained priority while technology generally assumed a support role. With microminiaturization of computer components and the packaging of user-oriented functions into personal workstations, including organized 2-D display screens (windowing systems), interactive devices (e.g., the mouse), graphics, color, etc., it became feasible to design the interface to meet the needs and wishes of individual users. The advocacy of Period 2 was finally coming to fruition. However, the complexities of determining how best to design, measure, and evaluate HCI also became very evident. Even with state-of-the-art technology available, the interdisciplinary nature of HCI still makes it extremely challenging to "engineer" the interface for effective, efficient, and synergistic use by humans.

That challenge will undoubtedly be addressed by HCI researchers throughout the 1990s and well into the 21st century. The organization and contents of this book are purposely intended to anticipate and promote advancements in HCI. But, first, it is important to give special credit to certain visionaries and pioneers (next section) and also various organizations that were significantly involved (Section 1.3).

1.2. Notable Contributors

Several individuals deserve special recognition for having contributed in important ways to the development of HCI. Such recognition is particularly important for those few who, in the early years (Period 1, Fig. 1.1), had the insight and foresight to stimulate researcher thinking in the direction of a potentially powerful partnership between the human information processor and a computer-based information processor. A good historical perspective on various early contributions to HCI has been drawn by Baecker and Buxton (1987, Chapter 2).

In any assessment of the history of the young field of HCI, differences of opinion on the list of most notable, early contributors are inevitable. Personal experiences are significant and tend to color one's views. Accordingly, my list at this point only highlights a subset of those identified by Baecker and Buxton (1987) and other sources they cite. The work of many more individuals is given credit in later sections of this book.

For my personal view of early HCI, I ask the reader for his/her indulgence. My dissertation research was completed in 1970, entitled "Supplementing Human Memory by Means of Interactive, Computer-Based Associative Storage and Retrieval." As the title implies, it was directly influenced by Vannevar Bush (1945). In that famous article about the hypothetical "memex," he recommended that we take advantage of the associative nature of the human mind and design a machine accordingly:

> With one item in its grasp, (the mind) snaps instantly to the next that is suggested by the association of thoughts, in accordance with some intricate web of trails carried by the cells of the brain.

In every attempt to design such an association-based information system to assist the human mind, however, it became very apparent that the human and the computer were not to be treated as equally qualified, limitless information processors. This fact was symbolically encapsulated by the psychologist George A. Miller (1956). His magical number "seven plus or minus 2" suggested that a limit exists on how many chunks of information can be accommodated by the "channel capacity" of the human mind (or memory):

> There seems to be some limitation built into us either by learning or by design of our nervous systems, a limit which keeps our channel capacities in this general range, . . .

with a mean of 2.6 bits of information.

Since the human mind has such constraints, HCI researchers should realize that the computer interface must be structured accordingly, that is, to present information that is not overwhelming (e.g., according to G. A. Miller) and that it must be organized in a manner conducive to being followed (e.g., according to V. Bush). In other words, the logical next step is to enable and encourage the human and the computer to become suitably interdependent. In particular, from the human's standpoint, the computer should ameliorate the human limitations. J. C. R. Licklider (1960) called this kind of cooperation "man–computer symbiosis," which is a

> living together in intimate association, or even close union, of two dissimilar organisms. . . .

The organisms, for our interest, are the human user and the computer. Licklider hoped that these two would ultimately be coupled together very tightly and that

> the resulting partnership will think as no human brain has ever thought and process data in a way not approached by the information-handling machines we know today.

Indeed, one person who seemingly adopted both Licklider's and Bush's ideas as a personal challenge was Douglas C. Engelbart (Engelbart, 1963; Engelbart and English, 1968). He led a research group toward designing and implementing a system for "augmenting human intellect." His research objective encompassed

> concern not only for the technology of providing interactive computer service, but also for changes both in ways of conceptualizing, visualizing, and organizing working material, and in procedures and methods for working individually and cooperatively.

With the help of his interactive device called a "mouse," Engelbart enabled each user to display, manipulate, and associate nodes of hierarchically structured, textual files. These files were, in turn, uniformly accessible for collaborative use by all members of the user group.

Engelbart was truly ahead of his time. He did not really start to get credit for what he accomplished until about two decades later. Not until the second half of the 1980s did professional interest groups get started in such areas as "hypertext" and "computer-supported cooperative work." Engelbart and his group had already paid substantial attention to those topics in the mid-1960s. His work was remarkable.

In addition, on a very personal note, I was privileged to get to know both Engelbart and Licklider. As a young HCI researcher in the early 1970s, I was able to visit their respective labs, at SRI and MIT, and to enjoy their "tours." Most impressive to me was the fact that both were very down-to-earth, attentive, and responsive. Unlike other persons of similar (or presumed similar) stature, neither one felt that it was beneath him to spend a lot of time with a junior person like me. Both retained that kind of commendable attitude during the later years of their careers.

Finally, from my perspective, one more notable contributor to early HCI development should be acknowledged. In January, 1971, John L. Bennett chaired what, to my knowledge, was the first really comprehensive attempt to look at issues in HCI (Walker, 1971). Among the attendees was Engelbart. As indicated in the next section, this workshop was oriented more to computer applications in information science (as represented by the professional society, ASIS) than in computer science (ACM). Hence, it did not get as much coverage in the computer science community as was warranted. But it was a very noteworthy occasion, and Bennett has continued to work very productively, although with little fanfare, to further the causes of HCI. Like Licklider (1968), he wrote one of the early review chapters on user interfaces (Bennett, 1972). Since then, he has especially pursued the objective of achieving "usability" in interactive systems (e.g., Bennett, 1986).

1.3. Organizational Involvements

The importance of HCI ultimately had to be recognized by organizations and groups of interested or affected persons in the different sectors of society. Following is an account of three of them.

1.3.1. Professional Societies

The pioneering work in HCI that was accomplished prior to 1970 resulted mostly from individual efforts by a small number of persons. In the early 1970s, that number of individuals started to grow somewhat. But organizational involvements in HCI studies, especially by industrial corporations and universities, remained conspicuously scarce.

Indeed, the area of HCI was not yet viewed as important or credible. Computer scientists were still totally absorbed by and enamored of computer technology itself. To them and to the computer designers and manufacturers, the user interface was, at best, of secondary concern. Furthermore, it surely did not represent an appropriate specialty area for any computer science department. It was deemed to be inadequately rigorous, excessively subjective, and too encumbered by user psychology.

At the same time, while computer scientists and their departments frowned on HCI, one might have expected greater attention from psychologists. However, collectively, they also were not yet prepared for what was to come. Interactive computer use had not yet advanced to the stage of really affecting and impressing many nontechnical people. In fact, the prospects of relating to computers psychologically seemed absurd, if not threatening. Hence, psychologists and psychology departments attended mostly to their traditional areas of study, not to how those areas might be significantly impacted by, or have impact on, computer-based information processing.

In the early to mid-1970s, some important steps were taken by several professional groups. These are identified in Fig. 1.2. First, in 1971, the previously mentioned workshop was conducted in Palo Alto, California,

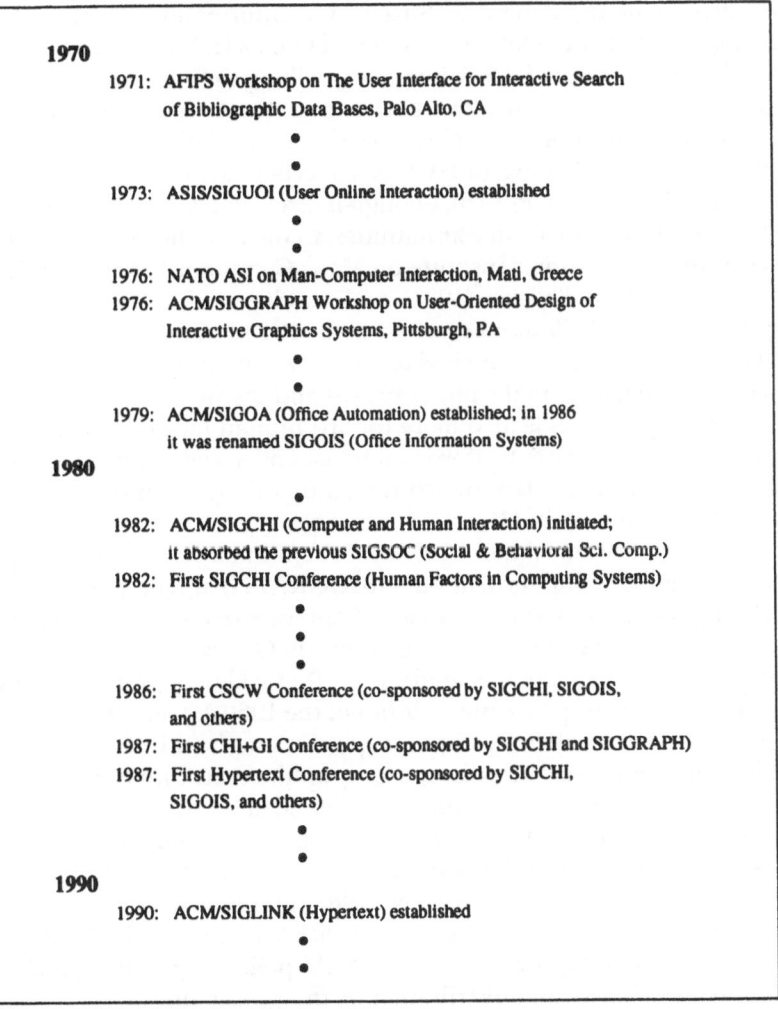

1970
    1971: AFIPS Workshop on The User Interface for Interactive Search
            of Bibliographic Data Bases, Palo Alto, CA
            •
            •

    1973: ASIS/SIGUOI (User Online Interaction) established
            •
            •

    1976: NATO ASI on Man-Computer Interaction, Mati, Greece
    1976: ACM/SIGGRAPH Workshop on User-Oriented Design of
            Interactive Graphics Systems, Pittsburgh, PA
            •
            •

    1979: ACM/SIGOA (Office Automation) established; in 1986
            it was renamed SIGOIS (Office Information Systems)
1980
            •

    1982: ACM/SIGCHI (Computer and Human Interaction) initiated;
            it absorbed the previous SIGSOC (Social & Behavioral Sci. Comp.)
    1982: First SIGCHI Conference (Human Factors in Computing Systems)
            •
            •
            •

    1986: First CSCW Conference (co-sponsored by SIGCHI, SIGOIS,
            and others)
    1987: First CHI+GI Conference (co-sponsored by SIGCHI and SIGGRAPH)
    1987: First Hypertext Conference (co-sponsored by SIGCHI,
            SIGOIS, and others)
            •
            •
1990
    1990: ACM/SIGLINK (Hypertext) established
            •
            •

FIGURE 1.2. Organizational involvements in HCI.

organized and chaired by John L. Bennett. The workshop title was "The User Interface for Interactive Search for Bibliographic Data Bases" (Walker, 1971). Although the invited participants were mostly active in information science environments, they exhibited an uncommon (at that time) appreciation for the importance of interdisciplinary collaboration.

One consequence of that workshop was the establishment in 1973 of the Special Interest Group for User Online Interaction (SIGUOI), under the auspices of the American Society for Information Science (ASIS). Among its leaders were John L. Bennett, Thomas H. Martin, and James H. Carlisle. To the credit of ASIS, it was very willing to foster this kind of new group. At the same time, the Association for Computing Machinery (ACM), the major professional organization representing computer scientists, was not yet receptive to HCI as a specialty area.

Several years later, in 1976, enough interest in HCI had evolved, both in European and American communities, to warrant the organization of a NATO Advanced Studies Institute on Man–Computer Interaction. It was directed by Brian Shackel (1981) and conducted in Mati, Greece, in September of 1976. A number of notable HCI researchers from Europe and the United States were invited to attend. A significant diversity of HCI interests was reflected in the presentations and discussions. In general, the European researchers leaned more toward human factors/ergonomic designs (e.g., physical layouts of workstations) and social implications, while American interests tended toward the study of cognition-oriented functions and capabilities in HCI.

At about the same time, in 1976, the ACM finally took a small step. Its Special Interest Group for Graphics (SIGGRAPH) agreed to sponsor the workshop on "User-Oriented Design of Interactive Graphics Systems." It was conducted in Pittsburgh, Pennsylvania, in October, 1976 (Treu, 1977). Attendees and speakers included: J. C. R. Licklider, John L. Bennett, Robert B. Miller (response time studies in the 1960s), James D. Foley (e.g., paper with Wallace, 1974; computer graphics text: with Van Dam et al., 1990), William M. Newman (computer graphics text: with Sproull, 1979), Raymond S. Nickerson (e.g., paper with Elkind and Carbonell, 1968; book on Using Computers, 1986), Thomas P. Moran (e.g., Command Language Grammar: 1981; GOMS Model: with Card et al., 1980b, 1983), Phyllis Reisner (BNF for command language: 1981), and Ronald M. Baecker (e.g., Readings in Human–Computer Interaction: with Buxton, eds., 1987). Because this workshop was "by invitation only," ACM policy regrettably precluded widespread publicity and distribution of the proceedings.

Enough serious interest in HCI by enough notable researchers, including both computer scientists and psychologists, made it increasingly likely that other HCI-oriented and ACM-based professional groups would be formed. The first new group, originally named SIGOA (for Office Automation) and later renamed SIGOIS (Office Information Systems), was started in 1979. It was chartered to address the variety of technological means for serving human workers in office environments. HCI was included as one of its major focal points.

A few years later, in 1982, SIGCHI (Computer and Human Interaction) was created, by transforming the name and focus of the previously existing SIGSOC (Social and Behavioral Science Computing). Unlike SIGOIS, which defined HCI as a subset of its research agenda, SIGCHI made HCI its all-consuming mission. HCI had finally "arrived" in the computer science community. SIGCHI and its associated annual conference have become increasingly popular. Its membership has grown significantly. It has become one of the most active, model SIGs in ACM, along with the very prominent SIGGRAPH.

In the late 1980s, SIGCHI, SIGGRAPH, and SIGOIS took on a number of leadership roles to stimulate and support various interdisciplinary and intergroup efforts. These are indicated by the cosponsored conferences listed in Fig. 1.2. By virtue of the interdisciplinary nature of HCI, such forums are extremely important and bode well for future progress in the area. Successful conferences on each of computer-supported cooperative work (CSCW), hypertext, and document processing systems suggest that a number of branch areas (and SIGs) are likely to be spawned. Each may bring with it a different perspective, but all are collectively and variously impacted by HCI, and vice versa.

Indeed, a new ACM SIGLINK, resulting from the above-indicated hypertext initiative, was created late in 1990.

1.3.2. Private Organizations

Because professional societies are public in nature and few in number, it is fairly easy to characterize them in relation to HCI. However, the same is not feasible here for the numerous and diverse private organizations that were concerned either with providing (designing, manufacturing, selling) or with acquiring computer technology for human use.

Nevertheless, some generalizations are possible. With reference to Fig. 1.1, during Period 1 the computer providers (IBM, Univac, DEC, etc.) essentially disregarded HCI. Highest priority went to attaining computer efficiency, both in hardware and software design. As a result, the customers had to accept and tolerate whatever inconvenience and cryptic interaction techniques and languages were imposed on them.

But then, as users became more knowledgeable and demanding during Period 2, the computer providers learned the hard way. Slowly but surely, poorly designed HCI stimulated users to shop for better alternatives. As a result, a computer provider was likely to lose major customer accounts. Perhaps there was validity to the needs for "user-oriented design" and "usability" that were claimed by some people!

Several very innovative interface designs came about by the early 1980s. They were typically produced by smaller computer companies (e.g., Xerox Star, Apple Macintosh), but they surely drew the attention and competitive reaction of the major firms. Engelbart's old "mouse," designed in the late 1960s, magically became a popular input device and was recognized as a commonly accepted household name.

Such progress, in turn, impacted the HCI advancements of Period 3 (Fig. 1.1). Powerful PC-based systems and workstations were configured with graphics, special I/O devices, and "user-friendly" software, in a manner far more conducive to human use than was experienced with the mini- and maxicomputers of earlier years. Again, some smaller companies (e.g., Xerox, Apple, Sun) took the lead. But their big brothers soon followed with their own competitive versions.

The end results are that, on one hand, computer providers in the 1990s should be far more sensitive to the importance of effective HCI. On the other hand, computer users have every right to expect such sensitivity by now. A number of very illustrative interface systems have set the precedent. User-oriented interface designs should henceforth be the norm, rather than the exception.

1.3.3. Government Agencies

Any discussion of how agencies of the U.S. government may have participated in the historical development of HCI can be dichotomized into two roles: (1) active in-house studies of techniques and tools for HCI improvement and (2) financial support for universities and other organizations in the private sector to carry out such studies.

With few exceptions, the first role was rarely adopted by a government agency. One exception was the Institute for Computer Sciences and Technology, National Bureau of Standards (recently renamed NIST). In the 1970s, it undertook the design, implementation, and testing of special interface systems (e.g., the Network Access Machine, the Network Measurement Machine) which could facilitate user access to heterogeneous systems and which could enable convenient measurement and evaluation of user-observable performance characteristics, such as response times experienced by the users. The ICST also acquired and utilized an interesting assortment of interface technologies for purposes of user authentication (recognition of fingerprints, voiceprints, handshapes, etc.).

Far more significant to HCI as a field was the government role of giving, or not giving, financial support for HCI research. For many years, such agencies as the National Science Foundation did not recognize HCI as a legitimate, fundable area. During Periods 1 and 2 (Fig. 1.1), the NSF criteria for awarding grants pretty much reflected the (previously discussed) attitudes prevalent among computer scientists: HCI was seemingly not substantive enough in technical content, or it was too interdisciplinary in nature, to deserve funding. Even in the 1980s, it was still rare for an HCI researcher to succeed in obtaining an NSF grant.

The fact is, of course, that HCI research is so difficult, in part because of the complexities of being interdisciplinary, that it should be a prime candidate for government support. Now that the importance of effective HCI seems to have been acknowledged in the scientific community, it is hoped that the typical lag by funding agencies, in reacting to and accommodating this research need, will be minimized.

1.4.   Current Status

The above-characterized historical perspective leads to several questions: Where does our knowledge of HCI design stand today? How much do we know? Where are the frontiers?

The largest section of this book, Part II, is entitled "Prerequisite Knowledge Areas." It can be interpreted as providing a structured portrait of what we already know. By now we have learned a fair amount about the capabilities and limitations of computer users (Chapter 3); we have various tools and techniques available for collecting and analyzing information about users; and we can utilize the results for constructing meaningful user models.

The user would not be "turned on" to interacting with a computer, were it not for having interest in various computer-based applications (Chapter 4). Those applications are increasing both in number and complexity. We know quite a bit about them and about how they may be rendered more or less conducive to human use. To a large extent, the usability of a computer-based application is dependent on the capabilities and limitations of the computer (Chapter 5), in terms of both the software and hardware facilities it offers. We understand the different types and the technical performance characteristics very well. How they can be selected and configured for effective HCI is the much more difficult task.

This is addressed in part by the mounting knowledge about HCI techniques and styles (Chapter 6). Given the composite profiles of the capabilities of both user and computer (Chapters 3 and 5) as well as the nature of the application of interest (Chapter 4), we can by now select from a number of viable alternatives in interaction technique/style. They range from command line and natural language-based interaction to graphic/ iconic representation and so-called direct manipulation.

To provide more formal underpinnings for the characteristics of user, application, and computer, as well as HCI techniques, researchers have developed a number of useful representation models and methods (Chapter 7). In particular, various specification techniques (e.g., extended BNF) are available. These are, furthermore, supplemented by supportive tools (Chapter 8) that are designed to assist in modular HCI design (e.g., using the UIMS model) and also in the special-purpose measurement and evaluation of HCI.

Given this portrait of what is already fairly well known, what can be said about what needs to be done? Most accomplishments thus far have involved specialized models, tools, and techniques and very illustrative interfaces that instantiate them in various ways. These have been extremely valuable, and they point to the tremendous potential that exists for improving HCI. But they tend to be relatively restrictive and narrow in scope.

Much more comprehensive and integrative methodologies for HCI design are needed. We need long-term efforts at formulating what might be called *interface engineering*. As Gaines and Shaw (1986) suggested, we must provide for "foundations for engineering the human–computer interface as explicit and well founded as those for hardware and software engineering." That will not be an easy task; it will take many years to accomplish.

This book makes an initial attempt to construct such an approach. It and its companion book (Treu, 1994) are organized accordingly. Based on the observation that *interface structures* (Treu, 1992) are pervasive in HCI, both the design and development methods of this book and the measurement and evaluation methods presented in the companion volume become achievable in systematic, engineeringlike ways. In each case, a "structured approach" results.

1.5. Literature

The HCI literature, or, more correctly stated, the literature representing the various branches and niches of HCI, has been growing by leaps and bounds. This becomes particularly evident when writing a book like this and attempting to incorporate citations that might serve as helpful resources to the reader. The volume has become extremely large. Any interested person conducting a comprehensive literature review in HCI soon finds it necessary to become selective.

With respect to the major historical periods outlined in this chapter, it may be instructive to give a brief overview of the types of publication that evolved in HCI. In the 1960s (Period 1), there were relatively isolated efforts reported via published papers. Some notable examples were cited earlier. Others included the response time studies associated with time-sharing systems (e.g., Miller, 1968; Sackman, 1968). Most such publications appeared in proceedings of conferences. Sackman (1970) compiled results of his experimental work in a book. Understandably, no books that addressed the entire HCI design area as such were yet available.

At the start of 1969, a new journal was started. The *International Journal of Man–Machine Studies* produced its first issues, with the expressed purpose of bridging the gap between several disciplines that were becoming increasingly related to each other, including psychology and computing. The *IJMMS* has continued to publish ever since. For many years, Brian Gaines has been executive editor.

Throughout the 1970s, the IJMMS was the sole HCI-oriented journal. *Human Factors* published occasional articles of interest, but they mainly pertained to physiological considerations involving users working with computers. Except for books that were collections of conference or workshop papers, attempts at writing books addressing the HCI topic on the whole remained rare in the 1970s. Two early exceptions were Charles Meadow's (1970) *Man–Machine Communication* and James Martin's (1973) *Design of Man–Computer Dialogues*. These books primarily served reference purposes. The lack of formal courses in HCI precluded their more extensive utilization.

However, courses in computer graphics were being initiated at a number of universities. The first edition of a major book on that topic (Newman and Sproull, 1979) was written in 1973. Besides containing a chapter on user interface design, the inherent nature of the subject area covered, which includes the ability to create human-perceived (near-) realism, was a precursor of the user-oriented graphical techniques that are now widely available to HCI designers. Further, the manipulation of graphical objects on the interface surface really represented an early version of "DMI style" that is now so much in vogue.

In 1980, Ben Shneiderman's first HCI book appeared. Its title, *Software Psychology*, appropriately implied linkage between the two important disciplines. Included were chapters on "Interactive Interface Issues" and "Designing Interactive Systems." Then, continuing in the early to mid-1980s, a number of additional books hit the shelves. Included were Card and colleagues' (1983) *The Psychology of Human–Computer Interaction*, Spence's (1985) *Computer Usability Testing and Evaluation*, Nickerson's (1986) *Using Computers: Human Factors in Computer Systems*, Norman and Draper's (1986) edited work on *User Centered System Design*, Shneiderman's (1987) first edition of *Designing the User Interface: Strategies for Effective Human–Computer Interaction*, and Baecker and Buxton's (1987) edited collection of papers and many useful references in *Readings in Human–Computer Interaction—A Multidisciplinary Approach*.

An increasing number of books have been added to the HCI literature since then. Included are books *authored* by: Brown (1988), Booth (1989), Jones (1989), Thimbleby (1990), Bødker (1991), Shneiderman's (1992) second edition, Mayhew (1992), Barfield (1993), and Duffy *et al.* (1993), and books *edited* by Carroll (1987), Guindon (1988), Long and Whitefield (1989), Ackermann and Tauber (1990), Falzon (1990), Harrison and Thimbleby (1990), Carey (1991), Karat (1991), Klinger (1991), and Preece (1993). These and other books are cited as appropriate in later chapters.

With regard to new HCI journals, the *IJMMS* (in 1994, renamed *IJHCS*) by now has a substantial number of relatively young companions. They include: *Behaviour and Information Technology, Human–Computer Interaction, Interacting with Computers, International Journal of Human–Computer Interaction*, and *ACM Transactions on Human–Computer Interaction*.

Finally, many results of current work in HCI are published through the relevant conference proceedings. Particularly appropriate are the ACM SIGCHI conferences, as reflected by the many papers included in the Bibliography of this book. A number of other, more specialized conferences, symposia, and workshops also produce important proceedings to benefit the community of HCI researchers and developers.

The reader of this book, especially if a student using it as a text, will soon find out that many of the exercises appended to chapters require selected readings. Given the size of the HCI literature and the interdisciplinary nature of the field, that approach seems very appropriate. Designers and evaluators of human–computer interfaces must, as a matter of routine, be able to find and utilize the numerous resources that are necessary to support their tasks.

Exercises

1.1. Areas of research and expertise in the arts and sciences have traditionally been pigeonholed into strictly defined disciplines, categorized into the natural (or physical) sciences, the social sciences, and the humanities. In reflecting on the periods of progress outlined in Section 1.1, what can we learn about such strict lines of demarcation? Do you think that human-oriented interface design would have progressed more quickly if the disciplinary boundaries had been more flexible? Write a well-reasoned position statement on the advantages and disadvantages of disciplinary separation—in relation to the HCI field.

1.2. Read the two articles (co-)authored by Engelbart to determine any clues on the extent to which the augmentation of human intellect by computer is dependent on (a) human senses, especially vision, hearing, and touching, as opposed to (b) human cognition, thinking, and problem-solving. Does either set of capabilities seem to have higher priority? What are the general implications for interface design?

1.3. Distinguish the term "symbiosis," as used by Licklider (1960), from "synergism" or "synergy." Develop and write a position statement that is either for or against having HCI designers attempt to provide for such qualities.

1.4. Find the definition of "hypertext" from Nelson (1965). Why did it take 20 years for the ideas of people like Engelbart and Nelson to become acknowledged and accepted and to lead to developments of hypertext systems for general use?

1.5. Consider the "best" computer interface that is available to you in your organization. Characterize the types of (a) input/output devices, (b) widget-level software, (c) interaction techniques, and (d) interaction styles it supports. Use your own understanding of these terms at this point in time. Later, especially in Part II, they will be defined/clarified for use in Part III of this book.

1.6. With reference to Exercise 1.5, give a well-reasoned response to each of the following: Is the best interface that is available to you (a) synergistic, (b) non-overwhelming (in amount and organization of information displayed), and (c) easily usable? (Note: this exercise anticipates the need to evaluate the design result.)

DEFINITIONS AND DEPENDENCIES

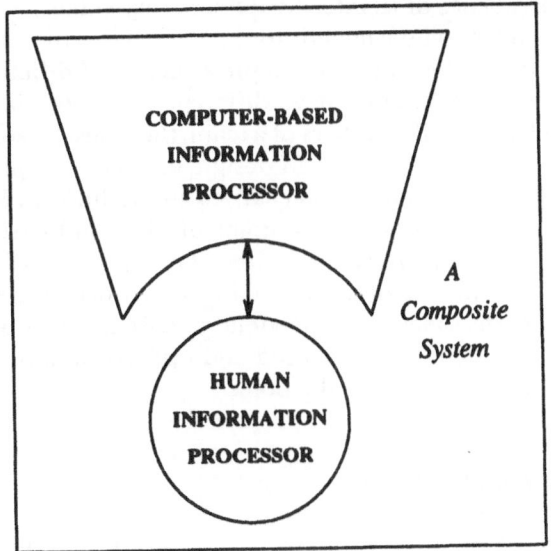

2.1. Overview

Unlike most other areas of computer-related study, HCI has been faced with a number of exceptional problems and hurdles to impede its progress. Not only were there difficulties in formulating a credible identity and in gaining acceptance in the scientific community, as discussed in Chapter 1; those difficulties were probably symptomatic of certain fundamental issues that had to be resolved.

One of these issues had to do with the long-standing confusion or, at least, ambiguity in definition of terms. HCI researchers often were less than clear in describing what they were doing. That is, their terminology was inconsistent and led to misunderstandings not only among them, but especially among those people immediately outside the field. Several important labels and definitions, as they changed over the years, are characterized in the next section.

But even if the terminology seems clear to an HCI researcher or research group, the confounding multifaceted nature of HCI makes life very difficult. Effective HCI is dependent on a number of disciplines and specialties. Which major disciplines should be viewed as contributors to HCI design? Which of the specialties in computer science should be called upon? The possibilities are discussed in Section 2.3.

As a consequence of its interdisciplinary dependencies, HCI is naturally also dependent on the qualifications and perspective of the designer or the design team. Not only do the representatives of different contributing disciplines and specialties have different points of view on what is important; collectively, if members of a team, they must be able to agree on what they want to achieve in an HCI design, or what their primary design criteria are to be. The general alternatives are outlined in Section 2.4.

In Section 2.5, the particular point of view and design approach advocated in this book are characterized. Finally, a symbolic, functional representation of design decision-making is defined in Section 2.6. It accentuates how decisions are dependent on specific types of knowledge. That functionlike dependence is used and updated in a thematic way in the various design chapters of the book.

2.2. Labels and Definitions

The study of HCI has undergone a number of label changes over the years. From its beginnings, it was basically viewed as a *relation between two entities*, as indicated by Fig. 2.1. But the two entities and their relation seemingly were variables that changed values (or labels), in accordance with changing attitudes and interpretations. Those changes did not take place with consistency or in chronological order. Nevertheless, it is interesting to construct a logical scenario of how labels were modified over the period of three decades. The pattern provides fuel for discussion of how different terms carry differing implications for the designer's model of the interface.

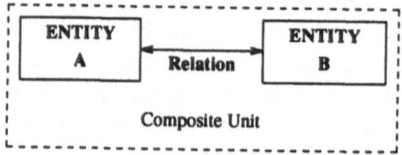

FIGURE 2.1. Binary relation.

Initially we had essentially a *man–machine system*:

> Entity A := *man*
> Entity B := *machine*
> Relation := *system*

For the two entities, the term "system" was not really used that often, but it was implied in the sense that man was subsumed by it, e.g., in a factory or in a transportation system. The "man–machine" label, however, was fairly prominent (e.g., Meadow, 1970; Hayes *et al.*, 1981) and, indeed, was retained until recently by the long-standing journal, *IJMMS*.

But while certain similarities exist between our use of any machine and our use of a computer, especially with regard to physiology-based manipulations, the computer was distinctive enough to warrant explicit emphasis:

> Entity B := *computer*

Accordingly, the "man–computer" label appears in a number of significant, early publications (e.g., Licklider, 1960, 1968; Miller, 1968; Martin, 1973).

In recent years, this label has also tended to subsume the interconnected, multicomputer alternative:

> Entity B := *computer network*

Entity A may have the option of accessing one or more computer resources within that network, either in parallel or in some coordinated pattern.

The labels for the Entity A side of the relation also changed. This was particularly motivated by societal preference for a more generic or gender-independent term. Several options have been used, to replace "man":

> Entity A := *person*
> Entity A := *user*
> Entity A := *human*

The term "person" has been used least often of the three (e.g., DeGreene, 1991); "user" became very prominent (e.g., Draper and Norman, 1985; Chi, 1985; Bødker, 1991) and is still in common use (including this book); but the "human–computer" label has become most prevalent in formal representations of the area (e.g., Harrison and Thimbleby, 1990; Karat, 1991). The Bibliography lists many other examples.

Analogous to substituting a computer network for Entity B, as indicated above, we can likewise use a plural or collective form for the user:

> Entity A := *user group*

On one hand, this may simply designate a *group of individuals* accessing Entity B for whatever (similar or different) purposes. On the other hand, the truly *collective user* interpretation is possible. It relates to characterizing certain kinds of computer-based applications as involving interhuman or intragroup collaboration (e.g., Greif, 1988; Rein and Ellis, 1991; Gaver *et al.*, 1992).

More interesting than what happened in the relabeling of either Entity A or Entity B is how the word denoting their relation was variously transformed. The idea of a composite man–machine "system," as if well-oiled and functioning meticulously like some machine, was undoubtedly intriguing. The term probably was reinforced by the use of terminology like "man–computer symbiosis" (Licklider, 1960). But the notion that a human user should simply act as a rigidly positioned and constrained part of a larger system, and could not depart from that role, was seemingly deemed unacceptable. It became preferable to have Entities A and B both become independent agents, each with the potential of emulating the other or of capitalizing on its own peculiar strengths. As a result, several different "models" for the relation were adopted. One of them was based on:

Relation := *communication*

It was used in a number of early publications (e.g., Licklider, 1968; Meadow, 1970). Connoting "the act of passing along or transferring information," by whatever means and methods necessary, the term may have lost some appeal because of its similarity to the technical transmission of bits and bytes in telecommunication and computer networking (e.g., Tanenbaum, 1988). Communication in that sense seems to impose a computer model on both entities, as if a human user could communicate in a manner analogous to a computer.

The opposite extreme was to impose the human model on the computer entity, giving rise to either

Relation := *conversation*

or

Relation := *dialogue*

The first term was used in earlier years (e.g., Miller, 1968; Foley and Wallace, 1974); the latter term was used more recently, especially in the 1980s (e.g., Gaines, 1981; Guest, 1982; Gaines and Shaw, 1983; Hanusa, 1983; Benbasat and Wand, 1984; Kobsa and Wahlster, 1989; Ulich *et al.*, 1991). Both terms imply that the computer should be able to act in a manner analogous to the user entity. But a case can be made that this is not necessarily desirable. The computer should not learn to emulate both the good and the bad features of human–human dialogue (e.g., Nickerson, 1977).

Thus, after trying both the computer model for the user and the user model for the computer, we apparently found a reasonably generic and innocuous alternative:

$$\text{Relation} := interaction$$

The titles of publications listed in the Bibliography certainly confirm its popularity.

Let us consider a dictionary definition of this term. Note that the *World Book Dictionary* (1975) was consulted for many of the nontechnical versions of definitions presented in this book.

Definition 2.1. **Interaction**: the action upon or influence on each other.

Interaction implies a binary relationship, that is, with one entity acting upon or influencing another, and vice versa. In so doing, the entities may very well "communicate" or "converse" with each other, but those terms are now subsumed, serving as alternative means for carrying out the more general "interaction." It is possible to extend Definition 2.1 to encompass more than two entities. Rather than focusing on one human interacting with one computer, we can consider collective entities in each place. For example, a group of users may interact with one computer, and thereby with each other, such as in computer-supported cooperative work. Also, either one user or a group of users may interact with a network of computers.

Let us restrict our attention to the binary version of interaction, leading to the terminology that is in common use today. The simple derivative of Definition 2.1. is:

Definition 2.2. **Human–computer interaction** (HCI): interaction between a human user and a computer.

But a more meaningful and purposeful version is:

Definition 2.3. **Human–computer interaction**: the combination of physical, logical, conceptual, and language-based actions between a human user and a computer, toward achieving some purpose.

Whatever subset of actions is employed, by either the human or the computer on the other, is dependent on their respective capabilities as well as the intended purpose of interaction.

The use of the term "interaction" enables designer and evaluator discretion on what role is being played by either the human or the computer. Interaction can be carried out as if between two totally "equal" parties. On the other hand, it can involve some form of dependence, even subservience, of one party on/to the other. So, this term gives a lot of freedom for interpretation.

Interaction also clearly represents an action word. It is the active or dynamic component of the relation. But it must be enabled by supportive physical and physiological means, namely, an interface. That may be defined as follows:

Definition 2.4. **Interface**: (1) a surface between two objects, forming their common boundary; (2) a connection of two or more objects in an association, partnership, or other relationship.

It can also be defined as a verb, namely, to operate together in close association. But the verb "interact" is considered preferable in this book.

Definitions 2.3 and 2.4 can be used selectively to compose the following:

Definition 2.5. **Human–computer interface**: the physical surface and facilities, between human user and computer, providing the medium through which they can connect and interact; the physical (visual, audio, tactile) means, methods, and patterns that support human–computer interaction.

It is also simply called the *user interface* or just the *interface*. Its meaning tends to be extended beyond covering only the physical medium for interaction; it is often used to encompass everything, including the conceptual framework of its user. The title of this book is an example. The structure and constituents of this interface are discussed extensively in later chapters. For now, we observe that the interface minimally supplies the passive or static component of the human–computer relation. It becomes active only when invoked, or activated, by the two entities, thereby causing an interaction across or through its boundaries.

Although Definitions 2.3 and 2.5 distinguish human–computer interaction from the interface, the HCI acronym can obviously and reasonably apply to both. For ease of reference, this book uses it interchangeably in that manner. At times, the context makes clear which version is intended. At other times, the distinction is drawn explicitly.

Related terms. HCI and its various predecessor versions (in terminology) are often being viewed as synonymous with "human factors" and "ergonomics." Actually, the so-called area of human factors has existed for many years, attending to concerns about human use of any equipment or machines, such as in factory environments. Primary attention was paid to the physical and physiological aspects of human use of machines, such as the dimensions and layouts of the physical interface and the resulting impacts on the users or operators. Impacts were assessed in terms such as required arm and eye movements, induced stress levels, and resulting performance. In general, the more cognitive aspects of human use of the equipment were not direct objects of study.

But that interpretation seems to have changed, to the extent that many authors now use the term "human factors" as subsuming HCI issues as a subset; included are "all aspects of the use of machinery by humans and the implications for the design of that machinery" (Jones, 1989). Many of the entries in the Bibliography deal with human factors (e.g., Sondheimer and Relles, 1982; Foley *et al.*, 1984; Simes and Sirsky, 1985). However, to reserve the term "factors" for its more literal meaning, in the context of the design methodology presented in this book, the use of "human factors" will be avoided except in the following sense:

Definition 2.6. **Human factors**: All human characteristics (psychological, physiological, social, etc.) that have the potential of influencing the design of human-oriented HCI.

Note, therefore, that interface features, which may have resulted from taking human characteristics (i.e., factors) into account in the design process, are not to be confused as also being "human factors." For example, if an interface is "easy to learn" or "easy to use" or "provides meaningful feedback," those are features that are representative of interface design *with respect to* certain human factors. They may also reflect specified user-oriented "principles" of design, but they should not themselves be interpreted as being human factors. They are the design consequences or effects, not the causes. The point behind these distinctions is to prepare the reader for corresponding methodological considerations developed later.

This discussion leads naturally to one more related term, "ergonomics" (e.g., Shackel, 1985). Again, it has often been used interchangeably with human factors and HCI. DeGreene (1991) has distinguished the two terms, along with describing their various pros, cons, and relationships. Also, "cognitive ergonomics" has come to the fore in recent years (Long and Whitefield, 1989). It seeks "to support the specification of knowledge conceived as the representations and processes required by humans to interact with a computer to perform work effectively" (Long, 1989).

Paraphrasing a dictionary definition of the term and orienting it to HCI, we get:

Definition 2.7. **Ergonomics**: the study of the relationship between individuals and their computer-based work and work environment, especially with regard to fitting the jobs to the needs and abilities of the computer users.

Designing the interface to "fit user needs and abilities" is the key to this definition. In other words, once we know which human factors are significant to HCI, ergonomics involves the study of how to suitably accommodate those factors in the design of an interface. The term itself is not used further in this book. However, its meaning is subsumed by the design methodology presented.

2.3. Contributing Areas

As already stated, the study of HCI is dependent on multiple disciplines and specialties, not in their totality but selectively, utilizing those topical areas that are directly relevant and that can have substantive influence. This means that effective HCI study is necessarily interdisciplinary in nature, and interface designers must be trained and oriented accordingly.

Which are those disciplines? With respect to the individual human user who participates as one of the two entities in the binary relation, several major disciplines become involved. Others could be mentioned as potentially useful (e.g., anthropology), but the following are deemed to be most directly relevant.

2.3.1. Major Disciplines

Psychology is the science dealing with the mind and mental processes, feelings, desires, etc. It, therefore, encompasses everything that a human being thinks and does, that is, the sum of a person's actions, traits, attitudes, thoughts, beliefs, etc. For a computer user, all of these can have a bearing on how the user thinks and behaves in interaction with the computer. In so doing, the user develops and utilizes a "mental model," which the HCI designer needs to take into account.

In all of this mind-based activity, knowledge is critical. Its importance is accentuated by using the adjective "cognitive" as a qualifier. **Cognitive psychology** is defined to be the study of how people acquire, remember, and use knowledge, for purposes of making decisions and solving problems. It is obviously very relevant to understanding how users can interact with computers and how the interface design should thereby be affected.

Physiology, on the other hand, is the science dealing with the functions and vital processes of living organisms and parts thereof. It therefore emphasizes the physical, rather than the cognitive, characteristics of the human being. For computer users, illustrative physiological factors are left- or right-handedness, arm length (to reach the CRT screen), typing speed (in using a keyboard for input), visual acuity (with regard to displayed font type, size, resolution), etc.

If the human entity is also interpreted as part of a collective unit, or user group, several other disciplines become involved. **Sociology** is the study of the origin, development, organization, and problems of people living together as social groups. Among its interests are the relationships that develop within human communities. With respect to computer users, social groups or user communities were already developed in the old days of batch processing systems. They helped each other out, they exchanged ideas, they commiserated about poor computer services, and they complained. Such social patterns have been greatly facilitated, transformed, and extended, particularly because of the much more convenient, interactive access now available to networked computer resources. Indeed, computer network-based socialization now includes a great variety of collaborative arrangements and management-required modes of interpersonal communication. Interface design should be affected accordingly.

Further, as just indicated, the organizational structure among people, as reflected by management science, contributes certain factors that influence HCI. **Management** is the art or manner of handling, controlling, directing, the personnel and other resources in an organization (such as the computing resources and computer users) for purposes of attaining various goals. Management can influence computer users, their attitudes and skills (e.g., through training), and their consequent performance. This can be borne out through measurement and evaluation methodology, as covered in the companion book. Management can also have significant bearing on the computer entity in HCI, e.g., in terms of establishing priorities and providing adequate financial support for the acquisition, design, and updating of computer facilities.

In order to be able to obtain, assess, and apply the data that represent the above-indicated, human-oriented disciplines, or the human entities involved in HCI, it is essential to know how to conduct **experimental design** and **statistical analysis**. Relevant techniques are defined and taught under the auspices of each of the various disciplines at the college level. While they are often thought of as most appropriate for obtaining information about human beings, they are also necessary for the study of computer performance and, most certainly, for evaluating users in their interaction with computer entities.

But, from a strictly technical standpoint, the computer entity is dependent on **computer science**, the study of computers, their underlying theories, and the principles, techniques, and tools enabling their useful application. This is the discipline that covers the design of the computer entity involved in the binary HCI relation. It is of necessity concerned with both the software and the hardware on which the software can carry out its intended functions. However, the physical computer equipment, including special-purpose input and output devices that affect HCI, is typically produced in **computer engineering** laboratories.

2.3.2. Specialties in Computer Science

A number of specialties that constitute computer science play contributing roles in HCI design. They include **languages**, especially for programming the computer, using statements with precisely defined syntax and semantics, to enable human expression of problem solutions (or algorithms) in a manner that can be processed by the computer. Such language relates also to design of language for interaction between the user and the computer.

Computer graphics is a specialty that can enhance that interaction language by means of visual, diagrammatic, and pictorial means. While its primary emphasis is on creating visible forms of output on computer display screens, it also gives rise to interestingly different and effective input devices and modes. As a result, HCI design can be significantly enriched.

Both the traditional language processing as well as the graphical types of interaction language must have appropriate support from the specialty known as **operating systems**. It consists of the set of software products (designed to utilize a particular hardware configuration) that control the resources and the processes that invoke those resources. The functionality and performance of a computer, as experienced by a user at the interface, are therefore directly dependent on the services provided by the operating system behind the visible surface.

Each one of the above-mentioned specialties is, furthermore, subject to scrutiny from the area of **software engineering**. It is concerned with the entire range of activities, or the process, of designing and developing software. It requires the designer to move systematically through a sequence of steps, including requirements analysis and specification, program specification and development, validation, verification, and testing. Certain well-known principles of software design are established and expected to be followed. The design of HCI software also is in need of such demanding methodology. As is pointed out later in this book, adherence to software engineering methods and principles, when designing the interface software architecture, is likely to produce significant benefits, both for the designer and for the user.

Modeling and simulation is a specialty that, in a sense, encompasses everything that is done in solving problems with computers. But it has special relevance to HCI. As is true of any other complex system, which may be too expensive and difficult to implement prior to assessing its prospective performance, it is important to be able to model each of the user, the computer, the interface, and their composite (HCI system) and then to simulate their respective behaviors or performance. The tools and techniques available from the modeling and simulation specialty can be very useful for such purposes.

Another important specialty is **artificial intelligence**. Some people treat it as if it were a part of computer science; others view it as an interdisciplinary area in its own right, somewhat analogous to the study of HCI. Artificial intelligence (AI) is concerned with the development of computer software that performs tasks requiring "intelligence" when carried out by humans. That is, the software-based artifacts it creates are designed to exhibit intelligent behavior. Example tasks are: game playing, learning, making inferences, plan formation, natural language understanding, speech understanding, visual perception. These have to do with language, understanding, learning how to solve problems, etc. Clearly, the computer user, an intelligent entity, is very much dependent on such capabilities when involved in HCI. Hence, the more intelligent the behavior of the user's partner, namely, the computer, if acting in deliberate alliance with the user's capabilities, needs, and wants, the better the interaction is likely to be. The utilization of **expert systems** technology within the interface architecture is one concrete way of taking advantage of AI. The emerging field of **cognitive science** is a close relative of AI. It is variously defined to be the study of the principles upon which intelligent entities interact with their environments. Its distinctions from AI are not very clear, and a number of researchers feel that the two areas will/should ultimately merge.

In addition to the above-outlined specialties that are either an integral part of, or dependent on, computer science as a discipline, some specialties that affect HCI design arise from replacing the relatively simple, single computer entity (in the HCI relation) with one or more **computer networks** or **distributed systems**. This has a number of complicating effects on how each of the other topics (languages, graphics, operating systems, software engineering, modeling and simulation, AI) must be tailored to render the interface suitably oriented (for the user) to a potentially massive network of computer-based resources. Even the area of **telecommunications**, which consists of the means and methods for electronic transmission of any type of data (including numeric, alphanumeric, voice, image, video) from one network node to another, and ultimately for display (or other form of output) at the user interface, must be brought into the design process.

The above-characterized list of disciplines and specialties that variously contribute to the study of HCI may seem overwhelming and un-wieldy. Each area is associated with a sizable and growing literature. Can any one HCI designer, or even a design team, realistically encompass all of those areas and their relationships? That is an important reason why comprehensive HCI design is so complex and challenging. Also, a book like this obviously cannot possibly cover all relevant areas to any depth. However, it can present a methodological framework, including pointers to other resources as appropriate.

2.4. Designer Orientations

In view of the multiple disciplines and specialties that contribute to the study of HCI, it is not surprising that a great variety of approaches to interface design have been prescribed. The approach that is selected is generally dependent on the background and perspective of the designer.

A broad characterization is presented in Table 2.1. The design orien-tation and outcome may either "favor" the actual user, or the computer being used, or some hybrid combination of the two. By "favoring" is meant the "rendering of HCI conducive to the capabilities, preferences, etc." of the user, the computer, or some combination of the two entities that are party to the binary HCI relation, as discussed in Section 2.2.

So, if the designer is also the user or deliberately represents the user, one would normally expect the resulting interface to favor the user. This is indicated by Perspective 1 of Table 2.1. It is also reasonable to expect that the user would be given highest priority by a designer with expertise in one or more of the human-oriented disciplines, as suggested by Perspective 3. However, if the designer is an expert in one of the technology-intensive

TABLE 2.1
Dependencies on Designer Orientation

	The likely DESIGN APPROACH:		
DESIGNER PERSPECTIVE: Representing . . .	User-favoring	Computer-favoring	Some hybrid
1. The user or user group	X Ease-of-use		
2. The supervisor or management		Efficiency	X
3. Human-oriented disciplines	X		
4. Technology-intensive discipline(s)		X	
5. Interdisciplinary expertise (3 and 4 above)			X

disciplines (Perspective 4) and has little sensitivity to user needs, the user will probably be relatively neglected. The interface may end up showing off the power of the computer (Perspective 4), possibly to the detriment of the user.

It is also possible for the designer to be asked to follow some other agenda, such as mandated by the user's supervisor or management (Perspective 2). In that case, the design approach might be constrained by overall HCI efficiency or cost, which can produce undesirable results both for the user as well as for the computer side of the relation. On the other hand, if management recognizes the importance of attending to the capabilities and the limitations of both the computer and the user, some more effective hybrid design may result.

The above portrait is an oversimplification. It may be very unfair, in any given instance, to a particular, conscientious designer. Nevertheless, for discussion purposes, we must recognize that designer qualifications and perspectives carry important consequences for user interface design. Ultimately, the message is that either an individual designer or a design team should have interdisciplinary preparation and orientation (Perspective 5), in order to do justice to the extremely challenging task of designing an interface for effective HCI.

2.5. Attributes of Methodology

Methodology for interface design is developed throughout this book. At this point, some of its important attributes are highlighted. It should be observed that, while primary emphasis is on interface *design*, the same attributes should also be applicable to methodology for interface *measurement* and *evaluation*.

First, with reference to the previous section, interface design should promote the *interdisciplinary* perspective (Table 2.1). This includes giving equal treatment to each of the user entity, the computer entity, and the various facilities and styles for their interaction. In effect, this also encourages a *symmetric* view of the user–computer relationship model, without precluding a distinct bias in favor of the user as desired.

Whenever possible, the design approach should be *systematic*. That means "being orderly in arranging things or in getting them done." It implies that

- The design decision-making
- The design process, and
- The design results

should all be clearly representable and describable. To accomplish this objective, several organizational mechanisms and constructs are introduced and utilized in thematic ways throughout this text. They include:

1. *A cause-and-effect framework,* encompassing the following and other paradigms; it is summarized diagrammatically in Chapter 9.
2. *Decision schematics,* to portray graphically how design factors and principles must feed into a design decision, leading to specification of design features; these are introduced starting with Chapter 3.
3. *Symbolic functional representation,* to suggest that the decision-making for HCI is like a mapping function, taking factors and principles as inputs and producing design outcomes (features); this view is introduced in Section 2.6 below and updated in various chapters later on.
4. *Interface structures,* inherent to the design features evident at the user interface; these conceptual, logical, and physical patterns are conducive to both user and computer; they are utilized in a number of places in this book.

If the design methodology is indeed systematic and well-organized, it is much more likely to provide the designer with the opportunity to be *comprehensive.* Having the ability to take all major HCI components and factors into account, as opposed to being forced to be arbitrarily *selective* (thereby possibly ignoring some significant aspects), has tremendous advantages. Of course, if the methodology truly supports systematic, comprehensive design, it should also give the designer the option to be selective, in a carefully controlled, deliberate way.

The approach should be as *objective* as possible. That is, it should be based on patterns and objects that are real, observable, and systematically confirmable. We should continue to strive to overcome the earlier image of HCI (Chapter 1), namely, that it is too *subjective* or soft in nature. This is not to say that subjective user and expert opinions should not be introduced and utilized when appropriate. They should retain an appropriate place in the methodology. However, any subjective data should be very carefully collected, analyzed, and invoked for design and for evaluation, using suitable experimental design methods. Unsubstantiated claims, e.g., that an interface is somehow magically "user-friendly," should no longer gain credibility without scrutiny.

Finally, the *design rationale* behind any design feature, including any significant decision-making criteria and priorities, should be recorded and subsequently be made accessible to interested parties. Doing this seems to be a natural corollary to all of the above-listed characteristics of a desirable design approach. The additional time and effort required can be alleviated by carrying out such recording as a matter of course, within the framework of a well-structured design methodology. If done and done consistently, it is likely to provide the highly desirable designer *accountability*. It should not only benefit the HCI design results, and hence the user, but also should help to advance the HCI field in general.

2.6. Symbolic Functional View

In order to accentuate the importance of carrying out HCI design in a systematic, well-organized manner, a functional representation of the decision-making is introduced at this point. It is defined below and then updated in subsequent chapters, contingent on additional material having been covered since the previous update. Thus, it serves as one organizational mechanism that ties the chapters together, leading to composition of design methodology in Part III.

Although this design decision function seems mathematical in nature, the reader does not have to be a mathematician to understand or appreciate it. In fact, the function is not really a true function (as the mathematician will observe immediately); instead, it is a functionlike mapping of various *inputs* to a design decision *into* the desired *outcomes*, or design features. Nevertheless, we will simply use the label "Function" to refer to the numbered mappings listed in this and later chapters.

Let us assume the following types of inputs, expressed in terms of one or more sets. They are treated as analogous to the independent variables (in the domain) of a mathematical function:

1. *Design factors*, representing influences from each of the entities or components of the system being designed. These factors will be characterized in Chapters 3 through 5. In general, they form a set, and its members are themselves sets. To avoid complicating the terminology, the following expression already assumes that only a *subset* of the total possible set of factors is used in a design:

$$\text{FACTORS} = \{\text{entity1\_subset,entity2\_subset,...}\} \quad (2.1)$$

2. *Design principles*, representing the goals in a design that are specified as desirable. These will be defined and illustrated in Chapter 9. Only a subset of the possible principles is selected:

$$\text{PRINCIPLES} = \{\text{some\_subset\_of\_principles}\} \quad (2.2)$$

3. *Designer knowledge*, to enable determination, analysis, and specification of the relevant factors and principles [Eq. (2.1) and (2.2)] for purposes of selecting and integrating the most appropriate inter-

face features [Eq. (2.3) below], resulting from carefully conducted decision-making [Function (2.4)]. Such design decisions must be based on substantial amounts of KNOWLEDGE. This entire book is organized to encompass the different types of knowledge required:

- *Factual knowledge*, presented as factors representing users, applications, and computers: Chapters 3 through 5.
- *Features knowledge*, representing the potential design outcomes and options with regard to the visible interface (Chapter 6), the helpful models that can be superimposed on it (Chapter 7), and the supportive software organization and tools (Chapter 8); this knowledge category also includes the structural paradigms, or interface structures, that undergird the factors and features of Part II.
- *Methodological knowledge*, involving the design principles, criteria, methods, etc., that must be understood to enable the creation of an interface product (features) based on inputs of relevant, enabling or constraining information (factors): Chapters 9 through 13.

In addition, the designer should have knowledge of how the design product can be evaluated. This is covered in the companion book (Treu, 1994). Finally, special knowledge beyond what is already implied is necessary in certain topical areas. These are illustrated by the designs described in Chapters 12 and 13.

If the above-outlined knowledge types are necessary as inputs to design decisions, we can likewise characterize the outputs. Assume that the following are the outputs, analogous to the dependent variables (in the range) of a mathematical function. Again, they are expressed as a set, with the understanding that members of the set will have to be suitably integrated into a composite interface system.

4. *Design features*, to be selected as the outcomes of design decision-making. As stated above, the choices available are covered in Chapters 6 through 8. The designer must select the subset of those features that are both possible and appropriate for a particular design:

$$FEATURES = \{some\_subset\_of\_features\} \qquad (2.3)$$

Finally, we need the mapping function itself. It is called the design decision function, denoted by:

$$D_{criteria,n}$$

It symbolizes the nth such decision based specifically on one or more decision-making *criteria*. These are discussed in Chapter 9. Combining the above-defined elements, the resulting high-level, functional view is as follows. For each (the nth) decision, we require the HCI designer to have a wealth of KNOWLEDGE and to use relevant PRINCIPLES and FACTORS in order to decide on the FEATURES that are most appropriate and desirable:

$$\text{FEATURES}_n \leftarrow D_{\text{criteria},n}(\text{KNOWLEDGE}_{\text{designer}}, \text{FACTORS}_n, \text{PRINCIPLES}_n) \quad (2.4)$$

The design-oriented chapters of this book will refer to this symbolic model, Function (2.4), and update it as appropriate. The relevant terms (factors, principles, features, and criteria) are illustrated in the following chapters, even though they are not defined formally until Chapter 9. Because they are commonly used terms, they are gradually introduced and exemplified in order to give the reader a sense of increasing dependency (in design decisions) on different categories of knowledge. This gradual approach to formalizing terminology will hopefully make the distinctions in definition (in Chapter 9) more convincing and acceptable.

Exercises

2.1. Based on your personal experience in interacting with computers, what characteristics of that interaction make it similar or analogous to human-to-human dialogue? In what respects are they different?

2.2. Contrary to Definition 2.3 of HCI, do you or others you know use a computer with no intended purpose in mind, even if it is only to be entertained (which is a purpose!)? Explain.

2.3. The interface between two very dissimilar entities, like user and computer, can be very elusive and in a sense misleading. The term "facade" can be applied, in that either or both entities may have reason to want to conceal, or "cover up," to the other some capabilities or weaknesses. For what circumstances and to what extent is it desirable (a) to design such a facade into the computer side of the interface, and (b) to encourage and enable the user to present a facade to the computer?

2.4. Consider the frequently used compound terms, "cause-and-effect" and "means to an end." For designing an interface, the designer should clearly distinguish (a) causal factors, (b) means or methods, and (c) results. From the literature cited in this chapter, determine and justify which of these three elements is/are encompassed by each of "human factors," "ergonomics," and "HCI design."

2.5. Consider the department in which you are a student (or for which you work). Which of the specialties in computer science outlined in this chapter are represented either by staff expertise and/or course offerings? Also, does your department either include expertise in one or more of the major disciplines (e.g., psychology) or have collaborative bridges built to corresponding organizational units? Discuss how the results of your analysis might have both positive and negative impacts on the study of HCI design in your particular environment. (Remember that it is quality, *not* quantity, which is most important!)

2.6. The orientation of an HCI designer undoubtedly can influence the design results, as suggested by Table 2.1. Adopt the perspective of each of the first four entities of that table, one at a time. For each, consider how you could deliberately try to achieve a more balanced, interdisciplinary perspective. What means or methods would you employ?

2.7. Function (2.4) is intended to be symbolic of the HCI design decision-making process. It is not to make the process seem unduly formal or mathematical. Assume each of the five perspectives listed in Table 2.1 and, in each case, write a descriptive paragraph of the three independent variables, with respect to how the perspective would be likely to limit the amount and types of design knowledge, factors, and principles known to and usable by the designer. (Note: If you are uncomfortable with the general form of a mathematical function, a brief look at a basic mathematics book that covers the subject should alleviate your concerns and clarify the intentions behind the functional model used in this book.)

PREREQUISITE KNOWLEDGE AREAS

The multifaceted, interdisciplinary area of HCI requires designers and evaluators knowledgeable with respect to several important topics, as *prerequisites* to understanding and utilizing the methodologies developed later. Accordingly, Chapters 3 through 5 define and model the characteristics (design factors) of each of the User (U-factors), the Application (A-factors), and the computer Interface (I-factors), respectively. These design factors are interpreted as the causal inputs to a cause-and-effect design paradigm, leading to specification of design outputs (the features). The major categories of design features are defined and modeled in Chapters 6 through 8. They include interaction techniques and styles, representation models for HCI, and special support tools and techniques.

USER CAPABILITIES AND LIMITATIONS

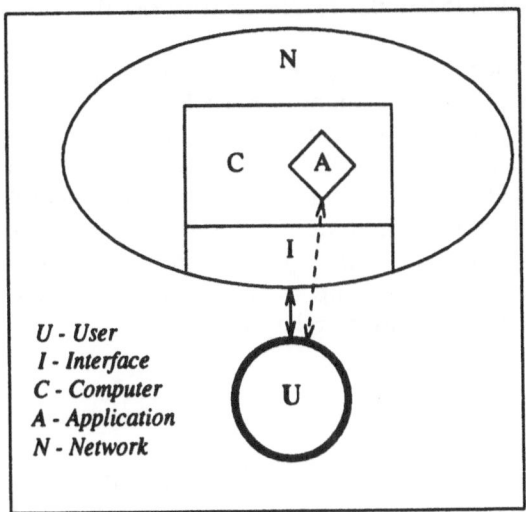

U - User
I - Interface
C - Computer
A - Application
N - Network

3.1. Overview

The interface designer must either already have the knowledge about what the user can or cannot do, and what the user needs and wants, or have the means available to ascertain that knowledge. This is far more easily said than done. It is complicated by the fact that there are so many different types or categories of users (Section 3.2).

Furthermore, depending on who is actually establishing the design objectives and what they are, some information about the user may be important while other information may be useless. In general, it is helpful for the designer to develop a user profile (Section 3.3.), which can then be completed and updated as necessary. That profile should contain various obtainable facts and opinions deemed important. Factors such as level of experience with target software, required response time, and preferred interaction style are examples. Such factors carry implications for interface design, as illustrated in Section 3.4. In addition, the designer must also be sensitive to whether indicated "needs" are consistent with user opinions (Section 3.5) and whether they are confirmed by user performance data (Section 3.6).

Based on information about the user, the designer must be able to construct a meaningful model of how the user thinks and functions, in interaction with the computer for a particular application. This means having to consider the human mind and having to understand mental and conceptual models (Section 3.7). Needless to say, that becomes especially difficult.

In preparation for utilizing the knowledge being characterized (in this part) for making design decisions in Parts III and IV, graphic schematics for representing the decision inputs and outputs are defined in Section 3.8. Those schematics are also inherent to the symbolic functional model (introduced in Section 2.6), which is updated in Section 3.9.

Finally, to enable the designer to acquire the above-indicated kinds of knowledge about the user, appropriate resources, tools, and techniques must be available for obtaining them. These are briefly mentioned in Section 3.10, with reference to relevant coverage later in this book.

3.2. User Categories

Interface design would be simplified greatly if the intended users all belonged to a homogeneous population. Because the user's knowledge and skills have important implications for human–computer performance and, hence, interface design (e.g., Trumbly *et al.*, 1993), we attempt to classify users. We cast people into well-defined molds, with labels like "expert," "master," "intermediate," and "novice," and even "parrot" (Koffler, 1986). Other terms include "stereotype" (Rich, 1979) and "discretionary" (Santhanam and Wiedenbeck, 1993). Throughout such attempts, we know that users are far from identical, either in their qualifications or their interests, even within any given user category. They tend to have tremendous individual differences. The designer must understand this fact and be able to determine the distinguishing characteristics of target users, in addition to the similarities that enable categorization.

Definition 3.1. **Target user**: the human user, or category of human users, to be served directly by a planned design; the user who will personally interact with the interface to be designed.

Notice that the target user is, therefore, distinct from any other person, such as a supervisor or customer, who might ultimately benefit from the results of interaction. However, in some special applications, the target user may also have the role of direct intermediary for someone else, e.g., a client looking over his/her shoulders. In that case, the latter may benefit from the design features at the same time.

A flowchart of high-level questions to be asked by the designer is depicted in Fig. 3.1. The questions can be used as a guide. For user-oriented design, it is preferable to answer the questions in the order indicated. A dependence on previous answers is generally inherent to the sequence. Each question is discussed below.

3.2.1. Source: User Population?

The source of the user(s) who is (are) to be the designer's target(s) should be identified in advance. Among the distinctions are whether the

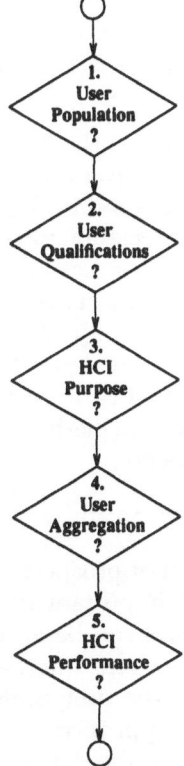

FIGURE 3.1. Designer questions about target user.

user belongs to (a) a *present* user population, accessible for collection of user data, (b) a *prospective* user population, from which meaningful user data may or may not be obtainable and, in case of the latter, may have to be hypothesized, or (c) some *idealized* or *statistical* user population, to which the real, future users will hopefully conform. The idealized user type may impose unrealistic expectations on a user. Such expectations may be much more indicative of what the designer thinks the user should be able to do than what the user in fact can do. Realism in the modeling of users is important (Sparck-Jones, 1989).

The statistical user type gives rise to such terms as *average* users and *worst case* users.

Definition 3.2. **Average user**: a composite model of a user category that is based on taking one or more factors representative of users, collecting data about each factor, and using the averaged result for each factor to guide the interface design.

Definition 3.3. **Worst case user**: a composite model of a user category that is based on taking one or more factors representative of users, collecting data about each factor, and using the worst resulting data to guide the interface design.

An analogous definition applies to the best case user.

Thus, if a factor of interest is user-required response time, the average among a sampled group of users may be 3 seconds. However, the worst (in this case, most demanding) expectation might be 0.5 second. Accordingly, if the target user is taken to be the indicated average user, the former figure would be a target value not to be exceeded in response time. On the other hand, if it is stipulated that the design should accommodate, i.e., should target, the worst case user, then the latter figure would be used.

As already implied, the identity of the source of the target users will significantly impact the means and methods for acquiring the data necessary for effective interface design.

3.2.2.   *Qualifications: Facts and Opinions?*

In the case of real (present or prospective) users for whom the design is to be carried out, various important data about their qualifications pertaining to use of computers can be acquired. Which aspects of the user's background, capabilities, and interests are important? They are indicated in conjunction with the user profile discussed in Section 3.3. How are the data obtained? Appropriate means for data collection are essential (Section 3.10). Some of the data may be factual; others may be based on opinions.

If the target user is not yet "real" and must be projected or statistically formulated, the designer must make suitable assumptions about anticipated qualifications. Depending on how representative (of the ultimate, real users) these assumptions turn out to be, interface performance will obviously be affected.

3.2.3. Purpose: Intended Application?

What does the target user want to do with the computer? The intended application may or may not correspond to what the user has already experienced. The need to analyze the computer-based application(s) must be recognized by the designer and taken into account in user-oriented design. That kind of analysis is discussed in Chapter 4.

The question of purpose continues the process of categorization of the target users. Thus far, in Questions 1 and 2, the designer has only considered the source and qualifications of the target users. How varied are their interests in using the computer? If all users are potentially interested in doing each of computer-aided design, computer programming, text editing, etc., all across the same interface, the designer's problem is more multifaceted and complex than if the users expect to do only one of those applications. Furthermore, the nature of one target application (e.g., involving computer graphics) when compared with another (e.g., involving text processing) has significant influence on interface design specifications.

3.2.4. Aggregation: Individual, Collective, or Collaborative?

It matters to the designer whether the planned interface is to accommodate one or more *individual users*, taking their idiosyncratic characteristics into account (Rich, 1983), or whether those same users are to be absorbed by a target group of users. In the first case, the design approach must encompass techniques that will tend to satisfy the needs of different individuals. In the group-oriented case, the designer can afford to construct a profile of a *collective user*. The word "collective" was implied by the group statistics underlying Definitions 3.2 and 3.3. Let us define the collective user type:

Definition 3.4. **Collective user**: a model of users that is dependent on utilizing selected factors representative of a group of users; distinguished from the individual user.

A collective user model should preferably maximize attention to commonalities among individuals and minimize their differences. It should provide a model of a user that is as close as possible to satisfying the needs of most, if not all, users (in the group), thereby recognizing that not everyone will be served adequately. This group-oriented design is clearly a close relative of the above-mentioned design based on a statistical user population. However, the average user may not be consistent with the collective user model suggested above. It depends on how many users are in fact close to the average figures used in design, as can be determined by analysis of the standard deviations and variances. On the other hand, if one can afford to produce a worst case design, all users should presumably be satisfied, unless some of them object to getting better than required performance (e.g., in response time), which indeed has been known to happen.

It must also be pointed out that it matters whether the statistics used for determining any type of user model (average, worst case, collective, etc.) are taken (1) from a user population at large or (2) from a particular target group. It can occur that a selected group is not represented accurately by the statistics of a more general user population.

The collective user is one kind of aggregate user. Another kind is the *collaborative user*. Such a user transcends the previously drawn distinctions between individual and collective user needs. This means that the designer must attend to HCI design features that will support, at the interface, interpersonal modes of collaboration, or user-to-user networking via intermediary computer facilities. Hence, network-oriented interface design (Chapter 12) becomes a relevant consideration.

3.2.5. Performance: Realistic Plan?

What level of HCI performance is expected, realistically, by or on behalf of the target user? This question becomes especially difficult to answer in advance of interface design. The reader may observe a certain ambiguity about it. After all, one would expect that the target user's ability to perform with the computer is already reflected in the user qualifications collected (Question 2 above). The user's level of experience, for example, should be a strong indicator of potential performance and should be usable as a guideline.

However, the question on performance is not only contingent on user qualifications, assuming these are accurately known. It also emphasizes the requirement that the designer be realistic and integrate the user's capabilities and needs (this chapter), as they relate to the target applications (next chapter), with those of the computer (Chapter 5). The user profile (Section 3.3) might suggest that the (individual or group) user requires a certain level of computer performance (e.g., maximal response time) in conjunction with a particular application (e.g., text editing). What if the target computer is incapable of meeting that requirement? Then, assuming that the designer is not personally responsible for computer selection and acquisition, his/her task is rather futile.

So, it is very important to understand and recognize performance factors pertaining both to the target user and to the target computer, as related to the one or more target application(s). Then, the designer can anticipate user–computer performance as it might be assessed in later stages, during and following interface design and development (Part III), and using appropriate measurement and evaluation methodology (Treu, 1994).

3.3. User Profile

If knowledge of the user is prerequisite to effective interface design, one must wonder how detailed and thorough that knowledge has to be. Is it really feasible for the designer to learn to understand the user capabilities and limitations, especially in view of the enormous individual differences existing among humans?

One can argue that people are too complex to be fully understood. Fortunately, all details about users are really not necessary in preparation for interface design. Yet, the HCI designer must construct and use some kind of appropriate user model. Several definitional models were already suggested earlier (Definitions 3.1–3.4). A generic version is:

Definition 3.5. **User model**: a representation of an individual user or of a group of users.

The literature on user modeling is growing steadily. Significant recent publications include the collection of papers edited by Kobsa and Wahlster (1989). Earlier contributions include: Rich (1979, 1983), Card *et al.* (1983), Dagwell and Weber (1983), and Williges (1987). Many different types of user models are possible, not only the ones defined in this chapter. The approach taken in this book is, first of all, to construct a comprehensive, representative profile of the user, incorporating those major factors that are expected to have either enabling or constraining influence on the design.

Definition 3.6. **User profile**: a concise description of a computer user's abilities, interests, preferences, etc., as confirmed by collectible data or measurements; a list of named characteristics or attributes that represent a user.

It becomes the designer's responsibility to select a *subset* of all characteristics that can be included in a user profile. He/she must choose the most relevant and important factors for a particular design, and then collect and analyze the corresponding data, thereby arriving at a particular, specialized version of the user model to be targeted.

Figure 3.2 presents a framework of factor groupings constituting such a general user profile. It is stratified into columns corresponding to the following three major categories:

- *Factual data*, representing information about the user's current abilities and interests, as they may be recorded for a particular user and/ or known to apply to human users collectively (based on scientific knowledge). These data are to be as *objective* as possible. They are to enable the designer to determine the needs that are implied and that, therefore, should be satisfied by interface design. Potentially conflicting or corroborating information may be forthcoming from the other two columns:

- *User opinions*, representing information about what the user personally thinks he/she wants or prefers in the interface. Indicated wants may or may not be consistent with what seems to be implied by the factual data (above). This category tends to be *subjective* in nature. Interviews and questionnaires are generally employed to collect the information. Although designers may appear presumptuous in possibly overruling a user's opinion, they have sometimes found that what a user wants is not necessarily the same as what a user really needs.

- *Measured or observed data*, representing information that reflects how the user actually performs in interaction with the computer for specific purposes. This category, therefore, transcends the relatively static, factual data (first category) by illustrating what the user's capabilities and limitations really are, or seem to be. Such information must be acquired by a third party. It is generally *objective* in nature, if based on measurements, but it may also include relatively *subjective* results, based on observations. It is possible to use these measured or observed results to modify the factual data and also even change the user opinions.

The factual data category is portrayed, in Fig. 3.2, as consisting of four groups plus a special group that variously combines and transcends the factors of the other four. Short lists of representative factors are displayed for each group. They are *not* intended to be exhaustive. In later chapters, a number of these are utilized while illustrating design methods. Also, the reader is asked in several exercises (at the end of this chapter) to expand and refine the lists. A large variety of such lists can be found among the indicated readings.

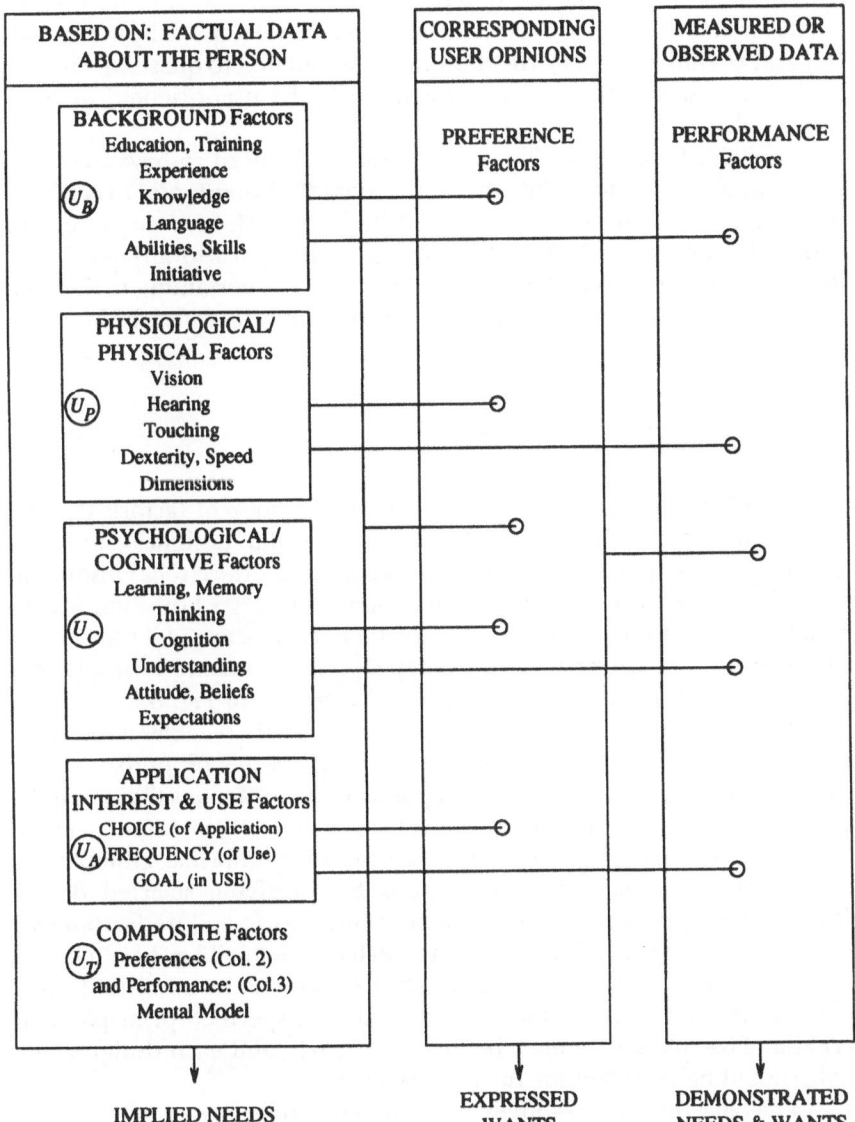

FIGURE 3.2. Stratification of factors in user profile.

The second category (middle column) of Fig. 3.2 can provide the designer with subjective input directly from the user. Instead of going strictly according to the facts, representing either the specific user or whatever knowledge exists about humans in general (especially in psychology and cognitive science), the designer is stimulated to question whether or not certain interface features might really be user-oriented or user-preferred.

The third column of Fig. 3.2 represents the need to have ways and means in place both to update the factual data (Column 1) and to confirm, deny, and/or update user opinions (Column 2). Effective measurement and evaluation methods must be utilized, with regard to any particular design factor or some combination of design factors pertaining to the user. They are relevant to this material *before, during*, as well as *after* the interface design process is carried out.

3.4. Illustrative Factors and Effects

At this point, it is important to justify each group of factors, thereby establishing an overall rationale that can be useful to designers. Justification is given by presenting illustrative cause-and-effect relationships in terms of IF–THEN clauses, in the succession of Tables 3.1 through 3.5. To facilitate reference to the examples, the table entries are identified mnemonically and by category. Thus, entry $U_{B,2}$ is the second example of a *U*ser factor pertaining to the *B*ackground category of Fig. 3.2.

The column entitled "Critique or rationale" in those tables is intended to emphasize the following, during this early stage of preparing for interface design: (1) the variability in possible design actions that might be taken in reaction to particular design factors and (2) the importance of remembering through recordings, even by using informal annotations, any points of comparison and reasons for justifying selected design features. We need to encourage designer sensitivity to and understanding of how user factors may/should affect interface design. The "best" choices of design features will later be seen to be dependent also on other factors (e.g., those covered in Chapters 4 and 5) and on specified principles and criteria. They ultimately must be justified clearly, and each design rationale should be recorded for future reference.

The tables only give samples. They are only indicative of the different kinds of factors that may become involved in a given design, subject to local priorities. Consistent with the title of this part of the book, we are talking here about one of the key, prerequisite knowledge areas that the HCI designer should understand. A wide range of factors is potentially eligible for consideration in a particular design. In Part III, the establishment of design principles (as goals) will enable the narrowing down of these factors to a selected, more manageable subset.

3.4.1. Background Factors

The user-based design factors can be categorized in a variety of ways. Most important is that the designer define the range properly and then deal with it effectively. In our categorization (Column 1 of Fig. 3.2), the first group represents the user's background. That set, U_B, encompasses the capabilities and traits that the user has already *acquired*, from whatever sources or for whatever reasons, at the time when a computer interface is to be designed for him/her. Using such information, the designer may be able to categorize or rank user abilities, e.g., into experts, apprentices, novices, and various gradations in between. Besides the commonly used factors (e.g., education, domain-specific experience), the set can include evidence of the user's willingness to take the initiative (in interaction) and even his/her level of assertiveness and patience with technology. We could also add the user's predetermined attitude toward computers but have instead opted to place it in the third category.

Note that some factors are missing. For example, user intelligence and cognitive ability are not included. They could be added. So could the gender distinction, although that can conceivably fit in one or more of the other categories, depending on what its purpose might be.

Table 3.1 lists some examples of the effects that background factors may have on the design. The reader is encouraged to supplement the table with other meaningful examples (see Exercise 3.8).

3.4.2. Physiological/Physical Factors

The second set of user factors, U_P (Fig. 3.2), relates to inherent characteristics, of users in general and/or of certain users in particular, that are physical in nature (e.g., Kriloff, 1977; Smith, 1984). It does not matter how these characteristics came about (i.e., whether inherited or resulting from training, conditioning, environment, etc.); the designer need not be concerned with their origins. However, it does matter that such factors be recognized and accommodated in the interface, assuming that they are found (during the design process) to be significant in a given situation.

Some examples listed in Table 3.2, such as giving the user a left-handed input device if he/she is so oriented, may be handled purely via hardware flexibility. Others, such as problems in user vision, may require special hardware and also special-purpose software support. Still others,

TABLE 3.1

Effects of Background Factors

Example	Condition (or cause) IF	Potential results (or effects) THEN	Critique or rationale
$U_{B,1}$	The user is NOT trained in the use of software tool A BUT has experience in using similar tool B for some application	Options (1) training exercises for tool A available on-line; (2) provide comparable commands with tool B, in parallel window	(1) takes user time; user may be impatient; but it supports learning; (2) also supports learning, but it complicates interaction and uses space
$U_{B,2}$	The user is totally unfamiliar with the local operating system	Options (1) use a different operating system; (2) provide a software shield; (3) train the user as needed	(1) may not be feasible; (2) requires special software development; (3) takes user time, but supports learning
$U_{B,3}$	The user has considerable experience with iconic or graphical interaction	Make a similar technique available for the target application	If it is feasible to do so on the target computer
$U_{B,n}$	. . .	. . .	. . .

TABLE 3.2

Effects of Physiological Factors

Example	Condition (or cause) IF	Potential results (or effects) THEN	Critique or rationale
$U_{P,1}$	The user is left-handed	Interactive tools should be organized accordingly	Switchability is desirable
$U_{P,2}$	The user is (partially) color-blind	The use of color distinctions and cues in the visual interface is not appropriate; use other cues, e.g. shape distinctions, positioning	Cues dependent on vision also relate to user psychology
$U_{P,n}$	. . .	. . .	. . .

such as adapting a workstation layout to the physical dimensions of the user (e.g., arm length, knee room), may necessitate more suitable arrangement of the furniture, including workstation components, rather than affecting either the interface software or computer hardware as such.

3.4.3. Psychological/Cognitive Factors

Analogous to what was stated for physiological factors in the previous section, the user also reflects a great variety of characteristics that are psychological or cognitive in nature (e.g., Anderson, 1985; Allen, 1982). This set is labeled U_C. Table 3.3 lists a sampling. Again, the designer must be aware of the possibilities and the effects they should have, if deemed significant, on the design features to be specified and implemented. Obviously, as before, those features should be aimed at ameliorating, if not overcoming, various user weaknesses and at supporting or reinforcing user strengths. An illustrative feature that compensates for a user's weakness, e.g., inability to spell ($U_{C,2}$), is to provide spelling correction (Durham *et al.*, 1983).

TABLE 3.3
Effects of Psychological or Cognitive Factors

Example	Condition (or cause) IF	Potential results (or effects) THEN	Critique or rationale
$U_{C,1}$	The user has a specified limit in memory capacity (e.g., in number of simultaneous items)	The amount of information displayed in parallel should be restricted accordingly	7 plus or minus 2 rule is significant here (Miller, 1956)
$U_{C,2}$	The user is prone to making many spelling mistakes	Provide spelling checking and correction either (1) automatically or (2) on demand	Such help should become standard, but requires suitable dictionary developments and software support
$U_{C,3}$	The user has a demonstrated difficulty in understanding a specific language or application	Consider alternative modes of on-line assistance, including context-specific (1) explanations, (2) guidance, (3) illustrations, (4) tutorials	The choice(s) should be based on user preferences (this chapter), the nature of the application (next chapter), and the capabilities of the computer (Chapter 5)
$U_{C,n}$	. . .	. . .	. . .

The reader is encouraged to scrutinize the factors listed (see Exercise 3.5). Notice that user attitude (i.e., way of thinking, acting, feeling) and belief (i.e., holding something as true or real), as they pertain to human interaction with a computer, are included in this category. Depending on how they are interpreted and how they might be used (e.g., in static ways or in dynamically changing ways responsive to user attitudes), they can also belong to the background factors.

The memory factor is also subject to question. It can be listed as a physiological factor as well. Physical memory cells and connections are needed to store information in some combination of spatial and temporal patterns within the human brain. Then, if the complex retrieval mechanisms are functioning properly, we are later able to remember.

3.4.4. Application Interest and Use Factors

This set of factors, U_A (Fig. 3.2), is somewhat different from the three pervious categories. It is to provide a portrait of what the user normally is (considered to be) interested in doing with a computer, given his/her area of expertise (perhaps reflected within the Background category). Alternatively, for users who have not as yet established a track record in using a computer for specified applications, this category must consider projected or prospective factors to be anticipated for new, inexperienced users. Besides indicating the choice(s) of applications to be designed for, the profile should also supply a guide on how frequently or regularly the user can/should be expected to interact with the computer [for the chosen application(s)]. Third, the nature of the application-specific goals pursued by the user can help the designer focus in on the features that are most supportive.

Two simple examples of this category are given in Table 3.4. More interesting examples are dependent on the distinctions among applications, as characterized in Chapter 4.

3.4.5. Composite Factors

This category of factors, U_T, involves subsets of the above-defined factors, considered together with special other factors. They may be combined with what the user says he/she wants or needs (i.e., preference factors, Column 2 of Fig. 3.2) and with results of objective evaluation of what the user actually seems to need (i.e., performance factors, Column 3). These two categories of factors are highlighted briefly in Sections 3.5 and 3.6, respectively. A special composite factor is the mental model that the user brings to bear on the interaction with a computer.

By "combination" of factors is meant their logical conjunction or

TABLE 3.4
Effects of Application Interest and Use Factors

Example	Condition (or cause) IF	Potential results (or effects) THEN	Critique or rationale
$U_{A,1}$	The user intends (or is expected) to carry out programming in a specified language	Convenient access to that language should be provided	Must be concerned about potential incompatibilities with the version known to the user
$U_{A,2}$	The user is expected to interact with the system only on an occasional, infrequent basis	Facilities must be provided to remind the user of details that might be forgotten between sessions	Automatic or on-demand help facilities are desirable but take time and effort
$U_{A,n}$	. . .	. . .	. . .

disjunction, using Boolean operators to relate two or more factors that may be mutually consistent and reinforcing in their effects, or they may potentially be conflicting. A generic expression of such a combination is:

$$\text{IF Factor A } AND \text{ (Factor B } OR \text{ Factor C) THEN ...?...} \qquad (3.1)$$

Such formulations can become very complicated. It is helpful to visualize them by graphical means, as is discussed in Section 3.8 and illustrated with the multifactor schematics of Fig. 3.3. The entries of Table 3.5 indicate some example combinations. Conflicts between/among factors are likely to occur. Priority-based choices and even compromises may have to be made. In any case, the designer must be able to deal with such situations in deliberate and systematic ways. In so doing, the rationale for making any design decision should be suitably recorded, for later recall both by the designer and by other interested parties, as suggested earlier.

Example $U_{T,2}$ in Table 3.5 refers to the special composite factor, namely, the mental model. It also combines various factors, but it involves the creation of some kind of meaningful, cohesive framework, as discussed in Section 3.7.

3.5. User Preferences

Interestingly, the user may disagree with his/her own factual profile and perhaps may wish to alter its contents purposely. For example:

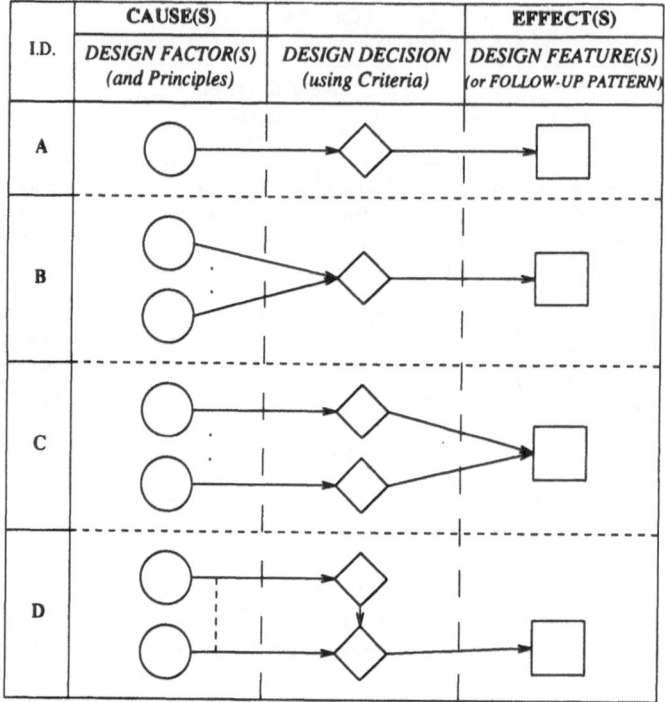

	CAUSE(S)		EFFECT(S)
I.D.	*DESIGN FACTOR(S)* (and Principles)	*DESIGN DECISION* (using Criteria)	*DESIGN FEATURE(S)* (or FOLLOW-UP PATTERN)
A			
B			
C			
D			

FIGURE 3.3. Factors causing features: some patterns.

- On *background*: the well-trained and experienced user, in some area of application, may prefer to be treated as a novice.
- On *physiology*: the left-handed user may nevertheless opt in favor of interacting with the computer in a right-handed manner.
- On *psychology*: even though the user may have difficulties learning certain language features, he/she may not want the interaction to be disrupted by various forms of automatically provided explanations and tutorings.
- On *application interest and use*: the occasional user, with an excellent memory, may want to be treated like the very regular, frequent user.

Many other examples can be cited. As is well known, user opinions can be very troublesome to designers. However, it is far better to be safe and purposely take them into account in the design process, than to ignore/evade them and suffer later consequences (e.g., criticisms, forced re-design).

TABLE 3.5
Effects of Composite (Considered Together) Factors

Example	Condition (or cause) IF	Potential results (or effects) THEN	Critique or rationale
$U_{T,1}$	The user has experience in using Language A, but revised application interest requires learning of a similar yet different Language B	Transition to that different language should be facilitated, using (1) repeated comparisons of language features, in parallel (real time), or (2) intensive training	Option (1) may be more expensive to implement, but it may be more effective than (2)
$U_{T,2}$	Background and performance factors with respect to an application imply a skilled user but out-of-date mental model	Options: (1) reinforce the mental model in new interface, or (2) provide training and tutorials	(1) is probably user-preferred but (2) may be easier for the designer
$U_{T,n}$	. . .	. . .	. . .

3.6. User Performance

The "Composite Factors" category can also include any performance data that supply evidence on how well a user does or can do with reference to some/all of the other factors outlined. Such data result from measurement and evaluation methodology.

Example $U_{T,2}$ in Table 3.5 is assumed to include use of selected data on user performance.

3.7. Mental Models

One of the most intriguing and difficult topics in HCI research is how to define the model that the user somehow learns and subsequently recreates and utilizes when interacting with a computer for some purpose. This is not merely a "mental exercise"; it carries important implications. The HCI designer has to appreciate the existence of such models, understand the range of different models that might be involved, and attempt to adopt or emulate the one(s) most suitable for particular users in specific situations.

First, let us define the term, as it applies to the user's vantage point:

Definition 3.7. **Mental model**: the framework of concepts, components, actions, and/or tasks that the user has constructed in his/her mind for subsequent visualization and use in interaction with a computer.

Notice that we are actually talking about a model within another model. That is, a mental model is couched in a user model (Definition 3.5). How does one describe such a model? The major alternatives for the basis or paradigm underlying a mental model are:

1. *Language*: to express what the user wants to do and how to do it, relative to the "objects" of interest in the system environment; also to understand the computer's responses. Language-based paradigms are inherent to various interaction techniques, as discussed in Chapter 6.
2. *Metaphors*: to relate to a known pattern of activity in carrying out the interactive activity with a computer. Examples are: driving an automobile; storing information spatially in a pattern of filing cabinets and drawers; working with a set of tools and a workbench. Each of these evokes a visualizable model that the user can emulate in his/her interactive activity.
3. *Task actions and objects;* to concentrate on application-specific tasks, relevant actions and objects, and how actions can manipulate (e.g., relocate, transform) the objects. Representation and analysis of tasks are considered extensively in Chapter 4.
4. *Spatial organization*: to arrange the various components, both those that are visible and invisible, in a coherent, logical visualization pattern within which the user's mind can function. Such arrangements relate to interaction techniques and styles (Chapter 6).
5. *Structures*: e.g., task structures; these actually pervade all of the other alternatives listed above.

In addition, various hybrid combinations of the above are possible. Each basis for a mental model must be driven by, or must provide the vehicle or platform for carrying out, the intended computer-based task, in the context of some application. Each model must be invoked using appropriate language and must be contingent on some relevant set of rules. The user must be able to handle both the language and the rules. In a sense, the user must be able to carry out a "mental simulation" of the system of actions and objects involved in an application.

It is clear, based on the great body of evidence about individual differences among humans, that many different mental models are possible. They do not only differ among users; they are also likely to differ within a particular user, even for the same computer application, from one interactive session to another.

Much has been written about mental models. Carroll and Thomas (1982) focused on the use of metaphors in cognitive representation. Gentner and Stevens (1983) proposed mental models for user understanding of a specific knowledge domain. Norman (1983) distinguished the user's mental model (of how the system works) from a designer's conceptual model (of how the system should work for some target group of users). Waern (1987) discussed how mental models apply to the learning of computer-based tasks. More recently, Van der Veer *et al.* (1990) have related metaphors and metacommunication to mental models. Metacommunication involves both explicit forms (e.g., help, error messages) and implicit forms (command names, icons, screen layout) of communication between user and computer; such communication supplements the task-specific variety. Eberts and Bittianda (1993) have studied the mental models evoked by the command-line technique and the DMI style (both described in Chapter 6) to determine which models are preferred by users. Other resources on mental models include Tauber (1988), Ackermann and Tauber (1990), and Staggers and Norcio (1993).

3.8. Decision Schematics

The variable combination of design factors can be both cumbersome and confusing. Visual help is desirable. Figure 3.3 lists several, simple schematic alternatives to portray graphically how design factors are influential in determining design features. The examples are only generic. As we define more types of factors in the following chapters, they are made more specific and interesting.

The term "factor" is being used as causal in nature. The resulting outcome, or effect, is called a design "feature." However, a particular factor, depending on its importance, may in practice:

1. Be the primary cause for specifying some feature; this is implied by Pattern A, Fig. 3.3.
2. Contribute, along with one or more other factors, to a decision on a design feature that has collective, multifactor justification; this alternative is implied by Pattern B.
3. Be used in conjunction (e.g., in a set, in parallel, or in sequence) with one or more other factor-based decisions, toward selecting the design feature to be implemented; two alternative patterns for this are C and D.

The parallel decisions in Pattern C, perhaps made independently by two collaborating members of a design team, can be logically collapsed to render Pattern B. Pattern D is a special version involving time-sequenced decisions with the first (upper) one deferring to the second one.

In addition, each of the patterns of Fig. 3.3 can be viewed as possibly providing input to some follow-up decision schematic, i.e., they may not in themselves lead to final specifications of design features until after other schematics are invoked.

The factors–features terminology is illustrated further in the following chapters and then is formally defined and elaborated, with regard to overall HCI design, in Chapter 9.

3.9. Decision Function: Update

As promised in Section 2.6, the view expressed by Function (2.4) is to be updated wherever appropriate in this book. Thus far, we have characterized the factors representing the user entity only. The entire collection of U-factors can be expressed as follows:

$$U_{\text{factors}} = U_B \cup U_P \cup U_C \cup U_A \cup U_T \qquad (3.2)$$

Therefore, all of the user factors, or U-factors, that may have a bearing on interface design are, in general, contained in a set that is the union of the subsets profiled in Fig. 3.2. However, for a specific design, the designer is expected to select a subset of the above. To simplify terminology, we will refer to that chosen subset by:

$$\{U_i\} \subset U_{\text{factors}}, \qquad \text{for } 0 \leqslant i \leqslant n_u \qquad (3.3)$$

without distinguishing the subsets from which these are drawn. The specific selection will be the responsibility of the designer.

Now, to update Function (2.4), all we can do thus far, after the material in this chapter, is to specify one of the sets that should be contained among the factors [see Eq. (2.1)] used in a design decision:

$$\text{FACTORS}_n = \{\{U_i\}, \ldots, \ldots\} \qquad (3.4)$$

So, factors representing the user must enter the decision-making process. The functional model is clearly consistent with the schematic representation given in the previous section. Other sets of factors, representing the application and the computer/interface, will be added to the formula after the next two chapters, respectively.

3.10. Obtaining Data

The left and middle columns of Fig. 3.2 and the many IF–THEN pairs (tied to factors from all three columns), as illustrated in Tables 3.1

through 3.5, are in need of data to support, confirm, or reject the indicated conditions and claims. Therefore, we must have ways for collecting such data:

1. *Questionnaires and interviews*, to collect user opinions
2. *Measurements and observations*, to determine evidence of user behavior and performance
3. *Published guidelines*, to utilize known information about humans in general and about computer users in particular

The first two means must be included in any comprehensive measurement and evaluation methodology. With regard to the third means, the literature in psychology and cognitive science, as well as in user modeling, is replete with facts and guidelines on what the human user can or cannot do. It is obviously not feasible here to review all of those results. To help in guiding the designer to useful resources, a number of selected references are made throughout this book.

Exercises

3.1. How should "worst" in worst case user be interpreted: being (a) untrained and unskilled, (b) prone to making errors, forgetting things, etc., (c) very demanding of the computer/interface, (d) some combination of the above, or maybe (e) some other distinctions? Answer the same question analogously for the "best" case user. For each case, illustrate (using selected interface features) how the design specifications will be affected.

3.2. The distinctions between individual and collective users bring up the issue of right of privacy in HCI. To what extent should the interface designer ensure that an individualistic user, who does not want to be "bothered" by other users, should have suitable protection? What design features could reflect such protection? Or does a person who becomes a computer user (in a multiuser environment) necessarily have to become part of and participate in that user community?

3.3. The sequence of high-level questions of Fig. 3.1 gives up-front attention to the user. But the sequence can be rearranged depending on motivation and priorities for a design. In realistic interface design efforts, what sequence is more likely to be used? Why?

3.4. Where does "cognitive style" belong in the user profile of Fig. 3.2? Why?

3.5. Do user attitudes, beliefs, and expectations about computers and computer use really belong in the psychological category? Or should they be moved to the background factors grouping? Why?

3.6. Which factors, if any, would you add to each of the five categories of the user profile? Why? Which, if any, would you omit? Why?

3.7. Is there any correlation between the general categories of the user profile (Fig. 3.2) and the high-level design questions (Fig. 3.1)? Explain.

3.8. For each of the five categories of factors in the user profile, hypothesize two more cause-and-effect entries for each of the corresponding tables. Justify each one.

3.9. What effects might the user's (a) frequency of using and (b) goals in using a particular application have on interface design? Explain.

3.10. Construct a Boolean expression that is at least as complicated as Statement (3.1), using a mixture of factors you select. Hypothesize a composite result, along with suitable justification for it.

3.11. Represent the expression resulting from Exercise 3.10 using a schematic pattern selected from Fig. 3.3.

3.12. Based on your experience with computers, describe whether you are aware of creating and using a particular kind of "mental model." If so, what is it based on? Is it application-specific? Do you have an all-inclusive type of mental model as well? If you are not aware of using a mental model of any kind, on what basis do you remember what to do each time you log in?

3.13. Assume that the user's mental model is based on driving an automobile. Describe how such a model might affect the interface design, both in terms of (a) physical and (b) logical features. Justify the features with respect to the user profile of Fig. 3.2.

3.14. Repeat Exercise 3.13, but use a mental model based on a tool kit in a carpenter's workshop.

3.15. Repeat Exercise 3.13, but use a mental model based on a pattern of filing cabinets and drawers in an office, for purposes of information storage and retrieval.

3.16. Read the cited publications on metaphors. List and briefly describe the types of metaphors that have been proposed for HCI design. Does a metaphor differ from an analogy?

3.17. Assuming you have an existing group of target users (e.g., the members of a department), what means would you use to collect the data for each of the factors listed in Fig. 3.2? In each case, how would the means change if the target users were not available to provide information, e.g., when the target users are not yet identified and are only projected to adhere to some specified user model?

COMPUTER APPLICATIONS AND TASKS

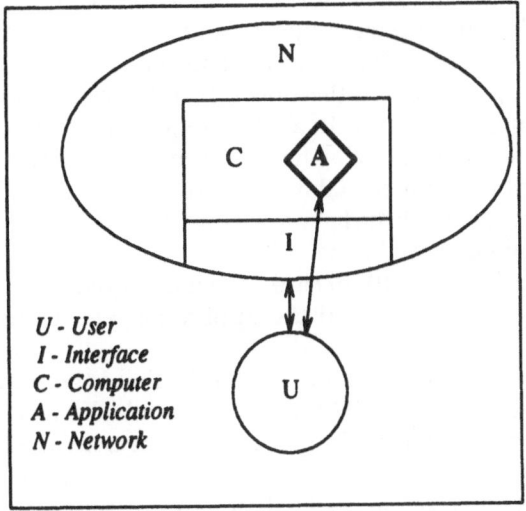

U - User
I - Interface
C - Computer
A - Application
N - Network

4.1. Overview

The factors in the user profile (Chapter 3, Fig. 3.2) include user interest in one or more computer-based application(s). Prior to designing an application-specific interface, the designer should know how the application has been and can be carried out, preferably both *with* and *without* a computer. A good understanding of the target application and how to deal with it successfully is contingent on familiarity with computer-based applications in general. The latter will enable more insightful comparisons and decision-making by the HCI designer.

It is possible to characterize the distinctions among applications, thereby contributing to the design factors and criteria that must be used in a particular design. Such distinctions are drawn in Section 4.2. Included is the fact that all applications are dependent on constituent "tasks," as discussed in conjunction with the multilayer model presented in Section 4.3. A task represents only one part, or one aspect, of the work that the user needs to carry out in a computer-based application. Sections 4.4 and 4.5 emphasize the importance of "task analysis" and "task plans," respectively. In Section 4.6, a broad characterization of applications and tasks is presented by means of a profile of factors.

It is also necessary for the designer to find out whether the target application is feasible, contingent on both the (current, prospective) target user's capabilities (Chapter 3) as well as the (current, prospective) target computer's capabilities (Chapter 5). This is reflected in Section 4.6 in terms of application-specific support requirements (in data storage, processing, I/O) and status. The effects of various factors are illustrated in Section 4.7. Expert opinions (Section 4.8) and performance data (Section 4.9) also play important roles. In a sense, requiring the designer to be able to answer the feasibility question has a preventive purpose. It is to preclude an HCI design that is predictably inappropriate or unrealistic. Also, it is useful in preparation for the later tailoring of the computer configuration to the application, or vice versa.

Finally, in Section 4.10, decision schematics that now involve factors representing *both* the user and the application are discussed and illustrated.

Before continuing at this point, clarification is necessary on the role intended for the designer. The designer should be able to analyze an application thoroughly, including its constituent tasks and task plans, and recognize the requirements it will impose on each of the user, the computer, and the interface in an HCI design. To support that role is the primary purpose of this chapter, *not* to prescribe how to develop application software.

The HCI designer may or may not also be responsible for designing and implementing the application software. Separate software developers can be called upon to do that work. On the other hand, such development may not be necessary, at least in part. For some designs, an acceptable software module may already be available. Reuse of available software modules is a goal in software engineering. However, even if the application software is already in place or can be acquired, the HCI designer should thoroughly understand its functioning and how to interface with it, both in terms of the modular interface architecture and with regard to encompassing the characteristics of the application and its impact on the user within the overall design method (Chapter 10). Hence, the material in this chapter is important regardless of who develops the application software.

4.2.   Distinctions in Applications

First, we should define what we mean by a computer application. That may seem obvious, but it is nevertheless important. It should not be considered as synonymous with a "task," as is often done in the literature.

Definition 4.1. **Computer application**: the activity or the way of using a computer to accomplish something; employing or utilizing a computer for some purpose.

This connotes only a general, high-level category of work carried out by a user on a computer. Example applications are listed in Table 4.1. Most of them have become commonplace. Acronyms are only assigned to facilitate references from the text; they are not necessarily in common usage.

Many other applications can be added to this list (see Exercises 4.1 and 4.2). In contrast to the relatively traditional applications, a small

TABLE 4.1
Example Applications

Name	Acronym
Information Storage & Retrieval	IS&R
Programming (in some language)	PROG
Text Editing/Word Processing	WP
Document Processing Systems	DPS
Database Management	DBMS
Data Analysis & Display	DA&D
Graphic Representation & Manipulation	GRAPH
Design & Engineering	CAD&E
Computer-Aided Instruction & Learning	CAI&L
Financial & Banking Systems	F&B
Modeling & Simulation	M&S
Scheduling & Planning	S&P
Decision Support Systems	DSS
Inventory Control	INVC
Real-Time Process Control	RTPC
Machine Learning	ML
Natural Language Processing	NLP
Robotics	ROB
Architectural Design, Storage & Retrieval	ADS&R
Home-Based Shopping	HBS
Building Tours/Viewing	BTV
Facilities Monitoring & Control	FM&C
Computer-Supported Cooperative Work	CSCW

selection of more unusual applications, which are gaining increasing acceptance in our society, is also included in Table 4.1. Again, others can be added.

The HCI designer must determine whether the application of interest is one that is already established, or is some composite or something altogether new and different.

Definition 4.2. **Target application**: the computer application that is identified to be of interest to the target user (Definition 3.1).

Regardless of how the target application is described for the designer, and regardless of the source of the description, it now becomes subject to analysis in preparation for design. The reader will observe that some of the applications in Table 4.1 are dependent on others, suggesting hierarchical relationships among them. For example, all are initially based on PROG, which is, in turn, dependent on WP. Further, CAD&E, M&S, and certainly BTV are typically dependent on GRAPH; HBS is dependent on both IS&R and GRAPH; FM&C is dependent on a form of RTPC. CSCW is purposely included in Table 4.1 as a kind of meta-application; it is like a higher-level "application of applications"; the type of "work" involved is variable; multiple users can cooperate or collaborate on a number of different applications (e.g., Greif, 1988). The designer must, therefore, extend his/her perspective from a single-user interface to a multiuser interface providing access to whatever application is of group interest.

In considering all applications collectively, several important observations can be made. First, it is apparent, as already illustrated above, that each is dependent on, or consists of, various pieces of lower-level work. Thus, an application must undergo careful refinement; it is divisible into smaller units or chunks of activity. These units are described in terms of subapplications and tasks in the next two sections. Also, toward being able to complete any application, from starting point to finish, it should be possible somehow to "string together" or organize such low-level work units into sequences or scenarios or other patterns. This is discussed in Section 4.5. Third, at a lower level of activity, various applications can be found to exhibit commonalities in requiring similar types of operations to be carried out. This observation provides some of the impetus for the sharing of software modules in multiapplication environments.

The major distinguishing features among different applications can be characterized with reference to the generic model of Fig. 4.1. That model was used initially to represent a command language "action primitive" (Treu, 1975a), but it can be applied to any level of action or activity in HCI. Carter *et al.* (1991) have extended it with more specific definitions of

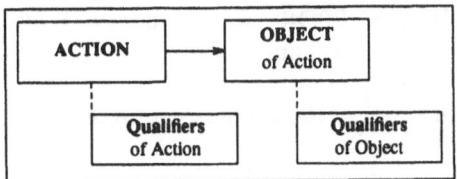

FIGURE 4.1. Generic action–object model.

the qualifiers and for purposes of producing a taxonomy of user-oriented functions.

For HCI design purposes, an application should undergo both *classification*, to determine the kind of work involved, and *quantification*, to estimate how much work it will entail. Classification of the kind of work involved can be carried out using the following profile of questions, tied to the model of Fig. 4.1:

1. ACTION(S): what type(s) of work need(s) to be carried out, at some level of activity, both from the vantage point of the user and the computer. The "qualifiers" of such action(s) include:
   - *HOW* to do them, in terms of method, plan, style, etc.
   - *WHERE* to do them, i.e., with respect to locality of work, e.g., on the visible interface surface, or behind that surface (not directly visible to the user)
   - *AT WHAT LEVEL* of detail, to be discussed in Section 4.3
   - *HOW MUCH* work is to be done; this relates to quantification below.
2. OBJECTS of those actions, in terms of the organizational units of data/information and their representative data types, formats, etc., which must be entered, stored, manipulated, output etc., in the course of application-specific interaction between user and computer. The object qualifiers include:
   - *HOW* they are constituted and organized
   - *WHERE* they are located, i.e., in what storage medium or vehicle, inside or outside of target computer
   - *AT WHAT LEVEL* of detail, or which component/surrogate of the total information object is to be acted upon
   - *HOW LARGE* is(are) the object(s); again, this relates to quantification.

The above-implied process of trying to classify an application leads naturally to questions about the quantities of work and of data involved:

1. PROCESSING SUPPORT with respect to both
   - Computing work, and
   - User work
2. DATA VOLUME in the (above-mentioned) data objects, with regard to both
   - Computer storage, and
   - User memory, perception, etc.

The kind of analysis of the target application that is suggested by this outline should be carried out by the designer on behalf of the user. Thus, the designer is expected to understand both *what* the user will have to do and *how much*. Design decisions must then reflect *how*, i.e., with which features, the work can be performed on the target computer.

Analysis of this type requires a kind of sizing, or estimation, in advance of interface design, of the work that the interface is to support. This is much more easily prescribed than done. Indeed, the state of the art is very limited in this area. Some investigators (e.g., John and Vera, 1992; Gray *et al.*, 1992) have studied the predictability of user behavior and performance at the keystroke level in carrying out very specific tasks (e.g., in text editing) using the GOMS model (Card *et al.*, 1980a,b, 1983). Others suggest that the effectiveness of such models for predicting interface performance accurately has not as yet been demonstrated (e.g., Gugerty, 1993). In any case, we are *in general* not yet able to size up the amount of work entailed by a selected computer application, e.g., in terms of numbers and types of interrelated tasks and data objects modeled at whatever level of interaction. In the future, we should be able to access a comprehensive handbook for HCI design that gives the designer reliable models and formulas to use for such purposes.

In the meantime, this topic is typically given minimal attention during the design process. Instead, trial and error and guesswork are employed, at least during first iteration of design. Then, when it is determined during evaluation that the interface features selected are simply not very conducive to, or supportive of, the type and quantity of interactive work required, adjustments in the design are made.

Many variables are involved. Embedded in the above-outlined analysis questions are *choices* on different ways or styles (e.g., Chapter 6) for doing things, and on different sizes or parts of data objects and procedures to be accommodated by the computer (Chapter 5) using different representation models (Chapters 7 and 8) for access and manipulation by the user, depending on his/her capabilities (Chapter 3). Although the previous sentence is complicated, it accurately represents the design complexity faced by the designer. The ultimate HCI performance will most surely be affected by how well the designer can handle that and how well he/she can integrate all of the different design inputs.

Some exercises at the end of this chapter suggest illustrative analyses of several applications. User-oriented analysis of M&S is described as part of the prototype design in Chapter 10.

It is clear from the above classification + quantification outline that "level" of detail is relevant to both actions and objects of those actions. With that in mind, we next discuss the multiple levels of HCI.

4.3. Multilevel Definition

To clarify and develop the above-outlined distinctions, we must first place a given application into the context of the multilayer model displayed by Fig. 4.2. This model is a variation (and composition) of several other layered HCI models found in the literature. Levels 1 through 3 are essentially equivalent to the command language structure defined by Foley (1979). Then, supplementing that model with the Task Level basically results in the Command Language Grammar (CLG) of Moran (1981).

Some of the terms used in Fig. 4.2 should be explained. "Subapplication" is included as an optional layer (in dashed rectangles), subject to the nature of a particular application and the number of levels it contains. The term emphasizes the fact that an application may consist of two or more lower-level applications that are each deserving of separate identity and design attention. For example, one can view IS&R as consisting of several distinct phases, or subapplications, such as (1) data entry and storage, (2) information search, (3) response output/presentation, and (4) database maintenance/updating.

Likewise, the M&S application can be separated into several subactivities, including (1) constructing and modifying a model (e.g., a graphic version of it), (2) searching for a suitable existing model in a database, (3) transforming a graphic model into a programmed model, and (4) executing the programmed version (i.e., conducting a simulation).

Whether or not the subapplications are carried out sequentially or in parallel depends on the particular application and the interdependencies involved. This is analogous to the execution of software modules either in sequential or parallel modes. In either case, appropriate coordination or, if necessary, synchronization must be effected among the subapplications. From the perspective of the user, this means that clear and harmonious functioning and transitions among the subunits of work must be in evidence across the interface.

The distinction between application and subapplication is, in practice,

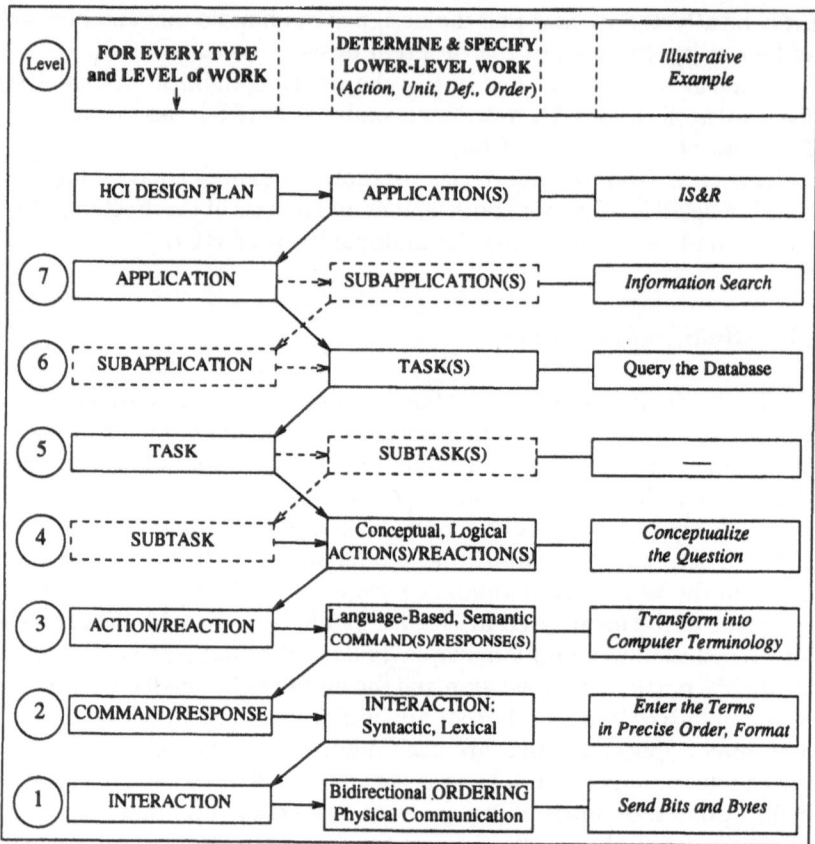

FIGURE 4.2. Layered structure of HCI design.

a matter of semantics and/or preference on the part of the designer. Some people may prefer to treat certain subapplications as if they were high-level tasks. For the purposes of this book, however, it is useful to try to restrict the term "task" to an application-independent level, if possible. The motivation for this is to encourage HCI designers to look for those tasks that are logically similar, or are shared, across different (sub)applications. Opportunities for greater efficiency in HCI software design can result through modular, task-oriented organization of the software.

Let us define "task." Under the umbrella of a computer (sub)application, things must actually get accomplished somehow, by means of tasks:

Definition 4.3. **Task**: any piece of work of a particular type that the user wants or needs to get done, as part of an application; types of action applied to one or more (types of) objects to achieve some (interim) result (or state); a type of action carried out repeatedly.

As implied by Fig. 4.2, a task normally encompasses more than just one fundamental action or command. We can relate this definition to the one given by Miller (1977) for a human task: "a progression of information states from a starting condition of information and goal concept to goal state which completes a work cycle, or what the human perceives to be a meaningful segment in a work cycle." Notice that this endorses some lower-level structure within a task. On the other hand, a task itself plays a role in a higher-level (multi)task structure, as discussed in the next two sections.

An (incomplete) range of application-independent tasks is listed in Table 4.2. The set is fairly representative of most tasks that users must carry out with a computer. Just as was pointed out for different applications, tasks are also dependent on each other. For example, the user must express his/her intentions (with T1) and then move (T2) or enter (T3) the data. Likewise, Task T9 is variously dependent on Tasks T1 through T8. Task T9 can be treated as synonymous with Tasks T7 and T8, in combination. Further, it can be upgraded to the application level (WP).

The action–object model (Fig. 4.1) can be meaningfully superimposed on every level of Fig. 4.2. This is illustrated only for the task level in Table 4.2. In general, every level requires a certain amount of work to be carried out, either by the user and/or the computer. Historically, most attention has been paid to user work performed at the task level and lower levels. The next two sections consider the analysis of tasks (Section 4.4) and the construction of task plans (Section 4.5).

4.4. Task Analysis

The literature has dealt with tasks and task definitions extensively. Examples are the efforts on task-oriented dialogue design (e.g., Ulich *et al.*, 1991) and formalisms for incorporating tasks in input language in consistent ways. Illustrative of the latter is the task–action grammar (TAG) (Payne and Green, 1986; Schiele and Green, 1990). In all cases, some kind of task analysis (e.g., Drury *et al.*, 1987; Carter, 1991) is necessary.

To understand exactly what a particular task entails and how it can be carried out, it must be analyzed. Questions similar to those outlined for application analysis, in Section 4.2, can be oriented to the task level and used as a guide.

Definition 4.4. **Task analysis**: the careful, detailed study of a task to determine its nature, purpose, and component parts (subtasks and/or basic actions) and the order in which they must be carried out.

TABLE 4.2
Range of Tasks

I.D.	(Sub)Task ACTION	Potential OBJECTS	Comments or qualifiers
T1	Formulate or express	Commands, queries, responses, i.e., action objects	For processing by computer
T2	Move or relocate	Data objects, action objects	From one storage area or medium to another
T3	Input and Output	Data objects, action objects	To or from external form from or to internal storage
T4	Represent, structure, or arrange	Data objects, processes, products	For computer-internal storage
T5	Represent, structure, or arrange	Data objects, processes, products	For user-visible input or output
T6	Find, seek, browse, or determine	Data objects, facts	Using appropriate T1
T7	Change or modify	Data objects, processes, programs, display screen	To update the contents or alter the organization
T8	Delete or omit	Data objects, processes, programs, display screen	One special form of T7
T9	Edit	Textual data, tabular data, graphic objects	To make changes, corrections, extensions, reductions
T10	Transform or translate	Data objects, programs, interface layout	From one version (e.g., data type, language) to another
T11	Analyze or evaluate	Data, programs, interface layout	Relative to some criteria
T12	Calculate or compare	Data objects	Using appropriate expressions
T13	Compose or synthesize	Data objects, processes, products	Into multisource, multimedia, etc., results, e.g., after T4
T14	Model	System objects and processes	For dynamic representation, e.g., for execution with T15
T15	Execute	Modeled objects and processes	For computer-based simulation
T16	Correct or remedy	Errors, error conditions	In conjunction with the other tasks
T17	Decide or select	Options, alternate paths	Pertaining to any tasks

Tools such as graphs and matrices have been suggested as useful (McGrew, 1991). It should be possible to express and represent the nature of a task using actions and objects like those listed in Table 4.2. Then, a task can either be repeated, in a loop pattern, or be linked to other tasks in different patterns.

The intertask dependency observations made in the previous section lead to composition at Level 5 (Fig. 4.2) of a collective view of how a task is accomplished *within a pattern of (sub)tasks*. This is illustrated by Fig. 4.3. Note that, for purposes of this discussion, tasks and subtasks are treated as interchangeable. Given the 2-D layering of Fig. 4.2, the reader may visualize the entries of Fig. 4.3 as providing an expansion, or a third dimension, at Level 5. That is, in support of a selected application, the user must be able to invoke one (sub)task after another, from the currently applicable (and legal) set and use them in a clearly defined pattern.

One approach to task analysis is at a relatively high and logical level (Level 2 or higher, in Fig. 4.2), avoiding lower-level details that are dependent on the characteristics of particular computers. Physical/physiological, keystroke-level modeling and analysis were considered extensively in the 1980s. The reader is referred to the GOMS model of Card *et al.* (1980b, 1983), and others who have analyzed or utilized that model. Several such studies were cited in Section 4.2.

4.5. Task Plans or Scenarios

Analysis of applications and their constituent tasks soon leads to the following realization: some are much more "structurable" than others,

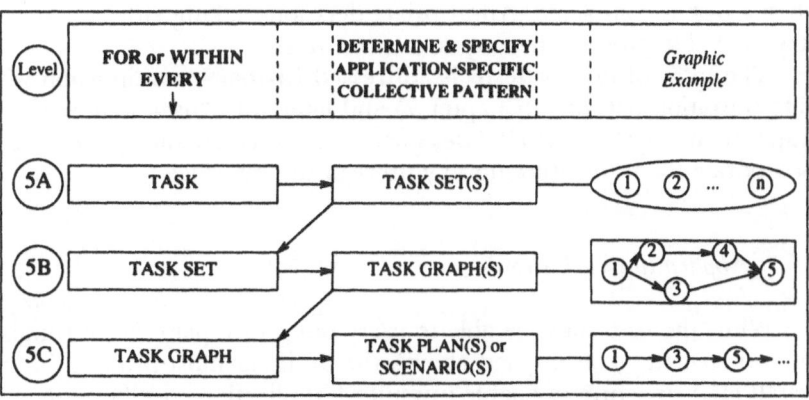

FIGURE 4.3. Composing patterns of (sub)tasks.

when it comes to arriving at a plan, or a scenario, through which the user might be guided toward arriving at a desired task goal and, ultimately, to the goal of completing a particular application, or job. In the literature, therefore, various distinctions have been drawn between *structured* and *unstructured* tasks and how they can be best accommodated (e.g., Bennett, 1977; Miller, 1977).

Depending on user needs and preferences (Chapter 3), resulting HCI designs can indeed be significantly different. The unstructured alternative can give the user, if adequately knowledgeable, much greater freedom to navigate through the application domain. However, less experienced users become easily lost, frustrated, etc. Therefore, in keeping with the structure theme that pervades this book, it is safer to attempt to arrive at general forms of superimposed structure, including state-specific forms of context (discussed in Section 6.2 and Chapter 12), and then provide for the user option to loosen or even eliminate any appearance of task-oriented structure.

We can consider a particular application as involving a sum or sequence (or some other pattern) of specific tasks. These result from analysis of both the individual tasks and the ways in which those tasks can be combined to serve a particular application.

Definition 4.5. **Task plan**: the sequence (or other pattern) of steps (or subtasks, task states) required to accomplish a task or to solve a problem.

Analogous to what Miller (1977) pointed out, such a plan or scenario involves the process or action sequence that is designed to reach task conclusion (or problem solution). It is indicated briefly in the graphic example at Level 5C of Fig. 4.3. But it must also be accompanied by supportive information along the way, involving (1) input to the task problem, (2) reference data during the task, and (3) criteria for deciding when a task is completed. Appropriate decision-making rules are necessary to enable progress from task start to finish.

The topic of task patterns is addressed further in conjunction with state transition networks (Chapter 7) and later with "user state scenario graphs" (Chapter 11). The HCI designer must anticipate such patterns and incorporate them for utilization by users at the interface.

4.6. Application/Task Profile

While the user must be able to carry out a task plan, given suitable support structures (as implied above), the designer must provide for the overall HCI structure to enable pursuit of application-specific goals. For that purpose, the cause-and-effect approach is again usable, with various factors representing the target application and its subservient tasks influencing designer decisions on which system/interface features are necessary.

Such factors are profiled by Fig. 4.4, in a manner analogous to what was done for user-based factors in Chapter 3. They are illustrated in the next section. The columns of Fig. 4.4 correspond to the following three major categories:

- *Factual data*, representing information about the impacts or demands made (or implied) by the nature of the application on *both* the computer and the user. These data are generally *objective* in nature. Depending on any other corroborating or conflicting information (from the other two categories below), they should enable the designer to determine whether and how the target user and the target computer must be suitably accommodated or prepared in order to handle the target application.

- *Expert designer opinions*, representing information about what the expert, who has experience with the application(s) of interest, thinks about it(them). These opinions may or may not be consistent with what seems to be implied by the factual data (above). Because it involves human judgment, this category tends to be *subjective* in nature. A computer application can be viewed and reported very differently by different people.

- *Measured or observed data*, representing information that reflects experimental or operational data on the application-specific performance of the target computer and also the target user. This category can supplement (and possibly contradict) the information obtained from the first two categories. It may be either *objective* (if based on measurements) or *subjective* (if based on expert observations).

The factual data category is portrayed, in Fig. 4.4, as consisting of four groups plus a special group that variously combines and transcends the factors of the other four. Several representative factors are displayed for each group. The groups are subject to being revised and extended (see exercises).

4.7. Illustrative Factors and Effects

As was done for the user factors (*U*-factors) in Chapter 3, we now illustrate the categories of factors that are based on the type of application of interest. The tables (4.3 through 4.7) are identical in format and again

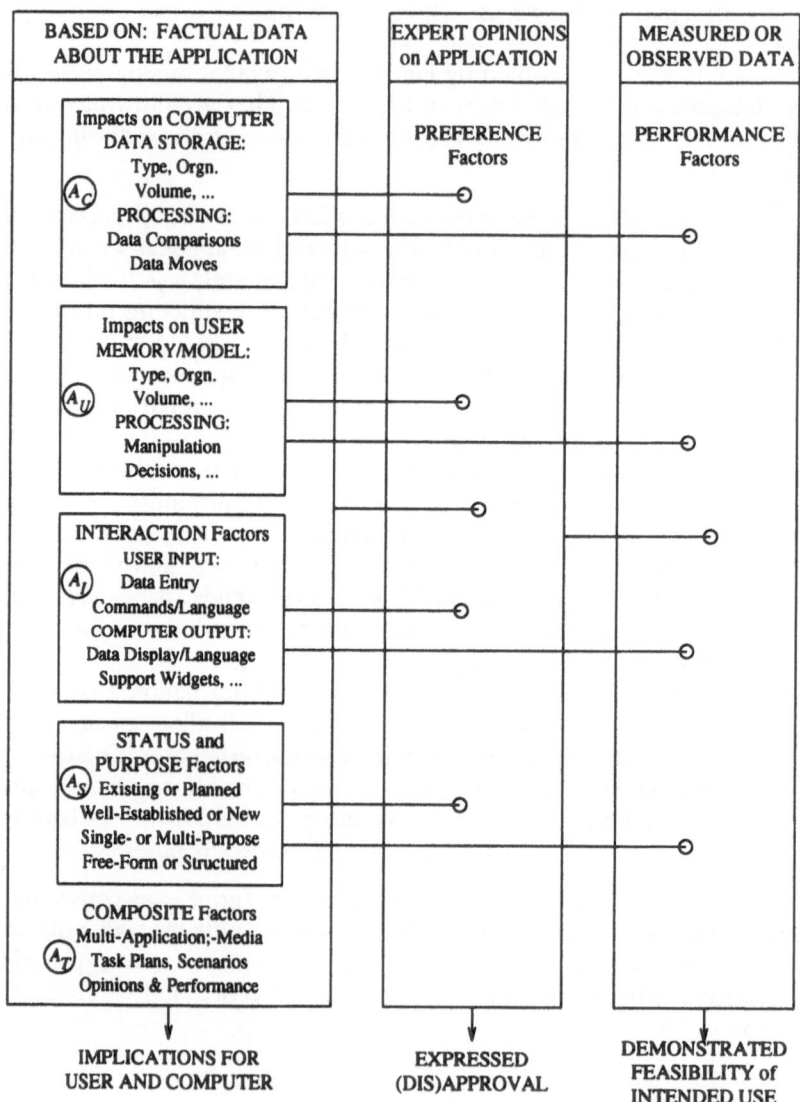

FIGURE 4.4. Stratification of factors in application/task profile.

label the entries for easy reference. For example, $A_{1,4}$ refers to the 4th entry in the *I*nterface category (Fig. 4.4) of *A*pplication factors (*A*-factors).

After the designer understands the *A*-factors that pertain to a particular user-oriented design, the decision-making becomes multifaceted. That is, both *U*-factors and *A*-factors must be taken into account within one or more of the schematic patterns modeled by Fig. 3.3. This combination is illustrated later, in Section 4.10.

4.7.1. Impacts on Computer

The nature of the planned application necessarily impacts what the computer must be capable of doing, especially in terms of the data storage and processing requirements it (the application) imposes. With regard to data storage, it matters greatly whether the application calls for storage of relatively simple data types, e.g., numeric or alphanumeric, or whether it requires more complex forms of visual data, e.g., diagrams, plots, graphics, pictures, videos, and also nonvisual types of data, e.g., audio (speech, music), tactile. Various combinations of these may be desirable.

Besides the data type, the structure and volume of stored data are also significant. They have potential effects on both the computer hardware and software that must be made available. For example, large volumes of data may necessitate a computer configuration with modularly expandable disk storage as well as main memory. Or, altogether special hardware for storage, e.g., for video and/or audio data, may be needed.

Above-indicated application factors, relating to data type, structure, and volume, also impact the data processing efficiency imposed on the computer. Such considerations are dependent on exactly what is involved in a particular application. If it requires a lot of data manipulation, including reorganization (Tasks T3 and T4), searching (T6), and/or computation (T12), and the data volume is large, the processing support must be very efficient. On the other hand, if the application involves less data volume but high-frequency user–computer interaction (T3) and data presentation (to the user), the processing efficiency may become far less significant than the I/O-intensive dynamics and display organization.

Several examples of application impacts on the computer are listed in Table 4.3.

4.7.2. Impacts on User

The nature of the application clearly also affects the user. In analogy to what was said (above) about the computer, the user's storage capabilities (human memory) and information processing capabilities (cognition,

TABLE 4.3
Impacts on Computer

Example	Condition (or cause) IF	Potential results (or effects) THEN	Critique or rationale
$A_{C,1}$	The application involves high-volume text	Substantial computer storage is required	May be costly but is essential
$A_{C,2}$	Graphic representation of the application objects is indicated	Must make graphics hardware and software available	Current technology makes this increasingly feasible
$A_{C,1}3$	Large-scale, repeated sorting must be carried out	Either (1) the hardware or (2) sort algorithm must be very efficient	To prevent undesirable delays noticeable by the user
$A_{C,n}$	. . .	. . .	. . .

thinking, etc.), as portrayed in Chapter 3, may or may not be adequate to meet the demands. If they are not, or perhaps even if they are, the designer should consider ways to provide suitable help. Some examples are listed in Table 4.4.

4.7.3. Interaction Factors

An application also impacts how the user and computer must/should interact with each other. The optimal means, methods, and modes for user

TABLE 4.4
Impacts on User

Example	Condition (or cause) IF	Potential results (or effects) THEN	Critique or rationale
$A_{U,1}$	The application requires many different commands and command versions	Should provide well-organized menus (of command choices)	To facilitate user search and selection
$A_{U,2}$	Many detailed user decisions must be made to accomplish the required tasks	Help is needed at various choice points, either (1) user-requested or (2) interface-volunteered	To give context to the user making informed decisions
$A_{U,n}$	. . .	. . .	. . .

input as well as for computer output must be considered and related to what the application seems to call for, in accordance with user-oriented design principles. Several examples are outlined in Table 4.5. Choice of interaction technique and style (Chapter 6) certainly is important here. Further evidence of factors in this category is presented in conjunction with the illustrative case study in Chapters 10 and 11.

4.7.4. Status and Purpose Factors

Status factors for making the application available, assuming it seems feasible to do so, include whether an application already exists or is being planned. In case it already exists, should it be implemented according to well-established methods (and available, importable software modules), or

TABLE 4.5
Effects of Interaction Factors

Example	Condition (or cause) IF	Potential results (or effects) THEN	Critique or rationale
$A_{1,1}$	The applicaton requires a number of distinct but interrelated phases	The interface should present an overview of the phase structure either (1) using a verbal outline or (2) using a graphical diagram or flowchart	To guide the user through the relevant transitions
$A_{1,2}$	Many, meticulous editing operations must be carried	The user should have effective options available for editing: (1) full-screen editor, or (2) line-oriented editor, or (3) some other familiar version	Based on knowledge of user backgrounds (U-factors)
$A_{1,3}$	Requires entry of large amounts of printed, textual information	OCR may be required	If it is affordable and reliable enough
$A_{1,4}$	The results of processing are in purely numeric form, with complex relationships inherent	Data should be presented in (1) tabular or, preferably (2) diagrammatic or even (3) graphical ways	To help the user in visualizing and understanding the data patterns
$A_{1,n}$	. . .	. . .	. . .

be considered in a new, different, novel manner? That may depend on its effectiveness (Table 4.6, Example $A_{S,1}$). In case it is being planned and is to be treated as new, it can be useful to consider ways in which the application can be carried out without computer help and then to map or transform the results into a computer-based implementation. However, this approach may not be desirable if it prevents discovery of an interesting and effective new way of utilizing a computer to implement an application. So, the designer must have the insight and ingenuity to consider both routes, before deciding on the preferred choice.

Also among the status factors are questions about how multifaceted in purpose the application is to be and whether or not it lends itself meaningfully to superimposed structure.

4.7.5. Composite Factors

It is one thing to design an interface to accommodate one application; it is obviously more complicated when two or more applications are to be available, in a user-oriented manner, across the same hardware and software package (Table 4.7, Example $A_{T,1}$). The increasing prospect of needing multiapplication HCI designs is one important reason for advocating not only structure-based design methods but also, within those, attempts to discern commonalities (e.g., in required tasks) that can enable software sharing and hence more efficient, integrated software organizations.

Also, the design becomes more difficult when not only one data type must be stored, processed, and displayed, etc., but multiple types of data and data presentations are involved. Such cases necessitate differential treatments (both by computer and user) and also demand significantly more versatile and powerful multimedia I/O support.

TABLE 4.6
Effects of Status and Purpose Factors

Example	Condition (or cause) IF	Potential results (or effects) THEN	Critique or rationale
$A_{S,1}$	The task already exists and is being carried out effectively	Use the existing software package	No need to unnecessarily redevelop the software
$A_{S,2}$	The task is new and novel	Must develop support for it from scratch	Expending the requisite resources for it
$A_{S,n}$	. . .	. . .	. . .

TABLE 4.7
Effects of Applications-Based Composite Factors

Example	Condition (or cause) IF	Potential results (or effects) THEN	Critique or rationale
$A_{T,1}$	A multiapplication is to be made available via a single interface	Must provide for consistent and uniform interaction, as possible, as well as easy transitions between applications	Assuming these respond to the design principles specified
$A_{T,2}$	The application has a multimedia requirement	Need a versatile interface, including parallel display via different output devices	Careful coordination and integration are essential
$A_{T,n}$	. . .	. . .	. . .

4.8. Expert Opinions

In the case of U-factors (Chapter 3), the users themselves may be treated as if they were "experts" in understanding their wants and needs. Hence, it is suggested that their opinions be taken into account. Now, in the case of A-factors, it can be very helpful for the designer to have access to experts who are thoroughly familiar with an application and are able to articulate the pros and cons of implementing it on a computer in various ways. Such consultation can provide insights and suggestions to prevent potentially shortsighted or inappropriate designs. But it should not be taken to extremes, to replace an attempt to arrive at an original and promising new type of design that no expert has yet created.

4.9. Performance Information

Likewise, as was done in scrutinizing U-factors through obtaining real user performance information, it is helpful to have application-specific performance data made available. Such data can be oriented either to how an application has been found to impact particular computer configurations (e.g., in storage or processing requirements) as well as particular kinds of users (e.g., with regard to the patterns of application-specific commands issued over a time period). Performance factors may end up having determining influence, when the designer is faced with making choices on desired design features. This is illustrated graphically below.

4.10. Decision Schematics

Figure 4.5 gives two example schematics, using the last two generic patterns of Fig. 3.3. Each involves a U-factor and an A-factor. In pattern C, Factor $U_{C,1}$ pertains to the user's limited memory capacity for keeping track of too many items or chunks of information. That in itself would suggest a decision to provide a suitable help feature. Separately, the designer (or another member of the design team focusing on the application module) could determine that Factor $A_{U,2}$, requiring many detailed user decisions, also calls for giving user assistance in remembering the choices to be made. So, while the two factors independently suggest the need for memory help (in the two separate decision diamonds of Fig. 4.5), they can/should actually be combined to cause multipronged, concerted design action to cover both needs.

Likewise, pattern D indicates that the user may have spelling difficulties (Factor $U_{C,2}$). If a particular application requires the user to do very little spelling, a decision in favor of a correspondingly supportive design feature may not be justified. However, if the application is such that significant amounts of textual data must be input by the user (Factor $A_{I,3}$), then a feature that alleviates the spelling problem (and also other related factors involving input efficiency) must be prescribed. For example, optical character recognition (OCR) on the input side might be appropriate. Short of that, at least a very effective spelling checker/corrector may be indicated.

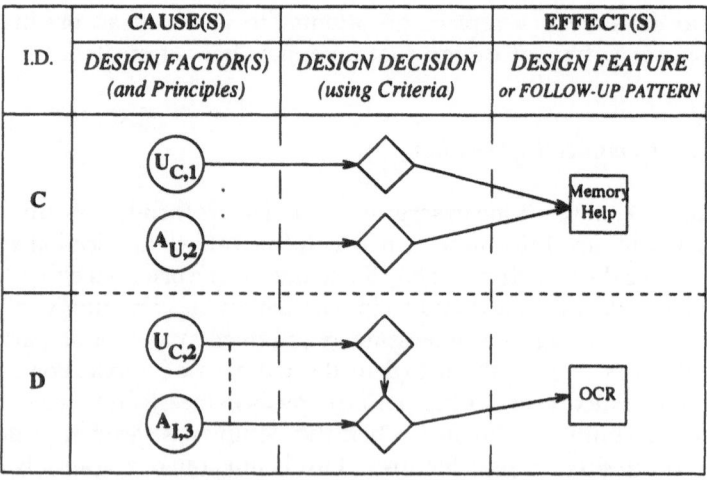

FIGURE 4.5. Example effects of U-factors and A-factors.

Notice that pattern D in Fig. 4.5, unlike pattern C, does not involve two decisions that select the same kind of feature independently and then can be merged. Instead, pattern D has one decision diamond (top one) that leads to a tentative (non)result. It then defers or becomes subsumed by the lower decision box, which ends up specifying a feature.

As is undoubtedly apparent to the reader, such decisions need further supportive means, that is, the criteria that enable the designer to resolve conflicts and select one choice as preferable over another. Design criteria are defined in Chapter 9. Also, many other examples of decision schematics will be implied/indicated in the remaining chapters of this book. The more original and multifaceted a design, the more complex the decision schematics are likely to become.

4.11. Decision Function: Update

With reference to Sections 2.6 and 3.9, the update of Function (2.4) can be done briefly as follows. The entire collection of A-factors is the following union of sets:

$$A_{factors} = A_C \cup A_U \cup A_I \cup A_S \cup A_T \qquad (4.1)$$

This is consistent with the profile of Fig. 4.4. If the subset selected by the designer is simply denoted by:

$$\{A_j\} \subset A_{factors}, \quad \text{for } 0 \leqslant j \leqslant n_a \qquad (4.2)$$

then Equation (3.4) is updated to be:

$$FACTORS_n = \{\{U_j\}, \{A_j\}, ...\} \qquad (4.3)$$

4.12. Obtaining Data

Information about how to design the interface in support of a particular application can be obtained through the following means and methods:

1. *Using published guidelines* on how to carry it out with a computer and in a user-oriented manner; other designers, who have experience with the application of interest, may have good ideas and models on how to proceed.
2. *Modeling and simulation* of how an application might be accessed and carried out via the interface; this can involve new and novel approaches, different from those already tried.
3. *Analysis* of the application to determine its essential patterns and

ingredients, with regard to how they might affect both the user and the computer; taking a detailed, systematic look at an application, whether it is already in existence or not, can produce new and refreshing insights on how to do things differently and perhaps better.

4. *Experimentation*, using the results of some combination of the above, to determine how well the application-specific design might in fact work; this can involve a sample of users as experimental subjects and preferably a prototype version of the interface envisioned.

Some of these means are illustrated in the design chapters later on. They can also be pursued further through the references made to the literature. The entire topical area of task analysis, as discussed in this chapter, is very prominent in the HCI literature.

Exercises

4.1. Prepare a critique of Table 4.1. Which other applications would you add to the list? Are some of the listed examples inappropriate? Would you combine some of them or break some of them up into separate applications? Why?

4.2. In looking to the future (e.g., beyond 2000), what computer applications (other than those in Table 4.1) are likely to become commonplace, even though they may still seem somewhat exotic now?

4.3. Give three examples of dependencies among computer applications, other than those indicated in Section 4.2. Justify each example.

4.4. Select the application in Table 4.1 with which you are most familiar. Analyze it using the action–object model of Fig. 4.1 and relating to the corresponding questions on classification and quantification outlined in Section 4.2. Tabulate your results, by describing the types of actions and objects and giving a general assessment of the interactive work involved.

4.5. With reference to Exercise 4.4, critique the profile of questions you used. Is it adequate to classify the application you analyzed? To quantify it? What else seems necessary (e.g., some kind of mental model to provide a cohesive framework for the sets of actions and objects)? Should the analysis be restricted to a particular level of detail or granularity of objects being worked on?

4.6. Select one of the applications in Table 4.1 (other than IS&R and M&S) that is conducive to being defined in terms of constituent subapplications. Break it down accordingly. Draw a flowchart to indicate the order in which the subapplications can/must be carried out. Include any parallelism that is appropriate.

4.7. Select two of the subapplications resulting from Exercise 4.6 and define them in terms of "application-independent" tasks. Try to find them in Table 4.2; add your own as needed. Are any tasks common to the two subapplications? Are any of the selected tasks dependent on other tasks or subtasks?

4.8. Select a fairly high-level task (e.g., T9) from Table 4.2. Assume you want to achieve two different editing goals on a text file in your directory. Draw illustrative flowcharts to indicate which patterns of (sub)tasks can lead to each of the two goals.

4.9. Compare the tasks of Table 4.2 with the AMOA classification of Carter *et al.* (1991). Does that classification suggest additions or deletions to the table? Identify them and explain.

4.10. Did the flowcharts resulting from Exercise 4.8 end up to be representative of (a) Level 5B or (b) Level 5C, in Fig. 4.3, or (c) some other pattern? Explain.

4.11. Consider the issue of whether and which computer-aided tasks should be *structured* or *unstructured*, in the sense of whether or not the user must follow some restricted, prescribed pattern toward reaching a goal. In your opinion, which of the tasks listed in Table 4.2 are conducive to being structured? Which ones are not? In each case, why?

4.12. Answer Exercise 4.11 with regard to structured and unstructured applications, among those listed in Table 4.1.

4.13. Analyze the profile of A-factors given in Fig. 4.4. Are the five categories adequate to cover the implications of any application for both user and computer? What would you change in the profile?

4.14. Add two more cause-and-effect entries to the illustrations of each of Tables 4.3 through 4.7. Justify each one.

4.15. For each category of A-factors (Fig. 4.4), identify which means/methods outlined (in Section 4.12) for obtaining data is most likely to be successful. Explain.

COMPUTER
CAPABILITIES
AND LIMITATIONS

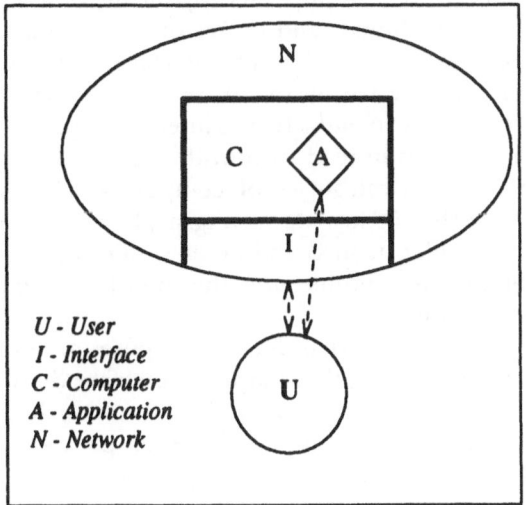

U - User
I - Interface
C - Computer
A - Application
N - Network

5.1. Overview

The two major entities in HCI are both information processors. They are to interact with each other, as if they were partners, in a manner supporting the accomplishment of selected applications (Chapter 4). The model of user–computer symmetry is appealing, at least in theory. It is utilized in a number of ways throughout this book. However, whenever the question of dominance arises, the user is the clear-cut choice; the computer capabilities are to be subservient.

In order to enable successful, user-oriented design, the designer must obtain information about the user entity. This was described in Chapter 3. The resulting user information should be restricted to only those characteristics that are relevant to HCI and that have potential influence on interface performance. Analogously, we can focus on the characteristics of the computer entity. Only those capabilities and limitations that affect the computer's support for the user's interaction with it are of interest. Such characteristics and their roles in HCI design are portrayed in Sections 5.2 through 5.6, in a manner remarkably similar to what was done for the user entity in Chapter 3. This chapter is, therefore, not to be viewed as a detailed technical survey of everything that different types of computers can or cannot do. That would be neither feasible nor desirable for the purposes of this book.

The relevant factors are presented by means of a logically defined computer profile. The brands and makes of computers are deliberately kept anonymous. In trying to develop interface design methodology, it seems undesirable and restrictive to talk about it in emulation mode, that is, by using some specific manufacturer's interface design as the way to go. The computer profile is instead to provide a general-purpose gauge of whether or not certain categories of computers, and their functional capabilities, are sufficient for supporting a planned HCI design. This means that a particular, named computer system can be assessed with reference to the computer profile, *after* the latter has been defined, not as a precursor to defining it.

The reader will observe that, for the purposes of developing design methodology, we are treating the computer interface (hardware and software) as equivalent to "the computer," and the resulting design characteristics are labeled I-factors. This is to avoid the complication of dividing the computer into two (physically and/or logically) distinct modules, one visible and one invisible to the user. Although such separation becomes relevant in some places of this book, it is deemed unnecessary for the user-oriented design methodology itself.

After the computer interface factors (the I-factors) have been identified with regard to the needs of a particular user population (U-factors) wanting to carry out a specific application (A-factors), the design decision-making can be elaborated accordingly. First, it is done using decision schematics, in Section 5.7. Then, the symbolic functional view is updated, in Section 5.8.

Finally, toward implementing the design specifications in either prototypical or operational interface form, the designer and/or developer must obtain data about specific candidate computers. Access to technical specifications and other reference materials must be provided, as mentioned in Section 5.9, in order to reach a conclusion on the suitability of a particular kind of computer.

5.2. Computer Categories

Unlike human users (Section 3.2), computers *can* be categorized into rather homogeneous groupings. There is no need to worry about individual computer peculiarities and preferences, as is generally necessary for individual users. Differences within and among computer groups are describable, in very objective terms, using various quantitative measures (e.g., execution speed in MIPS, memory capacity in bytes), various architectural labels (e.g., RISC—reduced instruction-set computer), and various interface-oriented service features (e.g., event-based, interrupt-driven). Distinctions may also be based simply on modular expansions (e.g., to gain memory capacity), replacements (e.g., to get a faster processor board), or connections (e.g., with different I/O devices, or with network communication equipment).

Such computer distinctions are mostly *hardware-based*. Computers are also categorized using *software-based* criteria. A major distinction is whether a system runs under one particular operating system (e.g., UNIX) as opposed to another (e.g., DOS). Interface designers should be well informed of the technical capabilities, both in hardware and in software, which may have impact on HCI performance. However, the ever-increasing modularity and versatility evidenced by computer design tend to make one type of computer seem (to the user) compatible in behavior to another type. Manufacturer names and model numbers are not necessarily that revealing, as far as HCI design is concerned. It therefore is preferable to use the following more generic categorization. Designers as well as users can relate to these groupings:

- *Computer terminals (CTs)*, not really computers as such, with limited local intelligence, connected (or networked) to some mainframe computer system or possibly a multiuser workstation, for purposes of obtaining computer processing support.
- *Personal computers (PCs)*, stand-alone or networked, representing a variety of manufacturers, sizes, configurations, etc., but many of them compatible with each other with regard to user-observable facilities and performance.
- *Workstations (WSs)*, normally within a network of other workstations and computers, representing generally more powerful and sophisticated systems than are most PCs. However, the distinctions seem to be getting increasingly blurred. Workstations can be PC-based; PCs can be expanded or enhanced to become, or act like, workstations.
- *Other computers (OCs)*, not encompassed by any of the above, but also

requiring suitable interface design. Illustrative are various special-purpose systems, e.g., featuring parallel processing architectures.

Given this broad categorization of computers, the HCI designer must determine and specify the target computer:

Definition 5.1. **Target computer**: the type of computer that is to provide the platform and the environment for implementation of the target application (Definition 4.2) for interaction with the target user (Definition 3.1).

Notice that the target computer does not need to be specified by manufacturer name and model number. In fact, it is preferable to have the designer focus mainly on determining its desirable characteristics. The question of which specific computer models may satisfy those characteristics can then be dealt with on a follow-up basis.

In general, the target computer can be identified with reference to five major questions that are analogous to those asked about the target user, in Section 3.2. The binary relationship model for HCI, developed in Chapter 2, encourages such symmetry. The succession of questions is identified in Fig. 5.1. Each question is discussed below.

5.2.1. Computer Category?

If the target computer is known, because it was already acquired and possibly even installed, it can be considered a given at the startup of design. Alternatively, specification of the target computer can be delayed until after the target user (Chapter 3) and the target application (Chapter 4) have been determined and analyzed. The general computer categories were outlined above (CTs, PCs, WSs, and OCs). Several possibilities exist with regard to making a choice for a particular HCI design: (a) the computer can be *prescribed*, either because it already exists (and maybe is paid for) or because management has somehow decided to go with a certain category, perhaps for economic, political, or other (nontechnical) reasons; (b) the computer is *selectable*, either based on technical grounds (i.e., pick the best available for the user and the application) or based on cost–benefit analysis (i.e., get the computer that is not necessarily the best, but it would deliver the best value for its cost).

5.2.2. Technical Capabilities?

Analysis and determination of which computer to select for HCI design, given the case in which the choice is open to the designer, requires a thorough assessment of the alternatives that are actually available in the marketplace. The different aspects of a computer's technical capabilities

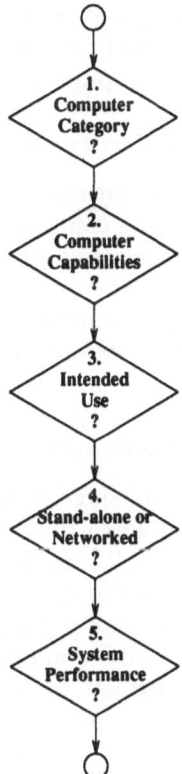

Figure 5.1. Designer questions about target computer.

and facilities, as they are important to serving the user at the interface, are outlined in the computer profile described in Section 5.3. In addition, the necessary technical data must of course be obtainable for specific candidate computers (Section 5.9).

5.2.3.   Purpose: Intended Use?

This is where the designer's task starts to merge with what was already done in studying the target user (Chapter 3) and the target application (Chapter 4). That is, the target computer is to support the target user in carrying out the target application. However, the designer must be able to discern the kinds of tasks and tendencies natural to the user and be able to map or fit them into a supportive environment to be presented by the computer. In general, this is not easy. It involves taking the results of the application analysis (Chapter 4) and trying to arrive at a solution that is mutually convenient and possible (if not optimal) between what the user needs or wants and what the computer is able to give.

5.2.4. Stand-Alone or Network Environment?

Just as we did in talking about aggregating users in various ways, a complication arises in considering computers for HCI, based on whether or not the computer is to be designed for use in stand-alone mode or in a networked environment. The former option tends to make things easier. The designer need not consider communication with and dependencies on other computers, nor the complications resulting from a network-oriented user perspective (Chapter 12).

5.2.5. System Performance Requirements?

Finally, it is necessary to consider, in advance of actual design and development, any expectations about the combined performance of computer and user. The performance factors that are established as representing user needs or wants (Section 3.3) must be accommodated, if possible, by the computer to be used, assuming it is affordable (by management). Such anticipatory performance evaluation should have direct influence on the selection of the most appropriate category of computers.

5.3. Computer Profile

The discussion thus far has already implied that it is highly desirable for the HCI designer to construct a model of the target computer, rather than simply select one by brand name and number.

Definition 5.2. **Computer model**: a representation of a computer or of a type of a computer.

This definition parallels Definition 3.5 for the user entity. Computer models have been presented to introductory computer science students for many years. Typically, a diagrammatic portrait of the major components (CPU, memory, control units, external storage) and their relationships is used. However, our interest now is in modeling the computer in terms of those characteristics that have direct, user-observable effects at the interface. We want to profile the computer accordingly.

Definition 5.3. **Computer profile**: a concise description of a computer's capabilities and limitations, as confirmed by technical specifications, collectible data, and measurements; a list of named characteristics representing a computer, with emphasis on the interface with the user.

Figure 5.2 presents a framework of factor groupings constituting a computer profile. It is stratified into columns corresponding to the following three major categories:

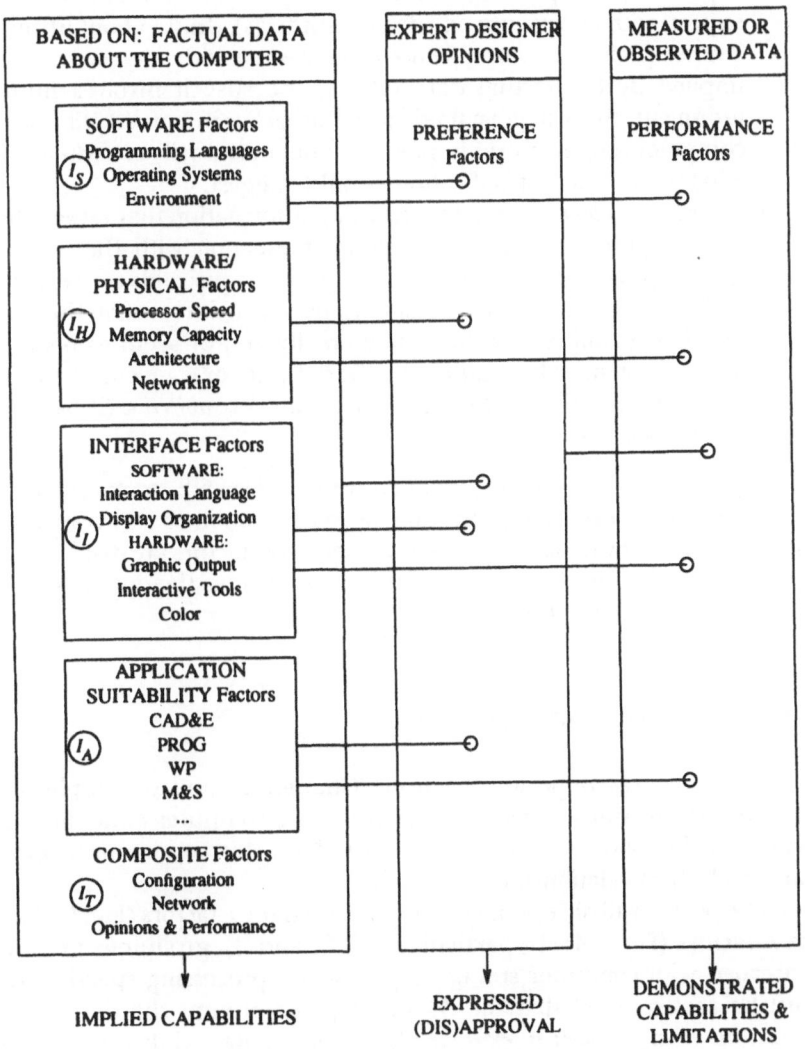

FIGURE 5.2. Stratification of factors in computer profile.

- *Factual data*, representing information about the computer's current abilities and limitations, as they may be recorded for a particular computer and/or known to apply to a class of computers. These data are generally *objective* in nature. Subject to any other corroborating or conflicting information (from the other two categories below), they should enable the designer to determine whether and how the computer can serve the application-specific needs of the user.
- *Expert designer opinions*, representing information about what the expert, with experience on such computer(s), thinks about it(them). These opinions may or may not be consistent with what seems to be implied by the factual data (above). Because it involves human judgment, this category tends to be *subjective* in nature. The way a computer actually works in practice is not necessarily consistent with what its technical specifications would suggest.
- *Measured or observed data*, representing information that reflects how the computer actually performs in interaction with the user for specific purposes. This category, therefore, transcends the relatively static, factual data (first category) by illustrating what the computer's capabilities and limitations really are, or seem to be. Such information must be acquired by the designer or someone else and is either *objective* (if based on measurements) or *subjective* (if based on expert observations).

The factual data category is portrayed, in Fig. 5.2, as consisting of four groups plus a special group that variously combines and transcends the factors of the other four. Several representative factors are displayed for each group. Exercises (at the end of this chapter) give the opportunity to expand and refine the lists.

5.4. Illustrative Factors and Effects

Again, as was done for the user (Chapter 3) and the application (Chapter 4), illustrative factors representing the computer entity are presented, in the following subsections. As before, this is done in terms of cause-and-effect relationships.

The reader will observe an overlap between the I-factors (Fig. 5.2) and the A-factors (Fig. 4.4). In particular, the I_H and A_C groupings are both concerned with computer storage capacity and processing speed. But it must be remembered that the A_C group is to prompt the designer to determine *what computer support the application requires*, while the I_H group focuses attention on *what a/the computer is capable of providing*. Subsequently, the designer must compare the two, in the context of appropriate decision schematics, and arrive at a feasible design result. Depending on whatever design criteria are employed, that result may end up to be a compromise (e.g., the application cannot be fully accommodated because of limited computer capability, and because the cost of the more capable computer is prohibitive), or it may provide more than adequate computer capability, or it may in fact be a (nearly) exact match.

5.4.1. Software Factors

Software packages that are available for many different types/models of computers tend to be (with reference to the acronyms in Table 4.1) in the areas of:

1. Fairly standardized applications or support tools, e.g., text editors to support WP, even though there may exist significantly different versions (full-screen, line-oriented, etc.)
2. Standardized language processors, e.g., compilers to support PROG in some language
3. Software for more specialized needs, reflecting reasonably standardized approaches to applications such as information storage and retrieval (IS&R, DBMS) or to visual data representation and presentation (e.g., GRAPH) or to other special-purpose applications (e.g., CAD&E, CAI&L)

In addition, certain well-established operating systems are widely available.

The more special-purpose, variable, and different the application gets, the more difficult it becomes to find already existing software packages and tools available on any particular computer. As a result, the designer must be prepared to consider the lack of suitable software and the possibility of having to (1) design new software for a selected computer, (2) convert software from another computer to the selected computer, or (3) switch to a different computer on which the software has already been implemented. A few cause-and-effect examples involving I_S-factors are listed in Table 5.1.

5.4.2. Hardware Factors

Because of amazing trends in the 1980s toward modular componentry, microminiaturization, and cost reductions, the computer hardware configurations that are potentially available to HCI designers nowadays provide much greater flexibility and expandability than used to be the case. Nevertheless, in any given designed situation, in which software

TABLE 5.1
Effects of Software Factors

Example	Condition (or cause) IF	Suggested results (or effect) THEN	Design comments
$I_{S,1}$	A compiler for the desired programming language is not available on the computer being considered	Options: (1) have someone convert or adapt the compiler; (2) consider a different computer	Writing an altogether new compiler is probably not feasible
$I_{S,2}$	The target computer only runs an operating system that is not user-oriented	Options: (1) develop a software shield or frontend; (2) give the user training; (3) provide good command explanations on-line	Assuming it is conducive to the application, and the user does not prefer some other operating system
$I_{S,n}$	. . .	. . .	. . .

factors (see above) or administrative factors (e.g., cost constraints) may have dominating influence, a computer under consideration must be thoroughly analyzed and matched or modified to meet indicated requirements. Some examples are shown in Table 5.2.

5.4.3. Interface Factors

Because HCI design should place high priority on the user-visible interface, it is natural to expect those software and hardware factors that have a direct bearing on the interface and the user's interaction with it to be accentuated as most significant. The double-I denotation (I_I), although seemingly redundant, confirms this emphasis. From the user's standpoint, the internal functioning and efficiency of the computer hardware and software may be totally irrelevant, as long as they do not adversely affect what he/she wants to do and see. Some examples are indicated in Table 5.3.

The interface factors represent those capabilities of the computer, both in hardware and software, which become conspicuously and intensely involved in a user's interaction with the computer. Ideally, they should accommodate both (1) what the user is capable of doing and wants to do (U-factors, Chapter 3) and (2) what the application seems to require (A-factors, Chapter 4).

With regard to interface hardware, a range of interactive tools and devices is available (e.g., Foley et al., 1990). In general, they must enable the user to:

TABLE 5.2
Effects of Hardware Factors

Example	Condition (or cause) IF	Suggested results (or effect) THEN	Design comments
$I_{H,1}$	The main memory comes with twice the storage capacity that is currently envisioned for the application	Options: (1) determine whether a smaller model is available; (2) consider other possible uses or enhancements	Given that the cost is reasonable, the excess capacity may be useful in the future
$I_{H,2}$	The computer has only one disk drive, when two have been determined to be essential	Find another model or a replacement, if possible	Assuming that analysis of the application is valid
$I_{H,n}$	. . .	. . .	. . .

TABLE 5.3
Effects of Interface Factors

Example	Condition (or cause) IF	Suggested results (or effect) THEN	Design comments
$I_{I,1}$	The interaction language is based on typed commands when menu selection is user-preferred	Options: (1) design a menu-based interaction language; (2) enable hybrid interaction	It may be possible to provide either or both, depending on the computer selected
$I_{I,2}$	The display area is full-screen, but without area organization	Acquire or design a windowing package	Assuming the computer can support it
$I_{I,3}$	The interface hardware does not support graphics	Replace the display component, if possible, or find a different computer	Knowing that graphics probably means greater expense
$I_{I,4}$	The interface currently includes a mouse, but not a lightpen (with which the users are familiar)	Options: (1) try to exchange the tools; (2) make both availble; (3) train users on the mouse	The pros and cons of these tools should be considered
$I_{I,n}$	. . .	. . .	. . .

1. Obtain *output of any types of data* relevant to the application of interest and conducive to the user's information processing capabilities; included are the major types of visual data (textual, numeric, diagrammatic, iconic/graphic, pictorial) and also audible information (signals, sounds, music). For purposes of supporting visual outputs, the major alternatives are:
   - Hardcopy devices, e.g., printers and plotters, and
   - Softcopy devices, including cathode-ray tubes (CRTs) and other display technologies

   Distinctions must be drawn between outputting (relatively) *static* data (e.g., text, numeric plots) and *dynamic* information (e.g., as in interactive graphics; motion pictures). If the hardware supports the latter, it normally also handles the former, but not vice versa. That is, a simple, alphanumeric CRT cannot be expected to do sophisticated graphics and animation.

2. *Input any types of data*, again in a manner relevant to the application and conducive to the user. For the visual types of data, the major choices are:
   - Manual devices, e.g., keyboards and special tablets for keying, typing, writing, and drawing
   - Automatic devices, e.g., optical character recognizers (for printed text), digitizing devices (for facsimile recording of text, diagrams, pictures), and video cameras, and
   - Devices for interactive manipulation of the data displayed via appropriate output devices (see below)

3. *Interact with the output medium*, for purposes of:
   a. Identifying or selecting data objects, among those on display
   b. Positioning or relocating data objects, within the visible display layout
   c. Requesting or commanding that selected data objects be transformed, connected (associated), stored, retrieved, etc.
   d. Signaling or gesturing what actions are to be applied to which data objects
   e. Entering selected data, including parameter values, as necessary or as requested by the computer

In summary, the user must be able to carry out any type of manipulation of whatever data type (on current display, in computer storage, or to be entered for subsequent display), as is necessitated by the application and as is meaningful and conducive to the user. The major categories of hardware choices to support such interaction are:

- *Cursor-control devices*, such as *mice, joysticks, lightpens*, etc., and
- *Special input tablets and surfaces* [mentioned under (2) above]

Good descriptions of interactive devices and their user-oriented advantages and disadvantages can be found in the literature (e.g., Shackel, 1987; Foley *et al.*, 1990; Jacob and Sibert, 1992). Various taxonomies for sorting out the bewildering variety have also appeared (e.g., Card *et al.*, 1990). Besides hardware devices, the interface is of course also dependent on software that can effectively and efficiently control and service those devices. Included must be device drivers and software that helps to organize the interface layout at the widget level, e.g., with windows and menus. Such support is discussed in Chapter 8.

For now, it is most important to reiterate the fact that interface factors, as depicted above, must be related to both the user (*U*-factors) and the application (*A*-factors). They are, therefore, very instrumental in determining the type of interaction technique or style that is possible and appropriate. Chapter 6 deals with interaction technique/style at considerable length.

5.4.4. Application Suitability Factors

In addition to looking at the different software, hardware, and interface factors separately, it is also reasonable to expect the designer to analyze how well-suited a computer might be for the target application. This means that, based on analysis of how the application is expected to impact the computer (Fig. 4.4), the designer should determine how well (or for how many of those *A*-factors) the target computer will do the job. Examples are given in Table 5.4.

5.4.5. Composite Factors

The last category of factors in the first column of Fig. 5.2 again involves composites, this time for the computer. If the user or the application requires more complex configuration of computer components than is normally the case, or if a computer network environment is being called for, then the designer must be able to consider such factors as well. Table 5.5 indicates some examples.

5.5. Expert Opinions

Besides taking the responsibility of analyzing the various *I*-factors that appear relevant in a given design situation, the designer should also

TABLE 5.4
Effects of Application Suitability Factors

Example	Condition (or cause) IF	Suggested results (or effect) THEN	Design comments
$I_{A,1}$	The computer has been used for the target application with much success	Select it for the HCI design being planned	This is an easy decision
$I_{A,2}$	The computer meets all identified A-factors for the application, except it does not support graphic modeling	Options: (1) consider doing without graphics; (2) see Example $I_{1,3}$	(1) may be acceptable
$I_{A,n}$	. . .	. . .	. . .

take advantage of any available persons who are experts on the computer(s) under consideration. Useful information can be solicited about a computer's potential suitability and effectiveness for the application of interest. This need is implied by Column 2 of Fig. 5.2. An expert can be very helpful in expressing opinions and in pointing out problems that are known to exist in the hardware or software of a particular type of computer. Ancillary issues, such as maintenance service and documentation quality available from a computer's supplier, can also be addressed.

TABLE 5.5
Effects of Composite (Computer) Factors

Example	Condition (or cause) IF	Suggested results (or effect) THEN	Design comments
$I_{T,1}$	A multiscreen arrangement at the interface is desired but presently not available	Determine whether the particular computer can be so configured, or find a computer that can be	This could also include multimedia interaction
$I_{T,2}$	The computer is tied into a LAN, with the potential of extending the application domain	If the target application does not require this, the designer may nevertheless take it into account as a positive factor	This is anticipating wisely what might become desirable in the future
$I_{T,n}$	. . .	. . .	. . .

5.6. Computer Performance

The opinions expressed or the evidence provided by experts should be interpreted as special I-factors to be included in the decision schematics (Section 5.7) composed for HCI design. So should any specific performance data (third column, Fig. 5.2) that can be obtained about the functioning of a computer system. Such evidence, especially if based on computer performance involving the intended kind of application, supplies objective demonstration of what the computer can or cannot do.

Some information may be available from published papers on performance studies. Often it has to be gleaned from other sources. If the design study is of high priority and in view of the potentially high costs of computer acquisition, it may be necessary to conduct selected (benchmark) performance tests as part of the design effort.

5.7. Decision Schematics

At this point in the coverage of this book, the prospective HCI designer is expected to recognize the need to identify factors representative of all three major modules (U-, A-, and I-factors) and to utilize them to compose decision schematics. Thus, the reader is asked to consider various meaningful combinations of the three classes of factors (Figs. 3.2, 4.4, and 5.2) and to hypothesize their effects. Again, the factors are viewed as causes. They must be taken in logical combination toward reaching design decision on HCI design features. Some simple, schematic patterns were indicated in Fig. 3.3. They can get far more involved.

Two examples of slightly more complicated schematics are shown in Fig. 5.3. They involve at least one factor from each of the U-, A-, and I-factors categories. In addition, a "management factor" is introduced as a miscellaneous yet important input into the second schematic. The point of the first example is to show how a user's experience with a specified application ($U_{B,1}$), coupled with the facts (causes) that

1. The user has nevertheless had difficulties with the application-specific software ($U_{C,3}$)
2. The application inherently requires a lot of different commands to be understood and utilized ($A_{U,1}$), and
3. The user him/herself has indicated a preference for getting away from command typing to a menu-based form of interaction ($I_{I,1}$)

lead the designer to decide in favor of a menu technique. That is an "effect." It is used, in turn, together with the knowledge that the target

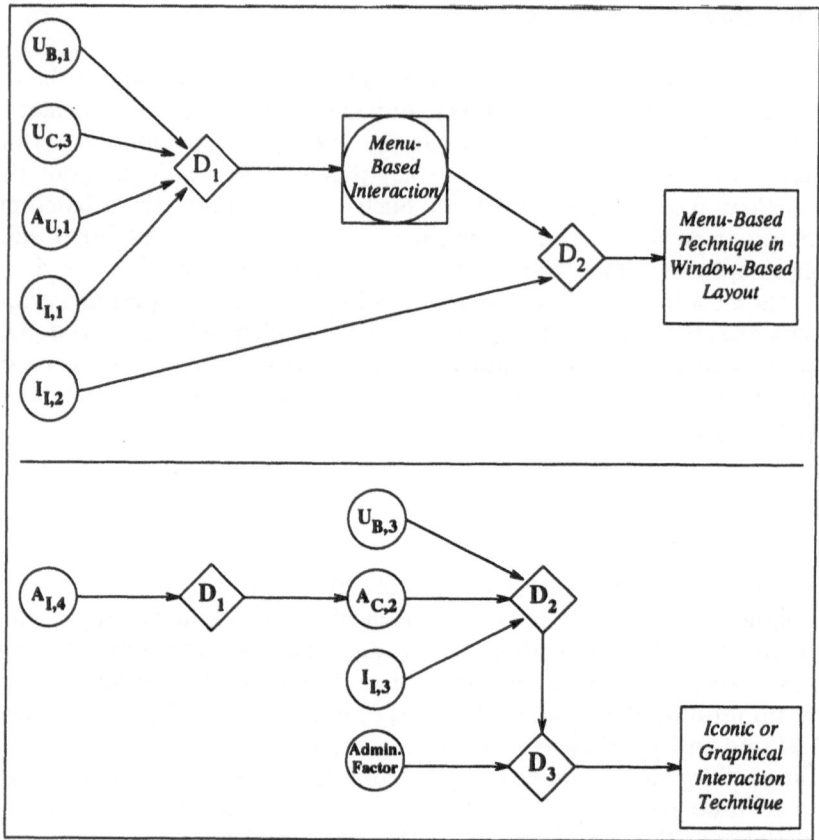

FIGURE 5.3. Example schematics involving U-, A-, and I-factors.

computer currently only offers an unorganized, full-screen display area $(I_{I,2})$. The end result of the schematic is to superimpose a windowing scheme on the menu-based interaction technique.

The purpose of the second schematic in Fig. 5.3 is to illustrate a succession of decisions followed by a deferral to a decision dependent on an administrative (management) factor. First, the designer realizes that the application $(A_{I,4})$ inherently encourages a more visual form of output, in order to make it more user-oriented. This decision in itself becomes the equivalent of a new application factor $(A_{C,2})$. The latter is used together with knowledge that

1. The user has experience with graphical interaction ($U_{B,3}$), and
2. The target computer's hardware does *not* currently support such interaction ($I_{I,3}$)

to decide in its favor. But it is not finalized until endorsement from management has been obtained. In other words, the decision to provide iconic/graphical interaction is deferred until that administrative factor has been cleared.

Numerous other examples can be constructed (see the exercises). It must be reemphasized that the design must be selective *within a comprehensive design framework*. Not all U-, A-, and I-factors can possibly be considered for any particular design. The choice of relevant factors has to be guided by designer skill and judgment, along with prespecified design principles and design criteria. These terms are defined in Chapter 9 and then illustrated in subsequent chapters.

5.8. Decision Function: Update

With reference to Sections 2.6, 3.9, and 4.11, a brief update of Function (2.4) can again be done. Recalling that I-factors are used to denote mnemonically the computer Interface factors, the set of such factors is the following union of sets:

$$I_{\text{factors}} = I_S \cup I_H \cup I_I \cup I_A \cup I_T \tag{5.1}$$

This is consistent with the profile of Fig. 5.2. The subset selected by the designer is simply:

$$\{I_k\} \subset I\text{-factors}, \qquad 0 \leqslant k \leqslant n_I \tag{5.2}$$

Then, Eq. (4.3) is updated to be:

$$\text{FACTORS}_n = \{\{U_i\}, \{A_j\}, \{I_k\}, \ldots\} \tag{5.3}$$

5.9. Obtaining Data

To find out about the capabilities and limitations of target computers, the designer (or his/her representative) is expected to acquire all available and directly relevant documentation. Manuals, books, published articles, and technical reports about particular computers are potential sources. In addition, the evidence provided by experts (Section 5.5) and through performance measurements and observations (Section 5.6) can be viewed as parts of the designer's data collection.

Exercises

5.1. Based on what you know (and have heard) about the four different computer categories (Section 5.2), rate them with regard to their general capabilities for serving users with (a) a well-organized interface, (b) useful and varied functionality (software support), and (c) adequately fast response time. Explain each rating. Given your ratings and explanatory comments, does it matter to you (significantly) what type of computer you are using? Why/why not?

5.2. For each of the five categories in the computer profile (Fig. 5.2), add at least two more factors that you consider important.

5.3. Add at least two more cause-and-effect entries to each of Tables 5.1 through 5.5. Justify each one.

5.4. Find one or more publications that compare the user-oriented performance of (at least two of) the major interactive input devices: mouse, joystick, lightpen. Report on their pros and cons.

5.5. In Section 5.4.3, only the interactive devices for input/output of visually oriented information are outlined. Is there such a thing as tactile information? If so, are there devices for it? Explain.

5.6. Construct and explain a decision schematic, similar in pattern but different in detail from those in Fig. 5.3, which has as inputs at least one from each of the U-factors, A-factors, and I-factors, respectively. The pattern should involve a negative U-factor (i.e., some user limitation), which must be accommodated (or compensated for) by a positive I-factor (i.e., a computer strength) in order to be able to meet a particular requirement (A-factor) of the target application. The result should be to decide on a particular design feature that you identify.

5.7. Repeat Exercise 5.6 for (at least) one positive U-factor, one (or more) negative I-factor(s), as they relate to one (or more) A-factor(s) to be enabled, if that is possible. (If necessary, the causal factors force the designer to select a design feature that is less than desirable, resulting in a compromise design solution.)

5.8. Repeat Exercise 5.6, using at least two conflicting U-factors (e.g., user opinion about something needed differs from empirical evidence about what the user needs). Other factors are unchanged.

5.9. Repeat Exercise 5.8, using at least two conflicting I-factors.

5.10. Is it also possible to have conflicting needs among the A-factors? If so, give an example, retaining the other factors as defined in Exercise 5.6. If not, explain.

5.11. Which (sub)categories of factors in the computer profile (Fig. 5.2) seem to have a general correspondence to (sub)categories in the user profile (Fig. 3.2)? Are there advantages in treating the two major entities in HCI design as both being information processors that have a number of similar (or analogous) characteristics? Any disadvantages to doing so? What are they?

5.12. Carry out a general, comparative analysis of the user and computer entities with respect to the following factors: (a) approximate memory storage capacity (in bits); if they have different types (other than in the physical/physiological sense) of memory, distinguish them; (b) sequential processing speed (e.g., number of simple calculations or data moves per second); and (c) parallel processing speed [e.g., time required to recognize the image(s) in a complex picture]. (Note: relevant information can be obtained from several books/articles on human and computer memory and processing capabilities; such sources should be available in a library in your vicinity.)

INTERACTION CHARACTERISTICS AND OPTIONS

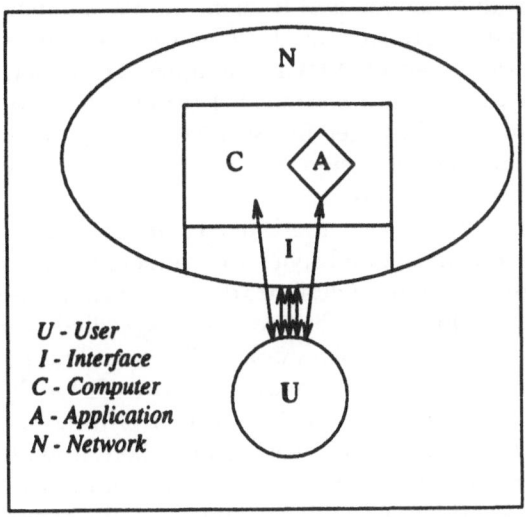

U - User
I - Interface
C - Computer
A - Application
N - Network

6.1. Overview

Thus far we have mainly considered design factors. After the HCI designer knows the target user (Chapter 3), what that user wants to do with a computer (Chapter 4), and the relevant capabilities of the (selected or prospective) target computer (Chapter 5), he/she must consider the characteristics of the binary human–computer relation that was discussed in Chapter 2. That is, the designer needs to understand the ways in which the user and the computer might interact.

Some of those ways may be application-independent, in that they typify natural tendencies on the part of the user and/or computer regardless of the task at hand. Others, however, may be very much hinged on the peculiar nature of the target application. In any case, the way of interacting and the success in doing so are necessarily tied to the capabilities and limitations of the two communicating entities involved. Those capabilities and limitations become the enabling and constraining factors in the HCI design process (Chapter 10). The previous three chapters emphasized identification of U-, A-, and I-factors and illustrated how those factors might suggest certain outcomes. The outcomes that are possible must be made more precise and cohesive. In this chapter, we refer to them as interaction *features* that should be selected and then provided in a design, to accommodate specified design factors.

A profile of relevant definitions is presented in the next section. In Section 6.3, the different kinds of human–human language and communication capabilities are portrayed along with how they have directly influenced the development of HCI techniques. The major, representative techniques are described in Sections 6.4 through 6.8. To facilitate their comparison, they are illustrated in a succession of figures using a selected application [architectural design and information storage and retrieval (ADS&R)] as a common thread.

The relationship between interaction techniques and styles is clarified in Section 6.9. Techniques and styles are presented as the primary, high-level features that result from designer decision-making, as pointed out in Section 6.10. Each high-level feature that is specified requires, in turn, refinement and specification of lower-level features. This pattern is consistent with the well-known, top-down design approach. On the other hand, a number of low-level features may lead to their synthesis, or integration, into a high-level feature, thereby suggesting a bottom-up design pattern.

Finally, this chapter concludes with elaboration of the decision schematics, in Section 6.11, and with an update of the symbolic functional model, in Section 6.12.

6.2. Definitions

Human use of computer technology has led to the adoption and application to HCI of well-known terminology from other areas of discourse. However, as usual, if those terms are not clearly defined, they may be used incorrectly or interchangeably (when they should not be) and hence tend to confuse rather than clarify important design considerations in HCI.

Examples of such terms are style, technique, and mode. It is helpful to define these terms first in their commonly used, dictionary-provided senses. This exercise demonstrates that the words are indeed very much related and hence lend themselves to causing confusion. Nevertheless, good reasons exist for distinguishing them, especially for use in HCI design. Each such definition is, therefore, succeeded by a version tailored to HCI. References are made to Fig. 6.1 throughout the discussion.

6.2.1. Style

We begin by looking at what it means to have a style:

Definition 6.1. **Style**: the manner, method, or way of speaking, writing, doing, etc.; writing or speaking with reference to form and expression as distinct from its subject matter.

What are we typically referring to when we talk about a person's style of behavior, including communication, but not including physical appearance? On one extreme, descriptions such as being pompous, demanding, intolerant, self-centered, come to mind; on another extreme, a person may be undemanding, passive, and very patient. Other expressions connoting overall style include whether the individual

1. Exhibits curiosity or inquisitiveness
2. Is intent on learning or prefers to minimize it
3. Likes to do things directly and promptly with minimal delays
4. Is inclined to be superficial rather than probing into things deeply
5. Wants to work in a systematic, well-organized manner, and
6. Tends to be analytical and evaluative of whatever is being done

The reader is invited to add other styles to this list and to consider how they might impact the interface design decisions (Exercises 6.1 and 6.2).

Notice that all of these descriptive terms and phrases are independent of the subject matter that is the object of attention. A person's style may, therefore, be evident consistently across different application domains. Accordingly, a working definition for our purposes is:

Definition 6.2. **Interaction style**: a manner or way in which one entity, human or computer, wants to do things with the other, based only on form or expression, not on the type of application.

6.2.2. Technique

However, style is an empty shell if it is not supported by appropriate, detailed means for instantiating its "form" and "expression." Because of this fact, technique, and later also mode, come into the picture. Figure 6.1 confirms this dependency.

Definition 6.3. **Technique**: the method or way of performing the mechanical details of some art; any special method or system of doing something.

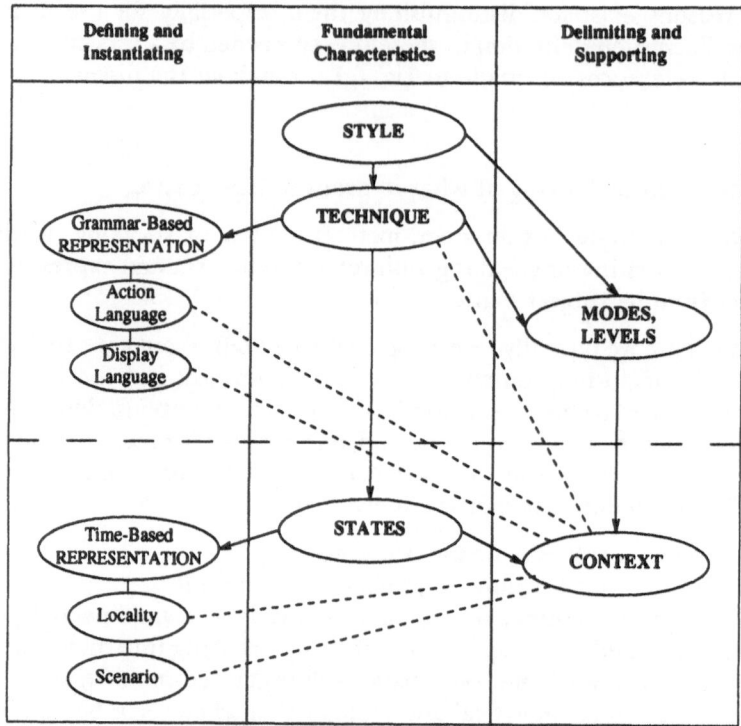

FIGURE 6.1. Interaction characteristics and support.

For purposes of HCI design, this definition is reworded as follows:

Definition 6.4. **Interaction technique**: a specific method for carrying out the details of interaction between user and computer, toward completing one or more applications or tasks.

Although interaction style, in its most general sense, is defined as transcending different applications, it does not suggest that changes in style are precluded when desired. For example, a user might show a less aggressive and more passive style in accessing a totally unfamiliar software package than in reusing software in which he/she is an expert. However, in general, it is reasonable to expect a user to retain a certain style across different applications, unless factors beyond his/her control dictate otherwise.

On the other hand, when similarly discussing interaction technique, that kind of expectation becomes unrealistic. This is because of the increased dependency on the nature of the application. Although some interaction techniques (e.g., menu-based) may be sharable across different applications, others will have to be distinct. The differences are clarified in Sections 6.4 through 6.8.

Any technique must be clearly describable and representable, in ways discussed in Chapter 7. This is implied by Fig. 6.1. It must also be definable in terms of its language-based components and actions.

6.2.3. Mode

Next is the term "mode," which is frequently used in HCI as well as in traditional, natural language grammar. What does it have to do with either style or technique?

Definition 6.5. **Mode**: the manner or state of existence of something; the property of verbs indicating whether the act or state is thought of as a fact (indicative), a command (imperative), or a wish (subjunctive); a style, fashion, custom that prevails.

To make it more clearly distinguishable from technique and style, we can give it the following interpretation for HCI:

Definition 6.6. **Interaction mode**: the locality or neighborhood of inter-action, which delimits or restricts what can be done and how that is done, by means of a partition into a subset of available techniques or functions or types of commands.

Partition is the key word. On one hand, it can be viewed as horizontally oriented, e.g., providing access to one of several alternative pieces of software, available in parallel. On the other hand, it has a vertical inter-pretation, that is, relating to the frequently used "level" of interaction. So, in this discussion, the term level is a close relative of mode (Fig. 6.1). Indeed, it is an example of mode. But, because of its frequent appearance in patterns of interaction, it deserves separate definition.

Definition 6.7. **Interaction level**: the layer of discourse between user and computer, which is distinguished or delimited by the relative abstractness versus concreteness, or generality versus specificity (or detail), required.

The more abstract and general the interaction, the more high-level it is said to be. For example, the decision to invoke an editor, a compiler, or a DBMS, while in the operating system mode, represents relatively high-level interaction. However, after accessing a text editor, the detailed edit manipulations require low-level interaction. Even lower is the keystroke level of interaction. These distinctions are consistent with Fig. 4.2.

To enter some other interaction level, or some other mode in general, requires an explicit transition or action. However, more than one mode may be simultaneously available and selectable. Notice, therefore, that interaction mode and level can be related to interaction techniques, in that they can restrict a user to one or more of them. For example, the technique for carrying out detailed, character-by-character editing of a file clearly implies different support needs (manipulations, command granularity, etc.) than does the technique requesting a compiler to compile, load, and execute a computer program. Also, a mode can mean having access to only certain functions, or to the software modules supporting those functions. Third, a mode is interpreted as activating only a certain category or family of commands, or a subset thereof, regardless of which techniques might be used to invoke them.

Given such criteria for distinguishing modes, it is evident that mode can enable or constrain different styles of interaction. This fact is implied by Fig. 6.1. For example, you would expect a user with a demanding style to want to use an imperative category of commands. Likewise, an interaction technique can be inhibiting or reinforcing to certain styles of interaction. For example, a relatively passive user would be expected to prefer a technique that displays available options (e.g., by menu) for easy selection, rather than requiring him/her to recall and key in selected commands.

Throughout this section, it has been implicit that preferred interaction style, as well as interaction techniques and modes, are very dependent on user capabilities and limitations (Chapter 3). For example, a novice, inexperienced user is likely to exhibit a different interaction style and to prefer techniques and modes that are most suitable to compensate for his/her limited abilities. But what about the computer? Does the computer also have interaction style and favor certain techniques and modes? Consistent with the symmetric treatment (in this book) of user and computer, the answer is "yes." Each of the above definitions can be rendered applicable also to the computer. However, the computer of course reflects the style, techniques, and modes that were designed into it, given whatever capabilities and limitations (Chapter 5) that were attributed to it, rightly or wrongly.

This fact presents definite problems to HCI design: the style, techniques and modes representative of the user may be different from those of the computer, especially a computer that is already in place and to which the user is obliged to adapt. Then, part of the challenge in HCI design is to ensure that user and computer are compatible in style, technique, and mode. Compatibility may mean matching, accommodating, or complementing each other. Matching each other in style, technique, or mode is conceivable, but, if taken literally, it is likely to cause problems. For example, analogous to what happens in human–human communication, if *both* are very aggressive or if *both* are very passive, the results of communication tend to be less than productive. Likewise, having both entities use the same interaction technique, literally, may not be conducive to both. It may not even make sense. Consider, for example, a user presenting to the computer a menu of possible actions from which the computer (not the user) can choose.

Accommodation is desirable when it comes to providing one party with what is preferred, regardless of whether it is suitable to the other party. Third, complementing each other, e.g., one party taking the initiative while the other is passive and willing to be led (perhaps temporarily), may be the most effective approach. The leadership can change using mixed initiative.

6.2.4. State

Interaction styles, techniques, and modes, and how they are constituted can be defined and discussed; but we need more than that. Their time-dependent dynamics must be determined, in order to understand how selected techniques and modes will support particular styles. Clearly, there must be a connection between the kinds of language components (words, icons, actions) that are used to instantiate an interaction technique and the way the user can utilize them to carry out an application. The latter means being able to move or transition through the application domain in a systematic manner, performing whatever tasks are required toward reaching whatever desired goal.

The two key terms needed to make that connection are state and context. Their relationships to each other and also to technique and mode are broadly indicated in Fig. 6.1.

Definition 6.8. **State**: the condition or situation of a person or other object at a certain time; condition with respect to composition, form, structure, phase or stage of existence; the form or way in which something exists, especially as affected by circumstances.

The concept of a state has been useful in computer science, especially in operating systems and networks, for a long time. State transition diagrams are used to carefully represent how a system moves from one state to another (Chapter 7). Detailed, time-specific situations, such as a system waiting for an input signal from some terminal or process, are frequently modeled in terms of states and transitions among them.

However, states can be used to encapsulate a great variety of time-dependent conditions, ranging from micro-level situations (e.g., the above-mentioned wait state) to much more macro-level or global situations. From the standpoint of the user in HCI, the state (at whatever level) that has a direct effect on him/her is of greatest interest.

Definition 6.9. **Interaction state**: the condition and circumstances shared by a user and a computer in interaction at any point in time, as reflected by the interface in terms of its current composition, functionality, structure, phase, and level of interaction.

Thus, the interaction state is an encapsulation of everything that the user can presently do (and has just done) and what the computer can presently support (or has just supported). What the user, and consequently the computer, can do includes transition to one or more other states. A state may be high-level, such as when the user is interacting with the operating system and trying to decide which software package to employ. On the other hand, the state may be low-level, such as when the user is utilizing detailed edit commands in interaction with some text editor. A state may also be confined to or by any mode.

In any case, whether it is high-level or low-level, or whether it is packed with a large assortment of actions available and results achieved or is rather narrow and limited in scope, an interaction state should be completely definable. However, that does not imply that the entire state is necessarily revealed to the user at the interface, nor is that necessarily desirable (in view of user capabilities, preferences, etc.) or even feasible (in view of limited display area, excessive information volume, etc.).

This brings up the notion of "user-visible" interaction state, or simply user-visible state. It is used here to refer to everything about a current state that is made visible and recognizable to the user, or that the user can at least request, either explicitly or implicitly, to be made visible when desired. Implicit requests are meaningful when system adaptation to user needs is available.

6.2.5. Context

How well a designer actually makes a state visible and, more importantly, understandable to a user is subject to evaluation (Treu, 1994). But, at this point, that question justifies introduction of another significant term.

Definition 6.10. **Context**: the parts that are directly before, after, or surrounding something; the immediate environment; the conditions and circumstances that may explain something.

Motivated by the above-suggested limits on the information that is or should be revealed to a user about an interaction state, we tailor Definition 6.10 as follows:

Definition 6.11. **Interaction context**: all information that is provided or providable at the interface, about an interaction state, at whatever level; information that envelops or is associated with the current state and that may render it user-recognizable and user-understandable.

Notice that interaction context may or may not be effective. Depending on what is presented and how, it may be more confusing than helpful to the user.

Because different levels of state exist, interaction context is applicable to different localities or neighborhoods in an interaction state graph. In other words, interaction context can range from being very localized, e.g., surrounding a simple action command available within an interaction state, to being very global in scope, e.g., encompassing an entire application-specific state transition graph. A hypothetical example is given in Chapter 7 (Fig. 7.2). With reference to a selected state, context may relate to constituents of that state (state-internal context), the neighborhood of adjacent, preceding and succeeding states (state-adjacent context), and, with increasing (logical) radii for the surrounding neighborhood, the entire state transition domain (state-surrounding context, or layers thereof).

Within that kind of global perspective, one further term is important:

Definition 6.12. **Interaction state scenario**: a sequence of interaction states, within an interaction state transition diagram, defined for purposes of reaching an application- (or task-) specific goal.

Interaction context, then, relates to interaction scenario in that, for a user situated in whatever state, it is highly desirable to have the following kinds of contextual information available:

- What alternative scenarios are selectable (to reach the user's current goal)
- Which scenario is currently being used
- Which state (in this scenario) preceded the current state
- Which state (in this scenario) may succeed the current state

In other words, an interaction scenario is a special, directed subgraph, which gives rise to the need for a very useful form of linear interaction context. It is, therefore, different from the contextual neighborhood (or locality context) discussed earlier, in which adjoining states are considered to be available in parallel, without being restricted to any particular scenario.

A different but complementary interpretation of interaction context is presented in Chapter 12. It involves a refinement of context into multiple layers, some of which surround a specific task (in a current state) while others reach beyond, to network-based, supportive resources.

6.3. Language for Interaction

An interaction technique can be defined and formally represented to enable a user to accomplish an application-specific task, perhaps restricted to some mode. However, the technique must be implemented by means of an interaction language (grammar), as implied in the left column of Fig. 6.1. The user should not be asked to invoke constituents of a technique in some arbitrary, illogical pattern. Carefully structured grammatical rules should be applicable.

Definition 6.13. **Interaction language**: the language for bidirectional communication between a user and a computer, based on one or more interaction techniques.

Interaction language in effect superimposes a (consistent) model on the elements of an interaction technique, as is discussed in Chapter 7. Numerous interaction techniques have been and continue to be developed, largely in analogy to what can be done using the capabilities of humans for representing information and for communicating it to each other. The techniques are then enveloped by the rules of language. As a result, an interaction technique is often treated as equivalent to interaction language.

6.4. Range of Interaction Techniques

The audiovisual elements of human–human language include spoken, written, drawn, and gestured forms. They are also subject to being "visualizable" (Treu, 1992). Tables 6.1 through 6.4 present a profile of how the different forms of interhuman communication and representation, indicated in the left columns, have influenced the creation of HCI techniques that correspond to or are dependent on those capabilities. They range all the way from writing in natural language to visualizing and viewing 3-D representations, thereby experiencing what is seemingly "real."

Besides being influenced by human capabilities, interaction techniques have also benefitted from advancements in computer-based processing. Some of these exceed human abilities, at least in speed and consistency. On the other hand, techniques have also been constrained by computer limitations in certain ways, and by human limits in knowledge of how to use the computer effectively.

The major techniques are described in the next four sections in the order listed in the sequence of tables, starting with Table 6.1. To illustrate their commonalities and differences, the application of "architectural design, storage and retrieval" is used as a common thread through the examples. The reason for selecting that application is its rich potential for drawing on the entire range of interaction techniques. We are assuming a model interface for ADS&R that can serve the multifaceted needs of the following users:

1. A user who is an *architect* wanting to make full use of both the design (AD) and the information storage and retrieval (S&R) functions of the application. He/she should be able to:
   a. Access architectural design tools and techniques and utilize them to create new designs
   b. Store the design results in the S&R part of the system
   c. Retrieve any previously stored architectural designs according to specified search criteria for viewing in various alternative forms
   d. Retrieve selected factual information about specified architectural designs, e.g., on dimensions, style, etc.
2. A user who is a *client* interested in the design product should be able to carry out retrieval operations also, ranging from getting questions answered to obtaining guided tours through 3-D architectural representations, perhaps even using virtual reality techniques.
3. A user who is an *intermediary*, e.g., a realtor, should be able to represent the client's interests in interaction with the system. This

TABLE 6.1
Interaction Techniques Based on Writing Skills

F_W	Human–human COMMUNICATION capability	Human–computer INTERACTION TECHNIQUE that builds upon it	See Fig.
1	Writing, full-form	Natural language, written —Input keying —Freehand printing —Freehand writing —Printed character recognition	6.2
2	Writing, imperative mode	Command line interaction	6.3
3	Writing, answer mode	Question–answer interaction	6.3
4	Writing, inquiry mode	Query languages	6.4

may only be necessary when the client is not able or willing to access it directly. The intermediary should at least be capable of utilizing the S&R part of the system. Depending on how much user-oriented support is provided in the interface, the intermediary may also be able to work with the AD part of the application. For example, it might be reasonable to sketch out an architectural layout, as is broadly envisioned and described by the user. If appropriate graphic tools are available, such dynamic illustration of potential designs can be very effective.

6.5. Written or Printed Language

One significant component of the language for human communication is based on skills in expressing oneself in writing. Several major options apply, as outlined in Table 6.1. In the leftmost column, each technique is numbered as a feature ("F") with a subscript that indicates mnemonically the capability it is based on (e.g., "W" for writing). This is done for ease of referring to the entries.

6.5.1. Natural Language

The written form of natural language, when considered as a technique for HCI, remains fraught with difficulties. Such language, especially the English version, is very complex to process efficiently and reliably. It is extremely variable in structure and word forms and meanings, and it is filled with ambiguities and inconsistencies. Nevertheless, much progress has been made by researchers in natural language processing, and a case can be made in favor of its use. After all, would it not be nice if a human could communicate with a computer as if it were another human? Consider the simple example of natural language interaction portrayed by Fig. 6.2. The user (U:) is requesting the retrieval and display of an existing drawing of a house that exhibits a specified architectural style. The application (A:) reacts as necessary and possible.

Many people are not at all sure about the desirability of using natural language for HCI. They feel that more restrictive techniques are in fact preferable. While it may appear easiest for the human user to utilize the language that should be most "natural" to him/her, closer scrutiny suggests otherwise. Not only may the computer have serious problems understanding the user; it could also end up to be as vague, inconsistent, verbose, even incorrect in the use of language, as humans often tend to be.

The pros and cons of using natural language have been discussed at

Source	DISPLAY WINDOW
	.
	.
U:	*Give me an example of a split level style of house*
A:	Do you want to see the front, back, or inside?
U:	*The Front*
A:	From which corner?
U:	*Left*
A:	(See Figure 6.12 for sample output displayed in separate window)
	.
	.

FIGURE 6.2. Interaction with written natural language using input keying.

length in the literature (e.g., Rich, 1984). The issue of considering HCI as being potentially analogous to human–human conversation has been covered extensively (e.g., Nickerson, 1977). The goal of creating "graceful interaction" has also been suggested (Hayes and Reddy, 1983).

Two major alternatives present themselves to designers who would like something that at least approximates natural written language:

1. Use a subset of it, in some restricted way (e.g., the imperative mode), as discussed with regard to command language in the following subsection.
2. Use of various selector devices, such as menus and text string highlighting, to enable the user and system to "negotiate" with each other through clues and prompts, leading to natural language statements that represent what the system can do. The interaction techniques that are especially relevant here are discussed in Section 6.6.

As is true of natural language processing in general, the second alternative is of considerable interest to the artificial intelligence community. Illustrative is the work on explanations by Carenini and Moore (1993). With respect to the first alternative, it is important to recognize that command syntax that is based on natural language (English) is preferable to some kind of less familiar, notational syntax (Ledgard *et al.*, 1980).

As long as humans control the design of how the computer communicates, the pursuit of interaction language design to capture the best of both worlds is likely to continue. In general, this implies the need to use some form of limited or artificial language, or a composition of several different forms and features of language, to arrive at a technique that is efficient and effective, both for the user and the computer. Most of this chapter is devoted to such artificial language-based interaction techniques.

Different means are available for inputting written language. Most prominent by far is the use of keyboards to enable the user to type (or key in) words and sentences in response to system prompts. An example is implied by Fig. 6.2. However, an option is the *freehand printing* of characters. This requires special technology, such as a table for printing the characters distinctly enough so that each one can be uniquely identified (Newman and Sproull, 1979). For verbose inputs of natural language, this option becomes less than efficient or reliable. However, efforts are continuing to improve it, such as through use of recognition engines based on neural networks (Pittman, 1991). Facilitating its usability for both novices and experts is also of interest (Goldberg and Richardson, 1993).

A close relative to the hand-printed input is to *write* it in cursive on some tablet or *ink* it on a display screen. However, this requires analysis of writing style, which is potentially even more irregular and individualistic than is printing style. Merely recognizing a person's signature reliably, e.g., for user authentication, is difficult enough. Therefore, it is not surprising that the actual handwriting of natural language for computer input is not as yet a very feasible option. But improvements in recognizing cursive script are also being made (e.g., Pittman, 1991).

One more choice can be useful and should be acknowledged here, namely, optical character recognition (OCR) (Nagy, 1982). It is not really designed to serve dynamic HCI. Instead it is a form of data input when the volume of such data is considerable. If natural language text is already in printed form, using type font with clearly distinguishable alphanumeric characters, it can be read optically. State-of-the-art OCR technology can perform at rather high levels of recognition accuracy. In fact, it *must* perform at a high level in order to be superior to manual text entry (Cushman *et al.*, 1990). However, the fully reliable recognition of characters, in general, is still viewed as an "unsolved" problem (Chianese *et al.*, 1992).

Nevertheless, OCR can be used in limited applications to obviate the time-consuming and expensive human task of re-keying large quantities of text already in printed form. Further, in looking toward designs of increasingly versatile, multimedia, and multimodal workstations, it becomes more likely that an interactive user may on occasion want to introject the entry of a printed document, e.g., to append to a file or create a hypertext node, and then continue with the interactive session.

6.5.2. Command Line Interaction

Because of the difficulties with full-form, written natural language, it is necessary to restrict its use to special modes. This means that an artificially constrained language, or a language subset, is employed instead. Most prevalent has been the use of command line interaction. From the user's standpoint, it basically involves the imperative model of natural language.

Definition 6.14. **Command language**: the input language employed by a user to command a computer to carry out desired actions.

The use of "interaction language" (Definition 6.13) is preferred over "command language" because of its broader connotation (potentially encompassing any interaction techniques) and its emphasis on two-way rather than one-way communication. The bidirectional pattern is evident also in the technique called command line interaction, as illustrated in Fig. 6.3.

Definition 6.15. **Command line interaction**: the interaction technique that is based on a vertical sequence of alphanumeric lines, alternatingly representing user inputs and computer outputs.

The inputs and outputs normally consist of one or more lines each. The user keys in a legal command or other input consistent with terminology and syntax supported by the system. The latter then responds with whatever is possible and appropriate. The response may be substantive in nature, providing the user with a meaningful kind of result; it may instead be nonsubstantive, such as informing the user of an error condition; or it may initiate a *question-and-answer* interchange, requiring the user to clarify or delimit the requested action.

Command line interaction requires the user to distinguish vocabulary terms in an application domain as well as the command constructs that are legal. However, if the vocabulary is carefully selected (e.g., Rogers and Oberne, 1985), communication is simplified considerably. The technique can eliminate a number of problems associated with truly natural language expression. Further, because it is based on restricted grammar, it is easier to design an interface that provides context-specific assistance to the user who needs or wants it. If nothing else, the potential number of states and contexts during which the user needs help is reduced to a more manageable level.

Source	DISPLAY WINDOW
	.
	.
U:	**display** *house*
A:	style?
U:	*split level*
A:	which view?
U:	*front*
A:	other qualifier?
U:	*left corner*
A:	(See Figure 6.12)
	.
	.

FIGURE 6.3. Command line interaction.

With regard to technological support for command line interaction, the use of a keyboard is again very appropriate. Also, the freehand printing (or drawing) of commands and answers on some medium (e.g., a tablet) becomes more feasible, in view of the restricted vocabulary and syntax. In addition and for similar reasons, other interaction techniques discussed in following sections can be more effectively applied.

6.5.3.   Query Languages

A special version of command line interaction is based on languages tailored for retrieving information from structured databases. Such query languages (e.g., Vassiliou and Jarke, 1984; Gittins, 1986b) developed their own identities and research attention. This happened in conjunction with traditional IS&R systems, such as for retrieval of bibliographic citations (e.g., system descriptions in: Walker, 1971), and then also with DBMS applications (e.g., Wiederhold, 1983).

A database and its associated software must be structured to support searching for its information objects, e.g., employee records, surrogates of books, architectural drawings. This must be possible using terms that are legitimate members of the application-specific vocabulary. They might be words listed in a relevant thesaurus, or they may be any other allowable "keywords" or "search terms."

In any case, queries that are legal (with respect to the system) and appropriate (with respect to what the user wants to find) must be formulated by the user and then entered on the command line. Boolean logic is used, including conjunctions, disjunctions, and negations, to represent and qualify the relationships among terms in a multiterm query. An illustrative query is shown in Fig. 6.4. It has the same effect as the interaction techniques exemplified in the previous two figures. Alternatively, it could first given an indication of the number of responses satisfying the query and then enable the user to decide which ones are to be displayed.

The necessary logic for expressing a query, i.e., what the user wants to retrieve, is generally the same. Hence, even if a formal query language (e.g., with a DBMS package) is not available, it can be built upon whatever application, such as the ADS&R, which includes an organized IS&R component. The query becomes an implied command to *find* the desired information objects and to *display* them or some subset or surrogate versions. If correctly formulated, it tends to abbreviate the lengths and numbers of interchanges between the searching user and the system. Comparisons of Fig. 6.4 with Fig. 6.2 and 6.3 are indicative. "Query-by-example" assistance to the user can be provided (e.g., Zloof, 1975; Thomas and Gould, 1975).

6.6. Location-Based Interaction

The associative nature of the human mind (Hebb, 1949; Hunt, 1962) provides for a significant capability of associating objects based on spatial

Source	DISPLAY WINDOW
	.
	.
U:	*house* AND *split-level* AND *front_view* AND *left_corner*
A:	(See Figure 6.12)
	.
	.

FIGURE 6.4. Interaction using query language.

location and then remembering them accordingly (e.g., Ash *et al.*, 1960; Schulman, 1973). This even applies to the sequence of word objects contained in a grammatically structured natural language sentence. But it goes beyond that. Much effort has been expended in HCI design to reinforce or take advantage of that natural capability. As a result, we have a number of different interaction techniques (Table 6.2) that are dependent on somehow organizing the interface display area into regions. Then, information objects, including those that are integral components of interaction techniques, must be displayed in particular regions in a systematic, consistent manner.

Because the outputs are presented in spatially organized ways, not only must the output technology (e.g., CRTs and CRT-like devices) support such organization and related dynamics, but the input devices must be designed accordingly (Chapter 5). A simple keyboard for line-at-a-time input is no longer adequate. Interactive devices are necessary for direct access (e.g., cursor-controlled) to whatever usable location desired, either in 2-D representation or in perceived 3-D (e.g., Jacob and Sibert, 1992). In the following subsections, it is assumed that suitable hardware, both for output and input, is made available to enable the location-based techniques that are outlined. Technical descriptions of I/O devices and their human-oriented characteristics are found in a number of publications (e.g., Shackel, 1987; Foley *et al.*, 1990).

6.6.1. Menus

One problem that becomes evident in the use of command line interaction is that the user must know and remember exactly what is to be input. This is even implied by the simple examples in Figs. 6.2 through 6.4.

TABLE 6.2
Interaction Techniques Based on Spatial Reference Skills

F_s	Human–human COMMUNICATION capability	Human–computer INTERACTION TECHNIQUE that builds upon it	See Fig.
	Spatial viewing and referencing	Physical and logical location-based interaction	
1		—menus, for selection	6.5
2		—Forms, to fill in	6.6
3		—Windows, to organize output, input	6.7 & 6.8
4		—Templates, to select, enable, etc.	
5		—Screens, to stratify interface	

The user must not only enter the required language components, but also sequence them in the expected order or according to required syntax. Choices for language components involve, in general:

1. *WHAT TO DO?* That is, what action is indicated presently? Examples: find something, or display something.
2. *HOW AND WHERE TO DO IT?* That is, what adverbial information must be supplied to qualify the action? Example: display something only in a certain manner and/or in a certain area of the screen.
3. *RELATING TO WHAT?* That is, what is to be the object of the above-indicated and -qualified action? Example: the computer-based representation of a house.
4. *WITH WHICH FEATURES?* That is, which version and which other adjectival information must be supplied to qualify the object of the action? Example: a wire diagram version and frontal view of the house.

The above components are consistent with the action–object model (Fig. 4.1) discussed in Chapter 4. It should be noted that the adverbial and adjectival qualifiers may at times be interpreted interchangeably. For example, one might consider the "wire diagram" stipulation as qualifying the action (e.g., display in some minimal form) rather than the object of that action.

In addition to requiring the user to express the above-profiled kind of language components, in appropriate order, the system may initiate a question-and-answer mode of interaction. For this interchange, the user must know the relevant range or set of legal inputs. Of course, the system should be prepared to reject illegal responses and inform the user accordingly.

Whenever a limited set of choices is available, depending on support from the interface and the application itself, the potential exists for presenting those choices for display to the user:

Definition 6.16. **Menu**: a listing of choices available in a particular interaction context, involving a set of (1) actions, (2) objects of actions, or (3) descriptors that qualify either the actions or the objects; an arrangement of context-specific choices for user selection.

A menu may or may not be on current display; if it is, it may or may not be in active status; if it is active, it may or may not enable user selection of every one of its entries, i.e., some subset may be precluded from selection in the current context. In this section, which focuses on written/printed language, the entries in a menu are assumed to be represented by words or alphanumeric character strings. In Section 6.7, other data types are used instead.

Many different arrangements of menus are possible, both individually (within each menu) and collectively (among menus). Individually, the entries can be arranged horizontally, in a bar menu, such as is illustrated by the DESIGN, SEARCH, STORE, . . . choices in Fig. 6.5. Using some device to control the cursor, the user can click the device, thereby highlighting and making a selection. Alternatively, the menu items can be arranged vertically, as indicated by the other menus of Fig. 6.5. Other linear arrangements, e.g., diagonal through a display region, are conceivable and theoretically possible. Generally they are less efficient in space utilization as well as less conducive to utilization by the human mind. However, special 2-D patterns [e.g., pie menus (Callahan *et al.*, 1988)] can have certain advantages.

Besides differences in physical/spatial orientation, menu entries can also be organized in logical ways. Examples are: alphabetical order, ordered according to frequency of usage (probably high to low), ordered by category of entries based on some criterion meaningful to the user, or simply ordered according to user preferences. Various pros and cons of ordering menu entries differently have been reported in the literature (e.g., Somberg, 1987).

When considering menus collectively, they can be associated and invoked in either *linear* or *hierarchical* sequence. The linear approach

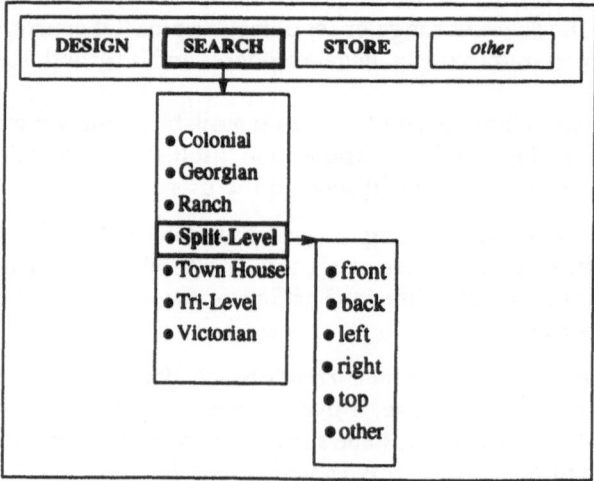

FIGURE 6.5. Horizontal and vertical menus.

simply involves making any selection from Menu 1, followed by any selection from Menu 2, and so on. The menus may either be displayed simultaneously (if enough space is available), e.g., left to right; or each new selection can cause the next menu to be popped up. The sequence of selections is complete after the final choice has been made, in the context of a well-formed input instruction. Alternatively, the sequence may be complete when the user explicitly signals the end, e.g., with a special key.

The hierarchical approach implies considerable dependencies between a selection just made and the options that consequently become available. Thus, as shown in Fig. 6.5, when SEARCH is selected in the bar menu, the corresponding menu of available objects or actions is thereby "pulled down" vertically and displayed. In the example, the menu displays the styles of houses represented in the current ADS&R database. If the user makes a selection from that menu (e.g., Split-Level), yet another lower-level menu can be pulled down to the side as shown. This could distinguish internal from external views (or tours) of the house; the example assumes different external viewpoints that can be selected for the style chosen. Many other possibilities (and hierarchical levels) exist, depending on the nature and complexity of the application. For example, for each major style represented, a submenu of alternative versions of that style could be presented. A selection of "Colonial" could trigger a menu containing "French," "Spanish," "Southern," and "New England" as a refinement of that style. In addition, more interesting viewpoints could be selectable, e.g., left or right front corners. Such capabilities of course depend on the sophistication of the application as implemented.

In addition, menus are typically contained within windows (see Section 6.6.3) and hence can take advantage of various window characteristics. For example, the borders surrounding windows may be activated so that they can be selected for purposes such as:

1. Enlarging or shrinking a menu, or the number of its entries that are visible to the user
2. Scrolling a large menu through a window region, because the latter is too small to enable its total display
3. Delete a menu or remove it from its display status
4. Pop up a menu from inactive to active status, when it is contained in a stack of (partially displayed) windows
5. Pop up some other menu that is dependent on the context provided by the currently active window

The possibilities for different menu arrangements and menu-based interaction patterns are great indeed. The HCI literature on menu designs and their comparisons with other techniques is considerable. Examples are the work by Paap (1988), Walker *et al.* (1991), and Benbasat and Todd (1993).

The menu-based technique is clearly a significant step in utilizing parallel display technology toward taking advantage of the user's spatial reference system and thereby helping the user remember what can be done when. But the whole thing must be carefully organized and controlled. It can become unduly complicated. Further, different users may have good reasons for preferring different menu systems for different purposes. The HCI designer should know how to accommodate those differences.

6.6.2. Forms and Text

Another interaction technique emulates the user's abilities to read text and fill in forms. Unlike menus, which present and discriminate among alternative items (Perlman, 1985), forms require the user to supply information within an integrated framework. Many applications lend themselves to soliciting information from users in a manner analogous to requesting entries in blank spaces on a hard-copy form. Examples are applications for driver's licenses, passports, mortgage loans, and many more. The technique also takes advantage of human skills for spatial referencing, especially in cases of users having to complete the same form repeatedly, such as clerks who act as intermediaries for various types of applicants. The human capability of writing or printing is also necessary.

Definition 6.17. **Form**: a document containing printed information and blank spaces to be filled in; an arrangement of printed words, phrases, and sentences, each followed or preceded by one or more blank spaces, and each one serving as a prompt to the reader for the information item to be inserted in the associated space(s).

This "document" is normally modularized into "pages," one page of it being presented to the user at a time. A form can provide the user with the context for what is to be supplied or entered into the blanks positioned at different locations. The context can be complete sentences, paragraphs, and lists of options; alternatively, one-word prompts, e.g., NAME:, may be adequate.

Figure 6.6 gives a simple example that relates to ADS&R. It implies that the user, who is a potential client, can place a request for architectural services to a named architect. A more realistic version of this form is obviously likely to be more extensive. However, the example demonstrates the basic ideas behind this interaction technique. The menu technique, which involves manipulation and "traversal" of some pattern of multiple

```
┌─────────────────────────────────────────────┐
│  REQUEST FOR ARCHITECTURAL SERVICES           │
│  TO: _____  (Name of Architect)    │
│  FROM: _____  (Client Name)          │
│  DATE: _____                           │
│                                               │
│   I am interested in having you carry out a   │
│   ┌ ─ ─ ─ ─ ─ ─ ─ ─ ─ ─ ─ ─ ─ ─ ─ ─ ─ ─ ─ ┐   │
│   └ ─ ─ ─ ─ ─ ─ ─ ─ ─ ─ ─ ─ ─ ─ ─ ─ ─ ─ ─ ┘   │
│     (search for information, design, other...) │
│   relating to the following style of house:   │
│   ┌ ─ ─ ─ ─ ─ ─ ─ ─ ─ ─ ─ ─ ─ ─ ─ ─ ─ ─ ─ ┐   │
│   └ ─ ─ ─ ─ ─ ─ ─ ─ ─ ─ ─ ─ ─ ─ ─ ─ ─ ─ ─ ┘   │
│    (Colonial, Georgian, Ranch, Split-Level,   │
│     Town House, Tri-Level, or Victorian)      │
│                                               │
│   Please prepare the results for display using│
│     the following viewpoint:  ┌ ─ ─ ─ ─ ┐     │
│                               └ ─ ─ ─ ─ ┘     │
│     (back, front, left, right, top, other ..) │
│                                               │
│                      ●                        │
│                      ●                        │
│                      ●                        │
└─────────────────────────────────────────────┘
```

FIGURE 6.6. Part of a form for filling-in.

menus, is potentially cumbersome to certain users. The forms technique, on the other hand, can be self-sufficient and more straightforward. If the form is properly designed, the user should only need to

1. Read the contextual information and remember much of it for future repetition (if appropriate) in completing the form
2. Select and highlight each blank to be filled in, one at a time and in whatever pattern is preferred (unless the system insists on a certain order)
3. Key in the information in the currently highlighted blank space, as if in command line mode
4. Signal the completion after each blank and after all blanks is/are filled in, using whatever key or other signal is so designated

The user should also be allowed to return to any filled-in entry in order to replace or correct it.

Of course, forms may actually not be as easy to use as implied above. What if the form does not indicate the optional responses and the user does not know or remember the legal set or range of choices for any particular blank space? For such situations, the ingenuity of the designer and his/her understanding of the application come into play. For example, upon focusing in any blank space, the user could be given the option of displaying a relevant menu of choices for selection. Included can be a request for further explanation of what is to be entered. Thus, the forms-based technique soon becomes a hybrid that is dependent on other interaction techniques.

It should be observed that the highlighting of words or phrases of natural language text, leading to feedback from the system on the meaning of those words and the relevant options available, can be interpreted logically as a special version of a form. In that case, the text constitutes the substance of the form (including the cues or prompts), and the user has access to "blanks" of variable length and contents. Hence, unlike the ordinary version containing actual blank spaces, this interpretation suggests that those spaces are already filled in with key words and phrases. It is up to the user to pursue their meanings in detail.

The literature on the use of forms is less sizable than it is on menus (previous section) and also on windows (next section). An example is the work of Jeffries and Rosenberg (1987).

6.6.3. Windows

The use of windows has become very pervasive in HCI. Most PCs and WSs have some version of a windowing package available. After those early years, when the full display screen was utilized inefficiently for simple command line interaction, things finally became better organized. Technology, as usual, progressed to enable such organization. Computer graphics specialists had "clipped" their graphic objects "to windows" on fairly expensive interfaces for some time. But then, a different interpretation of windows took hold and became applicable to less expensive (raster scan) CRT-based interface screens.

Definition 6.18. **Window**: a region on the interface screen that is normally rectangular in shape and is used to (1) encapsulate the display of any information objects and/or (2) provide the display region through which an available interaction technique can be utilized; a bounded display area that may be fixed or variable in both size and location and that may be currently (1) active or inactive and (2) fully visible, partially visible, or totally invisible.

Notice that a window is usable for containing a command line sequence, a menu, a form, highlighted text, or any other display-oriented technique for interaction. This is already evident from the earlier discussion of menus. Specific parts or subwindows can be rendered selectable.

These are normally its borders, consisting of narrow regions between parallel lines, and its corners, consisting of intersections of two such border regions perpendicular to each other. Purposes of such selections include:

1. Creating a new window and associating it with a particular function or interaction technique
2. Repositioning the window on the screen
3. Changing its dimensions, by extending or shrinking its borders, using the help of a temporary (e.g., dashed) and mobile window outline
4. Activating a window by appropriate selection, either within a tiled pattern or from a stack pattern in which it is currently situated and probably obstructed with respect to the user's viewpoint
5. Deactivating a window, either by direct signal or by default (resulting from activating some other window)
6. Scrolling the window's contents
7. Deleting the window

As was discussed for menus, and as implied by Purposes 5 and 6 above, windowing really becomes useful in multiwindow applications. It also enables multiple processes to be represented in parallel via the interface surface. The currently accessible set of windows can then be (1) tiled in some pattern, leaving no part of any window obstructed by another if at all possible, (2) overlapped in some pattern, either arbitrarily decided by the user or possibly appearing in a neat stack giving the user a 3-D perspective, or (3) some combination of the first two. A tiled example is illustrated in Fig. 6.7. Tiled windows may be preferred when a user wants

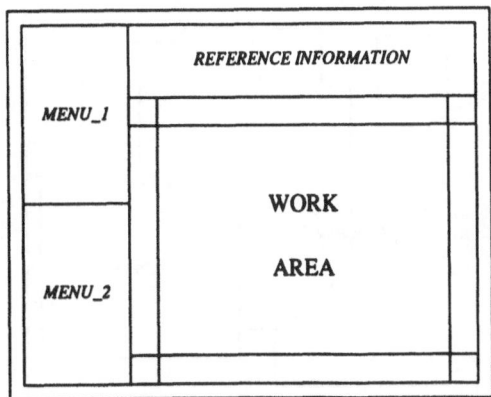

FIGURE 6.7. Example of tiled windows.

or needs to see all of them simultaneously and when they can be positioned spatially to be conducive to user memory and access for manipulation. In a critical, high-stress application, this approach may be the best way to go.

But it of course requires enough display area. For that and other reasons, overlapped or stacked windows are employed most frequently. An example pattern is shown in Fig. 6.8. Many applications do not require simultaneous display of all window contents. Further, the potential exists for too much information display, especially for novice users who may be overwhelmed thereby. Also, more experienced users may simply prefer to hide various windows from view. In any case, the HCI designer should be concerned about providing those windowing options and patterns that are most appropriate for the particular users to be served.

Bly and Rosenberg (1986) conducted a comparison of the tiled and overlapping window alternatives. Many other studies on windowing approaches and windows-generating software can be found in the HCI literature.

6.6.4. Templates

Another technique that can affect interaction is based on the template idea. Templates are dependent on both spatial and logical factors.

Definition 6.19. **Template**: any pattern, gauge, or model upon which something is based; any pattern that is superimposed on another pattern of information objects or interface components in order to (1) distinguish

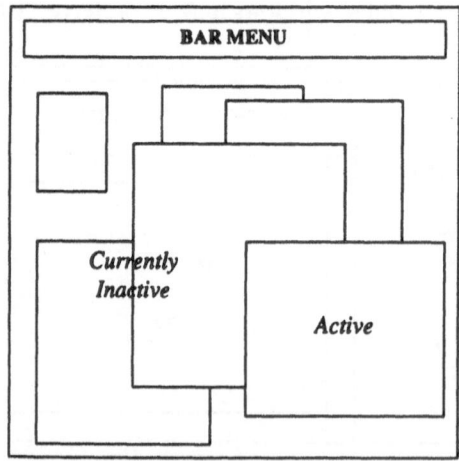

FIGURE 6.8. Example of overlapping windows.

the appropriate or legal ones from those that are inappropriate or illegal or (2) give different interpretations or meanings to the objects or components involved.

Alternative 2 of this definition can be illustrated by the physical superimposition of a template on the keys of a keyboard, thereby giving each one a current label and function. The first alternative is actually more relevant here to our interests in interaction techniques. A logical template can be specified as applicable to each of the techniques outlined in this section. For example:

1. In any *menu*, only a subset of choices may be highlighted as presently selectable; a superimposed template can prevent, e.g., by not displaying, the other choices for various reasons, such as not being useful in current context or to preclude problems that a novice user might have with them.
2. A *form* is, in a sense, a kind of template already; it channels the user into only making those entries that are necessary. But a form can also be made more dynamic, e.g., a superimposed template could prevent user entry of information into those spaces not applicable to him/her.
3. With *windows*, a template can be a particular pattern that is superimposed on the entire set, e.g., in a tiled layout, because the pattern has been determined to be particularly effective for a class of application-specific users.

Thus, the template can be seen to be a kind of *enabling and constraining mechanism*, used in conjunction with other interaction techniques, in order to render the result more suitable or effective for specified purposes.

6.6.5. Multiple Screens

A more macro-level technique for taking advantage of the spatial reference skills of humans (Table 6.2) is the use of multiple screens. In the last decade, much ingenuity was shown in trying to make the most out of a very small, single display screen for each user. One cannot display much in parallel on a screen that is typically less than one foot square. No wonder that the use of multiple, overlapped windows has become so popular.

The desirability of giving a user much more display area, perhaps stratifying an interactive application over several parallel displays, has been talked about for a long time (e.g., Treu, 1971). Now the technology has advanced enough to make such interfaces feasible.

Special-purpose interfaces, such as in conferencing and CSCW, have already illustrated the power of large, wall-size displays (e.g., Gaver *et al.*,

1992). Their emphasis has been on scaled-up output of different data types, including diagrams, pictures, and texts. However, for highly interactive, single-user applications, a multiscreen interface design is probably more appropriate. For example, with the ADS&R application, the architect may want or need:

1. A color graphics display with adequate hardware and software support, to be used as the actual design work area; on it any new design would be created, utilizing whatever gamut of available graphical tools and techniques; having the option of displaying the design result on a wall-size screen would provide additional benefits, especially to an architect

2. One separate screen, perhaps on the user's right side, to retrieve and display different views of similar architectural styles previously created

3. One separate screen, possibly on the left side, to enable retrieval and display of various relevant factual information; it could be used for referencing technical information, e.g., illustrative styles, shapes, dimensions, etc., and also technical contact persons

4. Another separate screen, maybe centered above the others, to provide various kinds of peripheral information to the busy architect; this could include display of information relating to arrival of messages from secretary or colleagues about scheduled appointments, status of projects, etc.

Such a multiscreen arrangement is now quite possible. For increasingly sophisticated users working on multifaceted applications, it may not only be desirable but necessary before long. We have already experienced analogous arrangements of multiple screens in critical areas, such as for the control panels on board spacecraft and in nuclear power plants. But even for more ordinary applications, such as ADS&R, their use is becoming increasingly reasonable.

Thus, besides knowing about effective utilization of menus, forms, windows, etc., as bases for interaction techniques, the HCI designer should ideally also be informed of the prospects of multiscreen interfaces. They have to be designed in patterns and sizes suitable for the user and effective and efficient for purposes of successful completion of the interactive work involved.

6.7. Drawing-Based Interaction

In the previous section, the onus was on the spatial layout of the interface to provide a pattern of displayed objects in a manner conducive to the spatial orientation of the user's mind. Those objects include menus, menu choices, forms, form spaces, windows, window contents, screens, screen contents, and also superimposed templates. For use of any resulting technique, main emphasis so far has been on written or printed data types, both for user input and computer output.

Actually, the same spatial layout techniques can also be applicable to I/O of other types of data, especially the graphic variety. For example, we can have menus and windows containing graphic shapes and forms. If so, the user is able not only to write but also to draw by using graphic representations. The major options are listed in Table 6.3.

6.7.1. Plots and Histograms

A fundamental type of graphic representation involves the portrayal of numeric data by means of visually meaningful, graphic drawings (e.g., Tufte, 1990). It has been in use in various ways for many years. The user obtains data from some source (e.g., an experiment) and wants to plot the results, analogous to what is done using graph paper with superimposed gridlines. The outcome can be a pattern of points drawn relative to a specified coordinate system (e.g., Cartesian). Whether or not it approximates a known mathematical formula, it indicates a relationship between a dependent variable and the independent variable. A different outcome is the display of a histogram in which the sizes of subareas in some selected shapes (e.g., rectangular bars, pieces of a pie) correspond proportionally to the sizes of the numbers or percentages. Those subareas may be shaded in or color-coded to make them more easily distinguishable and to associate them with particular data categories. Figure 6.9 gives simple illustrations of such graphic representations. They indicate relative cost factors involved in building a particular style of house.

TABLE 6.3
Interaction Techniques Based on Drawing Skills

F_D	Human–human COMMUNICATION capability	Human–computer INTERACTION TECHNIQUE that builds upon it	See Fig.
	Drawing 2-D and 3-D images	Graphic or iconic interaction	
1	Static, plotted	—Plots, histograms, etc.	6.9
2	Static, diagrammed	—Logical or physical objects	6.10
3	Static, modeled	—Iconic representations	6.11
4	Static, pictured	—Digitized images	6.12
5	Dynamic, changing of object images	—Full computer graphics	6.12

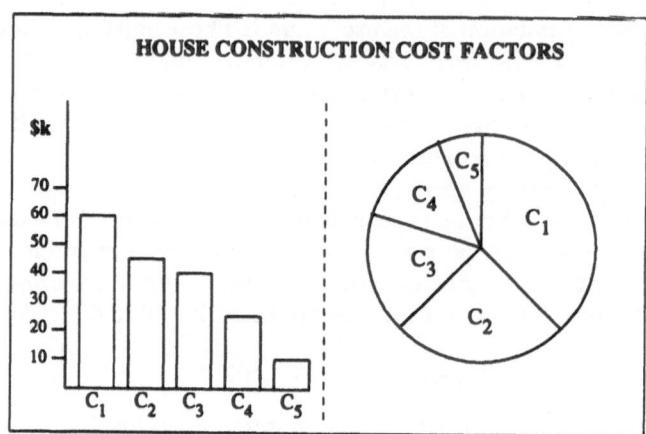

FIGURE 6.9. Graphic representation of numeric data.

Software for such graphic data representations, static in nature, has been around for a long time. In recent years, greater attention has been paid to interactive manipulation of data plots, including curves and surfaces in 3-D. Very complex mathematical relationships can be viewed and analyzed in this manner. However, to do so in truly dynamic form, the full power of interactive graphics has to be brought to bear. The graphical interaction technique is addressed last in this section.

6.7.2. Static Diagrams

A person typically can draw objects with pencil on paper. An interaction technique can enable the computer-assisted drawing of various objects. For example, assuming that the user makes appropriate selections (e.g., from a menu), he/she can draw in a selected window:

1. A wire diagram outlining a static view of a house, such as one of its sides; this might be part of the building plans prepared by an architect; it is a logical representation of what may be either a real (existing) or planned (conceived) object
2. A floor diagram showing the airflow directions (e.g., by arrows) of the heating/air-conditioning system of a house; this is also a logical representation of an object

Notice that in the first example the object of representation attempts to portray a potentially visible object; in the second example, the object (airflow) is invisible, although it is at least contained in the context of a visible object (floor plan). Such distinctions become important when dealing with visualization support models (Treu, 1994).

To accomplish the above, a PC or WS need only have basic graphic hardware and software. It must allow the user to specify coordinate points in a display area and to draw vectors or arrows, and maybe curves, to connect those points. There is no need for rotation and also for shading of the areas, although they are nice to have if available. Also, hidden line or surface removal is not called for, if the user only wants to make static drawings of one surface or view at a time. Obviously, for more advanced and dynamic drawing applications, greater graphics support becomes essential.

Figure 6.10 gives an illustration of a static side view of one part of a house. The ability to draw such simple diagrams is of course prerequisite to being able to do more advanced work, utilizing the full-blown computer graphics capabilities summarized in Section 6.7.5. Example studies of the effects of diagrams in HCI are the works by Larkin and Simon (1987) and Kieras (1993). Increasing interest in being able to manipulate diagrams using diagram editors has also been shown (e.g., Goettler, 1992).

6.7.3. Iconic Images

A special version of a static diagram is the following:

Definition 6.20. **Icon**: a diagram or image that is used repeatedly and without changing its shape or form, to symbolize a particular object or action.

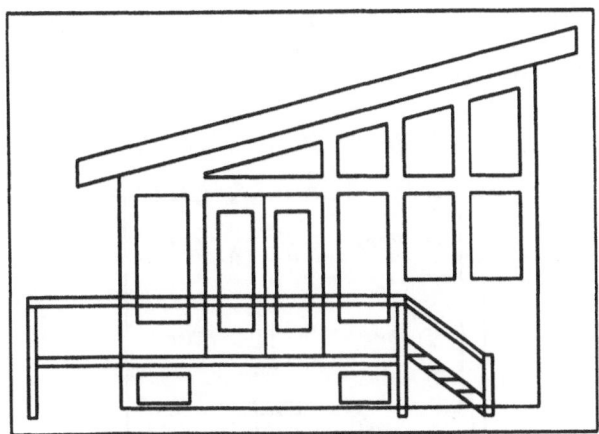

FIGURE 6.10. Example wire diagram.

Analogous to the variety of internationally recognized symbols used on street signs, to control and inform motorists and pedestrians, a number of symbols have become representative of objects or actions in HCI. Examples are symbols for mailboxes and filefolders. Several examples with relevance to ADS&R are displayed in Fig. 6.11. Some represent modular components (e.g., a door); others may also suggest a stylistic feature (e.g., an arch, a series of columns).

The motivation behind using such symbols is to convey meanings in graphical rather than textual form. They also play a role in the DMI style of interaction discussed in Section 6.9. If the icons are clearly recognizable and not too numerous to cause confusion, they tend to be conducive to human use, at least for application-specific purposes.

It may be possible to do simple scalings and translations on iconic images. These enable changing their sizes and locations on the screen. But, normally, icons are not transformed in any other way, such as by rotation. Their roles are intentionally limited. Formal consideration of icons for HCI began in the mid-1980s (e.g., Gittins, 1986a; Muter and Mayson, 1986). Their use also relates to the design of visual languages (Chang *et al.*, 1986; Chang, 1987). The more meaningful, unambiguous, and recognizable they are to users, the more effective the icon-based interaction can be expected to be. Iconic interaction is particularly useful for novice users. Effects of icon design have been studied, e.g., in terms of "articulatory distance" (Blankenberger and Hahn, 1991) and as cue enrichers (Lansdale *et al.*, 1990).

In HCI, the user is expected to recognize and select icons instead of the corresponding alphanumeric identifiers. Thus, they can be organized into menus as well and become an integral part of the menu-based interaction technique discussed earlier. Comparisons of iconic menus with text menus, and also with a combination of the two, have been carried out (e.g., Kacmar, 1991; MacGregor, 1992).

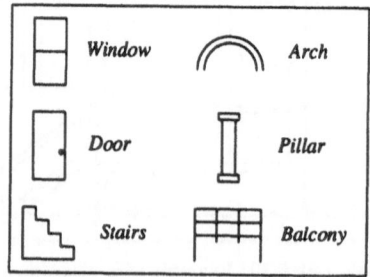

FIGURE 6.11. Possible architectural icons.

6.7.4. *Digital Images*

One further special technique depends on the powerful human ability to perceive, recognize, and understand pictures. A frequently cited assertion is that "a picture is worth a thousand words." Thus far we have only talked about approximating real objects by means of wire diagrams or icons. Using digital computer technology, much more realistic pictures are possible.

Such technology enables us to take a picture, even in real time using television cameras, and then to transform its continuous lines, shapes, and surfaces into digitized representations. The resulting digital data (discrete values) are storable in a computer. Using a finely grained grid, superimposed on the picture, numeric representations can be calculated for each addressable point at a gridline intersection. In computer graphics terminology, these are pixel values that specify the degree or level of shading (or color) applicable to each point (or intersection). Once such values are determined, the picture can be reproduced.

This process is analogous to what happens with facsimile (fax) machines that have become extremely popular in recent years.

Definition 6.21. **Facsimile**: an exact copy or likeness of a printed object, diagram, or picture; an electronic process for transmitting images from a sending station for reproduction at a receiving station.

A letter, a diagram, or a picture can be read in at one end of a communication line. A printed version of Fig. 6.12 or of any other figure or page in this book can be processed likewise. The item is scanned, one (superimposed) gridline at a time, and transformed into the digitized representation that is actually transmitted. At the receiving end, the digital data are then used directly to reproduce the original image. This process is of course dependent on telecommunications technology (Tanenbaum, 1988) and the conversion of analog data to digital data for digital transmission purposes.

It is important to note that the digitized image as described above is *not* structured in a way to enable knowledgeable manipulation of any of its parts by computer. The image is, in a sense, anonymous; that is, the computer does not "know" or "understand" what the image is or what it contains. To acquire that knowledge requires significant help, either from sophisticated pattern recognition software and/or from a user who looks at the displayed image and introjects the information needed to structure and identify it.

6.7.5. *Interactive Computer Graphics*

To generate pictures using a computer, either of real or conceptualized objects, and to be able to manipulate them dynamically, the full

FIGURE 6.12. Left-corner front view of a split-level house.

capabilities of computer graphics technology are necessary. If one wants to make the graphic images as realistic as possible, both in appearance and dynamic behavior (e.g., motion in 3-D), supportive graphics hardware and software are essential. Figure 6.12 is only intended to *imply* such dynamics and realism; there is no pretension that any of the graphically oriented figures in this book do justice to what can be accomplished with state-of-the-art technology, tools, and techniques in computer graphics. With greater realism, the corner view of the house architecture displayed by Fig. 6.12 would show the details of brick walls and aluminum siding panels, the shadows caused by the overhanging roof, reflections in the windows, shading and colors, and many other features. It could also portray the landscaping around the house. With dynamics and powerful transformations (e.g., scaling, translation, rotation, clipping), interactive graphics enables the user to change the viewpoint to any position desirable, thereby effecting visible movement of the represented object in any conceivable pattern and direction. Such dynamic motion contributes to realism and to the user's perception of perspective depth in and around the objects represented.

Techniques in computer graphics for achieving visual dynamics are not only usable for animation of real, physically measurable objects (e.g., people, dogs, houses) and how they move or change shape relative to other objects or different viewpoints; they can also be applied to logical entities and structures. For example, algorithms can be animated, although their utility in assisting learning has been put to question recently (Stasko *et al.*, 1993).

Graphical interaction techniques and tools have been variously characterized (e.g., Baecker, 1980) and the relevant human factors have been considered at length (e.g., Foley *et al.*, 1984; Jansen *et al.*, 1985). Also, a number of books on the subject have appeared. The most comprehensive resource for persons interested in full graphics is the text by Foley *et al.* (1990). It consists of nearly 1200 pages, including a large bibliography. An HCI designer, who wants to consider making the graphical interaction technique available to target users, perhaps in parallel to or combined with other techniques, is faced with having to understand much of the material in such a volume. But the effort is worth it.

Historically, an early article that deserves special recognition here is Foley and Wallace's (1974) study of "The Art of Natural Graphic Man–Machine Conversation." Although computer graphics had been initiated over a decade earlier, based on novel, new devices (e.g., Sutherland's Sketchpad, 1963), Foley and Wallace (1974) triggered interest in formalizing graphics as part of an interaction technique. Many of the concepts defined in that paper have influenced not only computer graphics but, more broadly, HCI design ever since.

Then, in 1976, a first-of-its-kind workshop was conducted on "User-Oriented Design of Interactive Graphics Systems." As mentioned in Chapter 1, many of the persons invited to attend would become key members in the HCI community. The workshop proceedings (Treu, 1977) discussed a number of the issues that are addressed in this book.

6.8. Interaction Using Other Skills

All of the techniques characterized thus far are dependent on the human sense of vision. In each case, the user must be able to see and perceive what is being written, printed, or drawn in some spatial location of the interface. If the technique is dependent on the effective use of colors (e.g., Thorell and Smith, 1990), the user should preferably be able to distinguish them. In any case, the images that result are either initiated by the user him/herself or by the computer according to its capabilities.

But most human beings are capable not only of seeing things, but also of *speaking* (one or more natural languages), *hearing* (sounds, speech, music), *feeling* (by physically touching and manipulating objects), and also *tasting* and *smelling*. Although all of these may conceivably play roles in futuristic HCI techniques, our primary interest at present is on capitalizing on our senses of vision, hearing, and touch. These are indicated in the entries of Table 6.4.

6.8.1. Pattern Recognition

Utilizing those three senses in some combination, we can take advantage of the mind's abilities to process complex, multisensory inputs. Inter-

TABLE 6.4
Interaction Techniques Based on Other Human Skills

F_o	Human–human COMMUNICATION capability	Human–computer INTERACTION TECHNIQUE that builds upon it
1	Gesturing, visual and tactile	Pattern recognition and display including computer vision
2	Speaking and hearing	Computer-generated speech and voice recognition —Limited grammar and vocabulary
3	Visualization and viewing in 3-D reality	Virtual reality

estingly, computer technology is being advanced to exhibit analogous abilities, especially in the areas of speech recognition (e.g., Schwab and Nussbaum, 1986a; O'Brien, 1993) and recognizing objects through computer vision (e.g., Schwab and Nussbaum, 1986b; Fisher, 1989). However, the general level of success is still quite limited. In the case of the user, the sensory input processing can be supplemented with a powerful facility to visualize, that is, to conceptualize things and form mental pictures of them. Computers are not yet prepared to come close to anything like that, although we can hypothesize how structure-based forms of object recognition might lead in that direction (Treu, 1989).

The desired outcome for either the user or the computer in HCI is the accurate recognition of what is being communicated by the other. Gesturing and recognizing gestures is one special skill that can help. Various types of visually instantiated and recognizable gestures were already implied among the techniques discussed. Before mentioning some of them, let us define what gesturing is about.

Definition 6.22. **Gesture**: any movement or activation of sensory signals through use of hands, fingers, eyes, mouth, or other parts of the body to communicate something, instead of using words.

Gestures can be made by either user or computer, within the limits of their respective capabilities. An explicit gesture from user to system is the hand-controlled movement of an input device, e.g., a mouse or lightpen, in the direction in which the cursor symbol or other displayed object is to be relocated. The resulting location may only approximate the position the user intended to convey. This fact is indicative of the frequently generic and less than precise nature of gestures. However, in graphical interaction, the system can be designed to recognize the imprecise signal from the user and to calculate the more exact coordinate values within the current context. That context might be the neighborhood surrounding the corner of an object to which some other object is to be attached.

Similar kinds of gesturing for indicating directions or locations can be based on touch- or pressure-sensitive technology. Special tablets and touchscreens are available for such purposes (e.g., Sears and Shneiderman, 1991). They can be placed in a keyboardlike position or even superimposed on a visual display screen.

Of course, gestures need not be restricted to communicating directionality. On one hand, they can be built-in, that is, implicitly contained in something being communicated. For example, in signature analysis and recognition, the angle, length, and speed of the written strokes are distinguishing features of a person's writing style.

On the other hand, gestures can be given whatever interpretations might be meaningful in a particular context. For example, an upward gesture can be considered a positive response, while a downward gesture can mean the opposite. The notion of a template (Definition 6.19) is relevant. Assume that a certain set of visual or tactile gestures is easily recognizable across the interface, either by user or computer. Then, if each gesture is attributed a distinct meaning within a particular application, the resulting pattern of meanings constitutes a superimposed template.

The "user action notation" (UAN) of Hartson et al. (1990) can be applied here to represent icon-oriented user actions and system reactions. In a sense, such high-level manipulation can be interpreted as a form of gesturing using special symbols. Both user and system must know exactly what the inherently imprecise gesture means and causes.

Gestures can be utilized in conjunction with a variety of tasks. For example, a recent study (Zhao, 1993) presented techniques for gesture recognition applied to syntax-directed diagram editors. The result is, therefore, a hybrid of the diagramming (Table 6.3) and the gesturing (Table 6.4) techniques.

More advanced forms of gesturing are based on visual motions or signals that can be "seen" by camera and then recognized using sophisticated techniques in computer vision. Some remarkable progress has been made in using modern technology for recognizing gestures. It is especially helpful for seriously impaired persons such as paraplegics. With appropriate hardware and with natural and unobtrusive incorporation of eye movements into interaction technique, the eye movements of any user can be detected and interpreted (e.g., Jacob, 1990).

6.8.2. Speaking and Hearing

One can also gesture using sounds. For example, a computer can output a pattern, e.g., a happy, upbeat tune, that suggests something positive. That can be contrasted with other sounds that evoke sadness or some other emotion. Many PCs have such simple sound patterns already provided, although most people probably consider them more as sound effects or fun gadgets than as potentially useful communication devices. Actually, the synthesis of "auditory icons" (Gaver, 1993) can have meaningful application to representing the events experienced by the user at the interface.

More significant to HCI seem to be the well-established human abilities of speaking and hearing. Except for the hearing-impaired who develop special skills for recognizing sign language and also reading lips, most people need to hear in order to try to understand someone else's spoken words. If the two skills are coupled with the far less well-developed but improving computer abilities to recognize human voice and to generate humanlike speech, we indeed have a potentially powerful interaction technique.

The state of the art of speech recognition (e.g., Schwab and Nussbaum, 1986a; O'Brien, 1993) is such that special-purpose interfaces for restricted application domains are becoming quite feasible. For example, we can now purchase a device that enables a TV viewer to schedule a VCR (for program recording) using speech. If the vocabulary and grammar required are strictly limited, in a manner analogous to what was said about restricted written language (Section 6.5), it is possible:

1. To store the primary characteristics and options for all legal words that can be input by a user, thereby enabling their analysis and recognition by computer, and
2. To store audio representations of all legal words, including the legal parameter values for any variables, to enable computer access to them in correct order for output of simple phrases understandable by the user

While the above imply a spoken (user) command language as well as a spoken (computer) response language, this mode can also be reversed. That is, the computer can employ simple speech in asking questions or making requests; the user is then in a position of having to respond in a manner that is not too complex for the computer to process and recognize.

Some interesting science fiction movies that featured computer-generated speech and voice recognition, such as "2001: A Space Odyssey" (Kubrick, 1968), were created during the early period of HCI development. They are now becoming increasingly realistic. They may add a significant component to the HCI designs of the future.

Among the current projects reported in the literature are the use of speech as data for taking voice notes via a hand-held computer (Stifelman *et al.*, 1993), and combining speech with gesturing (Hauptmann and McAvinney, 1993).

6.8.3. Visualization and 3-D Reality

Thus far we have linked the considerable range of interaction techniques to several major, physical senses. We can also capitalize on the human mental skills that exceed or transcend the processing and interpretation of sensory information.

A sighted person can see displayed objects or scenes and, utilizing various spatial, size, color, and other cues, perceive such characteristics as depth and motion. Knowledge of these human capabilities has had significant impact on the contents of any advanced course in computer graphics and the graphical interaction techniques. But the user is capable of even more. He/she can undergo total "sensory immersion" in interacting with computer technology, given appropriate interactive devices (Foley, 1987).

For example, a user can wear special headgear (covering the eyes) such that the stereo image is projected on a small screen before the eyes and the image is changed dynamically in response to user head movements. Coupling that capability with a microphone for speech input plus a so-called data glove, to enable sensing of finger and hand movements, provides a very intriguing combination of several human senses. As a result, the user's mind can experience the feeling of seemingly being there, that is, in the space and activity being represented dynamically by the computer at the interface. This is a remarkable kind of sensation or, if you will, illusion. One has to experience it to believe it. Static figures in textbooks obviously cannot even approximate it. The technique has been called "virtual reality." Actually it is more correctly termed "unreal but seemingly real reality." "Artificial reality" is another more appropriate label (Foley *et al.*, 1990). A separate branch of the literature is developing in this area. It exhibits both pros and cons, when compared with other techniques/styles and the demands they impose on the user (Treu, 1994).

Another capability of the mind can be argued as going beyond "artificial reality"-based interaction into a more independent and self-sufficient mode. It involves the ability to visualize representations of all kinds, whether or not the computer reproduces them at the interface or is even capable of doing so. Although it is dependent on the mind having learned and remembered various original representations provided by sensory inputs, it is nevertheless a special skill to be taken into account by the HCI designer. It can be related to "interface structures" deemed conducive to human use (Treu, 1992) and the user's ability to visualize objects in different spaces.

6.9. Styles Based on Techniques

A rich assortment of HCI interaction techniques is already available. The length of this chapter attests to that. In fact, it could have been much longer. Every technique could have been discussed and illustrated much more extensively, both individually and in combination with others. In addition, more techniques continue to be improved and developed. Of particular interest is the hybrid combination of different sensory-based techniques. Examples are: audio and spatial (Cohen and Ludwig, 1991) and speaking and touching (Bierman *et al.*, 1992).

But the purpose of this chapter is not to give exhaustive coverage to everything that exists and is on the horizon. It is hoped that the reader will instead attend to the overall pattern of capabilities and options introduced, starting with Fig. 6.1. Then, for a particular, new design, the considerable shopping list of techniques can be analyzed with reference to the needs of target users, nature of the target application, and capabilities of the target computer.

In addition to technique, the designer must look for any evidence of interaction style that may be preferred or required by the target users. For example, the levels of experience and knowledge required of users should have influence on how the interaction style is designed (e.g., Montazemi, 1991). The HCI literature is not always clear about the distinction. For example, is WYSIWYG or "what you see is what you get" interaction (Smith *et al.*, 1982) a technique or a style? (See Exercise 6.19.) Style should be interpreted as the high-level composite of various interaction techniques and other features.

Accordingly, it is meaningful to consider the direct manipulation interface (DMI) as an illustrative interaction style. Shneiderman's (1982, 1983) requirements for DMI were in essence:

- Continuous, visible representation of the objects of interest
- Rapid, reversible, incremental actions
- Causing actions through direct, physical indication (rather than using complex command language syntax)
- Requiring minimal user knowledge to accomplish the above

In analyzing these requirements in relation to the interaction characteristics and techniques profiled in this chapter, one can conclude that the DMI style can/should be built upon the following, among others:

- *Interaction techniques*, with the iconic and menu-based options being most relevant; they provide continuous, visible display of objects to be selected and manipulated

- *Interaction state transition graphs/scenarios*, to enable unambiguous and expeditious memory of and return to previous user-visible state, to reverse any user actions
- *Interaction context*, including the meanings inherent to objects displayed (e.g., icons), to make things as easily understandable for the user as possible

In addition, suitable *interactive devices* (hardware) must be made available, as discussed among the *I*-factors (Chapter 5), in order to permit direct, physical pointing, selection, and gesturing. Also, the *interactive software* support (Chapters 5 and 8) must exhibit the kind of structure (e.g., modularity) and dynamics that are demanded by the techniques, state and context definitions, and by the interactive devices mentioned above. Thus, a style such as DMI is truly a multifaceted composite. The designer must recognize the facets as if they were component features and then integrate them into a well-engineered whole.

Much has been written about DMI, its directness and its effectiveness. Illustrative are the publications of Hutchins *et al.* (1986), Ziegler and Fahnrich (1988), and Te'eni (1990). Various enhancements and extensions have been reported, such as 3-D interaction (e.g., Houde, 1992), including use of 3-D cursor control and sounds to accentuate what happens (Venolia, 1993).

But many other interaction styles are possible. As popular as DMI has become, it really should not be viewed as the end-all panacea goal of designers. It has definite limitations. HCI researchers should recognize these and endeavor to create significant alternatives to the DMI style.

6.10. Techniques and Styles as Features

The *U*-, *A*-, and *I*-factors discussed in earlier chapters are among the causes that should lead the HCI designer to select the most suitable options and then pursue them in detail, with the help of other resources. Consistent with Fig. 6.1, any technique selected must be representable through grammar-based language and time-based states and contexts. Any style should be describable in terms of techniques and other features that support it.

If an interaction technique or style is selected as the result of design decision-making [Function (2.4)], it is necessary to distinguish what, as a consequence, becomes fixed and what remains variable in the interface. For example, if a menu-based technique is specified for a particular application, it is understood that the user will issue commands and identify other inputs by selecting entries from menu widgets that must be displayed. So, that fundamental aspect of the technique is fixed. But there are lower-level design decisions remaining to be made, that is, other features must be specified within the context of the technique. Examples are: the size, contents, organization, relative location, and timing of the menus to be invoked. Similar statements can be made about any other interaction technique or style selected.

Hence, it is important to recognize that a high-level feature specification, in turn, necessitates decisions on lower-level features. The options among the latter are, in general, dependent on the nature of the former. There are more than two levels of interdependent features, as suggested by the lexical–syntactic–semantic levels discussed in Chapter 4. However, we shall focus only on any adjacent pair of layers by dichotomizing in relative terms as follows:

- *High-level features*, e.g., an interaction technique, which provides the framework or amalgam within which any lower-level features must be apparent and to which they must contribute
- *Lower-level features*, as indicated above

Likewise, a style (e.g., DMI) can be viewed as a high-level feature in relation to a technique (e.g., iconic) which is lower-level and must support it. This view is consistent with the hierarchy of Fig. 6.1. The above dichotomy is also reiterated in the decision function update in Section 6.12. Following chapters present other features that can be modeled in a similar manner.

6.11. Decision Schematics

The schematics portrayed in previous chapters can now be elaborated with greater emphasis on the effects than on the causes. For example, referring to Fig. 4.5, the first-listed schematic somehow led the designer to decide that the user needs mechanisms that will reinforce or supplement his/her human memory. This is a relatively low-level feature in the sense that the type of help and the manner of providing it are dependent on the context within which the help is given.

On the other hand, the second-listed schematic in Fig. 4.5 resulted in the selection of an interaction technique involving the automatic recognition of printed characters. This is included among the options in Table 6.1. It is a relatively high-level feature, which accommodates one mode of inputting data. One would expect it to be supplemented by other techniques, e.g., command line interaction. In addition, various lower-level features, such as giving the user help in remembering what needs to be done next within the chosen technique, must be decided as well.

Likewise, interaction techniques are the features emanating from the schematics of Fig. 5.3. Given the discussions in Sections 6.9 and 6.10, it is evident that such technique-specifying schematics should *both*

1. Be subsumed by a higher-level schematic that leads to decision on the desired/required interaction style, *and*
2. Subsume lower-level schematics that determine the detailed features supporting each technique (and, in turn, style)

6.12. Decision Function: Update

In Chapters 3 through 5, the function (2.4) that symbolizes the designer's decision-making was updated with regard to design FACTORS only. Now we can also define the FEATURES. In view of the multilevel relationships characterized earlier, design features can involve a variety of complex and interrelated techniques, higher-level style, and subservient characteristics that are to be in evidence at the interface. This is illustrated in Parts III and IV.

In the meantime, we want to continue our approach of building up the material gradually. This chapter has dealt with a range of interaction techniques and of the styles that are compositions of those techniques. Each one can be considered a high-level feature. With reference to Tables 6.1 through 6.4, the entire set of techniques at this level of definition can be expressed as a union of sets:

$$F_{TECH} = F_W \cup F_S \cup F_D \cup F_O \tag{6.1}$$

Likewise, the set of available styles includes unions and conjunctions of interaction techniques:

$$F_{STYL} = \{combined\_subsets\_of\_F_{TECH}\}$$

As a result, we conclude:

$$F_{T+S} = F_{TECH} \cup F_{STYL} \tag{6.2}$$

The FEATURES equation (2.3) can therefore be refined to the following extent:

$$FEATURES = \{\{F_{T+S,X}\}, other\_sets\_of\_features\} \tag{6.3}$$

where the indicated set is a subset of interaction techniques and styles selected by the designer. But, as discussed in the remaining chapters of this book, the various support features remain to be elaborated further.

Exercises

6.1. Consider each of the six expressions connoting user style (in Section 6.2) to be a U-factor. Assuming that the relevant I-factors and A-factors are not constraining the design decisions, what design feature(s) would be suggested by each stylistic factor? Why?

6.2. What other U-factors pertaining to a person's style of behavior and expectation can be added to that list of expressions (mentioned in Exercise 6.1)? What design feature(s) would they suggest?

6.3. Based on your experience with computers, do you exhibit different personal styles (e.g., demand more or less) depending on which application you are working on? To what extent does the answer depend on other U-factors (e.g., knowledge of the application and self-confidence in using it)? Explain.

6.4. In interacting with a computer, is it essential to have different modes to distinguish different applications or tasks and levels thereof? Or can you have truly "modeless" or "seamless" interaction? Consider the analogy in human-to-human communication of changing from one topic to another. To do so effectively, are minimal separators or transition signals required? Explain.

6.5. Designing HCI with user–computer compatibility in mind requires (a) matching, (b) accommodating, and/or (c) complementing their respective styles, techniques, and modes, as discussed in Section 6.2. By means of a 3×3 table, illustrate how that might be done (in general, descriptive terms) using each of a (selected) style, a technique, and a mode/partition to be used in an interface supporting at least two different applications.

6.6. Consider the use of state transition diagrams for representing the different states in a computer's operating system. Which of those states are of interest to (or have an observable impact on) the typical user? Which ones are not of interest? Why?

6.7. Imagine yourself sitting at your favorite computer interface and doing text editing with your favorite editor. Suppose you are in the midst of completing an editing task, but you have forgotten a particular command, or the correct syntax for it. To get you past this hurdle, what type(s) of interaction context (Definition 6.11) does/should your interface provide? Discuss the effectiveness. Illustrate by a specific example.

6.8. What types of applications might require a more rich "contextual neighborhood" surrounding an interaction state (providing a number of alternative paths to follow) than is suggested by a single, prescribed "state scenario"? Why? Illustrate.

6.9. Consider how humans communicate with each other, one to one, in written and spoken (English) language. Which characteristics of that communication should be emulated by the computer in HCI? Which ones should not? Justify your points.

6.10. For what purposes are horizontally arranged menus preferable to vertically arranged menus? Within a menu, what are the alternative criteria for organizing its entries and when is each approach useful?

6.11. Menu-based interaction ($F_{S,1}$) does not obviate the need to adhere to language syntax. How can the user and computer share that responsibility for deciding and controlling which language component should be selected when, or after which other one? Give a descriptive model of what must happen.

6.12. Do Exercise 6.11 for forms-based interaction ($F_{S,2}$). Does it seem to expect more or less of the user (e.g., in terms of knowledge of syntactic structure)? Explain.

6.13. Compare tiled and overlapping windowing ($F_{S,3}$). List and describe their respective advantages and disadvantages, using illustrative applications. For what purposes might a combination of the two methods be useful?

6.14. Assuming a single-user, personal workstation that supports the ADS&R application, consider the design of a multiscreen configuration ($F_{S,5}$) of the physical interface. For what purpose(s) might a large, wall-area display screen be useful? On the other hand, when might the user prefer to keep relatively small screens as part of the WS layout? (Note: assume that the computer technology is not a limiting factor in your WS design.)

6.15. Describe an application in which it might be useful to convert a static, iconic symbol into a graphic image that can be transformed and displayed with the full dynamics of computer graphics. Likewise, describe an application in which the reverse (i.e., converting graphic images to static icons) might be desirable.

6.16. Based on what you have read about iconic interaction ($F_{D,3}$), what type of computer application lends itself to the use of iconic images at the interface? Do you think that there is or should be a limit on the number of distinct iconic symbols that a user can (or should be expected to) recognize and distinguish in interaction with a given application? Explain.

6.17. In graphical interaction ($F_{D,5}$), primary focus is on the generation and display of graphic objects, followed by their dynamic transformation to create user-perceived realism and utility within a vision-intensive application. This requires structure in object representation. The discussion of menu-based interaction ($F_{S,1}$) suggested that a hierarchical dependence among menus can be meaningful. In analogous fashion, assume that you want to represent a house (e.g., Fig. 6.12) in a computer using graphical means. Regardless of details of internal representation, diagram and describe how the different parts (or modules) of a house (e.g., its windows, doors) are dependent on the enclosing objects (e.g., specific walls) and how the latter, in turn, depend on the next level of enclosing object, etc. Likewise, discuss this structured representation in reverse order, i.e., from total object (the house) down to the lowest level of enclosed graphical objects controlled (or invoked) at that level.

6.18. Graphical interaction fundamentally capitalizes on the human sense of vision. Visually oriented gesturing ($F_{O,1}$) does likewise. List and describe the specific kinds of features available in computer graphics that can be interpreted as representing gestures. Which of those could be replaced by audio gestures designed to take advantage of the human sense of hearing? Comment on their relative effectiveness.

6.19. The terms interaction "technique" and "style" are often used interchangeably. With regard to Definitions 6.2 and 6.4, decide whether WYSIWYG is a style or a technique (or both). Make convincing arguments in favor of your choice. Does it relate to the DMI style? If so, how? If not, why?

6.20. For each of the interaction techniques based on (a) natural language, free-hand printing $(F_{W,1})$, (b) menu-based $(F_{S,1})$, (c) iconic $(F_{D,3})$, and (d) pattern recognition of gestures $(F_{O,1})$ interaction techniques, make a list of lower-level features that must be decided.

6.21. Using each of the two decision schematics of Fig. 5.3, (a) encapsulate it in a box (decision module), which serves as one feature resulting from a higher-level schematic pertaining to interaction style; create and draw such a higher-level schematic as an example; (b) refine its result by creating and drawing a schematic that determines lower-level features supportive of that result.

REPRESENTATION MODELS AND METHODS

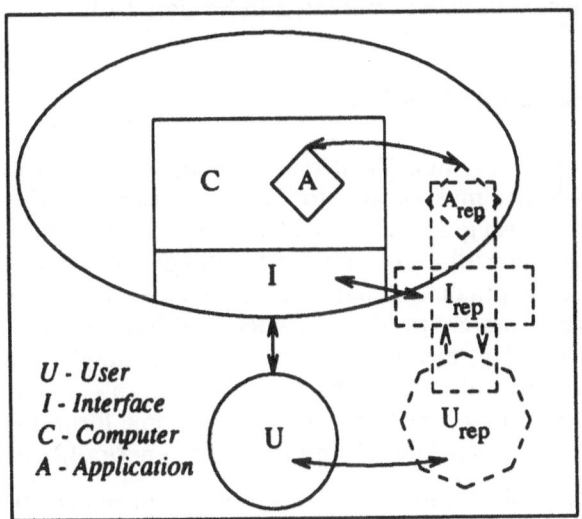

7.1. Overview

In previous chapters, we dealt with the characteristics of each of the major modules in HCI and with the ways in which the user and computer can interact. Understanding the kinds of potential design factors and the features that they may cause is treated as being prerequisite to HCI design. Knowledge about the factors and features is used in the design process described in Part III.

That knowledge can come in a variety of different forms. In this chapter, we first draw distinctions between the types of representation, or models, that can be applied to HCI, and how these contribute to specification techniques; in themselves, they constitute only part of HCI design methodology. Then, the major alternatives for representing HCI components and behavior are described and illustrated, in Sections 7.3 through 7.8. They range from purely descriptive models, to relatively static ways of specifying selected aspects of HCI, to carrying out dynamic modeling and simulation.

Schematic models that are supportive of HCI design and evaluation are reiterated in Section 7.9. They were introduced in previous chapters. An important goal of this chapter is to recognize that all forms of representation or modeling have limitations. While they play significant support roles (see also Chapter 8) in HCI design, they are only a means to an end. They should *not* be viewed as equivalent to HCI design. Finally, the decision function update is presented in Section 7.10.

7.2. Distinctions and Options

To represent anything, be it real or imagined, abstract or concrete, large or small, one must be able to identify it. Consider the well-known construct in English grammar that relates an action (transitive) verb to an object of that action (direct object). For HCI in general, we can have a user wanting to "conceptualize, visualize, . . ., utilize" something via the interface, a designer wanting to "design something" into the interface, and an evaluator wanting to "measure and evaluate something" about the resulting design and its utilization by humans. In each case, one has to have a representation of that something available, in some form. Let us refer to that "something" as an "object" and define it generically as follows:

Definition 7.1. **Object**: any unit of knowledge; an information entity or concept at any level of specificity or generality; any entity that is defined in physical, logical, or conceptual form and that is either static or dynamic in its behavior and/or appearance.

Because an object is dependent on the term "knowledge," the latter should be defined as well:

Definition 7.2. **Knowledge**: what one knows; all that is known or can be learned; range of information; familiarity with a subject.

Both of these definitions are used variously throughout the later chapters. It should be pointed out here that knowledge is, in turn, based on information, which is based on data. We use those terms without separate definition. Their meanings are assumed to be consistent with common usage in the literature of computer science.

For present purposes, objects can include users, computers, interfaces interaction languages, action commands, display screens, menus and windows on those screens, application programs, and uncountable other examples, all pertinent to the HCI design task. An object can serve as a component of another object, such as a user is part of the composite HCI system. Also, an object can itself consist of two or more component objects, e.g., multiple windows (containing whatever information objects) constituting the visible interface surface.

An HCI designer may not be able to work with the objects directly. It may not be feasible or desirable to do so (e.g., prospective users may not be accessible), or the objects may not even exist as such (e.g., a computer system is to be acquired). In other cases, the object may not yet have real, physical existence, but rather may require suitable definition or specification (e.g., an interaction language). Therefore, the designer must be able to represent relevant objects in a way that will support the necessary design process.

Definition 7.3. **Representation**: a likeness, picture, image, or model of an object; the process or faculty of forming mental images of objects.

But how do we represent human–computer interaction and the interface and other objects that support it? One way is to take a photograph of its physical appearance, or of selected images that are displayed on the interface screen. Such a "show-and-tell" approach is very prominent in HCI papers and books, illustrating what the named system does under certain circumstances. While it may be interesting and useful, a snapshot (or even a video) of the interface only gives the designer relatively superficial information about what happens in the interaction. Something more comprehensive and exacting is needed to help the designer in creating and using the object representation.

An important step is to consider different types of models. The term "model" is already associated with Definition 7.3.

Definition 7.4. **Model**: a conceptual, logical, or physical representation of an object and its functioning; an object to be copied, imitated, or instantiated.

Models are necessarily approximations of what they are supposed to represent. They may be used as a "substitute" or a "surrogate," that is, taking the place of or standing for the real object. On the other hand, a model may have a prescriptive purpose, for use in guiding the design and implementation of a new object, or an instance of that object.

Many different models have been created. A classification scheme for HCI models, based on what is modeled by/about (1) the program, (2) the user, (3) the researcher, and (4) the designer, has been presented by Whitefield (1990). A performance relationship model, encompassing user classification, attitudes, mental models, as well as interface characteristics, has been proposed by Arnett and Trumbly (1991). Many other versions of models can be found in the literature.

The general classification indicated by Fig. 7.1 is consistent with the

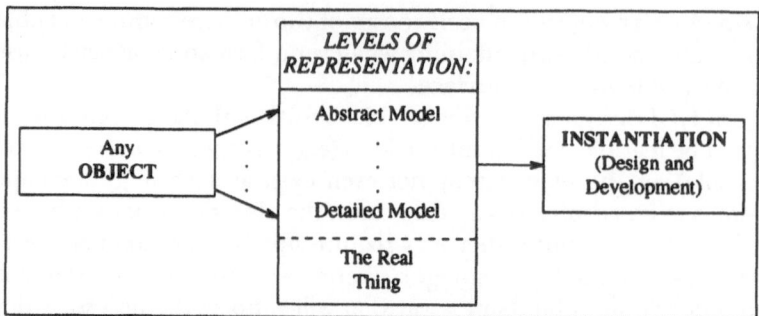

FIGURE 7.1. Range of representations.

way models are used in this book. On one extreme, they can be very general or abstract; on the other extreme, very specific or detailed; and there are many possible alternatives in between. Furthermore, they can be categorized into the following groups, with HCI-oriented examples cited in each case:

1. *Physical or Prototypical:* e.g., a mock-up arrangement of the physical components of a workstation interface
2. *Mathematical or Analytical:* e.g., a formula for the "pretty" arrangement of windows on the HCI screen (Gait, 1985)
3. *Descriptive or Verbal:* e.g., an organized description, or profile, of an HCI object, such as of the user in Chapter 3 or of the computer in Chapter 5
4. *Grammatical or Notational:* e.g., a precise, well-formed notation for the definition and construction of interaction language (commands and responses)
5. *Schematic or Diagrammatic:* e.g., a multilayer structure for interaction (Chapter 4); a diagram of the software components constituting the interface architecture; a graph representing various HCI states and transitions among those states
6. *Pictorial:* e.g., a digitized image of a real object (e.g., a building) displayed on the CRT screen; or an animated sequence of such images
7. *Graphical:* e.g., representation of any of the other models, generated using graphics software and displayed using graphics hardware; including iconic image models
8. *Mental or Conceptual:* e.g., the image of an HCI object as created in the user's mind and/or in the designer's mind

Thus, the possible models of objects can range from the physical form (1 above) to the logical (including rigorously mathematical as well as relatively subjective, descriptive) form (2 through 7) to the conceptual form of representation (8 above). A further distinction in these models and their usability for various aspects of interface design is that they are either

- *Static:* at rest; inactive; not in motion; acting by weight only; with no recognition of time
- *Dynamic:* relating to energy or force of motion; tending toward change; changing with respect to time

For each of the eight types of models outlined above, examples of both static and dynamic alternatives can be cited. A dynamic model requires the ability to move, or change state, possibly under computer-programmed control, such as in simulation of modeled systems and in visual transformation of modeled objects in graphics. Conceptual/mental modes, when dynamic, may therefore involve "mental energy" to cause changes in the representation.

Although the model types are basically intended to serve *representation* purposes, they may furthermore be conducive to use in design *specification* and also *simulation* of all or part of the HCI composite. Specification models are discussed in Section 7.3, simulation models in Section 7.8.

7.3. Models and Specifications

What are the implications of the above for HCI design? The HCI designer should preferably be cognizant of all the model types outlined. The most suitable and effective ones should then be employed in carrying out a design and also, as required, the evaluation of the design.

Which of the representations and models are most appropriate in a particular design situation? The answer depends on the design goals, scope, etc., as well as the designer's knowledge and skills. The designer may select and use one or more models for each of

1. Any *part or* component (e.g., the user) of the HCI system; or the *entire system*
2. The *dynamic behavior* and changing *appearance* (e.g., visible display screen) of any components, and the interactions between/among them (e.g., via interaction language)
3. *Specifying the requirements* imposed on the HCI design, including adherence to certain models and achievement of particular performance objectives
4. Organizing and guiding the *overall design methodology* itself

The last of these is characterized in Chapter 10. It is dependent on models available from software engineering and is also reflected by the structures-oriented coverage throughout this book.

In this section, our interest lies in 3 above, as it relates to 1 and 2. Software engineering includes specifications for everything from design requirements, to applicable standards, to stylistic considerations, to formats and notations, to user expectations. A variety of special-purpose languages have been created (e.g., Fairley, 1985) to support the precise representation and analysis of requirements specifications for software. Subsequently, all specifications are subject to verification and validation.

Specialists in HCI have learned to use software engineering techniques to produce formal representations of various limited aspects of HCI. The resulting specifications can actually be considered as equivalent to models.

Definition 7.5. **Specification**: a detailed description of the characteristics (e.g., structures, dimensions, materials) and behaviors of an object (e.g., application software package, interface software/hardware) to be designed; the detailed requirements imposed on such a design.

A specification, then, is a model that is formally prescribed and expected to be followed in a design. It has significant impact on the ultimate implementation (Swartout and Balzer, 1982). It may itself dictate the use of specified other models. Several important specification models now used in HCI have been prominent in other areas of computer science. Examples: precise grammars to represent the statements in programming languages and state transition networks to represent the dynamic states of operating systems. For HCI, formal specification techniques were tailored for use in representing interaction languages, as discussed in Section 7.5. Also, specifications of the functionality of the interface and of the flow of data and control across the interface have gained increasing attention. These are summarized in Sections 7.6 and 7.7. But first, in Section 7.4, we want to accentuate the need for separate modeling of the major HCI modules.

Abstractions and specifications pertaining to program development have been considered extensively (e.g., Liskov and Guttag, 1986). A book on formal methods applicable to HCI has appeared (Harrison and Thimbleby, 1990). Its coverage includes various types of specifications and abstract models.

7.4. Component Models

One important category of models was already used several times in early chapters of this book, to portray not only the interface and/or interaction (Chapter 6) but also the user (Chapter 3), the application domain (Chapter 4), and the computer (Chapter 5). The reason for calling them "component" models is the emphasis on the individualistic nature of a selected part of an HCI system. Consistent with the principle of modularity in software/system design, each major part is subject to being modeled separately and differently. Then, the different resulting models have to be composed into the total system.

Some component models may involve dynamically changing representations; others may be relatively static. In any case, component models are not restricted to only the descriptive profiles presented in previous chapters for the major HCI entities. In general, they may be represented by any one or more of the model types outlined earlier in this chapter. Depending on the success and nature of such models, they may also serve as inputs to the use of HCI simulation studies, as described in Section 7.8.

7.5.   Syntax Specifications

For programming languages, Bachus-Naur form (BNF) has been used for many years (e.g., Horowitz, 1983). The statements or sentences that form computer programs consist of sequences of words. These sentences must be composed or structured very precisely and unambiguously. Language *syntax* is a set of rules, or a notation encompassing those rules, to determine whether or not a sentence is "well-formed." BNF provides such a rules-based notation. The rules are also called productions.

BNF consists fundamentally of the following elements and rules:

- A set of *terminal symbols*, which are the individual words and special characters that are contained in a language
- A set of *nonterminals*, which are constructed using sequences of symbols, e.g., noun phrases or verb phrases
- A *starting symbol*, which identifies the particular sentence being constructed
- *Metasymbols*, which are not part of the language but are used within the notation to indicate legal word combinations and alternatives in sentences or phrases; for example, the vertical bar ("|") indicates the Boolean "OR" and enables specification of alternative strings
- The *rules* or *productions*, which utilize the above-outlined elements in representing the "well-formed" sentences within the language of interest

One of the features of this notation is that the rules may be expressed in terms of recursion. Second, a language defined using BNF is equivalent to a "context-free grammar." See Horowitz (1983) for further elaboration.

BNF can also be applied to the representation of interaction language in HCI. Reisner (1981) did exactly that in defining the action language for interactive graphics systems. By action language she meant "the sequences of button presses, joystick motions, typing actions, etc. performed by the user. . . ." Subsumed under the language specification is not only the exact prescription of how the user must command the system to carry out its functions, but also the identification of whatever functions (e.g., ability to draw certain shapes) are available to the user.

Reisner (1981) actually extended the basic BNF notation by adding "semantic restrictions," which are informal rules to restrict the use of a particular production. But her entire focus was on describing the user's side of the interaction. Bournique (1981) utilized her approach and also the related work by Hanau and Lenorovitz (1980) to encompass both user and system actions.

Following is an illustrative subset of Bournique's graphical interaction language (Bournique and Treu, 1985). It represents interaction language at a high level, rather than focusing on the low-level details. Nevertheless it is indicative of how an extended version of BNF notation can be usefully employed. The illustrative language subset is listed in Table 7.1. Let the (context-free) interaction grammar, G, be denoted by ⟨T, NT, S, P⟩, where T = set of terminals, NT = set of nonterminals, S = the starting symbol, and P = set of production or rewriting rules. S, the starting symbol, is a special nonterminal that represents the root of the interaction tree inherent to the notation. It is ⟨graphical interaction⟩.

Each nonterminal, in NT, is also enclosed in ⟨. . .⟩ brackets. It consists in general, of a string of ⟨nonterminals⟩ and/or "terminals." As implied thereby, the terminal symbols, in T, are enclosed within ". . ." delimiters. Included among them are the keywords, variables, operators, etc., that constitute typical language grammars. Members of NT and T are easily identifiable among the rules listed in Table 7.1. Those rules, in P, collectively and hierarchically represent the overall prescription of how various interactions can be legally constructed using members of NT and T, and starting with S. Optional strings are enclosed by square brackets [. . .].

Realizing that Table 7.1 only lists a subset, the pattern of language definition can nevertheless be appreciated by traversing the illustrative rules branch (of the tree) starting with ⟨command sequence⟩ and ending with ⟨locating response⟩. As already indicated, such a grammar is subject to much more detailed specification (e.g., of precise command syntax) as well as greater versatility (e.g., providing more alternative actions at various points). For example, for the syntactic class ⟨keyboard action⟩ the alternative of automatic command completion can be included, by appending to the string in Table 7.1: | "user types first unique characters of item followed by carriage return" [⟨keyboard response⟩] [⟨item completion⟩].

Emphasis in the language subset of Table 7.1 is on the action language

TABLE 7.1
An Illustrative Subset of Interaction Grammar[a]

⟨graphical interaction⟩ ::= ⟨initialized system⟩ ⟨command sequence⟩
⟨initialized system⟩ ::= ⟨initialized work area⟩ ⟨initialized command area⟩
                         ⟨initialized message area⟩ ⟨initialized input area⟩
                         ⟨initialized file system⟩
⟨command sequence⟩ ::= ⟨user request⟩ | ⟨user request⟩ ⟨command sequence⟩
⟨user request⟩ ::= ⟨button pressing action⟩ ⟨LINE⟩ "system draws a line"
⟨button pressing action⟩ ::= ["system prompts for user button action"]
                         ⟨button alternative⟩
⟨button alternative⟩ ::= ⟨keyboard action⟩ ⟨keyboard parse⟩|
                         ⟨function key action⟩ ⟨function key parse⟩|
                         ⟨menu action⟩ ⟨menu parse⟩|
                         ⟨valuator action⟩ ⟨valuator parse⟩
⟨keyboard action⟩ ::= "user types item at keyboard" [⟨keyboard response⟩]
⟨keyboard parse⟩ ::= "system rcognizes the typed item"|
                         "system indicates an error" ⟨keyboard action⟩
⟨keyboard response⟩ ::= "system echoes typed characters"
⟨LINE⟩ ::= ⟨endpoint specification⟩|⟨polar coordinate specification⟩|
                         ⟨rubberband specification⟩|⟨stroke specification⟩
⟨endpoint specification⟩ ::= ["system prompts for point"] ⟨locating action⟩
                         ["system prompts for point"] ⟨locating action⟩
⟨locating action⟩ ::= [⟨system prompts for a locating action"] ⟨locating alternative⟩
⟨locating alternative⟩ ::= "user positions physical locator"
                         [⟨locating response⟩]
⟨locating response⟩ ::= "position of locator is displayed on the screen"|
                         "system indicates an illegal position" ⟨locating action⟩

[a]Reprinted from Bournique and Treu (1985) with permission of Academic Press.

agents, namely, those that enable the user to effectively communicate *to the computer* the actions it is to carry out (Bournique and Treu, 1985). Likewise, display language agents must be defined, to enable suitable, visual output *from the computer*, in a manner conducive to human perception and cognition. Accordingly, a sample for the syntactic class ⟨menu response⟩ is:

⟨menu response⟩ ::= "chosen menu item is illuminated"|
                    "chosen menu item is blinked"
                    |"chosen menu item changes color"

The rule indicates that visual feedback is provided by means of brightening, flashing, or changing the color of the menu item selected by the user.

The above-indicated type of grammar enables simple and well-structured description of the interaction. An interactive session can be parsed to result in an interaction tree (see Exercise 7.5). The terminal nodes of the tree can be visited left to right, thereby revealing the scenario of user–computer events ordered in time. The particular bindings of logical actions with physical devices are left up to the designer. For example, the virtual locating action might be bound to a mouse or a joystick. The subset of an interaction grammar portrayed above is *not* presented here as being necessarily the most effective; instead it is to illustrate how interaction language and the supportive interaction techniques can be represented using extended BNF notation. The construction of an effective, user-oriented interaction (grammar) must ultimately depend on the designer's knowledge and skills in taking the various significant design factors (about user, application, computer, etc.) and features into account.

It should be noted that, until fairly recently, models such as extended BNF representations of HCI language were often treated as if they portrayed the totality of the HCI design problem. This suggested that if you knew how to represent interaction language in a formal way, you should thereby be able to implement it and, presto, the interface design would be achieved. By now we recognize that such representation is only one part of the large HCI design problem.

Nevertheless, it is a very useful part, both from the perspective of the designer and the user. The designer can be assured that, if the specified representation is adhered to in a meticulous, systematic manner, the design results will be correspondingly consistent and correct. On the other hand, the user can also expect consistency in the required formulation of inputs as well as in the system's responses. Consistency tends to be a good principle of design, although there may be reasons for accommodating certain user idiosyncracies that argue in favor of inconsistency in special contexts. This issue is mentioned again in Chapter 9.

7.6. *Functional Models*

Syntax specification models, as portrayed above, may already indicate the kinds of functions that are available to the user at the interface. After all, the language itself must be capable of expressing and invoking target functionalities, at least those that are specific to the application being accessed. However, the repertoire of functions that serve the user can also be modeled in other ways, utilizing several of the model types outlined in Section 7.2.

The descriptive approach involves the listing and definition of functions and associated operations that are to be accessible to the user (in a particular context). A number of taxonomies of functions have been produced and reported (e.g., Cohill, 1984; Carter *et al.*, 1991). Modeling the required functionality can also be accomplished in ways that are:

1. *Diagrammatic:* drawing the functional modules and how they relate to each other, either physically/visually (e.g., with respect to window positions on the interface screen) or logically (e.g., with regard to software-based support modules behind the interface surface)
2. *Event-Based:* whenever some significant activity starts or finishes, defining the function(s) that constitute or trigger those events, e.g., a procedure to process the arrival of a message
3. *State-Encapsulating:* within a particular time-dependent state (or context), identifying the currently available functions—using descriptive, diagrammatic, or other means
4. *Formal, Mathematical:* using rigorous notation based on some mathematical area, e.g., algebraic or set-theoretic techniques, to represent the functions, axioms, and operations that are available

Many different versions of diagrammatically portrayed functional models are possible. Several examples are included in this book. In particular, the UIMS model described in Chapter 8 is indicative. The UIMS also subsumes other models, such as event handlers and state transition networks, as mentioned there. It must also accommodate the multilayer model described in Chapter 4.

Event-based models, in which the required functions are embedded in event handling procedures, are prevalent in many areas including event-oriented simulation. So are the basic state transition models, in which the state contents are very narrowly defined. State-encapsulating models, on the other hand, have been less prominent. As discussed in Section 7.7, they are based on a user-oriented generalization of state transition networks. They are used heavily in the design method proposed in Part III of this book.

With regard to more formal, mathematically based models of available functions and associated operations, a number of alternatives present themselves. They include approaches based on algebraic axioms (basic and extended algebraic, and event algebra) and also based on more general set-theoretic specifications (Chi, 1985). Interface structures can be specified on behalf of the user and what he/she visualizes at the interface (Treu, 1992). Such specification is based on a set of applicable functions, each expressible as available operation(s). Underlying is a set of axioms, which are statements describing the semantics of those operations.

The choice of functional model should depend on the category of function to be represented. Functionality that is to be *user-visible* and *user-*

understood may suggest a diagrammatic version. An example is a diagram of the positional layout of the screen, which the user is expected to learn and remember. It may also require a state-encapsulating model, to emphasize how the user must move from one context to another. A state transition graph, discussed in the next section, is applicable.

On the other hand, if the functionality to be modeled is to be based on some formal notation, which may be rigorous but less than conducive to user comprehension, an algebraic or set-theoretic approach can be employed. Chi's (1985) detailed comparison of several such techniques is useful.

Third, if functionality is to be modeled more for the sake of high-level guidance to software designers, a diagrammatic approach identifying the software modules and their relationships may be satisfactory. However, if the HCI design is to be user-oriented, such a model must necessarily be refined and coupled with the above-indicated, user-conducive models.

7.7. Flow and Control Models

In traditional computer science theory, the notion of a "state" arises in the definition of a finite automaton (Cohen, 1986). Besides requiring an alphabet of possible input letters, which are to be read one at a time to form allowable character strings, a finite automaton must have:

- A finite set of *states*, including a start state and some (maybe no) final states, and
- A finite set of *transitions* that identify for each state (and each input letter) which state to go to next

In essence, the finite automaton then looks like a graph with its states (nodes) and transitions (arcs) appropriately labeled. It works by inputting to it a string of letters, which it processes very systematically, left to right.

But our interest here is not in dwelling on finite automata for HCI. Instead, we recognize that such formal models were subsequently interpreted and utilized for much more practical purposes. An example is its representation of the time-specific states, and the permissible transitions among them, within an operating system. However, that interpretation was still rather narrow, because very specific state definitions (e.g., waiting for input) were used. Wasserman (1985) then adopted and extended the state transition diagram model to HCI-oriented specification. The model has also been found useful in a number of other applications relevant to HCI (e.g., Jacob, 1985).

Various kinds of state transition diagrams or networks can be employed to represent the different "states" through which the user and the computer must pass, as they interact with each other. The states and transitions can be very narrowly defined, e.g., indicating merely that the user moves from a wait (for response) state to a read (the response) state. But we can enlarge the scope or contents of a state very significantly and meaningfully. By emphasizing what the user sees and must do within each state, rather than the back-and-forth switching from narrow, user-controlled state to/from computer-controlled state, we can encapsulate everything that is important to the user at any point in time. Even the lower-level, detailed transition diagrams can be included in each high-level state definition, as applicable. Further, every event that triggers a transition, or a change of state, can itself be defined with respect to the timepoint at which it occurs. As a result, event handling procedures can represent both (1) the relevant functionality and (2) the state transition dynamics of HCI.

Definition 6.9 in the previous chapter presented a special view of an "interaction state." It was then related to "interaction context" (Definition 6.11). Figure 7.2 displays a generic, high-level state transition graph. In

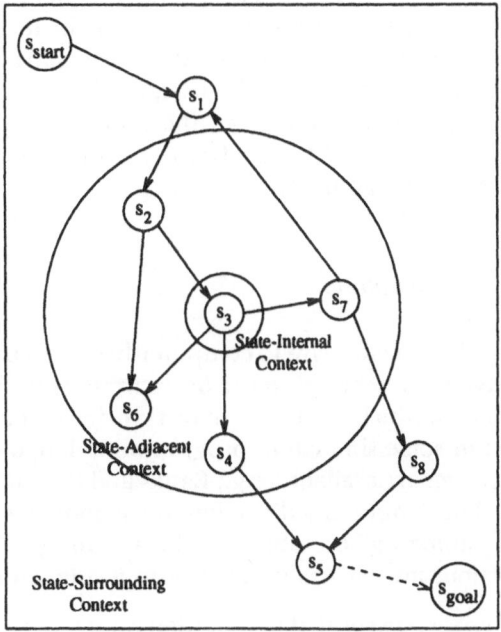

FIGURE 7.2. States, state scenarios, and contexts.

Part III, this kind of graph is used in a prototype interface design to represent user-identifiable states, state contexts, and scenarios (or paths) of high-level states through which the user must transition.

If a state is represented by a node in a state transition diagram, which is a directed graph, then a state scenario is a nodal path through that graph. An example in Fig. 7.2 is

$$[s_{start}, s_1, s_2, s_3, s_4, s_5, \ldots, s_{goal}]$$

More than one scenario may be available for reaching a desired goal state from some start-up state. In the above scenario, the user can branch from s_3 to s_7 (instead of to s_4). The states of a scenario may be repeated, by means of iterations (or cycles in a graph). Example:

$$[s_1, s_2, s_3, s_7, s_1]$$

Although that repetition is in terms of defined functionalities, the values of state variables, as produced by a user from one iteration to another of the same state structure, are of course likely to be different. One or another scenario may be selected, subject to what the user is planning to do and how the computer assists in task planning and scenario selection.

As was stated for syntax specification models, flow and control models are also useful for both designer and user. The designer gains a high-level organizing mechanism to guide the design both in terms of dynamic behavior (states and state transitions) and the functional capabilities to be made available in various contexts. The user, on the other hand, benefits from that same organization, but from the user-visible perspective oriented to answering: where did I come from? what is available to me right now? where can/should I go next?

7.8 Modeling and Simulation

Certain models are conducive to computer-based simulation. An HCI object and its dynamic behavior must be representable by means of a detailed, valid model, which, in turn, can be transformed into a computer program written in some simulation programming language. A number of different languages are available (e.g., Banks and Carson, 1985; Sanderson *et al.*, 1991). The programmed version of the model is then executed for purposes of "imitating" the object's behavior and performance. The following distinctions are especially relevant to a simulation model:

- *Analytical versus numerical:* if the solution cannot be obtained directly from a mathematical representation, a numerical method for specifying values of model parameters is necessary. The latter fundamentally leads to the alternative of conducting simulations of the objects being modeled.

- *Deterministic versus stochastic:* for example, instead of knowing exactly (deterministically) when an event will occur (e.g., when a user selects a menu entry), that timepoint is based on "random" (or stochastic) behavior (using a random number generator with reference to an appropriate cumulative probability distribution).
- *Continuous versus discrete:* instead of trying to model a user's continuous motion (e.g., with a lightpen drawing some curve), interpreting the action in terms of discrete decision points (e.g., user hits lightpen start button, followed by a sequence of other intermediate points, followed by a lightpen stop button).

For any substantial HCI-oriented simulation, all of these distinctions must be understood and may have to be invoked. A number of books on the subject are available (e.g., Fishman, 1978; Gordon, 1978; Lewis and Smith, 1979; Law and Kelton, 1991). If the designer determines that a valid simulation is possible, he/she can utilize it for purposes of assessing the *potential* results of an HCI design, prior to (or instead of) actually implementing it.

Simulation is primarily useful to HCI designers and evaluators. It enables analysis of the behavior and appearance of an interface without having to implement it, even in prototype form. However, if the simulation study is done well, the user is likely to benefit from ultimately improved design.

7.9. Decision Schematics

The decision schematics presented in previous chapters now can be extended to include an additional type of effect or outcome: the use of one or more models to represent the selected interface features. In other words, the featured outcome of a design decision is not only a specified interaction technique or style, as suggested by examples in Fig. 4.5 and 5.3. That decision should be coupled with a decision on which model will be used to represent that technique or any other parts of the interface design.

Any such model provides the means for careful organization and description of a design. Depending on the model chosen and what it is supposed to represent, both the user and the designer (and designers in general) are likely to benefit.

7.10. Decision Function: Update

In Section 6.10, interaction techniques and styles were included as high-level features. Each such choice represents a subset of dependent variables to be determined by the designer. Now, we can add another category of high-level features. They are those models (and related methods) that have a bearing on how the interface will look, feel, and behave. Accordingly, using an expression similar to Eq. (6.1), we have the following union:

$$F_{\text{MODELS}} = F_{\text{COMPS}} \cup F_{\text{SYNTAX}} \cup F_{\text{FUNCT}} \cup F_{\text{FLOW}} \cup F_{\text{ORGN}} \cup F_{\text{OTHER}} \quad (7.1)$$

The set labeled F_{COMPS} is used to encompass the component models, including both the relevant mental models of users and, more importantly for the design process, the conceptual models that are constructed by designers to represent those mental models. The set labeled F_{ORGN} consists of any organizational models, including diagrammatic and purely descriptive models, which help to organize the interface design in user-observable ways. The other sets of models should be self-explanatory. They are to contain the other models described in this chapter.

Any selected model, when used in conjunction with interaction techniques, selected from $F_{\text{T+S}}$, should be influential in the resulting interface appearance and behavior.

Accordingly, the FEATURES equation (6.3) can be updated as follows:

$$\text{FEATURES} = \{\{F_{\text{T+S,x}}\}, \{F_{\text{MODELS}}\}, \text{other\_sets\_of\_features}\} \quad (7.2)$$

Exercises

7.1. Read the Whitefield (1990) paper. Develop a correspondence or mapping between that classification of models described and the eight categories of models outlined in Section 7.2. Discuss the respective pros and cons.

7.2. Consider a physical, user-visible interface screen, with which you are familiar, as the HCI object to be modeled. Produce as many models of it as is possible, keeping them to reasonably brief presentations (i.e., give enough details to be convincing). Each model should represent one of the eight model categories (Section 7.2).

7.3. Repeat Exercise 7.2 for the interaction language with a particular application (see Table 4.1 for choices) available via your interface. The interaction language is now the HCI object to be modeled.

7.4. Repeat Exercise 7.2 for an airplane (as the HCI-produced object) that is to be designed and displayed using the CAD&E application.

7.5. Convert the interaction grammar (subset) of Table 7.1 into an interaction tree hierarchy. Which representation is more important to the user who must utilize the grammar? Explain.

7.6. Read the Reisner (1981) paper and compare its extended BNF with that indicated by Table 7.1. Which one is "higher-level"? Why?

7.7. Consider yourself sitting at your favorite computer interface, ready to invoke the e-mail system to send a message to a colleague. Utilizing the type of high-level state transition graph depicted by Fig. 7.2., model your interaction from start to finish. Include some nonroutine functions and actions, such as reading part of a text file into your e-mail message and editing the message after noticing earlier spelling mistakes. Besides the high-level model, use a different model to represent the user-visible contents of each numbered state.

7.8. Repeat Exercise 7.7 to represent your (imagined or real) interaction with some other well-defined application available in your computing environment. Examples: PROG or DBMS (see Table 4.1). After creating the model, test it by trying to follow it in real interaction with your system.

7.9. Design, implement, and execute a simulation model of the interaction described in Exercise 7.7. If possible, use a simulation programming language rather than a general-purpose programming language. By means of the simulation clock, the timepoints for transitioning between user-observable states should be explicitly represented. Notice that your simulation model is necessarily dependent on other models. For the system to be simulated, it must encompass (at least) minimally accurate representations of each of its major components, including the e-mail application, the interface-supported interaction (language), and the interacting user. For example, you must decide the rate or pattern of user interaction, e.g., the variable time intervals between user commands, or between user commands and system responses. The details depend on the objectives of the simulation. (Note: this exercise is subject to considerable refinement; depending on the priorities of your instructor, it can range from being a relatively simple, single-user simulation to becoming a very complicated, multiuser simulation.)

7.10. With reference to Exercise 7.9, elaborate Eq. (7.2) by listing all the design features that were (or could be) incorporated in the simulation model, including applicable (a) interaction techniques and styles and (b) representative models. (Note: here the design features are only being simulated to assess their potential effectiveness; ultimately, the designer must decide on a set of features, including any representation models, which deserve specification for implementation.)

SUPPORTIVE TOOLS
AND TECHNIQUES

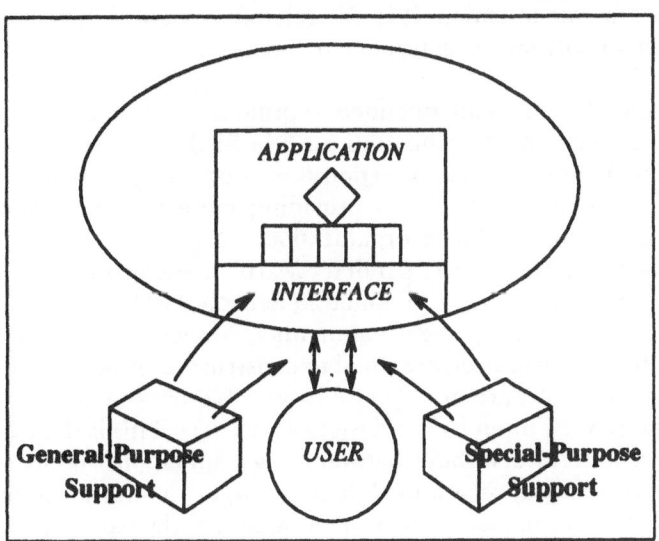

8.1. Overview

Part II of this book covers the major prerequisites to HCI design and evaluation. Thus far it has included knowledge of each of the target user (Chapter 3), the target application (Chapter 4), the target computer (Chapter 5), how the user and computer can interact (Chapter 6), and ways of representing the HCI components and features by means of static or dynamic models (Chapter 7). This chapter considers a variety of software tools and techniques that have been developed for purposes of assisting in the tasks of interface design and development.

Some of the tools depend on previously covered topics. In particular, Section 8.2 points out how the models of Chapter 7 can in themselves be viewed as useful tools for the design process. They can be used like templates. The term "supportive tools" is obviously defined very generically.

Section 8.3 describes prototyping as an interim step, producing a representation that approximates the final design. A prototype interface can be created through the normal design process emphasized in this book. Its creation can also be expedited in certain ways, such as through "rapid prototyping" and automatic software generation (Section 8.6).

Section 8.4 presents several tools that can support the modular and object-oriented design and development of interface software. Included is the special model for interface software organization, namely the UIMS. While it can be inserted in the range of models described in Chapter 7, it deserves separate attention. It is also related to the widely acknowledged approach to software organization in general, namely, object-oriented design.

Besides those that are intended to organize and facilitate the design, some tools and related techniques have been developed in response to particular design principles (Section 8.5). Accordingly, they are special-purpose in nature, rather than providing more general-purpose help, such as in interface software organization.

Efforts have also been expended toward "predetermined" generation of the interface software, as outlined in Section 8.6. Short of creating an original, new interface in the usual manner, special software packages (or models thereof) have been designed to construct interfaces automatically. They generate software in response to variable parameter values or options that must be input by the designer (or user). This is done either for the "entire" interface, within whatever design limitations and for whatever application intended, or as a module of a "larger" interface. An important example of such a module is the window manager, discussed in Section 8.4.

Although this book is not about implementation as such, some relevant considerations are outlined in Section 8.7. It is also important to recognize that all design results should be subject to effective documentation, both to aid users and to guide prospective designers. Suitable "tools" for that purpose are essential. They are mentioned in Section 8.8. Finally, a brief update of the functional view of design is given in Section 8.9.

8.2.　Models as Templates

The range of models presented in Chapter 7 can serve as a special kind of tools kit for the designer. If he/she determines that an existing model of the interface functionality, or of the interaction language, or of the interactive state transitions closely approximates the components or behavior of the planned interface, it makes a lot of sense to take advantage of that model.

How does one utilize any such model? Toward instantiating something in an HCI design, or toward evaluating a design result, one can view it as a template. That is, it can be a pattern to be applied or emulated, consistent with Definition 6.19. A template is itself a model. But emphasis here is on practical utilization. When used as a template, a model becomes a tool that can guide the designer toward achieving a desired result, by enabling the comparison of its appearance and behavior against the model. For example, if a CLG-based model (Moran, 1981) is used, it can become a design tool for checking the consistency and validity of design (Firth and Thomas, 1991).

To use models as templates is generally not easy. It demands that the designer have the skills to employ the template in a very deliberate, systematic manner. It also assumes that appropriate validation and verification techniques are employed, consistent with what is done in modeling and simulation (Section 7.8). In other words, the model must be valid in that it closely resembles the interface (sub)system to be designed and instantiated; further, the resulting, model-based design must be verified to ensure that its behavior and performance accurately represent the goals planned for the (sub)system.

8.3. Prototyping

Because the design and implementation of an interface can be very complex, time-consuming, and expensive, there are good reasons for wanting to obtain evidence, *prior to full implementation*, that the design indeed carries the potential for meeting its goals. The major reason is of course to prevent the expenditure of resources toward implementing a design that may turn out to be less than satisfactory.

Obtaining evidence to predict or project interface performance is not easy. One approach to assessing the potential performance of at least selected components of an interface design, short of actual implementation and testing, is to conduct modeling and simulation studies. These were mentioned in Chapter 7 as representational methods that can assist in the HCI design process. However, the purpose of using modeling and simulation is typically to avoid *any* implementation, even partial, until one is very confident in the design.

Another approach is called prototyping. It is based on the view that software development is evolutionary in nature, aided by experimentation and experience (Budde *et al.*, 1992). This approach results in the implementation of a prototype of the system (HCI design) or some significant part(s) thereof:

Definition 8.1. **Prototype**: the first or primary version of an object; the implementation of an original or model representation.

Prototypes have been built in various engineering fields for many years. As Budde *et al.* (1992) point out, however, a prototype that is the first specimen of a product series is technically not the same as a software prototype intended to demonstrate the design features of a system.

Notice that the word "model" again appears in Definition 8.1. However, it now refers to a model implementation of something. In our case, that something is all or part of an interface. By definition (Definition 7.4), a model is only a representation, not the real, final thing. It is, therefore, expected to provide an approximation to the appearance and behavior of the finished object being represented.

In practice, this means that an interface prototype is not expected to be fully developed, debugged, and utilized in operational settings. It is instead like an experimental, trial version that is implemented relatively quickly, in order to give the designer and the users, as well as management, the evidence deemed necessary to either commit to or refrain from full implementation. To this end, so-called "rapid prototyping" tools have been developed (e.g., Rouff and Horowitz, 1991; Miller-Jacobs, 1991). In general, it is wise to implement an illustrative, proof-of-concept prototype whenever feasible. This is especially true when full implementation is expected to require much time and many resources.

However, prototype implementation must be viewed as an interim step in the full implementation sequence. It should constitute a step in a systematic development process. In that sense, the implementor should ensure that the prototype product itself can serve as the base for continued development toward full implementation. In other words, the prototype should exhibit the software engineering principles that will enable the refinement, expansion, replacement, modification, etc., of the HCI software, and ideally also of the hardware platform on which it runs, in order to transform it into a final product. It should *not* result from designers being so enamored of the various existing software construction tools now available that they abandon careful design processes and use trial and error to arrive at a product of questionable quality and usefulness (Budde *et al.*, 1992).

8.4. Design and Development

Generally applicable tools and techniques for effective software design have their origins in the area of software engineering (e.g., Pressman, 1988; Fairley, 1985). Modularity is certainly significant; so is the need to separate the abstract definition of what a piece of software (e.g., a search procedure), or a data structure (e.g., an event queue), is to be able to accomplish, from the corresponding implementation details. As long as the operations of the software/data structure are consistent with the abstract specifications, and as long as they are accessible to the user, the typical user should have no need to care about the low-level details of implementation.

The above should also apply to interface software. However, that software is not merely one application program implementing some algorithm, nor even a set of system programs (e.g., a compiler) implementing the processing of application programs written in some language. Instead, the interface software is a complex package that must be able to cope with all of:

1. Facing the computer user (U) on one side
2. Facing the application (A) software on the other
3. Utilizing its own internal functionalities and capabilities to accomplish 1 and 2, both
   a. *Individually*, that is, understanding the characteristics of the user and the application and dealing with each accordingly, and
   b. *In conjunction*, enabling the user–application communication to take place in ways that are deemed effective, efficient, synergistic.

Doing this is no small feat. For years, the designers and developers of interface software endeavored to approximate the above-outlined, descriptive model. The resulting degrees of success varied greatly. Often the approach to interface software organization was very ad hoc. By now, we have some well-established tools to enable us to be more systematic. Myers and Rosson's (1992) survey indicates that various tools, including the UIMS, are used extensively (by three-fourths of the respondents); few use no tools. Software tools are available for dialogue design (e.g., Guest, 1982; Wong and Reid, 1982); they are also used for various other interface design features, both at high, all-encompassing levels (e.g., UIMS) and at lower levels (e.g., widgets). These are discussed in the following sections.

8.4.1. UIMS Model

In the early 1980s, the importance of interface modularity was recognized (e.g., Schvaneveldt *et al.*, 1984; Draper and Norman, 1985), and a high-level organization was proposed (e.g., Pfaff, 1985; Green, 1985). It was called "user interface management system" (UIMS). Although the term "management" may be something of a misnomer when focusing on design, the UIMS label has become commonplace. With reference to the model distinctions drawn in Chapter 7, a UIMS is a diagrammatic and

174 CHAPTER 8

descriptive, functional model superimposed on the software organization of an interface system.

A diagrammatic version of the UIMS model is depicted in Fig. 8.1. It exhibits desirable modularity, thereby promoting (1) software/hardware exchangeability and portability, in general, and (2) independence between the application software and the interface software, in particular. The latter has been advocated by a number of investigators (e.g., Hurley, 1993). Ideally, each of the modules of the UIMS model (Fig. 8.1) should be replaceable with alternative implementations. The alternatives available of course depend on the nature and functionality of the particular module:

1. *Presentation* (PM): this module is the physical interaction component; it basically represents the lexical level, including the device-specific and token-based input, output, and control, and the display arrangement (e.g., via windows and menus) and management. This component
   a. Encompasses Level 1 of the seven-layer model shown in Fig. 4.2, thereby supporting Level 2
   b. Interacts directly with the user, on one side, based on whatever I/O devices are in place
   c. Provides input tokens to and receives output tokens from the Dialog Control Module, on the other side
2. *Dialogue Control* (DCM): this module is the logical interaction component; it represents the language-based, semantic level, which interprets, constructs, and controls inputs and outputs to/from either of its neighboring modules. This component
   a. Encompasses Level 2 of the seven-layer model shown in Fig. 4.2, thereby supporting Level 3 and, indirectly, the higher levels
   b. Interacts directly with the PM, on one side, utilizing it to instantiate whatever interaction technique is to be available

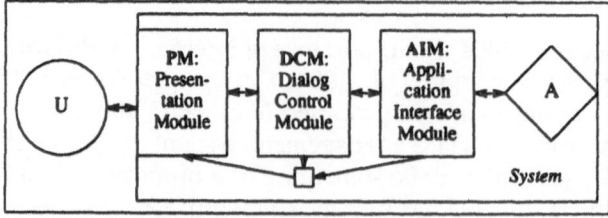

FIGURE 8.1. Basic UIMS model.

    c. Interacts indirectly (via the PM) with the user, conducting a dialogue in accordance with the interaction technique(s) it is designed to support

    d. Provides inputs to and receives outputs from the Application Interface Module

The interaction techniques to be supported by the DCM are those characterized in Chapter 6. Figure 6.1, Definition 6.4., and Tables 6.1 through 6.4 are especially relevant. But, to prepare the DCM for such a support role, suitable dialogue models must be created and used. Three models for this purpose were discussed in Chapter 7: syntax specification-based (Section 7.5), event-based (Section 7.6), and state transition-based (Section 7.7). These three represent major notations for dialogue design (Green, 1985; Olsen, 1992).

3. *Application Interface* (AIM): this module is actually a "model" of the application and how to access it; it represents abstract, logical-level information about the routines, (procedures, functions) and data structures accommodated by the application software; it must know about procedure names, parameters, etc., but not the implementation details. It also represents information about a special kind of interaction mode, that is, about which software unit is to be the initiator of interface–application communication.

    Three choices are: the user interface calls on routines in the application; the application calls on routines in the interface; or, in the mixed-initiative mode, both are independent, communicating processes and neither has control over the other. In the last case, the two can be treated as concurrent, interleaving processes or co-routines.

    The AIM component

    a. Provides definition of what the application contains and what it can do, to enable independence between the interface software and the application software

    b. Interacts directly with the DCM, mapping what the dialogue requests into appropriate action(s) by the application

    c. Interacts directly with the application software, providing the necessary calls and parameter values and returning results, under DCM control (see Fig. 8.1), for display by the PM

    d. Establishes which software unit, if any, is to be the initiator of interface–application communication

We should note that the UIMS can be and has been used for different purposes (Green, 1985; Ero and van Liere, 1988). It can be useful in developing the detailed design specifications for an interface; it is also used for producing the executable run-time system for it, consistent with the design specifications (e.g., Buxton *et al.*, 1983). In either case, however, we can interpret the UIMS to be a model that is superimposed in order to gain the resulting organizational and functional advantages.

8.4.2. UIMS Variations

But, while the basic UIMS model is useful, a number of HCI investigators have found it necessary or desirable to extend it for various reasons, or to tailor it for special purposes. Examples are the interface systems reported by Hill (1986), Foley *et al.* (1988), Sibert *et al.* (1988), and Manaris and Dominick (1993). In Chapter 11, another extended version of the UIMS model is presented.

Further, some people have suggested that HCI designers' reliance on UIMSs may be altogether excessive or misdirected. For example, Johnson (1992) feels that the UIMS (and various UI tool kits) tend to be oriented primarily to widgets. He encourages greater attention to higher-level semantics and "selectors" that are dependent on semantics rather than on widget-based appearance and layout of the interface.

8.4.3. Object-Oriented Software

Definition 7.1 attributes a broad meaning to the term "object." As it implies, an object can take on a variety of different forms and be useful in a wide range of contexts. With regard to HCI design, some objects are physical constituents of the interface system itself, others are information entities that the users can view, conceptualize, or visualize, and still others are logical modules that make up parts of the interface's software architecture. Indeed, the modular UIMS can be "object"-oriented (e.g., Sibert *et al.*, 1988).

Above-indicated examples of objects suggest that they all share the characteristics of

1. *External definition or identity as a unit:* delimiting the entity, part, or module as it is situated in some medium or as a component of a larger, containing object
2. *Internal definition or structure within the unit:* information that defines and associates the lower-level components of the object
3. *Relationship(s) to other object(s):* excluding those implied by containing and contained objects above (1 and 2) but including
   a. Degree/level of independence from or dependence on other objects
   b. Connection to or communication with other objects

The set of major HCI modules (U, A, I) can be discussed with reference to the above characteristics; so can other objects, including those that are conceptually defined by the user as well as those that are logically defined within the confines of a computer system.

For present purposes, the software organization designed to support an interface system can be based on software objects, as is well-known by software engineers. The resulting "object-oriented software" consists of units that are specifically defined with separate, external identities, each capable of performing certain functions within its domain. Relationships with other units include possible parent–child dependencies, that is, a child object inheriting specified characteristics of its parent object. Such patterns clearly suggest hierarchical dependence. Also, such software units must be able to communicate with each other, if necessary, in certain prescribed ways, e.g., using messages (Goldberg and Robson, 1983; Pinson and Wiener, 1988).

Such object-oriented software design carries with it considerable advantages over more traditional techniques (e.g., Kim and Lerch, 1992). It has become so important that a separate professional conference on the topic of object-oriented programming systems, languages, and applications (e.g., OOPSLA, 1992) has flourished for a number of years.

Object-oriented software organization is also advisable for HCI software. However, that is suggested not only for reasons known to software engineers. Given our broad definition of objects, we are also interested in how objects that are logically contained in, or represented by, software can be mapped into either (1) objects rendered visible on the interface screen, or even (2) objects that are conceptualized by the user (Treu, 1992). Such correspondences can have positive effects on interface design.

This does *not* mean that the characteristics of object-oriented software, such as the inheritance feature, are necessarily assumed to apply to objects that are viewed or visualized by users. As was pointed out by Rumelhart and Norman (1988), it remains unclear whether such software features also have utility in knowledge representation techniques of interest to the human mind. But, regardless of how that question is ultimately answered, the object-oriented approach to HCI software organization is certainly very important. It is a supportive "tool" that can make the power of object-oriented representation pervasive throughout the interface system.

8.4.4. Widget Software

In addition to using the various types of models, including the UIMS, as template tools to support HCI design, a number of other tools and techniques can become involved. Unlike the models, which tend to be higher-level features in a design, these software features are lower-level in their applicability and support.

To enable the user to interact with a computer, he/she must be able to *input* commands, queries, data, signals, etc. The most basic (token-level) input activity is carried out at Level 1 of the layered interaction model (Fig. 4.2). It requires the availability of some reasonable set of input devices, typically including at least a keyboard and a mouse. Lightpens, joysticks, tablets, and other special devices, such as OCRs, may also be useful for certain applications. In addition, more advanced input equipment, such as video cameras for hand gestures and microphones for voice input, will become increasingly prominent in the future.

In any case, the HCI designer must know about how the selected input devices can be connected to the interface hardware and then rendered operational using supportive software. Generally, any such device requires a *device driver*. This is a software module specifically designed to control the operation of peripheral equipment, including input devices employed by the user at the interface. Depending on the characteristics of the device hardware as well as the interface system's operating system intended to serve the device, a device driver and any necessary interrupt handler may already be provided. If not, it will have to be written as part of the HCI design implementation, using whatever implementation language is available and in accordance with the requirements of the operating system involved. Numerous books and manuals are available to help. Most books on the design of computer operating systems in general (e.g., Peterson and Silberschatz, 1985) or on a particular operating system (e.g., Bach, 1986) give descriptions of device driver designs and illustrative code for implementing them.

Likewise and in keeping with the definition of the Presentation Module of the UIMS model (Section 8.3), the *output* side of HCI also needs low-level support. This too is relevant at Level 1 of the interaction model (Fig. 4.2) and involves the display of various so-called widgets, such as menus and windows. Window management has been considered and categorized extensively (e.g., Hopgood *et al.*, 1986; Myers, 1988; Funke *et al.*, 1993), and specific named *window managers* have been created (e.g., Scheifler and Gettys, 1986; Goodfellow, 1986).

Availability of such widgets provides the HCI designer with options tied into choice of interaction techniques (Table 6.1). The designer should be aware of any special support package that may already be installed in a candidate interface system or that can be acquired for it. If widget support is not already available, or if its functionality and performance are deemed inadequate to meet the designer's specifications, the HCI developer will again be obliged to create it from scratch. A variety of documentation can be found to aid in this task. However, while widgets are essential, designers should not be excessively preoccupied with toolkits that provide widget-level design support. As Johnson (1992) has pointed out, too much focus on widgets tends to distract designer attention from the more important, higher-level design issues.

8.5. Goal-Specific Software

In deciding on the major features to be instantiated in a particular interface, the designer must choose from a great variety of design principles. These are discussed in Chapter 9. Principles of design are treated as synonymous with high-level design goals.

Depending on which goal is chosen, some appropriate tools and techniques may already be available. The designer should know about them and about the literature describing them. This does not mean that relevant software modules are necessarily obtainable or usable. It does mean that pertinent models may at least have been specified and tested, thereby giving the designer a head start on understanding the options available.

For example, suppose that the planned interface is to be *adaptive* to user needs and preferences. This goal is addressed in detail in Chapter 13. It should prompt the HCI designer to become thoroughly familiar with the tools and techniques related to *expert systems*, a subarea of artificial intelligence. Included must be understanding of:

1. Different types of knowledge in general (e.g., Buchanan and Shortliffe, 1984) that can be represented
2. The particular, domain-specific types of knowledge upon which an expert system is dependent (Rolston, 1988)
3. Schemes for knowledge representation, including production systems and their constituents (e.g., Jackson, 1986)
4. How to build expert systems using above-suggested knowledge and tools (e.g., Harmon *et al.*, 1988; Chadwick and Hannah, 1986)

Using the above, one or more expert systems have to be integrated into the interface software architecture, as illustrated in Chapter 13.

For a second example, suppose that the planned interface is to provide an interaction language that appears *uniform* to the user, even though different languages are in fact required for access to different versions of the same application (e.g., Shepherd and Watters, 1985). Those different software versions may be located in one computer system or be distributed over a number of systems in a network. For example, it can be useful to have an intermediary (human or computer) be able to search several different IS&R systems in a uniform, composite manner (e.g., Marcus, 1983).

Again, it is useful for the HCI designer to know that this kind of goal has been pursued before. An approach previously taken involved (Treu, 1982):

1. Determination of whether the goal of language uniformity is reasonable for a particular application, e.g., bibliographic information retrieval
2. Analysis of the similarities and differences in the language syntax and semantics (of individual commands) reflected by different versions
3. Modeling of the intermediary module that must be designed to transform different languages into one that appears to be uniform, or at least as uniform as possible
4. Specifying the types of functional capabilities that the intermediary module must have in order to carry out the two-directional transformations

As is true in the expert system example given earlier, the language uniformizer module would also have to be integrated into the interface software. In the former case, the intermediary module invokes changes based on (changing) knowledge about the user, application domain, etc.; in the latter case, transformation of interaction language is based on (unchanging) knowledge of the different instantiations of language versions.

A simpler example than either of the previous two is based on merely wanting to *facilitate* user access to different systems in a network and also access to target software packages in those systems. After gaining such access, the user is then on his/her own. There is no attempt to do more, such as through uniformizing transformations. The point is simply to enable the user to bypass potentially frustrating and time-consuming login (and possibly also logout) procedures.

Each such procedure can be easily represented and stored in an intermediary module for every system of interest to the user. The user can then access the intermediary, identify the target system, and let the intermediary take care of the relevant protocol automatically. An early example of such a tool was the Network Access Machine developed at the National Bureau of Standards (Rosenthal, 1976). That tool, after being suitably extended, was also used to demonstrate feasibility of the language uniformizer discussed above (Treu, 1982).

8.6.   Software Generators

Bournique's Generator of Interactive Graphical Languages (GIGL) was a software tool designed to instantiate a variety of personalized interfaces, in response to user-supplied choices among available options (Bournique, 1981; Bournique and Treu, 1985). Among the options were: specification of screen layout, virtual actions (bound to physical devices), keywords for user functions, and prompts and error messages. In the INTERROGATE Mode, the user (or the HCI experimenter) could select the desired graphical language features. The resulting profile was used by the language generating tool (written in PASCAL) to create a user-specific language *interpreter*. The latter was then invoked on the graphics system by the user, during INTERACT Mode, to experience the personalized kind of interface that was generated automatically.

Buxton *et al.* (1983) used a preprocessor, called MENULAY, to enable interactive specification by the designer of the desired graphical layout and functionality of a menu-based user interface. Using the data from the resulting module, in conjunction with the University of Toronto version of a UIMS, the code for the required run-time support package was generated automatically. The specifications from MENULAY were converted to software (in C), compiled by another module, called MAKE-NEW.

Another generator of graphical interfaces was described by Olsen and Dempsey (1983). It was called SYNGRAPH. Since then, a number of additional generators have been created. Instead of requiring the designer to instantiate an interface model independently, a software tool is specifically prepared to generate the target model automatically. The graphical user interface (GUI) design area has been especially active. Exemplary is the de Baar *et al.* (1992) tool designed to generate the interface (widgets) directly from the specified application (data) model, rather than having to specify both of them in separate efforts. It is based on an interference engine that uses style rules for selecting and positioning widgets, thereby defining the run-time layout of the user interface (for each of any number of GUIs).

Generator software is available for several of the HCI models outlined in Chapter 7. An example is the use of a context-free grammar model for the automatic generation of the dialogue module of the UIMS model (Scott and Yap, 1988). Many other such tools will undoubtedly appear in the future, just as happened in the past with other software generators in computer science, especially in the languages and systems areas. If interface software generators match some subset of the intended HCI design, and if the generated software can be fit, or can be integrated, into its overall (preferably modular) framework, they have the obvious potential of facilitating the design and implementation tasks. This is one of many factors motivating the need for an effective software organization model.

8.7. Implementation Considerations

The actual implementation of the interface only constitutes one or two steps in the design sequence. However, it is obviously very important; the "proof is in the pudding." The HCI designer should exert his/her influence in the direction of ensuring that the design "recipe," assuming that it is good, leads to "tasteful" results. Accordingly, this section highlights several implementation-oriented considerations that should be taken into account in planning for the instantiation of an HCI design. These are special "tools and techniques" that are significantly hinged on implementor knowledge and skills.

8.7.1. Staff Qualifications

Both HCI designers and implementors, who may be the same persons or at least serve on the same project team, should be suitably qualified. The knowledge areas that are prerequisite to carrying out a good design have been presented in the chapters of Part II, including this one. Assuming that a good design results, the implementation of that design is also critically dependent on appropriately qualified personnel. But what are the required qualifications, as they relate to essential technical skills and techniques?

First, as discussed in Chapter 2, the orientation and background of the designer tend to influence the nature of the design specification. Likewise, the orientation and background of the implementor can influence the resulting product. That influence should not be as great, assuming clear-cut specifications are provided (from the design process), with the expectation that the implementor must fully adhere to them. Nevertheless, enough variability may exist to enable the implementor to place his/her own stamp on the result. Thus, if it is possible to do so, it is preferable to have user-oriented persons carry out the interface implementation. A good understanding of Chapter 3 (User Capabilities and Limitations) should be part of that orientation.

But that alone will obviously not do it. The implementors need to be technically competent. This must include the following, briefly outlined:

- Understanding of all the prerequisite knowledge areas (for HCI design), as presented in the chapters of Part II. Especially important are the technical aspects of Chapter 4 (Computer Applications),

Chapter 5 (Computer Capabilities and Limitations), Chapter 6 (Interaction Characteristics and Options), and Chapter 8 (Supportive Tools)
- Ability to follow and adhere to design specifications, including understanding various representation models and methods (Chapter 7) that may be used by the designer in stipulating the interaction language, dynamics, etc., that are expected
- Thorough knowledge of software engineering principles and practices and ability to apply them effectively and efficiently in the programming, integration, testing, debugging, etc., of the interface software within the selected hardware configuration

8.7.2. Software Engineering

The implemented interface should correspond to the designed interface. To that end, the implementor should fully understand and adhere to well-established software engineering principles. He/she must be knowledgeable in the general UIMS architecture and in the models and algorithms required to implement UIMSs effectively (Olsen, 1992).

Particularly critical are the following principles. They relate to the macro-level vantage point of implementing and then, later, modifying or extending the implemented interface package:

1. *High-level modularity*, as discussed in Section 8.3, both in terms of using some (tailored) UIMS organizational structure as well as in the lower-level, constituent modules, or software "objects," of whatever function and size
2. *Object-oriented software organization*, superimposed on or integrated into the high-level software organization (of 1 above).

Taking care to provide a well-organized software framework will enable the introjection of various design objects, including definition and presentation (to the user) of the application-specific interactive states, together with relevant syntax, semantics, context, and transitions to neighboring states.

If such software organization is followed, it will also significantly facilitate software maintenance and subsequent redesign, including expandability and exchangeability of software modules/objects to provide new or improved functionalities to the user at the interface. An example is the addition of an adaptive interface capability, as discussed in Chapter 13.

8.7.3. Software Acquisition

Not every HCI design needs to be implemented totally from scratch. This is true whether we are talking about a prototype or an operational implementation. Indeed, for some people, it may be possible to satisfy their HCI needs by simply adopting, or acquiring, someone else's already completed and tested product. That is of course fine, and it is to be encouraged when it is satisfactory in meeting the needs of a particular user population.

However, to the extent that it obviates much of the design material in this book, the case is obviously not very interesting. We, therefore, assume interest in at least designing and implementing parts of an interface, while other parts of the total software package may be acquired. The implementor's challenge then becomes the following:

Definition 8.2. **Integration**: taking a set of parts and making, or composing, it into a harmoniously functioning whole.

There are different forms or degrees of integrating software parts:

1. *Combination of independent modules,* toward constructing the total interface package, utilizing both new, original modules as well as already existing and tested modules. This can be done when the overall software architecture is properly structured and when both new and acquired modules are independent of each other, in terms of correct separation of abstract definition and implementation. But the modules must be compatible with each other for communication or message-passing purposes.

2. *Nonmodular integration* of the newly implemented and the acquired software pieces. This means literally intertwining the logic (and code) of the pieces being combined. The result might lead to an integrated, independent module. This type of integration is obviously more difficult, risky, and consequently discouraged. However, it can become essential when the designer/implementor can acquire a piece of software that partially meets the needs of the interface but that must be modified in order to incorporate some other functionality not yet contained.

3. *Interrelation of dependent modules,* in order to cause new and acquired modules to become functionally dependent on each other, even though they are to retain their respective modularities. This means that two or more modules may be altered for purposes of sharing application-specific functioning.

Acquisition of an existing text editor can be used to illustrate the above-outlined alternatives for integrating it into an interface software package. Its use can range from remaining an independent module that is separately accessible from another, parallel module (in same environment), to being integrated (in whole or in part) into another module. An example is an editor that can be invoked from within an electronic mail system module.

8.7.4. Integration and Testing

One category of software integration options has already been outlined above, with regard to acquisition of existing software packages or modules. However, as is evident from the multicomponent and multifaceted nature of HCI design discussed in previous chapters, the implementor of such a design is not merely writing some large, modular program; he/she must accommodate all aspects of the total user–interface–application software and hardware framework.

That is quite an undertaking. The composite integration task involves all of the following:

1. Analyzing the HCI design specifications, including interaction technique and style, and any stipulations on how the user-visible presentation should relate (or map) to what is being done behind the interface surface
2. Constructing the required/desired interface software organization or architecture
3. Providing for the user-oriented support functionalities in the interface software (resulting from 2 above)
4. Providing for the application-specific functionalities to be accessible to the user via the interface software, which may or may not be independent of the application software
5. Creating the means for dynamic user-visible presentation and user-workable input at the interface surface

In order to do all of the above successfully, the implementor must not only have the skills of a software engineer working on a substantial software development project; his/her job is further complicated by having to satisfy the interdisciplinary requirements of attending both to the software to be executed by the computer and to the software/hardware that must serve the real-time interaction with the user. It is reasonable to assert, therefore, that the tasks in "interface engineering" generally form a superset of the tasks in software engineering.

Besides the challenge of integrating the pieces of an HCI product, to be designed according to methodology in Part III, the result must also be tested very carefully. As a result of testing and evaluation, preferably carried out in an iterative manner at various steps of the interface implementation process, the design should then be modified to improve its performance. Finally, the interface software must be properly maintained.

8.8. Documentation Tools

The role of documentation in HCI (e.g., see Clement, 1984) has often been neglected. It should not be. Various types of documentation can substantially eliminate user difficulties and enhance interface usability.

It is important to distinguish the documentation of the interface layout, devices, operations, and functionality, all intended to explain and facilitate what the user sees and can do, from the documentation of the software and hardware platforms that must be understood by designers, developers, and systems support personnel. The former has to be much more oriented to the target user, preferably taking different user backgrounds and capabilities (Chapter 3) into account. The latter variety should be able to assume technical knowledge on the part of technical experts, thereby becoming somewhat less concerned about user-oriented writing style.

The range of alternatives for documentation means or media include: (1) the traditional variety, producing hard-copy manuals; (2) making those (relatively static) manuals available on-line; (3) providing a sophisticated retrieval interface between user and documentation, to enable queries about many different topics; and (4) enabling context-specific access to alternative versions of explanations, either provided in response to explicit user requests or as a result of interface functionality that involves adaptation to the user's current needs.

The above options are mainly intended to serve target users. The importance of providing the user with helpful documentation, preferably on-line, has been recognized (e.g., Sondheimer and Relles, 1982; Houghton, 1984). It is consistent with several user-oriented design principles, discussed in Chapter 9. However, some of the documentation options can also be used to support technical experts. In particular, the person interested in HCI design decision-making should be given on-line access to recorded rationales on design features that were chosen. This need is formalized in Chapter 9.

8.9. Decision Function: Update

The use of some of the support tools and techniques discussed in this chapter can be interpreted as resulting in design features, similar to the models of Chapter 7. We could therefore simply add them to the feature sets, especially to F_{ORGN}, already identified there. However, those models were oriented more to organizing the interface in a user-observable manner. The features discussed in this chapter tend to be of greater interest to

HCI designers. For example, whether or not the UIMS model is employed may not be of particular concern to the user, but it is to the designer.

Therefore, the functional update again seems worthwhile. It only need involve Eq. (7.2). The profile of possible sets of features specified for a design is extended to:

$$\text{FEATURES} = \{\{F_{T+S,x}\}, \{F_{MODELS}\}, \{F_{SUPPORT}\}, \text{other\_features}\} \qquad (8.1)$$

Exercises

8.1. Consider the use of models as templates in an engineering area such as bridge design. A fairly complete collection of bridge models, representing most bridges in existence, can be available in an engineering library. So, if an engineer wants to copy or emulate the design of the Golden Gate Bridge in San Francisco, a detailed model of its design could be utilized and adapted to the span size and other conditions relevant to the new bridge site. Do you think it is feasible to develop an analogous collection of models for use in HCI design? Discuss that possibility with emphasis on the range of different types of computer applications, both existing now and projected for the future, when compared with the (relatively limited) applications for which bridges are designed.

8.2. With reference to Fig. 4.2, identify *for each layer* of that structure those tools and techniques that have been developed to help HCI design (at that level of interaction). Which tools and techniques transcend two or more of those levels? Do you notice any patterns? For example, have some layers received much attention while others are comparatively neglected? Explain.

8.3. The term "prototype" can be used as an excuse for a design that is implemented in an inadequately thorough, structured, debugged, etc., manner. While the intended design may or may not be good, the implementation ends up less than respectable. Yet, prototyping plays a very useful role. What should be the minimal requirements imposed on an HCI design and implementation that is labeled a prototype? Assume that a prototype should be a step or a stage on the way to designing and implementing a full, operational version.

8.4. According to Fig. 8.1, the UIMS model is seemingly oriented to a horizontal partitioning of modular functions between user and application. Is it possible (and maybe preferable) to achieve the equivalent modularity through a model that is hierarchically structured, with dependencies between vertical layers? If so, diagram and describe such a model. If not, explain.

8.5. Suppose you want to design an interface to be consistent with the basic UIMS model. However, it is to include a module that represents (or models) various characteristics of the user entity, to be used for changing the interface's behavior toward the user. Where would you position that module in the model of Fig. 8.1? Explain.

8.6. With reference to Exercise 8.5, does the basic UIMS model encompass special models of the interface (*I*) and the application (*A*), but not of the user (*U*)? Discuss.

8.7. Among the features of object-oriented software is that the attributes of parent objects can be inherited by child objects. Such inheritance patterns can be meaningfully applied to software objects in the interface (*I*) and the application (*A*) in HCI design. In view of our generic use of the term "object," could it make sense and be useful to also consider user (*U*) objects as inheriting certain attributes from each other? If so, what could be the logic and the means for doing so? If not, explain.

8.8. Given your particular computer system, identify each of the I/O devices (e.g., keyboard, CRT, mouse, lightpen) you have available at the user interface. Then, determine how each of them is controlled by the operating system. For each device, distinguish (a) whether and how it needs to get the system's attention (e.g., via interrupts or polling), and (b) what constitutes an "event" that must be processed.

8.9. If you have the facilities available to do so, write and implement a device driver, not yet provided in your system, for an input device that can be attached (e.g., a different type of mouse or joystick to control the cursor).

8.10. Read about window managers (e.g., see citations in Section 8.4.4). If you have the appropriate facilities available in your system, do the following: select an application and create your own tailored windowing layout and support, by either (a) utilizing the window manager already installed, and/or (b) writing your own window manager software. Can the resulting manager provide either an overlapping or a tiled window layout? Explain.

8.11. What is a software "workbench"? Given all the tools and techniques outlined in this chapter, and others you might think of, describe (or model) what would be an ideal workbench for HCI design.

III

DESIGN AND DEVELOPMENT

After gradually building up the prerequisite knowledge about design factors and features in Part II, this part is intended to "put it all together" by composing an overall methodology for design and development of interfaces. Chapter 9 formalizes definitions of terms that were already introduced in previous chapters, along with other concepts and terminology constituting the cause-and-effect design framework. Particular emphasis is placed on design *principles* as the goals of HCI design. Design principles and design factors are portrayed as the significant inputs to designer decisionmaking that must lead to specification of the required or desired design features. Chapters 10 and 11, then, develop the methodology, focusing on design methods and illustrating them by means of a prototype interface case study.

DESIGN TERMS AND DECISION CONSTRUCTS

9.1. Overview

Toward defining and utilizing "methodology" for HCI design, the relevant terminology must be made very clear. As stated earlier in this book, many terms have been used interchangeably, when they should not be. Some have also been used inconsistently or even totally incorrectly. This chapter presents a series of definitions that are useful for design decision-making. Some of the terms and constructs are illustrated. The cause-and-effect framework that was already implied by the use of decision schematics in earlier chapters is more fully developed in the next section. Then, after distinguishing, in Section 9.3, what is meant by design and the products thereof, the causes and effects are considered in the following order: inputs to a design decision in Section 9.4, and outcomes of such decisions in Section 9.5. But how do the inputs lead to the outcomes? Section 9.6 deals with criteria and constructs that can help in the decision-making process.

Section 9.7 provides another update of the functional, cause-and-effect pattern inherent to HCI design. It is based on the high-level model introduced at the end of Chapter 3 and then extended in subsequent chapters.

Individual, feature-specific design decisions must be carried out within an all-encompassing methodology. The latter is to produce a concerted, integrated set of specifications for features of an interface. Accordingly, definitions of such higher-level, methodological terms are formulated in Sections 9.8 and 9.9. They are also related to "interface engineering" in Section 9.10. Finally, this chapter concludes with recognizing the importance of coupling interface design methodology with evaluation methodology.

9.2. Cause-and-Effect Framework

The use of decision schematics and related terminology can be placed into the context of the cause-and-effect model displayed by Fig. 9.1. It emphasizes the fact that the characteristics of any HCI design product are necessarily dependent on the clear specification of input conditions and parameters. As is true in software engineering, you cannot expect the design process, as effective as it might otherwise be, to arrive at anything other than meeting the requirements that were specified in advance. Although a well-conceived design process may be able to trigger certain questions about required inputs and, hence, compensate for failure to be thorough in specifying what is expected of a design, it cannot be expected to perform magic. In other words, to achieve an HCI design in a deliberate, systematic manner, it is essential for the designer to know the (mini-

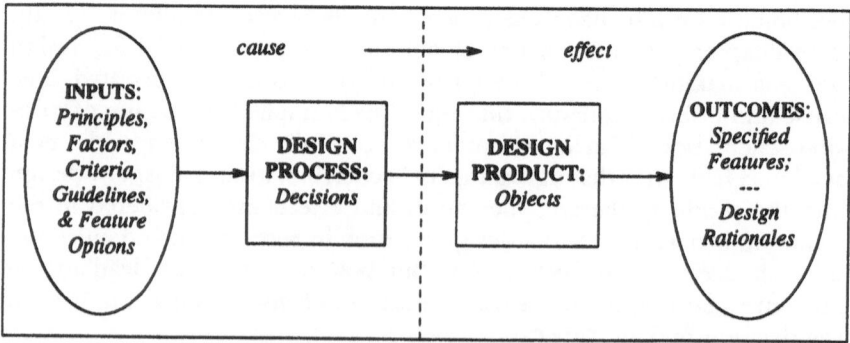

FIGURE 9.1. Cause-and-effect design framework.

mal) requirements and goals in advance. This will be evident from the description of design process in the next chapter.

If the reader looks back at the factor-causing-feature patterns illustrated in the tables of Chapters 3 through 5, those patterns are now encompassed (or subsumed) by the broad framework of Fig. 9.1. The elements of the framework are defined in the following sections.

9.3. Design Product

The HCI designer should be fully cognizant of the framework depicted by Fig. 9.1, including the "design process" that is to instantiate it in a particular design. That process is considered in detail in Chapter 10. At this point, we focus on what the designer has to work with (inputs) and what the results (outcomes) are to be. The latter will be representative of the intended design product.

What is the expected product of a design process? To clarify, let us consider what is meant by "design" of an interface or part thereof. If for no other reason, we should do so in order to distinguish it from interface implementation. This is analogous to distinguishing an abstract specification of a software module (e.g., a procedure) from its programmed implementation.

Definition 9.1. **Interface design**: the detailed characteristics that are specified for the interface object(s) to be built; a process for building the interface object(s); the product(s) of such a process.

The term has multiple meanings, in that it can connote each of (1) what is to be built, (2) how to build it, and (3) the result, i.e., the design object after it is built. The design product is itself an "object" (Definition 7.1). Simply stated, design can therefore refer to (1) the specification, (2) the process, or (3) the product. With the understanding that an interface specification should reflect, or be reflected in, the implemented interface product, our interests in this book are primarily focused on the first two interpretations; the details of how the product is implemented (programmed) are beyond the scope of this book. Indeed, consistent with software engineering practice, the HCI designer may very well turn his/her design specifications over to staff experts capable of implementing them.

9.4. Design Inputs

The most important inputs to the design "process" are the specified principles, applicable factors, and any useful criteria and established guidelines. Consistent with Function (2.4), these must be surrounded by designer knowledge of the options that are available for use as features in the interface. That is, the alternative techniques for interaction, interface representation, and other interface support must be well understood by the designer before it makes sense to ask: which principles and factors call for which features? Various feature options were outlined in Chapters 6 through 8. They are discussed further as design outcomes, in Section 9.5.

Here we take a closer look at design factors and principles. They are treated as independent variables in the design process. Criteria and guidelines, on the other hand, while also listed as inputs (Fig. 9.1), are viewed as logical devices supportive of decision-making; they are described later, in Section 9.6.

9.4.1. Factors

In Part II, a variety of factors were presented and discussed. They include the U-factors, A-factors, and I-factors. Their gradual introduction seemed logical in the context of material organized as prerequisite to HCI design. Now, in this part, we want to formalize their inclusion as major elements in the design framework.

Definition 9.2. **Design factor**: an element or characteristic that is causal in nature, either enabling or constraining the attainment of a design goal.

Notice that factors, therefore, can have either positive or negative influence on how the design ends up looking and behaving. For example, suppose that the interface is to be "helpful" to the user. There may be factors that may not be fully supportive of rendering the interface helpful, at least in the manner desired. In the case of I-factors (Chapter 5), the computer hardware may not be powerful enough or the software to be used may not have the required functionality to provide help as desired. On the other hand, if those factors meet the minimal requirements of the kind of help to be provided, the design can proceed accordingly.

As implied by the many factors discussed in Chapters 3 through 5, pertaining to users, applications, and computers, the designer's mission includes (1) taking advantage of positive factors and (2) ameliorating or overcoming the effects of negative factors. In addition, the designer must take into account other factors that are administrative or preemptive in nature. For example, constraints on allowable cost might be imposed, or someone in authority might stipulate that a particular interface feature must be included in the design regardless of other design considerations. Such factors are realistic; they may have positive, negative, or neutral effects on the design outcomes.

9.4.2. Principles

In addition to finding out all about the relevant design factors, the designer must have the design principles specified. In fact, depending on which principle(s) is(are) chosen, different design factors have to be considered. For example, the above-cited goal of making an interface "helpful" motivates the designer to look at those factors that have a bearing on whether it can be met. A very inexperienced user (*U*-factor) trying to work with a very complicated application (*A*-factor) may need much more sophisticated help than a particular computer (*I*-factor) is capable of providing. Especially because of that principle–factors relationship, it is highly desirable for principles of design to be determined and specified from the outset.

The HCI literature is not consistent on the meaning of design principle. Some used it to encompass methodological rules. For example, Gould and Lewis (1985) identified the following as key design principles: early focus on users and tasks, empirical measurement, and iterative design. Those are very important, as confirmed by the design methodology presented in Chapter 10. Draper and Norman (1985) distinguished quantitative principles from qualitative principles and favor the former variety, including "quantitative assessments" such as design trade-offs affecting user satisfaction. Such assessments can be dealt with under measures of evaluation (Treu, 1994).

The use of the term "principle" is reserved in this book for the following meaning:

Definition 9.3. **Design principle**: a fundamental truth or belief about a design; a rule explaining the expected behavior or appearance of a design object; a rule of action or conduct for a design object.

The designer should consider the *adherence to selected design principles* to be equivalent to the *pursuit of a design goal*. In other words, the principles should be used to determine the desired characteristics of the planned design product. This enables analogous treatments of the design goals oriented to each of the user, the interface, the application, and their combination.

Design principles, especially for HCI design, should preferably not be retrofitted, after the design is complete. If at all possible, they should guide the designer throughout the design process. Normally one expects such principles to be framed in idealistic, positive terms. They can be very broad in nature. For example, the principle may stipulate that the interface be rendered "user-oriented" or "user-centered" or "user-friendly." On the other hand, some designers may be asked to be less user-oriented and more intent on creating an interface that is "efficient" and/or "effective." General terms like these are very helpful for categorizing the performance aspects in evaluations of interface designs (Treu, 1994).

But, to enable more *specific* decision-making during HCI design, broad terms like "user-oriented" are inadequate. They are subject to many different views and interpretations and hence must be refined to a more detailed level. Then, after that is done, only a subset of the resulting design characteristics may be realistically attainable or even desirable.

An incomplete list of such (relatively more exacting) principles is displayed in Table 9.1. They are expressed as adjectives that modify (or describe) the intended design product. The format of each principle is therefore: "make the design object <selected characteristic>." A characteristic can of course be expressed instead as a noun. This is analogous to stipulating a principle in software engineering. For example, "modularity" essentially means "make the software modular."

Certain popular, user-oriented combinations, such as ease-of-learning-and-use (ELU) discussed in the literature (e.g., Lindquist, 1985), are included as separate principles (P26 and P44). Some principles are synonymous or nearly so (e.g., P7 and P40; P16 and P34). Some, such as consistency (P12), have been considered extensively (e.g., Polson, 1988) but have generated a certain amount of disagreement (e.g., Grudin, 1989, 1992). Others, such as P21 and especially P44, are probably viewed s desirable by everyone. Nevertheless, we could write a whole chapter exclusively on considerations pertaining to "usability," or to rendering the

TABLE 9.1
User-Oriented Design Principles

I.D.	Adjective: desirable characteristic	Qualified object or intended purpose
P1	Accessible	To enable user interaction via the interface
P2	Accurate, correct	With regard to values of objects output
P3	Adaptable	Interface is changeable
P4	Adaptive	Interface adapts to user
P5	Aesthetically pleasing	In color, appearance, etc.
P6	Associative	Providing explicit and implicit association links among objects
P7	Clear, concise	In choice and meaning of vocabulary and other objects used in interaction
P8	Comfortable	Making user feel at ease (see also P34, P39)
P9	Compatible	With specified user factors

TABLE 9.1
(*Continued*)

I.D.	Adjective: desirable characteristic	Qualified object or intended purpose
P10	Complete, comprehensive	In functional capabilities, etc.
P11	Congenial	Agreeable, suitable, etc.
P12	Consistent	In commands, spatial location, etc.
P13	Context-providing	In surrounding layers of support for the user
P14	Continuous	In interactive behavior, and output of changing objects
P15	Controllable	Providing user override, etc.
P16	Correctable	When errors occur
P17	Error-preventing or -minimizing	To avoid the need to correct errors (P16)
P18	Expressive	To enable clear, concise communication
P19	Extendible	To add other functions, commands, etc.
P20	Facilitative	Making it easy to use, learn, get things done
P21	Fail-safe	When user commits mistakes, serious consequences are precluded
P22	Feedback-providing	Acknowledging user input, and informing the user of current state
P23	Flexible	In interface layout, devices, scrolling, etc.
P24	Forgiving	After the user makes mistakes or takes other undesirable actions
P25	Helpful	With error messages, explanations, feedback (P22), tutorials, etc.
P26	Learnable	With respect to user capabilities and limitations
P27	Meaningful	Use of mnemonics, logical actions, etc.
P28	Memory-supporting	To supplement or obviate user memory
P29	Network-oriented	To give the user a network perspective
P30	Nonoverwhelming	In display density, action choices
P31	Organized or structured	In interaction language, display layout, functions, state transitions, etc.
P32	Powerful	To support more complex tasks
P33	Precise, exact	In relative positioning of objects, etc.
P34	Recoverable	From undesirable actions and states
P35	Responsive in content	With respect to information in system response
P36	Responsive in time	With respect to system time taken to respond
P37	Reliable	In advice, performance, etc.
P38	Simple or simplified	To avoid unnecessary complexity
P39	Stress-reducing or -minimizing	With regard to user stress
P40	Unambiguous	Similar to P7
P41	Unconstraining	To encourage or enable learning
P42	Uniform	In available functions, etc. (see also P12)
P43	Understandable	In phraseology, expectations, etc.
P44	Usable	Toward achieving desired goals
P45	Versatile	Offering different input devices, etc.
P46	Visualizable, conceivable	Reinforcing conceptualization, imagination, and viewing of objects

interface "usable" (e.g., Lindquist, 1985; Spence, 1985; Bennett, 1986; Harrison and Monk, 1986; Whiteside *et al.*, 1988; Guillemette, 1991). Usability is variously defined as encompassing several other principles in some combination.

A number of the principles listed 'in Table 9.1 need more precise definition and refinement, to enable a designer to know exactly what goal is to be pursued. But most of them are fairly self-explanatory. The reader can immediately confirm that it is extremely difficult, if not impossible, for any one design to adhere to all of those principles. In general, both designers and users have to be selective and decide, in advance, which principles are deemed to be most important. Notice that user-oriented, user-friendly, user-satisfying, and other, similarly broad principles are not included. All of the principles in this list are potential contributors to making the interface more oriented to the needs and wants of users. Many of them will also make the interface appear more "friendly." Whether or not a user ends up feeling "satisfied" is a major topic in itself, dependent on all or some subset of the other principles, including P39. User satisfaction can be defined in a very multifaceted way (Mullins and Treu, 1991).

The success of an interface in meeting the user-oriented principles can be considered under one of three major evaluative aspects: synergism. The other two aspects for evaluating interfaces and creating measures for doing so are "efficiency" and "effectiveness" (Treu, 1994). Actually, all three terms are potentially applicable to each of the user, the computer, and their (synergistic) partnership. But we could distinguish principles that are primarily indicative of either efficiency or effectiveness. A separate table, similar to Table 9.1, can result for each of these (see Exercises 9.9 and 9.10).

In the case of efficiency, several of the listed principles (e.g., P32, P36) tend to be supportive. Another related principle is the goal of designing the interface to be "productivity-increasing." Several of the other principles, taken in conjunction, can contribute to it.

Making the interface effective, by contrast, is used to represent qualitative (rather than quantitative) features. For example, principle P5 in Table 9.1, when applied to the results of interaction, is illustrative of one form of HCI effectiveness.

As implied earlier, design principles are not uniform in what they encompass or connote with respect to design goals. They can be defined at different levels of specificity (e.g., Smith, 1986), and also at different levels of complexity. Some are elemental in nature, while others can be constructed as dependent on combinations of elemental principles. This hierarchical structure inherent to design principles is evident from numerous suggestions made in the literature. For example, among the principles of good design proposed by Norman (1988) is to provide the user with continuous feedback. This principle can be interpreted as a conjunction of P14 and P22. Other such examples can be created (see Exercise 9.4). We must learn to analyze and specify the more complex goals in HCI in terms of their fundamental constituents. Then we can better address the means for achieving them in design.

The discussion on design principles thus far has been almost exclusively user-oriented. This is consistent with the main thrust of this book. But other principles, oriented to the design of the application software as well as to the computer interface software/hardware, are also important. In particular, they involve terminology adopted from software engineering, such as *modular*, *objected-oriented*, *robust*, and many others. Further, some of the principles listed in Table 9.1 are relevant. Examples are P19, P21, and P37. (See Exercise 9.11.)

9.5. Design Outcomes

It was assumed throughout the early chapters that the product of HCI design would have to be specified as some collection and integration of design features. We need to look at those features more closely. Also, the need to record the rationales used in deciding on particular design features should be advocated; those rationales should be viewed as a natural outcome of design.

9.5.1. Features

Although feature is a frequently used term, let us define it, based on the meaning we have attributed to it in previous chapters. This will facilitate categorization of features in a manner helpful to designers.

Definition 9.4. **Design feature**: a characteristic in content, appearance, or behavior of a design object, or in the representation of an object with regard to one of those characteristics.

A feature or a combination of features that is selected for a design should be consistent with the specified design principles, which are the guiding goals, and should be enabled by the relevant design factors. Design decisions should be based on appropriate design criteria, possibly aided by established guidelines, as defined later in Section 9.6.

Design factors were characterized and categorized in Chapters 3 through 5; the same was done for design principles in the previous section. Factors and principles are inputs to a design, as portrayed by the symbolic decision function (2.4). Features, on the other hand, are among the design outcomes. The major features were described in Chapters 6 through 8. But we need to become more specific about how the features can be organized, composed, and refined. General feature groupings identified thus far have been:

- Interaction techniques and styles (Chapter 6)
- Models superimposed on various parts of a design, including the interaction techniques and styles, especially in user-observable ways (Chapter 7)
- Other supportive models and techniques reflected by a design, especially those of interest to designers (Chapter 8)

Further, we have distinguished high-level features, like those above, from the relatively lower-level features (Section 6.10). Consequently, a selected high-level feature, such as an interaction technique that is suitably modeled, must be refined and supported by lower-level features, such as the input devices and widgets that are appropriate and preferred.

In addition, the features can be distinguished according to whether they contribute in a *task-specific* or a *task-independent* manner. This dichotomy will be developed further in Chapter 12, with regard to providing the user with task-surrounding and network-oriented context, beyond what one normally expects in a user's direct interaction with an application-specific task.

In either case, whether a feature is high-level or lower-level, task-specific or task-independent, it can be classified as variously affecting each of the following HCI dimensions:

1. *Information content*, in terms of substantive information actually communicated, within the "packaging" provided by the other dimensions below
2. *Form or structure*, in terms of organizational patterns and paradigms inherent to the information communicated
3. *Behavior*, in terms of the dynamic and static aspects of communicating information
4. *Appearance*, in terms of the quantitative and qualitative considerations pertaining to the individual dimensions (information content, structure, and behavior) as well as to their composite whole

It is conceivable that the appearance of the HCI composite might create some kind of "gestalt" in the mind of the user, suggesting that the entire interface gives the impression of doing more than one would expect of the sum of its parts. Perhaps that would only be a reflection of how much the user knows about it. In any case, that topic is not our interest here. In fact, the terms above are purposely chosen to seem neutral, in the sense of implying whether or not the interface performs well.

We want to be able to characterize how any selected design feature might contribute to the design outcomes in other than general terms. For example, suppose the graphical interaction technique, one of the high-level features (from set F_D), Table 6.3, is to be scrutinized. It certainly communicates information (graphically), using a variety of structures for its information objects. Its behavior includes dynamic transformations (e.g., motion in 3-D) of the objects on the output side, with real-time participation by the user with one or more devices (e.g., lightpen) on the input side. The overall communication pattern is itself structured according to which entity (user or computer) can or must take what action and when. Finally, the appearance of the interface, and of the dynamic inter-action via that interface, is dependent on whether or not a myriad of smaller features is attached to the higher-level feature. Examples are: color, 3-D perspective, realism in objects displayed, realism in the movement of objects, layout of the screen areas for designated purposes, and many more. These are the features that ultimately must result from careful designer decisions, based on the types of detailed schematics (or their equivalents) introduced and illustrated in early chapters. This is where designer knowledge, skill, ingenuity, etc., really come into play and can shine. All the resulting features, influenced by the many possible factors, must then be integrated into the context provided by the higher-level feature.

9.5.2. Rationales

Design approaches and processes are defined in Section 9.8 and then illustrated in the next chapter. Whether or not the process is executed in a way that adheres to the specified principles, criteria, etc., is of course subject to the qualifications of the designer. Especially because of that significant dependence, and in order to enable any interested parties to find out (and learn about) *why the designer did what* on any particular HCI design object, it is very important for us to advocate that the designer record the reasoning behind various design decisions.

Definition 9.5. **Design rationale**: an explanation of what was done, how and why, in the design of an interface object and its noteworthy design features.

What is "noteworthy" is generally what is of importance to (and noticeable by) the user, from his/her perspective in interacting with the system, as well as to other designers, from their standpoints of representing user needs as well as system efficiency, etc. Of course this is a matter of judgment. Because of the rarity of going to the time and trouble of recording design rationales, preferably for on-line access, almost *any* such efforts are better than none. An example of such recording is indicated at the end of Chapter 11. The use of decision schematics (or their equivalents), illustrated in earlier chapters, is also recommended as part of the record.

The importance of recording and using design rationales has been recognized in recent years (e.g., MacLean *et al.*, 1989; Treu *et al.*, 1991; Bellotti, 1993). More generally, it is being suggested that various types of knowledge, not only design rationales, should be preserved in design projects (Loewgren and Nordqvist, 1992; Herbsleb and Kuwana, 1993). Included should be knowledge of the application domain (Chapter 4) and also scenarios of use (Chapters 6 and 11). Design scenarios are also relevant, as illustrated by Karat and Bennett (1991).

9.6. Design Decisions

Most of Chapter 10 is dedicated to describing a design method. Before we define those terms, several other methodological distinctions and comparisons must be made. They will hopefully serve to further clarify the design terminology developed up to this point.

In this chapter so far, we have only attended to the inputs and prospective outputs of design decisions. We have indicated in a number of places that those decisions can be made somehow, e.g., using "design criteria." But what kind of help is available to the designer to make those efforts more systematic and exacting? Can a logical mechanism be supplied that is analogous to a mathematical function [the big D in Function (2.4)]? It is preferable to avoid decision-making that is purely subjective or ad hoc in nature.

Indeed, some constructs to facilitate the process are available. Of course, the designer must understand them and be willing to use them, in order to render them useful.

9.6.1. Criteria

Given the (normally idealistic) design principles (Section 9.4.2) interpreted as goals, design decisions must be tempered with the (realistic, practical) design factors (Section 9.4.1). To do so, specific criteria are needed to help the designer in making the necessary design decisions:

Definition 9.6. **Design criterion**: a rule or standard for making a judgment on a design feature or on a combination of design features to be specified.

The word "rule" is common to Definitions 9.3 and 9.6. The implication is that a criterion rule should be consistent in its effect with a rule based on a design principle. But exactly how should such a rule be expressed and employed? A criterion should be a reasonably precise statement or formula on what is to be decided. A general format of a criterion is portrayed in Fig. 9.2.

But the figure provides only that, a format. How or on what basis does the designer use it to make a particular decision to select a subset of features? The criteria have to be grounded on logic or rationale that is instrumental in the decision-making. It would be nice to have a precise mathematical formula to help us, e.g., to tell us exactly how strong the bridge span must be to withhold expected weights of vehicles. Unfortunately, the "bridge" design in HCI is much more complicated. We should nevertheless attempt to do something analogous for HCI design.

With reference to the decision schematics that were introduced in Chapter 3 and then expanded in subsequent chapters, the diamond-shaped decision boxes (e.g., in Fig. 3.3) were left unexplained. We can analyze the causal factors (feeding into those boxes) that are relevant to achieving specified goals (i.e., the principles) and then rank them individually and "weigh" the result collectively. That is, for any particular design decision, the designer must consider either all relevant factors or some subset thereof; the factors that are relevant (and also considered) are either equal in importance or they are not. Table 9.2 is organized to follow this line of reasoning. We want to arrive at a logical and reasonable way of characterizing the "weight of evidence" or the decision-supporting strength of the relevant factors collectively. In so doing, it matters (1) how many factors were considered, i.e., how thorough was the designer, (2) what subset of those factors actually support, enable, or even demand a particular feature, (3) how do the factors compare to each other in importance, and (4) whether the factors are quantitative or qualitative in nature.

GIVEN each of the following:			SELECT and SPECIFY:
One or more Principles:	The relevant Factors:	Corresponding Individual Weightings, Composite Rankings, Decision Rationales	Some Subset of Eligible Features
$\{P_r\}$	$\{\{U_i\},\{A_j\},\{I_k\},...\}$		$\{\{F_{T+s}\},\{F_{MODELS}\},...\}$

FIGURE 9.2. Format of a design criterion.

TABLE 9.2
Example Rankings and Weightings of Factors

Category	Relevant factors		Ranking of factors	Weight of evidence
	Considered	Supportive		
Quantitative	All possible	All	Equal	Very strong
	Most (majority)	All	Equal	Strong
	Most	Most (of those)	Equal	Fairly strong
	Some (minority)	All	Equal	Weak
	Some	Some (of those)	Equal	Very weak
Qualitative	Most important . . .			
	Subset (majority)	All	Equal	Strong
	Some (minority)	All (of those)	Equal	Generally weak
	Some (minority)	Some (of those)	Equal	Very weak

The last of these distinctions tends to mean that more objective analysis and comparison of factors are possible if they are quantitative in nature. The differences between *threshold-oriented* and *judgment-based* decisions are noteworthy here. If a factor (e.g., a performance requirement) is quantitative in nature, thereby enabling comparison against some desired threshold value, the decision-making is obviously made easier.

The end result of the above is to reach a conclusion on whether the particular factors considered, with reference to specified design principles, constitute convincing evidence in favor or against some feature. Table 9.2 indicates several possible judgments. They involve generic cases that are likely to be faced by a designer. For simplicity in tabulation, the factors in each line entry are all assumed to be of equal importance. Realistically, that may not be true and the differences in ranking have to be taken into account (see Exercise 9.14).

Table 9.2 entries are obviously subject to a variety of interpretations. Most important is not that the designers agree; most important is that they make their own, reasonable interpretations, utilize them, and record them to explain their decision-making. The equivalent of Table 9.2 used together with the decision schematics (e.g., Fig. 5.3) and placed into the criterion format (Fig. 9.2) should render the design decisions more systematic and objective. They should also contribute to making the results more credible.

9.6.2. Guidelines

The word "guideline" tends to be used as a synonym for several of the previously defined terms. A guideline can also facilitate decision-making.

Definition 9.7. **Design guideline**: any instruction set forth, as a guide, on how to carry out a design.

Actually, a design guideline can be used to subsume any one or more of the other design terms already defined. This is indicated by Fig. 9.3 and means that guidelines can apply to a variety of elements in the design process. They are definitely not uniform. They can also be difficult to apply (e.g., Mosier and Smith, 1986; Tetzlaff and Schwartz, 1991). The literature is replete with guidelines interpreted in many different ways. Brown (1988) includes a long checklist. Other sources of guidelines include Shneiderman (1992), Mayhew (1992), and Barfield (1993).

It is important to distinguish a design "guideline," in the general sense of Definition 9.7, from each of the other design terms for which it is intended to provide guidance.

9.7. Decision Function: Update

Decision schematics were presented in Part II, with emphasis on factors causing features. In parallel, starting with Section 2.6, we also introduced a functional view of the decision-making process. That view [Function (2.4)] is repeated here:

$$\text{FEATURES}_n \leftarrow D_{\text{criteria},n} \ (\text{KNOWLEDGE}_{\text{designer}}, \text{FACTORS}_n, \text{PRINCIPLES}_n) \quad (9.1)$$

Then, in subsequent chapters, the variables in the above-portrayed mapping were explained and refined. First, the major design factors were presented in Chapters 3 through 5, to be supplemented by other factors, e.g., administrative in nature:

$$\text{FACTORS}_n = \{\{U_i\}, \{A_j\}, \{I_k\}, \text{other\_factors}\} \quad (9.2)$$

That coverage was followed by development of candidate features, in Chapters 6 through 8:

In Designing an Object in HCI:	
• adhere to	some principle
• take into account	some factor
• follow	some criterion
• achieve	some feature
• do	a combination (of above)

FIGURE 9.3. Format of various design guidelines.

$$\text{FEATURES} = \{\{F_{T+S,x}\}, \{F_{MODELS}\}, \{F_{SUPPORT}\}, \text{other\_features}\} \quad (9.3)$$

In this chapter, we have added the very significant methodological elements called "design principles." They set the design goals from the beginning of a design process. The principles selected should be a subset of those listed in Table 9.1 and other such collections.

$$\text{PRINCIPLES} = \{\text{some\_subset\_of\_principles}\} \quad (9.4)$$

Finally, in the previous section, we defined and formatted "design criteria," to be used in carrying out the big-D design decisions, denoted by Function (9.1) above. All of the above must become constituents of the designer's knowledge.

9.8. Approaches and Methods

The design definitions and constructs presented thus far can now be used collectively as building blocks for formulating a design "methodology."

Definition 9.8. **Design methodology**: the science of method for designing something; the system of means, methods, and approaches used in designing objects; the application of principles of design in the production of objects.

As this definition implies, methodology cannot merely rely on a loose congregation of means and methods, even if these are individually consistent with all the principles and guidelines discussed earlier. Included must be one or more design approaches that provide the designer with some kind of direction and coherence.

Definition 9.9. **Design approach**: a general way or an orientation through which a design (product) can be reached.

An approach can still be relatively imprecise in characterizing how a design is to be carried out. We, therefore, treat it as a precursor to a design "method," which requires that some plan must be followed:

Definition 9.10. **Design method**: a specific plan or procedure for creating a design (product).

A method is only a major part of a methodology; it is *not* equivalent to it. Another related term is "technique." It can pertain to design method; it can also be used to refer to a detailed, technical method incorporated as a feature in a design specification. The latter is favored in this book. An example is interaction technique (Definition 6.4).

An even tighter version of a design approach, than is method, is a process. It gives more exact instructions on tying the methodological constituents together, in a systematic, usable fashion:

Definition 9.11. **Design process**: a specific pattern of design actions or activities to be carried out to produce an object.

Examples of specific patterns are an ordered sequence and two or more such sequences coordinated in parallel.

Design approach, method, and process are often used interchangeably, even sometimes in this book. However, when asked to be precise, the above-indicated distinctions seem reasonable.

9.9. Design Scope

The discussion thus far may seem to imply that the entire interface is necessarily to be designed in its totality. That is not intended to be the case, although it is a bias conveyed when trying to develop comprehensive methodology. The scope of design is extremely variable, as suggested by the following:

Definition 9.12. **Design scope**: the area or space within or around a system object, on which the design activity is to operate; the object(s) to be designed within the context of the complete set of interrelated objects constituting a system.

As before, we use the generic Definition 7.1 for "object." If one or more such objects are to be designed in the context of a complete HCI system (object), the design methodology should allow for that to be done. It will obviously require that other parts of the system be kept constant (e.g., the already existing pieces of hardware and/or software). The methodology is then employed to design only the new or changeable object(s) contained within the design scope.

The process defined in Chapter 10 is illustrative of such flexibility. In essence, it should be possible for a designer to be either *comprehensive*, encompassing all (or almost all) possible design objects within an HCI system, or *selective*, in working on only a limited subset of objects.

9.10. Interface Engineering

It was pointed out in Chapter 2 that software engineering is one of the specialties in computer science that contributes to the subject of this book. The interface must also be software-engineered, using the well-known, prescribed sequence of steps, ranging from requirements analysis and specification to its ultimate testing (e.g., Fairley, 1985; Pressman, 1988).

But it is also instructive to consider HCI design to be analogous to other engineering disciplines. For example, can we not consider the "building of a bridge" between a user and a computer as having certain parallels to building a bridge of the conventional variety, e.g., to connect one side of a river to another? Engineering, in general, is defined to be the systematic application of knowledge of the mathematical and physical sciences to the planning, design, and construction of machines, buildings, bridges, and other systems. By analogy:

Definition 9.13. **Interface engineering**: the systematic application of knowledge of the computer sciences and the human-oriented disciplines to the planning, design, development, and evaluation of human–computer interface systems.

As is true for other fields of engineering, this definition includes the need for performance evaluation. It is essential to be able to determine whether the design result meets the stipulated design objectives, as acknowledged below.

9.11. Design and Evaluation

Important to emphasize is the fact that any HCI design, which is based on specified principles and other requirements to be met, must *anticipate evaluation* of the design. That is, the design PRODUCT and OUTCOME, as indicated by Fig. 9.1, must become subject to evaluation against the design INPUTS. The resulting performance assessment may carry implications not only for whether the inputs were realistic and appropriate, but also for whether the DESIGN PROCESS itself was effective or was carried out effectively.

It was not feasible to include a detailed presentation of interface evaluation methodology in this volume, and hence it is covered in the companion book (Treu, 1994). The designer should be fully cognizant of the typical design–evaluation–redesign– . . . iterations *during design*, not only evaluation after-the-fact. This should mean greater designer accountability (e.g., through recordings of design rationales); it should also facilitate the measurement and evaluation efforts, by means of incorporating the required data collection devices within the software architecture as possible.

Exercises

9.1. Which of the user-oriented principles listed in Table 9.1 do you consider to be too broad or vague in definition and, therefore, in need of refinement? Select three such examples and show how each of them could be "subdivided" into two or more lower-level principles that are more precise in meaning.

9.2. Which of the principles in Table 9.1 are seemingly redundant, because they are nearly synonymous? Explain.

9.3. Which user-oriented principles should be added to Table 9.1? Why? For example, would you add "trustworthy"?

9.4. Which of the principles in Table 9.1 can be meaningfully combined, in a manner similar to the (P14 and P22) example mentioned in the text?

9.5. Accept the following as a high-level principle: "accelerate the process whereby novices begin to perform like experts" (Baecker and Buxton, 1987, p. 212). Which lower-level principles from Table 9.1 can be used to support this principle? Are any others needed? Explain.

9.6. Carroll (1984) suggested "minimalist design," which basically involves giving the user at the interface only what he/she naturally wants and needs. Examples: present only as much to read as is essential; expect every kind of error. Express such a minimal design as a high-level design principle. Which principles from Table 9.1 can support it? Are any others needed? With reference to Chapter 3, what type of user (model) is assumed for minimalist design?

9.7. The symbolic view provided by Function (9.1) would seem to suggest that a design feature should be equivalent to a design goal. Would that be better than interpreting a design principle (Definition 9.3) to be equivalent to a design goal? As a consequence of the latter, what relationship results between design principle and design feature?

9.8. With reference to Exercise 9.7, does that interpretation of a design goal prevent the following from being a requirement imposed on a design: design the interface with a specified feature (e.g., DMI style) that supports a specified design principle (e.g., P7)? In the context and terminology of Function (9.1), what, in effect, is the role of any design feature that is stipulated in advance, rather than being determined as a result of a design decision? Explain.

9.9. Construct a table, similar to Table 9.1, which lists and briefly explains a set of HCI design principles that are not concerned with being user-oriented or synergistic as such but rather involve efficiency (i.e., quantitative) goals. Does your table overlap with Table 9.1? If so, is that reasonable?

9.10. Repeat Exercise 9.9 for HCI design principles associated with effectiveness goals (involving quality instead of quantity).

9.11. Tabulate the most important software-oriented principles that should be among the goals of the designers and implementors of HCI software.

9.12. Function (9.1) correctly positions "features" as outcomes, on the left side of the expression. The text in this chapter also advocates the recording of "design rationales" as outcomes, although they are really only by-products of design decision-making. If you were to refine Function (9.1), where or how would you include "design rationale" in the expression? Why?

9.13. For each of the two decision schematics diagrammed in Fig. 5.3, and assuming that the factors entering each decision (D_i) are equal in importance, select the line entries in Table 9.2 that could be applied to justify each decision.

9.14. Repeat Exercise 9.13, but assume specific rankings (e.g., using integral values, from 1 to i) for the factors involved. How, if at all, could the variable rankings change the design decisions? Explain.

9.15. Prepare a critique of Definitions 9.8 through 9.11. What role does/can Function (9.1) play in HCI design "methodology"? Explain.

DESIGN APPROACHES
AND METHODS

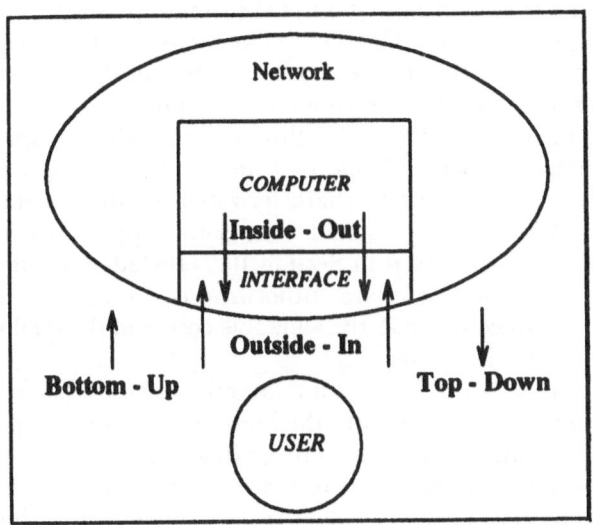

10.1. Overview

How should an interface designer describe a design approach or method or process for use by others? Thorough design descriptions are difficult to accomplish, especially within reasonable amounts of time and space. The design of an algorithm to solve a problem with a computer is a relatively limited and well-defined procedure. The design of a software compiler is substantially more complicated, requiring a number of different algorithms and software engineering techniques in effective coordination. The design of a complete interface system for HCI is even more complex. It must subsume the separate designs of component parts, including the applications software (at least the analysis thereof) and the various interactive tools and techniques required for taking advantage of that software. In addition, it must compose all of them into a cohesive whole, consistent with specified interface design principles and factors.

The task of describing the design method is facilitated by clear definition of what is meant by the term, in relation to other terms. As mentioned in Chapter 9, it should not be confused with specific "techniques," such as those for interaction between user and computer (Chapter 6) and those for specifying the interaction grammar (Chapter 7). These are features of the design and also contribute to instantiation of design features. But they do not represent methods for total interface design. Also, a user interface management system (Chapter 8), while useful in portraying the overall organization of the design product, is not synonymous with design method. UIMSs are among the methodological means. They are features of the software architecture, but they do not in themselves prescribe a plan for carrying out a design.

According to Definitions 9.8 through 9.10, design approach and design method are parts of the total design methodology. Further, an approach is a relatively loose characterization of the general flow and orientation adopted by a designer. Alternative approaches and related considerations are discussed in Section 10.2. Included are the priorities and objectives of those who are authorizing the design, the urgency in getting the design completed, the allowable cost, and the qualifications of the designer(s) or design team.

An approach can be refined into a design method (Definition 9.10). Illustrative methods described in the literature are broadly portrayed in Section 10.3. Then, a high-level, stepwise description of a design method, suggested as a generic model, is presented in Section 10.4. It is in some ways analogous to what one can find in software engineering books. It also contains elements of methods outlined in Section 10.3. But it encompasses the cause-and-effect model [see Function (9.1)] emphasized throughout this book. Also, a special version of that method, a three-pronged process model, is described in Section 10.5. To illustrate the use of that process, a case study is presented in Sections 10.5 through 10.7.

10.2.   Considerations

As implied by Definition 9.8, a design methodology can give the designer options, that is, the latitude to use different approaches in carrying out the design. On what basis should an approach be selected? But first, how can the different existing approaches be distinguished?

10.2.1.   Alternative Orientations

Analogous to what is done in designing software systems in general, we can characterize HCI design approaches in terms of high-level orientations. In effect, these provide the designer with a general flow, or order, for conducting design activities. The order is based on (1) what seems to be the most logical and effective progression in carrying out the design, (2) the perspective or viewpoint adopted by the designer, and (3) the established priorities (or principles) that are to be followed. Several major approaches can be distinguished.

Definition 10.1. **Bottom-up design approach**: a design approach that (1) starts the design with completing the low-level, detailed modules and facilities, (2) integrates and synthesizes those into a higher level of functionality, and (3) continues with that upward pattern until the composite design product is defined.

This approach may be deemed reasonable in some situations. For example, if some low-level interface features are already in place and are considered to be exactly what the designer wants (or the user needs), he/she can build on top of them. This tends to mean that higher levels of functionality become explicitly dependent on the lower-level details, rather than on abstract definitions of low-level functions that can be implemented in an independent manner. Also, this approach is fraught with other risks. If the interface design is to be comprehensive and driven by high-level principles and requirements specifications, the bottom-up orientation can lead to discrepancies between what was intended or preferred and what actually resulted.

A safer and sounder approach is to work top-down.

Definition 10.2. **Top-down design approach**: a design approach that (1) starts with high-level principles and requirements, (2) proceeds to define and analyze high-level modules accordingly, (3) repeatedly refines the resulting modules into lower-level units and functions, and (4) continues with that pattern until the composite design product is fully defined.

Notice that the design is "top down," both in terms of abstractly defined modules and in how they are to relate to each other. The actual implementation can follow a different pattern, e.g., "bottom up," as long as it is totally consistent with the specifications resulting from the top-down design approach.

An early prescription of a user-oriented, top-down (graphic) interface design is displayed in Fig. 10.1 (Treu, 1977). The top-down approach, by its very nature, is conducive to stipulating *at a broad, all-encompassing level* the kinds of features and performance goals that are to be achieved, and then insisting that the designer be guided accordingly until the lowest-level details are suitably worked out.

A number of top-down approaches to HCI design are described in

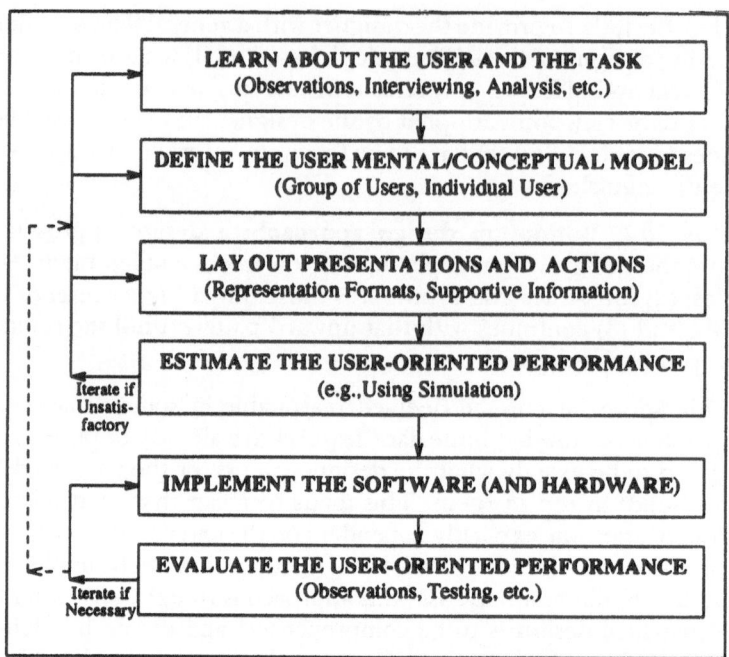

FIGURE 10.1. Top-down approach to graphics system design. [Reprinted from Treu (1977) with permission of ACM Press.]

the literature (e.g., see Baecker and Buxton, 1987). There are also some other approaches worth mentioning:

Definition 10.3. **Inside-out design approach**: designing with an internal-system perspective, by first considering how the system should function internally and then how the result will affect the outside.

As defined, this approach when used on interface design suggests that user-visible interface features and performance are treated as secondary in importance. The technology-intensive design factors would appear to get priority attention, possibly/probably to the detriment of the user.

On the other hand, the opposite orientation is possible. It has been interpreted by some researchers (e.g., Wasserman *et al.*, 1986) as preferred over the traditional top-down approach (Definition 10.2) for interface design:

Definition 10.4. **Outside-in design approach**: designing with an external-system perspective, by first considering the needs in externally observable performance before deciding how the system should function to meet the indicated requirements.

One additional approach is to compose a *hybrid* utilizing the above-indicated orientations. In a sense, an idealistic and comprehensive, user-oriented design needs a combination of at least the top-down and the outside-in approaches. The top-down orientation ensures that the designer is guided properly, from high-level considerations to low-level details; the outside-in orientation additionally requires that the designer adopt the perspective of what the user would experience directly in interaction with the system. The latter is also evident in the approach of Fig. 10.1, with respect to the need to attend to the user's mental model and performance.

But there are other significant considerations in selecting, or delimiting, an HCI design approach, besides using the above-characterized alternative orientations. The following questions are indicative of other influences:

1. What is the *administrative objective, mandate, or driving force* behind the design?
2. What is to be the *design scope*? (Definition 9.12)
3. What are the administratively imposed, quantitative *design constraints*, e.g., relating to urgency in getting the design completed and limits in allowable costs?
4. What are the *designer (or design team) qualifications*, and how can/ should they be utilized?

Answers to these questions are obviously contingent on administrative directions and limitations. They produce factors that necessarily supplement the U-, A-, and I-factors we defined earlier and used in decision-supporting schematics. Such factors can most surely affect the quality of the HCI design product. While they are not to be dwelled on in this book, they should at least be acknowledged briefly.

10.2.2. Administrative Objectives

With regard to what is expected by administrators, if the design is to be "done right," the full range of methodological considerations comes into play. This situation is delightful for the innovative designer, especially if the resources that might be required are also authorized. On the other hand, if the design is to be "quick and easy," then most of this book might as well be ignored. With such a directive, the probability of a successful design is very slim, unless one can simply import it. If administrators in essence request that an already existing design be acquired or emulated, because it has been determined to serve their intended purposes adequately, much of the HCI design methodology described in this book is obviated, and legitimately so. After all, we are then talking about only copying someone else's design, not creating our own, predominantly original design. That may be quite satisfactory, but it is not very interesting for us while considering comprehensive design of interfaces.

10.2.3. Design Scope

It is evident from the HCI literature that many interface design studies tend to address only a selected part of the composite user–computer system. For example, focus might be on how some user-preferred interaction features (Chapters 3 and 6) could be implemented within a particular interface; or, on how some modular interface system, e.g., based on the UIMS model (Chapter 8), might accommodate various interaction styles; or, on how a specified application software domain (Chapter 4) might be modified to enhance the user's ability to utilize it effectively.

The point is that HCI designs may be quite selective. They may emphasize mainly one component (e.g., the display screen organization) or one layer (e.g., interaction language syntax) or one evaluative measure (e.g., responsiveness) of the interface system, while assuming that all other parts are either fixed, have limited variability, or are relatively unimportant. This observation holds especially for HCI studies involving existing computer facilities, trying to improve these for the user. However, it can also be indicative of interfaces designed from scratch. For the latter, designers often acquire a piece of interface hardware and software, perhaps based on comparative analysis of products available in the market. Consequently, they are immediately "locked in." That is, the variability and freedom implied by designing an original interface are thereby diminished.

Such selectivity in design is of course very understandable. HCI design is an interdisciplinary activity that is extremely complex. Toward minimizing that complexity, attempts to build upon the successful hardware and software products developed by others are very prudent. But, for those interested in the range of possible design scopes, it is useful to develop methodology that can be effective for anyone who is in a position of truly creating an original interface system.

During the beginning phase of the case study, described in Section 10.6, we were fortunate to be given free rein with regard to design scope. However, as will be apparent, we later also took advantage of certain existing products that could appropriately fit into the design framework.

Basically, we had license to develop a high-level HCI design methodology that was to be systematic and comprehensive, without constraining the scope by preconceived notions about limitations in any existing interface. But, at prototype interface development time, the design scope had to be cut back; the design specifications had to accommodate a particular hardware/software platform.

10.2.4. Other Administrative Constraints

Management should be realistic. Requests for quality design must not be encumbered by impossible deadlines and inadequate resources. Expert designers should be consulted to determine what is reasonable. If a design effort is not affordable or achievable (within the time allotted), it should either not be undertaken at all or expectations should be appropriately reduced.

10.2.5. Designer Qualifications

The most significant resource is probably the designer or the design team. Even if enough financial resources are allocated and if the expected completion dates are generous, an HCI design is going to suffer if the designers are inadequately qualified. That is one reason for the organization of the material covered in this book: prerequisite knowledge (Part II) should be acquired *before* presuming to know HCI design methodology and how to use it.

10.3. Illustrative Methods

Several different methods (often called "methodologies") have been prescribed in the literature by means of step-by-step procedures. Ideally, such a procedure should enable a designer to follow it verbatim, with the promise of consequently leading to a good design. While "this ideal is unrealizable" (Baecker and Buxton, 1987), we should nevertheless endeavor to approximate it as closely as possible.

Methodologies proposed have been dichotomized (Baecker and Buxton, 1987) into those that are oriented to designing an entire application-specific system, including the user interface, and those that focus on the user interface design alone. Actually, the latter can be viewed as addressing a subset of the steps identified for the former, but they may do so in greater detail or using a different organizational paradigm. Illustrative examples (e.g., Treu, 1977; Shneiderman, 1983; Rubinstein and Hersh, 1984; Wasserman *et al.*, 1986; Foley *et al.*, 1990; James, 1991) generally use the following design steps, or they refine some subset of them:

1. *Preparation*: collection and analysis of information about the user, task, requirements, etc.
2. *Design*: definition, modeling, structuring, specification; this is the part that really constitutes the design plan; different authors describe this step in very different ways, using different levels of detail and emphasis.
3. *Development and Implementation*: either in prototype form, which is normally recommended, or directly in its intended, operational form.
4. *Evaluation*: of either the design specifications (e.g., using simulation) and/or the implemented system; hence, this step is not necessarily carried out at this place in the sequence.
5. *Iteration (as needed) and Follow-up*: including delivery to and support of the users.

Step 2 is where the detailed design methodology really comes through. For example, that is where Foley and colleagues' (1990) design levels (conceptual, functional, sequencing, and binding) apply. Notice that this general, five-step model does not differ very much from the software development life cycle models that can be found in software engineering books. It confirms the desired integration of software engineering techniques with HCI design (Sutcliffe and McDermott, 1991). But it may also imply that we should attempt to tailor the methodology more specifically to meet the more complex needs of HCI design. (See Exercise 10.7.)

10.4. A Cause-and-Effect Design Method

According to the theme established in earlier chapters (especially Chapters 3 through 5) and extended in Chapter 9, interface design should be significantly influenced, or "driven," by design principles and factors. Those must be determined and analyzed for purposes of establishing, via cause-and-effect relationships, the interface features that are indicated. The features, or "objects of the design," then end up affecting what must be implemented in software/hardware in order to bring them into existence. This pattern of influential links is displayed in Fig. 10.2.

It stands to reason then that any general "method" proposed for HCI design would include (in its prescribed steps) the pattern of Fig. 10.2. The cause-and-effect design method outlined in Fig. 10.3 gives evidence to it. The principles and factors must be identified early, in Step B, based on

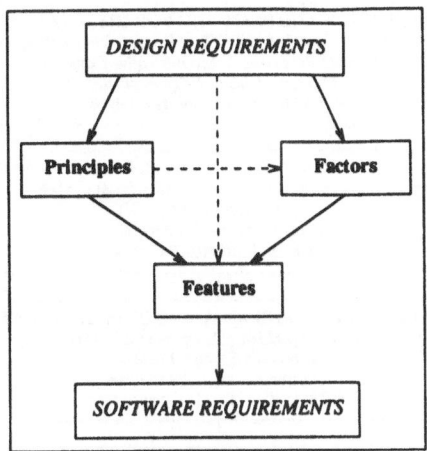

FIGURE 10.2. Features determination and impact.

whatever inputs from management and other sources are obtained in Step A. Besides the U-, I-, and A-factors, there may be other factors such as administrative restrictions or guidelines. Then, the suggested (or demanded) features must be determined, analyzed, and synthesized, toward accommodating all three major modules involved in the interaction. This happens in Step C. Design factors are not only considered in a module-specific manner; they must also be analyzed in conjunction, using pairwise and three-way combinations among the major modules. The decision-supporting schematics illustrated in early chapters can be useful in this step, as can the functional model [Function (9.1)] for decision-making.

  Step C is followed by the rather unusual step of asking the cause-and-effect question in reverse: *If the features identified and composed were in fact implemented, how would they affect each of the three modules?* In the interest of being comprehensive and careful, Step D gives the designer an opportunity to reflect on whether certain forms of preparation (e.g., user training) or modification (e.g., of the functionality of the application software) might facilitate and even alter the selection of design features resulting from Step C. In other words, carefully chosen changes in the characteristics of major modules may ameliorate factors that are restrictive and that make the design unduly difficult. It can be argued that this should be done earlier in the method. However, it is positioned at this point purposely. After a set of design features has already been determined (in Step C), the designer is likely to have a better appreciation for their implications.

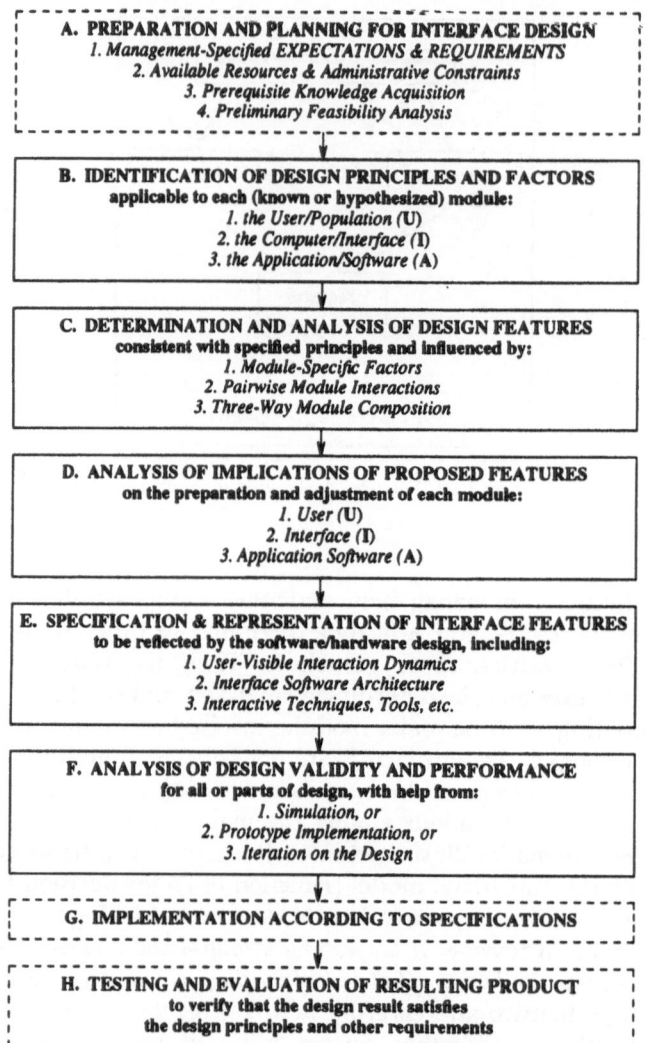

FIGURE 10.3. Cause-and-effect design method.

In Step E of Fig. 10.3, the results of the previous four steps are brought to fruition. The features and their combinations must be specified in terms of the necessary representations and models of software/hardware configuration, techniques, tools, and how they will be directly visible to and usable by the user. In this step, the software engineering methods are especially relevant.

Step F expects the designer to assess whether the specified design (resulting from Steps A through E) is in fact valid, with respect to initially stated expectations and requirements. Carefully planned simulation studies (mentioned in Chapter 8) can be used here. Also or alternatively, a prototype interface may be implemented. The complexity of the design specifications may give compelling reasons for turning to a prototype implementation first, and testing it thoroughly, before expending considerably greater resources on an operational interface that remains to be fully justified. Step F may, furthermore, lead to iteration in the design, by returning to earlier steps in the design method.

If the results of Step F are satisfactory, a full-blown implementation of an operational interface system can become the next objective, in Step G. Such an implementation should of course adhere to the design specifications resulting from earlier steps, including any revisions indicated after carrying out Step F. It may also be based on any prototype implementation, properly completed.

Finally, the interface product is subject to testing and evaluation in Step H. That topic is addressed in detail in the companion book (Treu, 1994). Notice that Steps A, G, and H in Fig. 10.3 are enclosed in dashed boxes. This is merely to accentuate the fact that they are not emphasized in the coverage of this book. The level of detail reflected by all of the steps in Fig. 10.3 is considered in Exercises 10.9 and 10.10.

10.5. Three-Pronged Process Model

A special instantiation of the method outlined above is implied in Fig. 10.4 (Treu *et al.*, 1990). It is consistent with the user–interface–application

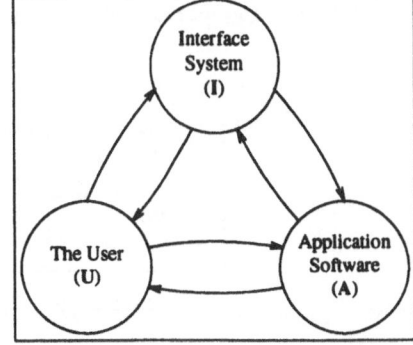

FIGURE 10.4. Triad model of parallel design processes. [This figure and Figs. 10.5 and 10.6 are reprinted from Treu *et al.* (1990) with permission of ACM Press.]

modularity emphasized throughout this book. With each circular area interpreted as a cross section of a design channel, the diagram represents an "end view" of a three-pronged design process. The triad of design subprocesses must be carried out in parallel. There is one process for each of the user (U), the interface system (I), and the application software (A). Important to note is that pairwise interactions are essential, to coordinate by means of information exchange and to synchronize and compare design considerations among the three processes. This characteristic promotes the comprehensive nature of the methodology. It is unlike the more typical $U \leftrightarrow I \leftrightarrow A$ view that is represented in Fig. 10.5. The latter model is very appropriate for the ultimate *usage* relationship between user and application domain, which is to be supported by the intermediary functionality of the interface system. But it is inadequate for representing the pairwise cross-linkage that must be ensured during comprehensive interface *design*.

The three-pronged parallel design process can be portrayed in tabular form, with directed links between design phases to indicate flowchart-like transfer of designer attention, or of interdesigner coordination (Treu *et al.*, 1991). This is done in the case study described in Section 10.6. However, an alternative is to model all three processes in a generic format. Each design process can then be instantiated in accordance with the particular module (U, I, or A) it represents.

Such a design process model is shown in Fig. 10.6. It represents any one of the triad of subprocesses of Fig. 10.4. Required interactions with the "neighboring" processes are indicated. Following is a description of the seven-step process. In each design step some example considerations and questions are cited to illustrate applicability to the three different modules.

This description is a refinement of a subset of the steps included in the general design method of Fig. 10.3. The mapping between the labeled steps of the two models is shown in Table 10.1.

STEP 1: *Design principles* are those that are identified at the start of an

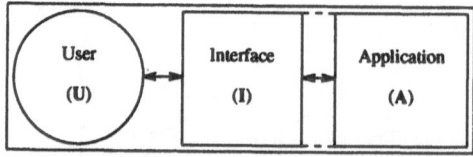

FIGURE 10.5. Typical HCI model.

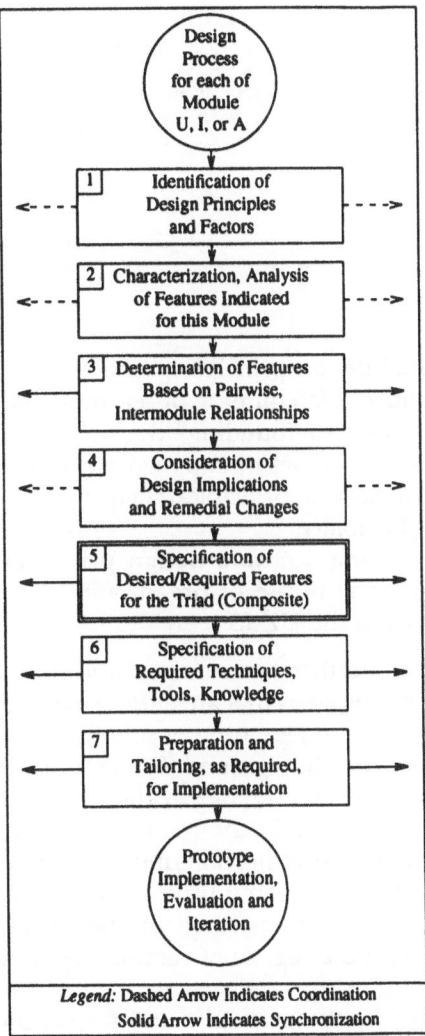

FIGURE 10.6. Seven-step module-specific design process.

HCI design, reflecting the desired evaluative criteria to which the ultimate design product should adhere. For a totally new HCI, the principles must be considered for each module. For an interface design that is based on one or more *existing* modules (*A* and/or *I*), the principles may (or should) already by inherent to those modules and hence are no longer variable.

TABLE 10.1
Mapping of Steps (Fig. 10.6 to Fig. 10.3)

Three-pronged process	Cause-and-effect method
1	B
2, 3	C
4	D
5, 6	E
7 . . .	F–H

U: User-oriented design principles, such as to render the interface both facilitative (P20), in ease of learning and use, and context-providing (P13), "surrounding" the user-visible displays and actions with various types of supportive information

A: Software engineering principles, such as modularity, object orientation, and flexibility

I: Some of the same software design principles as for Module A apply, in addition to use of organizational models for interface systems, such as the UIMS

In addition to principles that represent desired design goals, designers must identify those *design factors* that are either enabling or constraining in achieving those goals. Examples are any significant strengths and weaknesses in user knowledge or background (Chapter 3), as well as limits in the application software (Chapter 4) and in the target interface hardware/software capabilities (Chapter 5). Design factors become very evident in Step 7, in which the design specifications must be tailored for implementation. But they should be considered throughout the design process. Certain functionalities to be incorporated in the interface may have the specific purpose of ameliorating, if not eliminating, some of the constraining factors.

STEP 2: Guided by the principles and factors identified in Step 1, the designers must carefully analyze and characterize the capabilities, strengths and weaknesses, of each module of concern:

U: What exactly are the members of the target user population expected to want to do with the application software? How knowledgeable and experienced are they for doing so? What kinds of help or direction are they likely to need from the interface module?

A: What are the types of specific uses enabled by the application software?

I: What are the alternatives available in interface hardware, software, architecture, and anticipated user-visible interaction techniques and modes?

Each module may separately suggest that certain interface features are most appropriate for it.

STEP 3: Having considered separately the individual characteristics of the *U*, *I*, and *A* modules, specific pairwise, intermodule relationships must be determined in detail. Examples:

U↔A:
Does the application (software) exhibit inherent types of structural, visual, and other characteristics that can be exploited to better guide and direct the user?

I↔A:
Should modular independence (i.e., separation between *I* and *A*) be required? Or can the interface be designed to supplement the application software, without concern about that separation?

U↔I:
Is the intended user population qualified for, or in need of, a certain style of interface-supported interaction?

STEP 4: If Steps 2 and 3 have been successful, the designers now know what features seem to be indicated, without yet deciding precisely how they should be instantiated. Before expending the effort to specify the design in detail, this is a good time to attend once again to the module-specific design processes. The question is: how, exactly, do the agreed-upon results of Steps 2 and 3 impact on each module?

U: Will the user model have to be elaborated or supplemented somehow (e.g., with on-line solicitation of user preferences about some planned feature)? Should it be assumed that users will undergo training/tutorial sessions as prerequisite to using the design product?

A: Is the selected application software in fact adequate, or may it have to be modified to be more supportive of the planned interface features? Will software independence between modules *A* and *I* have to be ensured?

I: The composite list of desired interface features must be packaged, or "engineered," into one cohesive interface software environment; any potential conflicts or inconsistencies have to be removed.

Depending on results of this reconsideration of features proposed, some module-specific, remedial changes may be possible. The purpose is to facilitate thereby the remaining design effort.

STEP 5: In this step, the results of individual (Step 2) and pairwise (Step 3) analyses of the three modules, followed by consideration of design implications (Step 4) and any changes that might facilitate the remaining steps, must be integrated. This requires exact specification and representation of the *design features* that will encompass all three modules, in some combination. If, for example,

$A \leftrightarrow (U \leftrightarrow I)$:
> a structure inherent to the application (A-factor) will be used as a paradigm for providing visual confirmation and contextual guidance to the user, then

$U \leftrightarrow (I \leftrightarrow A)$:
> a specified capability required/desired by the user (U-factor) at each point (or phase) of such a structure should have determining influence on

$I \leftrightarrow (U \leftrightarrow A)$:
> the software designed into the interface system (I-factors) to supply that capability.

Step 5 requires intense interactions and brainstormings among all members of a design team. This design activity must be conducted very carefully, thoroughly, and skillfully. Designer skills must not be limited to ability to analyze individual parts of the complex system; it is essential that the designer be able to synthesize and integrate those parts into an effectively functioning whole.

STEP 6: This is where the detailed design specifications, representing the features determined in Step 5, must be translated into specification of design "objects" that are to be created. For example:

$U \; (\leftrightarrow I)$:
> How should the user-visible interaction be organized? Perhaps using a high-level version of a state transition graph superimposed on the selected interaction technique(s). This would focus on the states that are actually experienced by the user. The transition graph can be consistent with the goal-oriented structure of the application, and its "state objects" can map into the object-oriented interface software.

$(U \leftrightarrow) \; I$:
> What the user needs to know (but may not) must be available through appropriate help facilities, tied into the states of the high-

level transition graph. Such help can be extended by making the interface dynamically adaptive (P4). If possible, the user's task-specific plans and goals should be facilitated through intelligent forms of explanation, direction, and guidance.

I: The overall interface software architecture of the planned interface system must be specified to accommodate the above-indicated features, and all others impacting on it. It should be object-oriented and preferably adhere to an extended version of the UIMS model.

STEP 7: Finally, each of the three design processes must lead to combined implementation of prototype and/or operational version of the interface, using the targeted interface hardware and software. This step involves the preparation for implementation and also for any associated or follow-on testing and evaluation of the results.

As evident from the above, the three prongs of the design process, while described as if they were equivalent (Fig. 10.6), do not necessarily get equal priority in any particular design. If it is decided up front that the user module should get top priority, as one would normally expect, then the other two modules will have to take secondary or subservient roles. However, such a situation is often unrealistic. Expectations initially stipulated (e.g., by management) might include the utilization of a particular application module or interface module, thereby constraining the design methodology to adhere to corresponding characteristics, to the possible detriment of the user.

10.6. A Case Study

To illustrate the use of the above-defined three-pronged design process, an interface system called N-CHIME (NCR-sponsored Cohesive, HSL-oriented Interactive Modeling Environment) was designed (Treu *et al.*, 1991). A prototype version was then implemented by Pete Sanderson, Roman Rozin, and Ravi Sharma. This section describes specific utilization of the process, along with various methodological considerations. Some of the resulting features of N-CHIME are characterized in subsequent sections.

First, let us look briefly at the nature and purpose of N-CHIME. A basic model is shown in Fig. 10.7. The N-CHIME interface software was to serve as an intermediary module, positioned between the *user* and the application *domain* of interest. In our case, that domain was *modeling and simulation*, to be supported by the *HSL simulation programming language*.

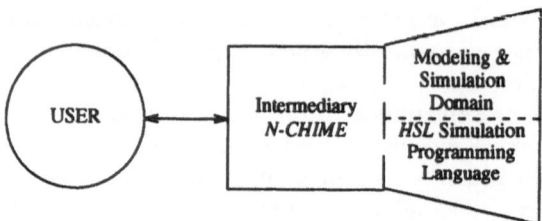

FIGURE 10.7. Intermediary role of N-CHIME. [This figure and Figs. 10.8 through 10.12 are reprinted (slightly revised) from Treu *et al.* (1991) with permission of Butterworth–Heinemann.]

HSL is a process-oriented language (Sanderson *et al.*, 1991) that is dichotomous in structure: each HSL program consists of an *environment* section, containing global declarations, object type definitions (including entities, resources, queues, statistics), and model control statements, and a *simulator* section, consisting of a set of processes and functions to perform the run-time activities. The processes represent the activity sequences undertaken by active entities in the simulated system.

It is important to point out that HSL was implemented as a two-phase interpreter (Rozin and Treu, 1991), not as a compiler. That interpreter status rendered an HSL program more conducive to interactive manipulation (e.g., interruption, modification, further execution) by a user, especially when assisted by an intermediary software package, such as N-CHIME. This intermediary was intended to make things easier and better for industrial users wanting to do modeling and simulation with HSL. Exactly what N-CHIME was to provide, and how, became dependent on specified design principles and factors.

As stated earlier, the three-pronged process is variable as to which prong(s) is(are) emphasized when. At the outset of the N-CHIME project, only two prongs determined the design: the characteristics of the user (U) and the application software (A). The target interface (I) software and hardware were initially not to have constraining influence. Accordingly, a high-level view of the design process is shown in Fig. 10.8. Mnemonic labels are again used for ease of reference from the text.

The process steps concerning the user (U-0) and the application software (A-0), in Fig. 10.8, are analogous and can each be refined as shown in Fig. 10.9. Basically, in each case, the input information must be utilized to transform a general, *conceptual* model (of a user; or of an application) into a clearly delimited, *practical* profile (based on various realistic factors), from which *specific* detailed requirements can be extracted, for input to the interface software design specifications. In effect, the conceptual and

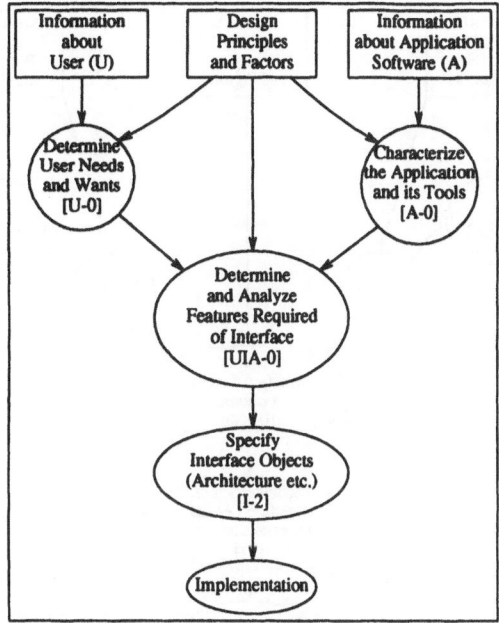

FIGURE 10.8. First high-level version of design process.

practical steps provide the IF part of the IF–THEN cause-and-effect patterns illustrated in Chapters 3 through 5. The specific requirements point to the design feature(s) (the THEN part) that is(are) called for.

After the refinement of Fig 10.9 is substituted in Fig. 10.8, with some minor changes, the process shown in Fig 10.10 results. The steps pertaining to the interface system prong (starting with composite step *UIA*-0) must

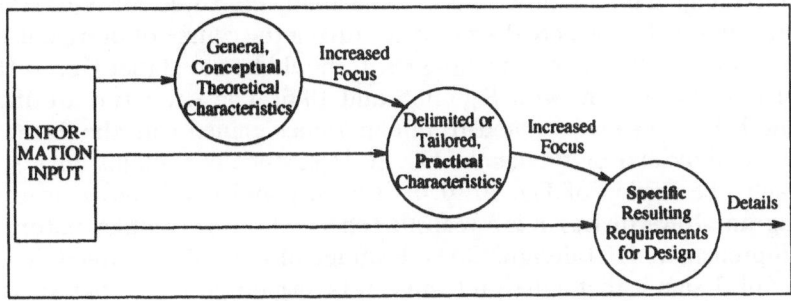

FIGURE 10.9. Refinement of preparatory steps.

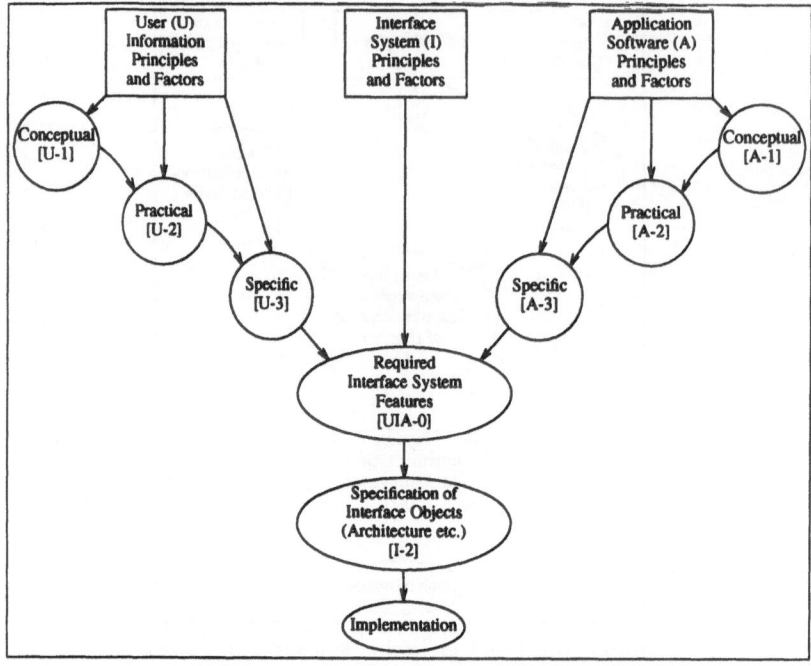

FIGURE 10.10. Process steps leading to interface specification.

also be further refined. This is illustrated in the description of the N-CHIME design study, found in the balance of this as well as in the next chapter.

10.6.1. Design Process: Overview

Figure 10.11 gives a more complete, high-level representation of the three-pronged design process that was actually employed for N-CHIME. The high-level steps were then refined during the course of design, using lower-level methodological techniques. It should be noted that Fig. 10.11 is not totally consistent with Fig. 10.3 and 10.6. The latter two are more generic versions that resulted from experience gained with the former.

As indicated by the labels, Fig. 10.11 essentially contains (as a subgraph) the version of Fig. 10.10. It is a busy and potentially confusing diagram. Nevertheless, it is a realistic reflection of the complex nature of comprehensive HCI design. One advantage of the three-pronged definition of design is that a design team can be organized into subgroups (of specialists) that work on separate tasks concurrently. Frequent coordina-

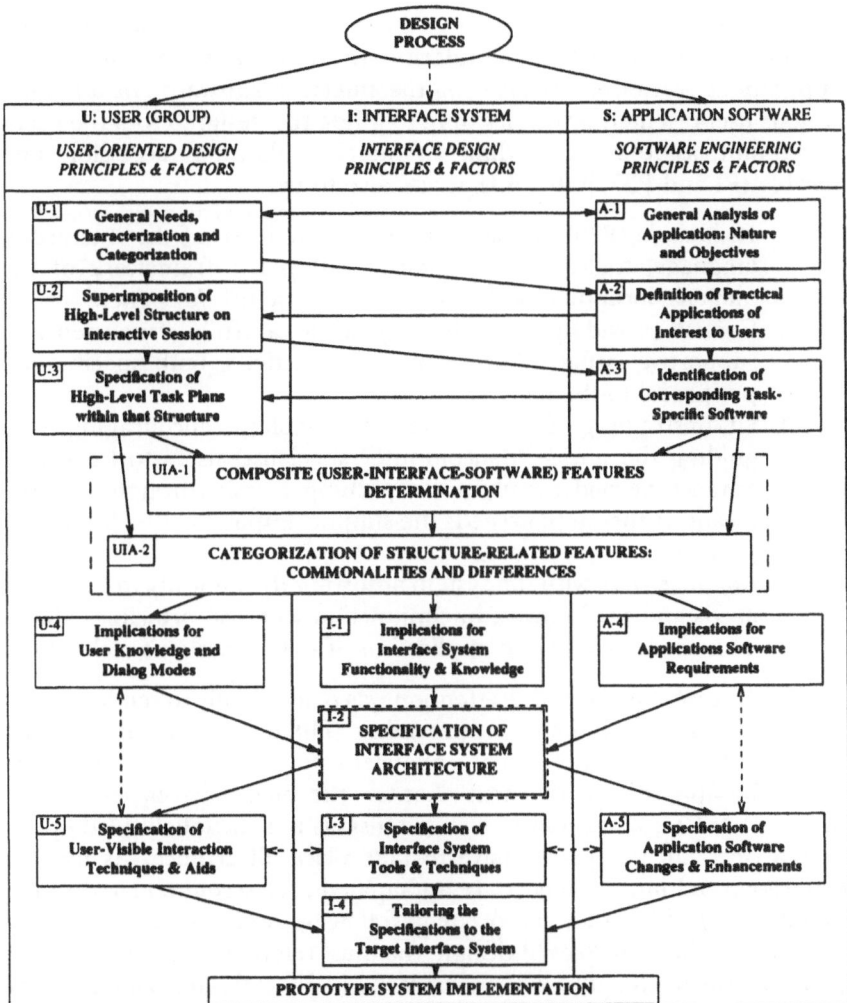

FIGURE 10.11. User-oriented and software-specific interface design.

tion and exchange of design ideas, decisions, and plans are essential, as indicated by the lateral arrows.

10.6.2. Design Principles

The N-CHIME design was to adhere to well-known software engineering principles, such as modularity and robustness, not only for the applications software, but also for the interface software. In addition, various user-oriented principles were to guide the design. From the user's standpoint, aside from needing an interface that was accessible and reliable (P1 and P37, Table 9.1), it was also to be:

1. Facilitative (P20), in ease of learning and use of the interaction language, tools, and techniques, within the framework of the mental/conceptual model employed by the user/designer.
2. Context-providing (P13), by displaying carefully structured and supportive visual information and directions, both specific and peripheral to the task.
3. Unconstraining (P41), deliberately enabling, encouraging, and guiding the novice (noncomputer specialist) users to learn and advance beyond merely accomplishing a task through minimal means. It therefore exceeds the support implied by the facilitative principle.
4. Adaptive (P4), with the system adjusting dynamically to the user's needs and preferences, in conjunction with the principles above. This requires effective application of expert systems technology.

In the case study, primary attention was paid initially to rendering the interface facilitative and context-providing. The other two principles became the focus of a subsequent enhancement phase of N-CHIME. As should be apparent in the next chapter, the modular, object-oriented design of N-CHIME supports such extensions in functionality. Complete design does not necessarily have to take place all at once. As long as extensions and improvements are anticipated and accommodated in the overall architecture, they can occur in follow-up design phases.

Besides the principles of design, the most relevant design factors had to be identified. Initially we were concerned only with analyzing the user and the application modules, as characterized below. The results led to determination of desired features, described in Section 10.7. The design factors pertaining to the interface module are inherent to the description of design "objects," including the interface software architecture, that were deemed necessary to implement the desired features. Those design objects are presented in Chapter 11.

10.6.3. Application Factors

Steps *A*-1 through *A*-3 of Fig. 10.11 represent our study of the application domain. The target application software, HSL, supports a domain that is very conducive to detailed analysis and structuring. We first considered the nature and objectives of modeling and simulation in general (Step *A*-1). Then, within that context, we defined practical uses of HSL (Step *A*-2) and related them to the specific, already existing functional capabilities and features of the HSL software (Step *A*-3). The following arguments provide insight into the software-specific analysis that was carried out. They illustrate how the applications software, or the designer's view of how the user should utilize it, must influence the structure and functionality of the interface software.

Among the familiar terms for traditionally defined uses of modeling and simulation software are: (1) system design projections, (2) capacity planning, and (3) systems tuning. At face value, these uses are not very consistent with each other, except that they all share some "system model" as the *object* of the implied activity. The first inclination might be to design the interface software with three separate tracks, one to support each of the three uses. But that would not lead to a very cohesive, integrated interface in which various system tools and techniques can be shared efficiently among different applications.

Upon further analysis, it was observed that each of the three uses is dependent on a combination of the following distinctions in modeling and simulation capabilities:

• Complete versus partial system (component) representation
• High-level versus low-level (detailed) system analysis
• Performance evaluation of an existing and/or planned system

These are examples of major qualifiers of the (modeling and simulation) actions or of the objects (i.e., system models) of those actions. The HSL software is equipped to support each of these distinctions. The question was: how should the N-CHIME interface software be designed to reinforce a cohesive interface perspective for the user? The user should preferably have the flexibility to transition from one applications track, or task plan, to another, rather than having them appear mutually exclusive. The above-implied object orientation became key to answering the question.

We decided that the following nontraditional distinctions among HSL uses would be more amenable to the modeler's mind. The essence of a computer-aided action conceived by a user is the previously mentioned action primitive (see Fig. 4.1). From the standpoint of someone trying to initiate actions within an application, such as modeling and simulation, it is the minimal surface structure, or syntax, of a user command. It results after stripping away any embellishments, inconsistencies, and extraneous words of natural language and regardless of computer-required syntax and semantics of the command and its components. Any such user-conceived command can be represented in the following format:

⟨action; action qualifier(s); object; object qualifier(s)⟩

To arrive at a design with such uniform object orientation, we adopted the view that

The user of N-CHIME may want to model, simulate, and evaluate (i.e., carry out some action), at whatever level of detail desired (action qualifier), any one of the following systems or system models (object of action) or part(s) thereof (object qualifier or attribute):

- Conceptualized system
- Real, existing system, and/or
- Previously specified or tested system model

This characterization of HSL applications is therefore contingent on the type of system (model) that is the *object* of the user's attention, not on the different *actions* the user wants to apply to those objects. A complete set of action capabilities is assumed to be available in any case.

10.6.4. User Factors

Steps U-1 through U-3 of Fig. 10.11 represent the user-oriented analysis carried out in the N-CHIME study. The above discussion on possible applications already implies a general categorization of users according to what they might want to do with HSL. It confirms the need to coordinate, and consider in parallel, both the software-specific analysis (Steps A-1, A-2, A-3) and the user-oriented analysis (Step U-1). For the case study, we only considered the commonly known distinctions among users (e.g., novice versus experienced) in the design decisions. In general, various other factors, reflecting specific user capabilities, needs, and preferences, should be identified at this point of the design, toward incorporating the user (or user group) in the design product more effectively.

As outlined in Chapter 3, the interface designer must somehow acquire a conceptual model of what the particular type of target user needs or wants (Step U-1), and a variety of different means are available for constructing such a model. In the case study, the conceptual model of what the particular industrial users needed was based on our own knowledge and experience plus a combination of:

1. Results of detailed discussions with senior staff persons (of the industrial sponsor), who served as *knowledgeable consultants* on the modeling and simulation application and expressed ideas and suggestions on which interface features would be important to prospective N-CHIME users
2. The agreed-upon, *user-oriented design principles* (outlined above), specified in advance, to guide the determination of interface features and support deemed desirable for/by the users
3. Using those principles to identify interface features that are both practical and specific (Steps U-2 and U-3), resulting in the observation that high priority should be given to *user-oriented interface structures*

The last of these topics has been addressed at length (Treu, 1992, 1994). Its implications for the case study are discussed next. It should be noted again that our "conceptual model" was constructed using only the above inputs. We, the designers, decided what the users were likely to need. The study did not permit us to elicit user preferences and needs, including existing "mental models," from target users directly.

10.6.5. High-Level Structures

Users in general, but especially those who are novices, are in need of guidance and direction toward completing application-specific tasks. This implies that they must be given a sense of orientation and context with respect to where they are in the task domain, where they are going or can go next, and what they can do there. Unstructured tasks tend to be too fluid and too variable. If a user is repeatedly faced with a myriad of possible options, and has no interface-supplied clues on currently logical and useful choices, then the problem-solving interaction tends to become confusing, especially for unskilled users.

An important, practical approach to dealing with this need is to analyze an interactive user–computer session and to impose meaningful, high-level structure on it (Step U-2), in correspondence to what is known about the application software domain (Steps A-1 and A-2). For N-CHIME, we assumed a previously proposed session structure (Treu, 1988a) and revised it. The result is outlined in Fig. 10.12, representing the major phases through which a user typically passes in modeling and simulating a system.

Structuring or partitioning an interactive user–computer session into phases must be done in correspondence to the goal-oriented functionality of the application software. Each phase is defined to play a specialized contextual role, supporting the user in making progress toward completing those subtasks and decisions that are inherent to it. First, the *concep-*

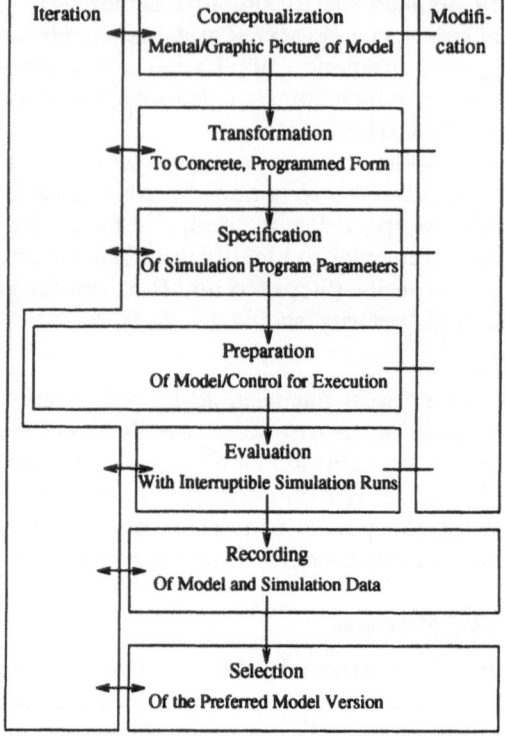

FIGURE 10.12. Phases of session structure.

tualization phase is very significant in modeling and simulation. In it, the user is in a discovery, innovation, or creativity mode. A user who does not yet have a clear idea of a (system) model in mind, must try to create or discover one. This requires somehow imagining, visualizing, or viewing the desired system to be modeled, at least at a very high level. Help for model creation includes stimulating the user with previously stored, relevant models. Further, user conceptualization and visualization can be supported by enabling the user to construct (or retrieve) a pattern of interconnected system entities (or graphic icons or symbols). Such help can be made available at the interface, both through procedural and explanatory means and by taking advantage of techniques in computer graphics.

Consistent with the nature of modeling and simulation, a graphical diagram of a system is itself a model. During the *transformation* phase, the user must be able to take such a high-level model, resulting from the conceptualizaton phase, and convert it into a more concrete representation, such as a shell of an HSL-programmed model. Alternatively, if the user is not experienced enough to do so, the system might be able to obviate this step by automatically producing HSL program shells as well as default parameters. In general, considerable user–system negotiation, involving a number of trial-and-error attempts and resulting changes of mind, may be necessary.

After a working high-level, HSL-programmed model has been created and is on display for further interaction, the user has to be given the opportunity to specify associated modeling parameters, criteria, and constraints. The *specification* phase affects such detailed parameter selections and model refinements. It also enables crystallization of the model environment, including any variables upon which the later evaluation phase may be dependent. During this phase, knowledge of the real capabilities of HSL becomes critical.

The next phase is *preparation* of the resulting HSL model and its control for actual execution. Any remaining details about the source program and its parameters have to be worked out. Then, the program must be compiled for use in the evaluation phase. Again, depending on user experience, some/most of the technical programming details may be obviated through some forms of automatic help or previously prepared model programs.

The *evaluation* phase encompasses the execution of the previously specified and programmed model for purposes of simulation and testing. Here the user must be able to manipulate and control the model. It must be possible to make changes and to stipulate how the performance data (simulation statistics) are to be displayed for the user at the interface.

Iterations (see below) may be required to fine-tune or modify the current system model. It is important to anticipate that the user may wish to return to and even select an earlier model version. This is a major purpose of the *recording* phase. In the interest of efficiency (avoiding repeated creation and simulation of the same system model), it should be possible to retain for later recall a record of the earlier results. This can be implemented as an option in cases of user uncertainty or when the user does not wish to reject a particular model out-of-hand.

The final sequentially ordered phase of Fig. 10.12 is for model *selection*. After a variable number of iterations and after several tentative choices may have been made and recorded for comparison, the user should be in a position to make a selection, if desired.

Two other phases, or phase-enhancing capabilities, are pervasive throughout the above-outlined session structure. They are indicated in the two adjoining, vertical regions of Fig. 10.12. To emphasize the importance of enabling a user to make frequent changes in the results produced at any point in the session, the *modification* phase must be explicitly identified. The interface should be flexible enough to let the user manipulate the diagrammatic model, the specified parameters, the HSL program as well as its simulation output quantities, formats, and forms of presentation. In short, to the extent it is reasonable and feasible to do so, the user should be able to change his/her mind during any of the indicated phases.

After simulation results are presented at the interface for user viewing, the user may want to change some of the specified parameter values or even return to modifying the representation of the system model itself. This is done in the *iteration* phase, enabling the looping back to earlier phases as many times as necessary. The phases to which iterations are most applicable are also indicated in Fig. 10.12.

The ability to provide guidance and direction to the user via the above-described session structure is further enhanced by superimposing specific task plans (Step *U*-3), or paths within a directed graph, on top of the session structure. Each such plan contains the steps required for carrying out one of the HSL-supported applications (Steps *A*-2 and *A*-3). Task plans are therefore distinguished according to which of the above-defined models is the object of modeling and simulation activity.

10.7. Features Determination

High-level structures in the interface, like the one illustrated in Fig. 10.12, are in themselves features caused by *U*-factors, e.g., the need for guidance or context. After they are determined and superimposed on an application-specific session, it becomes necessary to look for the supporting, lower-level design features.

In the N-CHIME case study, a set of desirable features resulted from lengthy discussions by the design team. The features were selected consistent with the established design principles, to support the user at the various points of the high-level structures (i.e., within different session phases or nodes of a task plan). This work is represented by Step *UIA*-1 (Fig. 10.11). Subsequently, the proposed features were carefully reconsidered, for purposes of:

- Identifying and distinguishing duplicates, i.e., those features that were suggested repeatedly, as applicable to two or more phases of a session: Step *UIA*-2
- Categorizing them with respect to their practical implications on the user (Step *U*-4), the interface (Step *I*-1), and the application software (Step *A*-4)

A subset of resulting feature groups is listed in Table 10.2. An example feature of N-CHIME is the ability it gives the user, during the model conceptualization phase, to browse through a library of stored graphical models. Another feature is the ability to create and edit original, graphic models of systems. Relevant *I*-factors include whether or not the interface system has the requisite graphics capabilities and also the storage capacity to support that feature.

Although we did not actually draw decision schematics during the N-CHIME study, our decision-making discussions and numerous tabulations accomplished the equivalent thereof. An illustration of a representative, partial schematic is given in Fig. 10.13. It shows how a decision (D_1) on superimposing high-level structures (e.g., the session phase sequence) was made based on the fact that we were primarily targeting relatively novice (non-computer scientist) users (a U-factor), coupled with knowledge of the importance of structure to the human mind (another U-factor) and the determination that the modeling and simulation application is very conducive to being "structurable" (an A-factor).

The result of Decision D_1, in Fig. 10.13, is an interim feature that is then interpreted as a hybrid factor ($U + A$ factor) for the next decision. It is coupled with another hybrid ($U + A$) factor, which asserts that in modeling and simulation the user must be able to *conceptualize* the systems to be modeled. To support the latter, the visually meaningful and effective

TABLE 10.2
Structure-Contained Features[a]

Session phase	Phase-specific feature groups
Conceptualization	Browsing of existing models in the database, Creation/Editing of graphical version of the model, Maintaining consistency in resulting model
Transformation	Transforming conceptual model into HSL shell (program)
Specification	Programmed model editing and specification
Preparation	Setting of model simulation control parameters, Detection/Correction of errors in HSL model
Evaluation	Actual execution of programmed model, Display of model output, Runtime error handling, Model execution interruption and debugging
Recording	Storing of model output, for later retrieval, Also storing of model itself
Selection	Comparison of results with other runs and experiments as well as with other models

[a]Reprinted from Treu *et al.* (1991) with permission of Butterworth–Heinemann.

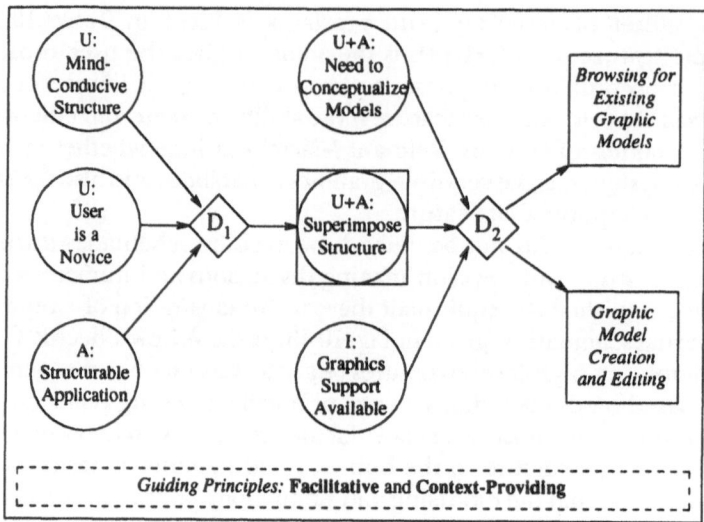

FIGURE 10.13. Illustrative decision schematic for N-CHIME.

techniques provided by computer graphics are suggested. Accordingly, using the *I*-factor that confirms the availability of graphics on a target computer, the second design decision, D_2, resulted both in (1) a browser tool for retrieval and display of existing, graphic models, and (2) a graphic editor, which enables the creation, display, editing, etc., of new graphic models in 2-D.

Actually, the schematic of Fig. 10.13 is a simplification of what really happened. Nevertheless, it represents in essence what our design team determined with regard to the particular features identified. Other schematics could be drawn to show the logic and rationale behind the other features, or feature groups, listed in Table 10.2. Throughout the many discussions on design decisions, the principles of design were repeatedly invoked for guidance. The two user-oriented principles most relevant to the features in question are indicated in Fig. 10.13.

Still other features, not included in Table 10.2, are not as specialized to the phases of the superimposed session structure. They are more pervasive. Examples are the constant need for screen organization (and windowing) and for system-provided explanation/help. These play "lower-level" support roles and transcend the structural boundaries. They are discussed in Chapter 11.

10.8. Features Specification

Determination of desirable interface features carries with it certain consequences, namely, the realistic implications on each of the user (Step U-4), the application software (Step A-4), and the interface system itself (Step I-1). These represent Step D in the general design method of Fig. 10.3. In the N-CHIME case study, such implications were taken into account in finalizing the features and reflecting them in the detailed specifications implied by Steps U-5, A-5, and I-3, respectively.

The proposed features were instantiated through appropriate software techniques and tools, in conjunction with the interface software architecture (Step I-2). The design objects that resulted are discussed in Chapter 11. At this point of the design, the interface-specific design factors (I-factors) became dominant. The capabilities and limitations of the target interface hardware and software were determined, for subsequent tailoring (Step I-4). Critical analysis of how the interface tools and techniques might influence the interface architecture, and vice versa, was carried out. Most importantly with respect to the user, it was necessary to arrive at a detailed prescription and analysis of the user-visible states and state transitions.

In this chapter, the N-CHIME study has been used to illustrate Steps B, C, and D of the cause-and-effect design method (Fig. 10.3). Chapter 11 presents how the resulting features of N-CHIME were incorporated in a set of design "objects." This is essentially Step E in Fig. 10.3 and also the prototype implementation part of Step F. The remaining major step covered in this book, namely, Step H, is addressed separately (Treu, 1992).

Exercises

10.1. With reference to Definitions 10.1 and 10.2, is it possible to both design and implement an interface (software/hardware) using the same approach? Why or why not?

10.2. Notice that the approach depicted in Fig. 10.1 includes not only design but also implementation and evaluation. Which of the indicated steps constitute "top-down design"? If you were a designer, what would you need for each of those design steps in order to be able to carry them out?

10.3. Construct and diagram a high-level inside-out approach (Definition 10.3) in a manner analogous to Fig. 10.1. Discuss the difficulties in doing so.

10.4. Repeat Exercise 10.3 for the outside-in approach (Definition 10.4).

10.5. Find at least three of the publications cited in Section 10.3. Analyze and compared the design methods they describe, to determine whether you agree or disagree with the observations that they all use the five-step method, or a subset of the five steps, outlined in that section. Explain.

10.6. Find a step-by-step description of a software development method from a software engineering book. Compare it against the five-step method outlined in Section 10.3.

10.7. Is James's (1991) "spiral" approach to interface design fundamentally different from the more common, sequential representations? Analyze it and explain.

10.8. Prepare a critique of the cause-and-effect design method depicted in Fig. 10.3. Is it significantly different from the other methods described in the HCI literature? Explain. Would it be easier or more difficult to use? Why?

10.9. If a design method is a specific plan or procedure (Definition 9.10) that a designer can follow step by step, can one argue that Fig. 10.3 is really not specific enough? Should each of its boxes, A through H, be accompanied by a detailed, lower-level procedure (or submethod)? At what point do detailed methodological instructions become excessive and constraining, taking away from the ingenuity and skills of the designer?

10.10. With reference to Exercise 10.9, try to characterize the dividing line between (a) following detailed instructions in a prescribed design method, and (b) utilizing one's design expertise within higher-level steps of such a method, while formulating the lower-level steps on one's own. The latter option suggests that the designer record not only design decision rationales but also the low-level steps leading to conclusions of the various design steps (as discussed in Section 9.5.2.).

10.11. Compare the three-pronged design process model, described in Section 10.5, with the cause-and-effect method (Fig. 10.3). What are their respective advantages and disadvantages?

10.12. In the N-CHIME case study, what other user factors should have been determined (directly from/about target users) and how might these have influenced the resulting prototype design?

10.13. Did the analysis of the modeling and simulation application, in Section 10.6, result in a "mental model" to be used by the user? Discuss.

10.14. Which interface structures (Treu, 1992) are in evidence in the results of the N-CHIME prototype defined thus far? Explain where and how they apply?

10.15. Figure 10.11 clearly indicates that I-factors were not of concern at the start of the N-CHIME design. If a specific computer system had been stipulated from the outset for use as the prototype platform, would that have changed the design results? Explain and illustrate.

10.16. A hierarchy of (interdependent) design features seems to have resulted for N-CHIME, consistent with the discussion of interaction techniques and styles in Section 6.6. To enable clear composition and integration of features selected and specified, do such interdependencies among features have to be made explicit, i.e., described and represented in unambiguous, usable patterns? If so, by whom and how? Illustrate. If not, how is the integration of interface features to be achieved?

DESIGN OBJECTS, MODULES, AND MODELS

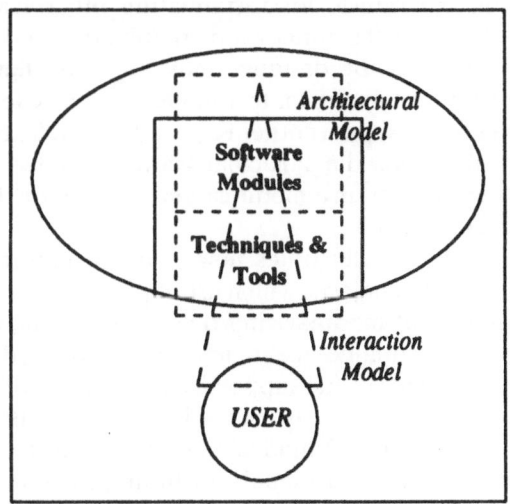

11.1. Overview

Numerous kinds of factors enable or constrain HCI design. They include the *U*-factors (Chapter 3), *A*-factors (Chapter 4), and *I*-factors (Chapter 5). Each of the three major entities is also dependent on structures (Treu, 1992). Although they may not be recognized explicitly, they become implicit features in design. In addition, there are other factors, e.g., administrative directions, which must be taken into account.

Because factors are causal in nature (e.g., Fig. 3.3), they as well as the stipulated design principles (e.g., Table 9.1) must be utilized by the designer to determine the required/desired interface features. Figure 10.2 confirms this pattern of influences. It is represented by Steps B and C of Fig. 10.3. Decision schematics were employed in several chapters to illustrate such factors-based determinations.

But a design feature can be realized in different ways or through different means. Suppose that a design principle requires that the inter-

243

face be rendered context-providing (P13, Table 9.1). To achieve this goal, one feature of the resulting interface must be that it provide the user with interaction context (Definition 6.11) in various states and points of inter-action. Therefore, the design result (feature) appears to be synonymous with the design goal (principle). That is good. But it does not yet explain how the goal was reached, or what means were used for doing so. For the context-providing feature, one can utilize an interaction technique (Chapter 6), which is itself a design feature. The latter becomes an "object" of design, providing the vehicle for instantiating other features such as context. Thus, as part of the anticipated combination and integration of selected design features, the designer must focus on how/whether the planned kind of interaction (style, technique, mode, states, etc.), as dis-cussed in Chapter 6, can support other required design features. Included must be concern about how the particular feature, if in fact implemented, will affect and perhaps require modifications in each of the U-, A-, and I-modules (Step D, Fig. 10.3).

The above discussion illustrates how a design naturally becomes a composite of interrelated objects, which are expected to instantiate design features. This pattern of modularizing the design solution is in keeping with well-established techniques for structured, top-down development of software. It relates to some of the supportive models described in Chapter 8. As a result, the designer can map each selected feature into one or more modules or into organizational models that transcend the modules.

We treat the modules and models, including interaction techniques and tools, as design objects, consistent with the definition of object (Defini-tion 7.1). Thus, we are not only referring to visible "interface objects" such as windows and menus, as discussed by Gieskens and Foley (1992). This chapter describes several significant objects specifically chosen to encapsu-late other desired design features. That is part of Step E, Fig. 10.3. While this material is intended to have general applicability, it is illustrated using the N-CHIME case study described in Chapter 10.

First, in the next three sections, design objects are considered that primarily address the user's direct involvement at the interface. They include an application-dependent user-visible state graph (Section 11.2), the contents and hierarchical structure within each state of that graph (Section 11.3), and the user–system interaction techniques (Section 11.4).

Second, the state-specific devices and tools that are to support various desirable features are characterized in Section 11.5. Then, the interface software architecture, that is, the all-encompassing, macrolevel object that envelops and supports the other objects, must be properly designed. It is discussed in Section 11.6.

Third, an abstract composite model of how various objects can be interrelated, both by the designer and by the user, is presented in Section 11.7. It includes a format for the recording of design rationales, as an object of design in its own right.

Finally, a methodological summary of the N-CHIME case study is outlined in Section 11.8.

11.2. User State Scenario Graph

An interactive system can be represented by means of state transition diagrams, as discussed in Chapter 7. These typically reflect the device-level actions and syntax of user inputs and system outputs, in appropriate alternating order. But an analogous technique can be applied at a high level, to represent the major states and contexts that the user can experience directly. The detailed, device-level types of transactions must then be specified separately within and among the localities of high-level states.

In the N-CHIME case study, the high-level "user state scenario graph" of Fig. 11.1 resulted. The nodes suggest only *which* functions or decisions need to be carried out by the user and *when*, relative to preceding or succeeding nodes in the graph. The *how* design details are relegated to directly associated lower-level support objects. Consistent with the title of this chapter, the term "object" can be applied to any module or model, including any self-contained state, node, or tool, at whatever level of definition and detail. This means that lower-level objects *may* be able to inherit selected characteristics from their parent objects, if the designer chooses to implement them that way.

The boxes of Fig. 11.1 are "High-level" states called H-nodes. The composite box, labeled H0, combines (for convenience) the hierarchy of goal orientations and selections through which the user must transition in preparation for modeling and simulation. Analysis of that application was discussed in Section 10.6. The user can then move through the substantive states, labeled H1 through H9. These are not only correlated with the phases of the high-level session structure (Fig. 10.12) indicated in the right column; they also reveal a number of different potential task plans (defined generically in Chapter 4) superimposed on (or integrated into) the graph. One such plan is implied by the bold-print path from the "Hypothesized System Model" choice, to programming the model directly HSL (in State H3), specifying it, etc. (in States H4 through H7), and finally storing it for future use (State H8). Such a task plan would probably be reasonable only for an experienced simulationist and HSL programmer, interested in producing a new model in an expeditious manner. A user like that may not need to browse (State H1) through the library of previously

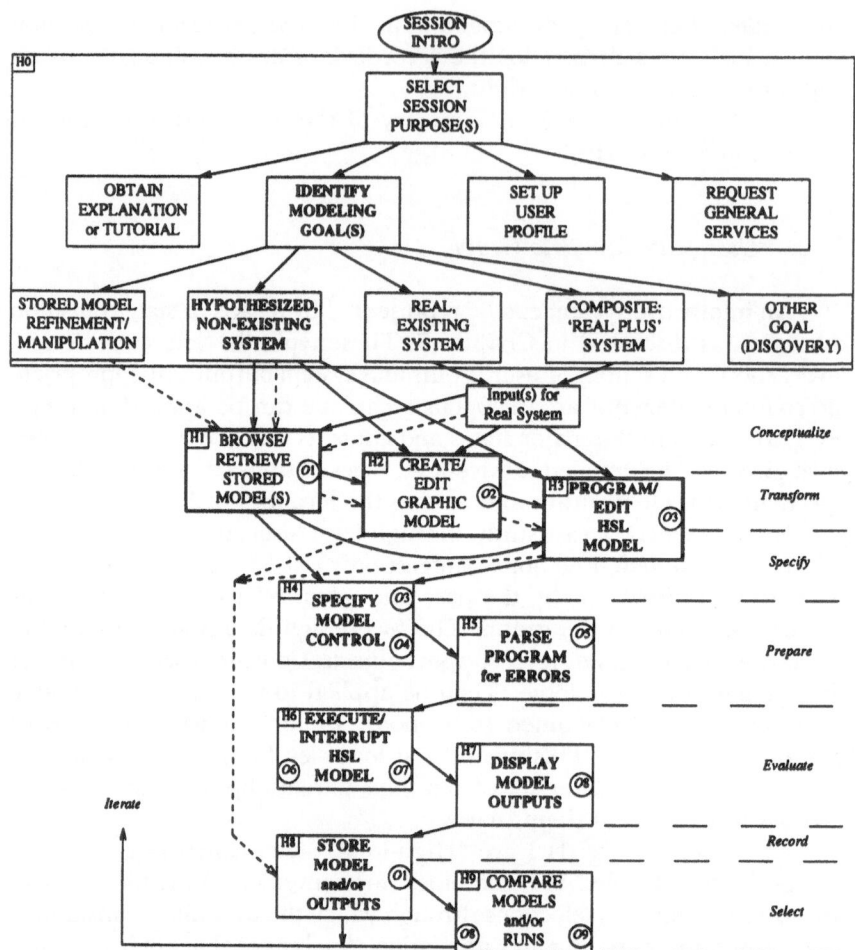

FIGURE 11.1. User state scenario graph. [This figure and Figs. 11.2 through 11.5 are reprinted (revised) from Treu *et al.* (1991) with permission of Butterworth–Heinemann.]

stored and analyzed models, nor create a graphical model representation (State H2), or obtain system help in transforming such a graphic representation (of any kind of model) into an HSL program (State H3). But other types of users may need or want to employ those features of N-CHIME. A number of different task plans are therefore possible. In particular, many users are likely to take advantage of the paths (indicated by dashed arrows) involving use of the library of stored models.

The decision schematic of Fig. 10.13 implies priority attention to novice (non-computer scientist) users and providing them with structures (e.g., the user state scenario graph) and other features (e.g., the graphics editor). But the N-CHIME design can actually accommodate the needs of other, more experienced users as well.

Although Fig. 11.1 is application-specific, pertaining to HSL and the area of modeling and simulation, a similar or analogous high-level plan should be possible for any other structured (or structurable) application. This assertion is reiterated in Chapter 13, which involves the extension of N-CHIME to make it also adaptive to user needs.

11.3. User-Visible States

At a high level of interaction with any system such as N-CHIME, the user is at any point faced with a display of information that should prompt, induce, encourage, and enable him/her to progress either to another high-level state or to accomplish some meaningful task(s) in lower-level state(s), within the current context. In other words, each high-level state or node (H-node) should present information, suitably organized, to support the user either (1) to move to another high-level state, along a desired path in the graph, consistent with one or more available task plans; or (2) to carry out some local action or activity, by invoking supportive tools and techniques and moving to lower-level (e.g., tool-inherent) states. The high-level states generally correspond to, and trigger events in, the dialog control (DCM) and application interface (AIM) modules of the N-CHIME run-time architecture (Section 11.6). Those modules were defined in Section 8.4.1.

Lower-level support nodes, which can be modeled as hierarchically supportive of the H-nodes, provide for the more detailed facilities and actions. They are required to assist the user in deciding or completing the function that is defined for the H-node in question. These L-nodes, not shown in Fig. 11.1, represent mostly physical or device-level functions. They generally relate to, and trigger events in, the device/presentation module (PM) of the interface run-time architecture. However, the DCM may also have to participate.

A general H-node must be supported by hierarchically subservient L-nodes as well as O-nodes (distinguished below). These relationships are portrayed abstractly later on, in Fig. 11.5. For example, an H-node that involves user choices among available options or branches (e.g., in H0 of Fig. 11.1) requires an L-node capable of presenting an appropriate "selector" device. Such a menu-based selector is designed to be used consistently with every H-node that has a similar need. Its contents (e.g., different context-sensitive menu commands) must of course be variable. But the same kinds of device-level actions (e.g., mouse clicks) will operate on it in every instance. L-nodes of this type, utilized by two or more H-nodes (and possibly also other L-nodes), are positioned in the "shared nodes" category of the total graph (Fig. 11.5). Another prominent example of a shared L-node is the frequently employed "windowing" capability, used for consistent screen layout and spatial location.

On the other hand, some L-nodes may be very specialized in nature, serving only one H-node. An example is the L-node that supports node H6 (Fig. 11.1). It has the capability to do run-time error handling. Nowhere else in the high-level graph is it required.

11.4. Interaction Techniques

Any interaction technique selected as a design feature of an interface must be suitably instantiated, within the context of an application-specific, user-visible state scenario graph. This is already implied above. It means that the designer must determine, for every H-node and for all such nodes collectively, whatever lower-level support objects (e.g., menus, windows) must be supplied to make a specified type of interaction uniformly available across all states.

Interaction techniques (Chapter 6) are of course among the most significant design features to be determined. For N-CHIME, we chose a combination of the following. Labels refer to entries in Tables 6.1 through 6.3.

1. *Menu-based interaction* ($F_{S,1}$), to give the user the ability to select among a variety of options available in different states
2. *Window-based interaction* ($F_{S,3}$), to enable the organization of the display screen into logical and consistently positioned regions/ entities
3. *Command-line interaction* ($F_{W,2}$), to provide for keying in of occasionally required input strings or parameter values, as well as for normal line-at-a-time outputs of HSL program statements.
4. *Diagrammed and iconic interaction* ($F_{D,2}$ and $F_{D,3}$), used for 2-D drawing, display, and editing of graphic representations (of modeled systems) plus the related use of iconic menu selection

In addition, we used plotted outputs ($F_{D,1}$) representing current queue lengths in simulated system operation. A succession of such plots, created in real time, can achieve the impression of animation by displaying the growing and shrinking queues associated with system resources, in a manner analogous to dynamically changing histograms. Some more details on several of the above-listed and other special techniques are outlined in Section 11.6.

Besides such interaction techniques, it is clear that higher-level design features, namely, representional models (Chapter 7), are necessary to compose the different features into one cohesive whole. That is exactly what the high-level state transition graph (Section 11.2) was designed to accomplish.

The reader may wonder about the "chicken-and-egg" syndrome that is evident. Which feature should be selected first? The interaction technique(s), or the high-level representational model(s)? The answer is: it depends. If the design features collectively call for a specific interaction technique (and style) to be available throughout an application-specific session, it may be most appropriate to select it first and then build higher-level definition (in terms of states, contexts) on top of it. On the other hand, if the design factors suggest variability in interaction techniques, as the user transitions among the different parts or phases of a structured application, it seems preferable to start with a high-level representational model and to engineer into its various phases/states those techniques that are locally most effective. The latter option was used in the N-CHIME study.

The above discussion implies that objects of interface design, which are to reflect and integrate the selected design features, may have to determined and specified either in sequence (top-down or bottom-up) or possibly in parallel. The approach is dependent on the particular circumstances (design factors) and most certainly also on the ingenuity and skill of the designer.

11.5. State-Specific Tools

In a highly modular architecture, some objects that are intended to encompass selected design features may be instantiated through software tools. The circled numbers displayed within the H-nodes of Fig. 11.1 refer to various software tools, or tool Objects. They are well-defined modules of software that are either pervasive or very special-purpose in nature. In either case, they prompt intense design efforts leading to tools that can be invoked, in a manner analogous to traditional procedure calls. Such modularity is even more important in the design of a complete, complex interface system than it is in the well-known structured programming area. For a variety of reasons familiar to software engineers, it makes sense to avoid designing a monstrous, unmanageable system of intertwined and integrated program code when, instead, the same functionality can be achieved by a well-engineered package of interfaceable, replaceable modules. This topic was discussed in Chapter 8.

For the N-CHIME case study, a number of self-contained functions were identified as belonging to the "tools" category. Some of them we decided to acquire and "plug into" the architecture; others we designed and implemented on our own. The nine tool objects labeled in Fig. 11.1 represent the following:

O1: Browser/Search and Retrieval Tool (Textual Mode)
O2: Graphics Editor and Transformer (Graphics Mode)
O3: Text Editor
O4: String Pattern Matcher
O5: Front-End of HSL Interpreter
O6: Back-End of HSL Interpreter
O7: Real-Time Model Interrupt Handler
O8: Graphical Output Generator
O9: Statistical Model Comparison Tool

Tool objects O1, O2, O7, and O8 were designed and implemented as part of our project; so were tools O5 and O6, which utilize the two previously implemented modules of HSL. O3 is a text editor that we acquired. It was also used for the special parameter search and exchange function envisioned for O4. The latter as well as O9 were not yet implemented.

Some of the tools get help from subsidiary tools functioning behind the user-visible interface. For example, we developed a transformation grammar (listed with O2 above) which can convert the internal representation of a graphic model (state H2) into a partially specified HSL program model (editable in state H3).

11.6. Interface Architecture

The interface software architecture should be designed (Step I-2, Fig. 10.11) as the all-encompassing system "object," which is directly influenced by the user-visible interaction objects discussed above, and vice versa. Hence, the discussion in Section 11.4, about which design object is to be determined first (interaction technique or high-level interaction representation), is also applicable here. But it depends on how the interface software model (a design feature) can best accommodate the user-visible design features collectively.

This section describes the initial software architecture that resulted from the N-CHIME case study (Treu *et al.*, 1991). It was later modified and extended (Sanderson, 1991; Sanderson and Treu, 1993) to render N-CHIME adaptive to user needs, as discussed in Chapter 13.

A high-level model of the N-CHIME architecture is shown in Fig. 11.2. It is an extension of the UIMS model. Such an architecture is obviously dependent on the preferences and judgment of the designer, subject to whatever design factors must be taken into account to achieve the desirable features. Different architectural versions are possible. Just as algorithms can be designed in a variety of ways, all toward reaching the same ultimate solution, there is no single "best" way to construct the interface software. The designer must endeavor to utilize all available design inputs to create the architecture that will hopefully be most effective. Then, after evaluation is carried out (Treu, 1994), it may become evident that certain characteristics should be changed or extended. In the case of N-CHIME, the version of Fig. 11.2 was later refined (Sanderson, 1991) into a highly object-oriented system, including distributed, micro-level dialogue control (for widgets) and centralized macro-level control (to relate to the H-nodes).

The major components in this version are the device interface, dialog control, HSL interface, and the tools package that supports selected

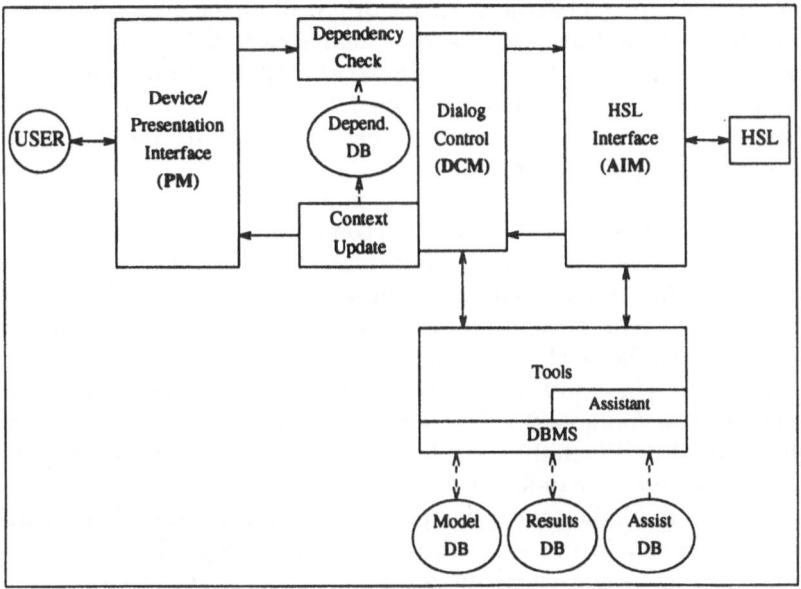

FIGURE 11.2. High-level N-CHIME architecture.

features. Interface modules communicate with each other through events. Functional operations are invoked by event handler routines. The device interface module includes software for handling interaction devices, such as the CRT display, keyboard, and mouse.

The DCM is the intermediary between the device level of interaction and the supporting tools plus the HSL interface. It collects from the user any necessary parameters required by HSL or by a selected tool, before invoking it. It also manages input and output between an executing tool and the device interface. Intermodule communication is through events. It always occurs within some context, not in isolation. The dependency check between the PM and DCM modules ensures that operations are performed only in the proper context. This prevents inconsistent situations during use of the interface, e.g., attempting to execute a programmed simulation model that has not yet been compiled.

The HSL interface module provides functional separation of HSL from the N-CHIME interface system. Theoretically, the HSL software should, therefore, be modifiable without affecting N-CHIME. It is the module to which the question of independence from the application software applies (e.g., Hurley, 1993). The decision on this issue depends on the designer's philosophy; not everyone believes that such independence is necessarily desirable.

The tools module contains interface system tools as design objects, including an assistance object capable of providing the user with information about N-CHIME, HSL, and related concepts. The support tools maintain several data bases with the aid of a DBMS. Information stored includes various forms of programmed HSL models (of systems to be simulated), output results from executed models, and the explanatory texts required by the assistant.

The run-time control module is modeled abstractly in Fig. 11.3. Events are contingent on messages that communicate information between software modules. Incoming events destined for a module are added to its list of pending events. The controlling loop, running independently, removes the event at the head of the list and invokes the event handler function. The choice of handler to be invoked is determined by the event parameters. The handler may choose to ignore the event, or it may generate new (outgoing) events and/or side effects such as modifying global variables. When the event handler terminates, the controlling loop repeats the remove-handle cycle.

Figure 11.4 indicates the modules of the run-time control mechanism that correspond to the N-CHIME architecture, Fig. 11.2. Device-level events are generated whenever the user presses a keyboard button or manipulates the mouse device. They can also be generated by event

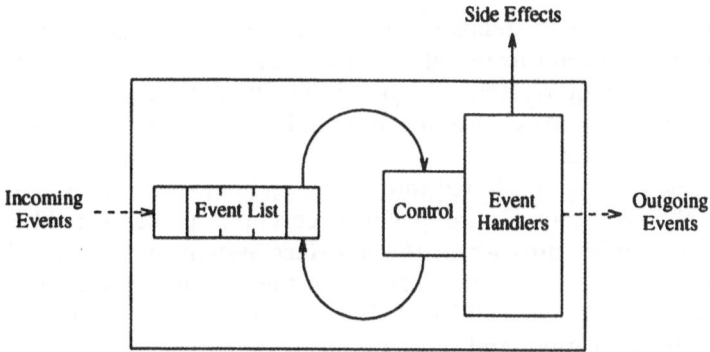

FIGURE 11.3. Structure of run-time control module.

handlers in a run-time control module. Dialog-level events are generated only by event handlers in a run-time control module. The HSL language processor and supporting tools are invoked by event handlers in the dialog-level run-time control module.

The specification of user-visible interaction techniques and aids (Step U-5 in Fig. 10.11) significantly impacts the interface software, and vice versa. As discussed in Chapter 6, interaction techniques are directly evident to the user, through output devices such as the CRT screen and input devices such as the keyboard and mouse. They are implemented through the PM of the N-CHIME architecture (Fig. 11.2). The DCM (and the rest of the architecture) should be independent of interaction technique. It should function according to the high-level model of language (dialog). For instance, the DCM is responsible for collecting the command and any parameters needed to invoke a support tool. It should not be concerned with how the command was selected, such as from a mouse-activated menu technique or from command line interaction with a keyboard. The mapping from the physical interaction activity to the dialog level is performed by the device-level event handlers. This mapping can be fairly straightforward when each command is involved in a single manner.

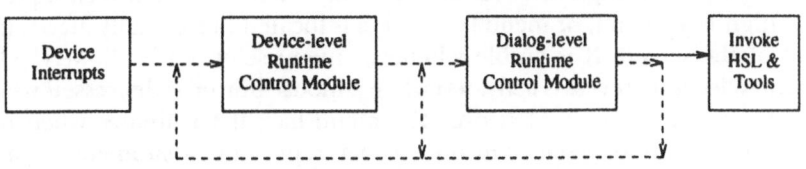

FIGURE 11.4. Event flow.

However, for a more complex design, e.g., incorporating adaptive capabilities, the decision to use alternative interaction techniques has to be dynamic and requires additional functionality (e.g., an intelligent agent), situated between the device interface and dialog control modules of the interface (Chapter 13).

Some aspects of selected interaction techniques are pervasive in the use of N-CHIME; others are specific to certain states or tools. The shared techniques apply throughout the interface system and act as bases for designing further interactive features in the future. They are ultimately dependent on the capabilities of the computer (*I*-factors), including the devices for user input and system output.

User-visible interaction in N-CHIME is undergirded by various interface structures (Treu, 1992), both at high and lower levels of representation. Illustrative are the high-level sessions phases (a vertical layering) and the state scenario graph (a network of states). At lower levels, organized layouts of the interface screen (in spatial reference patterns) must be combined with the bidirectional communication discipline (in half duplex or full duplex patterns). Such human–computer communication is of course intrinsic to the interaction dynamics and format. It must be effectively integrated into the interface, based on lower-level structures and within the confines or control of any higher-level structure.

All visible objects are shaped as rectangular windows. A window is not passive but is an active object with defined behaviors and attributes within the running N-CHIME software. Given N-CHIME's object orientation, a one-to-one correspondence exists between user-visible objects and internal software objects. A "responder" is a window which can respond to keystrokes and mouse events that occur when the text or mouse cursor is within its visible bounds. Complex visible objects can be composed from simpler ones. The window is the visible interface to N-CHIME tools. Within it the user can view and interact with the tools.

Interaction Techniques

Given these building blocks, a variety of interaction techniques were defined and utilized, as outlined in Section 11.4. Some of them are shared among different high-level states. The major item selection technique is the high-level menu, or menu bar, which is located horizontally across the top of the screen. It is visible whenever menu selection is allowed. The menu selection process is activated when a mouse button is depressed while the mouse cursor is located over the menu bar; it terminates when the button is released. Each item on the bar represents a submenu, which becomes visible when the mouse cursor passes over that item. Every item in this menu represents either an N-CHIME feature or a further submenu. The item at the mouse cursor position is visibly highlighted, and selection of an item occurs when the mouse button is released while the item is highlighted.

The main structure used to surround textual, command line interaction is the "dialog box." This is a window that appears on the screen under system control. It contains a prompting message describing the type of information required and a responder window to contain the entered text. The user types the required information, which is echoed in the responder window, then presses the Return/Enter key to terminate the interaction.

Some other interaction techniques are exclusively dependent on specific tools. For example, the HSL model browser ($O1$) allows the user to browse through a database of HSL models using the arrow keys on the keyboard to traverse lists of models. The feature-to-tool relationship may be one-to-one, many-to-one, or one-to-many. A one-to-one relationship suggests a feature is served by one particular tool; a many-to-one relationship implies a general tool can support several features; and a one-to-many relationship indicates a complex feature requiring two or more tools.

Another important feature is interactive assistance, which is invoked in special ways. N-CHIME offers two options: a tutorial available at the start and other forms of help available throughout an interaction session. Help is provided in a context-sensitive manner, dependent on the user's current goals (selected task plan) and current position relative to the defined session structure. The help feature is activated through a special key or, when a menu is available, through menu selection.

11.7. Hierarchical Interface Paradigms

As already asserted, the methodological steps of constructing a high-level, user-visible interaction scenario (e.g., Fig. 11.1) should be generalizable to other structurable applications. Also, the hierarchical relationships between high-level states (H-nodes) and their lower-level, context-specific support nodes (L- and O-nodes) can become generally useful paradigms in interface design.

They are depicted in Fig. 11.5 with regard to the "shared" versus "specialized" node dichotomy. The reasons for designer interest in this distinction are:

1. The resulting concentration of rendering a *consistent interface*, i.e., by requiring the same kinds of display formats and user actions for similar types of functionality

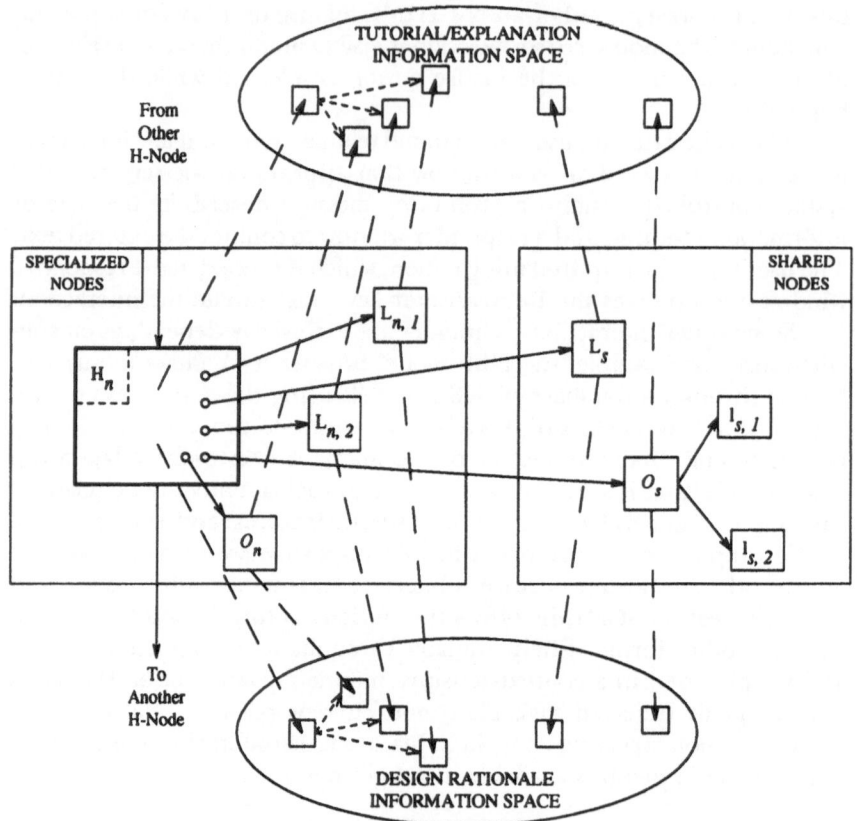

FIGURE 11.5. Design context for the *n*th high-level state.

2. More *efficient, object-oriented software design*, i.e., packaging the same
   functionality in a single, variable-content module, rather than
   redundantly duplicating it at different places
3. Together with (2), determining which types of repeatedly necessary functionality deserve special designer attention, either toward
   creating a corresponding *software tool* or, in case it might already
   exist as such, surveying the software area to locate such a tool for
   acquisition
4. Also in conjunction with (2) above, providing for more *efficient
   recordings of design decision rationales*, for those features and functions that are merely repetitions

The last of these leads to brief descriptions of the two state-specific information spaces depicted in Fig. 11.5 by the two oval areas. Although this model seems very abstract, it is nevertheless a legitimate design feature that can be integrated into the object-oriented software model of the interface. The two spaces are dedicated to providing usage tutorials and explanations and design decision rationales, respectively.

11.7.1. Explanation/Tutorial Space

Tutorial help can be made available, for the interested user, at the outset of an interactive session. It steps the user through an illustrative task plan. Then, both at the beginning and also at any other point (or state) of the session, the user can request an explanation. The object of that explanation can be global in nature, such as the total N-CHIME system or a selected H-node, or it can be oriented to low-level details, such as L-nodes, O-nodes, and HSL concepts and statements.

Explanation within any node provides information in the following general format:

1. *Locality*: identification of the state, or the context, within which the user's attention is currently focused
2. *Purpose*: what the user is able to decide or accomplish in this state, i.e., the state's objective(s)
3. *Actions*: the specific list of actions (or functions) that are available in this state for the user to select

These respond to the questions likely to be on the user's mind (Nievergelt and Weydert, 1980): Where am I? What can I do here? How did I get here? Where can I go and how do I get there?

11.7.2. Design Decision Space

With any high-level or low-level user state, represented by any H-node, L-node, or O-node, a special command is available for inquiry about the corresponding design rationale. Either a regular user or an interested designer can take advantage of this uncommon feature. Within the context of a user's current state (Fig. 11.1), the user can access and browse through the descriptions of locally relevant design decisions. For consistency, each state- (or node-) specific description is structured according to the format outlined below (in italics). Because the descriptions are rather lengthy (typically several typed pages each), an example is indicated only in abbreviated form, for the high-level state H1:

1. The *Design Object*, or the state identity: The current state/node (H1) is named, and a brief outline is presented of what the user can do locally (i.e., browse through a library of previously stored models; or obtain some local explanation) and what the options are as to where to move next (see arrows in Fig. 11.1).

2. Its *Dependencies* on any higher-level or lower-level states and tools: Identification of which states (preceding H1 in Fig. 11.1) can bring the user to the current state, with the resulting design implications. This state is dependent on certain local support nodes (type of selector, for presenting menu of choices; selector screen layout; and selection device, for input of user selection). It is functionally dependent on availability of the tool node, O1, designed to enable user browsing, storage, and retrieval of simulation models.

3. *Design Options* that were considered by the design team: Unique to state H1 are the design choices for providing BROWSING access to a library of models. The major options are outlined to include (a) searching through some SURROGATE level of model representation (e.g., model names, titles, descriptions, index terms), (b) displaying a GRAPHICAL representation of the model, and (c) displaying and scrolling through a PROGRAMMED representation.

4. *Design Decision* made: For state H1, it was decided that the initial BROWSER capabilities would be based on searching only on the model name (reflected by the file name), display of the corresponding HSL program and also a graphic version of the model, if someone previously created and stored it.

5. Design decision *Rationale*: Here the relevant design principles and factors as well as decision-supporting criteria (including any decision rules or thresholds) are pointed out. For state H1, the selected mode of browsing must be consistent with the forms of internal representation (of models) made available through N-CHIME. It was also influenced by the level of effort that had to be expended (administrative factor). The reasons for the design decision, therefore, are outlined to include the facts that the HSL-programmed models are stored in named files, which are organized hierarchically and alphabetically (A-factors). These, in turn, enable both the SURROGATE level screening by model name as well as the file access to display and scroll through the corresponding HSL PROGRAM. The latter is of course a result of user work carried out in state H3. Further, because state H2 enables user creation and storage of a GRAPHIC version of a model, the ability to display that in the current state, for user browsing, is also quite

possible. In any case, the feature provided in state H1 is consistent with the design principle of facilitating usage, especially by reinforcing a user's ability to conceptualize models.

It was not feasible, for the initial N-CHIME implementation, to provide for other modes of searching for existing models, other than through their representative names. However, such an extension is likely in the future.

Finally, a summary is given of the types of users (*U*-factors) who are likely to be served effectively by the implemented design options for state H1. They include (a) those who want to move expeditiously toward using a stored model (by simple scanning according to mnemonic name); they may not want to spend any time perusing them, (b) those who are well versed in reading and understanding HSL programs, perhaps without needing any graphic help to determine the model structures, etc., and (c) those who like or need to work by visual or graphic means, finding those more conducive to visualizing and understanding the nature of a stored model. In addition, the ability to present alternative browsing modes in parallel tends to make for an easily usable, powerful combination.

Recognition by HCI investigators that design decision rationales and other knowledge about interface designs should be recorded was discussed in Chapter 9. Although such recordings represent considerable additional effort, they lead to greater designer accountability and also facilitate transfer of designer knowledge to others. In view of having encouraged and illustrated decision-supporting schematics since Chapter 3, their inclusion in the recorded, on-line rationale is also highly recommended, when feasible. The portrait of how and why a designer decided in favor of a specific feature, in a particular state, is made much more vivid and recognized through graphic means.

11.8. Methodological Summary

The case study on the N-CHIME interface design can be summarized as follows:

1. *Design Method*: the three-pronged process of Fig. 10.11, which is a
   specialized version of the cause-and-effect method of Fig. 10.3.

Within that method and with regard to the parameters of Function (12.1), which symbolizes design decision-making:

2. *Design Principles*: P20, P13, P41, and later also P4 (Table 9.1), and various software engineering principles, as mentioned in Section 10.6.

3. *Design Factors*: A-factors resulting from analysis of the target application (Section 10.6) and U-factors resulting from characterizing the target (industrial) user; both analyses led to the need (or desirability) of giving structural support; identification of I-factors was carried out in conjunction with the design objects (this chapter) specified to instantiate the design features selected; other design factors were administrative in nature, e.g., directions given by the industrial sponsor.

Using those principles and factors as inputs, design decisions were reached with the help of design criteria. Following resulted:

4. *Design Features*: a composition of the following types:
   • A combination of several interaction techniques (Chapter 6), as outlined in Section 11.4; the resulting interaction style is a hybrid of those techniques; it is otherwise nondescript, except that it is composed/integrated by means of the following:
   • Superimposed representational models (Chapter 7), e.g., the user state scenario graph (Sections 11.2 and 11.3).
   • Supportive software organizational models (Chapter 8), involving an extended UIMS and object-oriented design (Section 11.6).
   • Special-purpose support model, transcending the other three feature types above, to provide context-specific explanations and to record design decision rationales (Section 11.7), including any relevant decision criteria.

It should be noted that the above summary of the N-CHIME design study was written after-the-fact. Consequently, it is not as thorough and concise as it could be. An objective of all HCI designers should be the careful, thorough, and comprehensible characterization of all major elements of methodology employed and the results achieved.

Exercises

11.1. Select an application (other than M&S) from Table 4.1 that you consider "structurable" and create a high-level user state scenario graph for it, analogous to the one of Fig. 11.1. As possible, identify different task plans (nodal paths) and distinguish their goals and applicability relative to different types of users.

11.2. Select an application from Table 4.1 that you consider to be (relatively) unconducive to being structured into a high-level user state scenario graph (like Fig. 11.1). Explain. Attempt to give it at least a minimal kind of structure (e.g., repeated loops between two prevalent states).

11.3. Focus on a generic, high-level state (or node) in a user state scenario graph. Any features that you, as a designer, specify for the user-visible interface should be either directly or indirectly associated with that state. If you treat the state as an "object," list all major types of features discussed in this book that can be (a) reflected by that object, as attributes, (b) contained or owned by that object, as components or subobjects, and (c) utilized by that object in association with other such objects, in a shared and transitional manner.

11.4. In previous chapters, the inputs to design decisions were depicted as requiring structure (e.g., via decision schematics). Now, in this chapter, the outputs of design, namely, the design features selected, are also presented as requiring structure. Discuss (and critique) the necessity and importance of this structure-oriented emphasis.

11.5. The state-specific "tools" of Section 11.5 should not be confused with the design "tools" of Chapters 7 and 8. However, the former can reflect the use of the latter. How can that be? What does that mean?

11.6. This chapter presents design objects (and modules and models) as representing the composite outcomes (features) determined from earlier detailed analyses (cause-and-effect) and decision-making. The latter involved taking relevant design factors (guided by design principles) and utilizing them to determine individual design features. Subsequently, we have been interested in composing and integrating those individual features into higher-level features (node objects). Which of the design approaches (Definitions 10.1 through 10.4) is/are representative of the pattern just described? Does your answer reinforce or contradict the design method portrayed by Fig. 10.3?

11.7. Given the description of the UIMS model in Chapter 8, how is the N-CHIME software architecture (a) the same, and (b) different?

11.8. Find and read a book about object-oriented software design, as it is defined in computer science. Is the abstract, high-level model of each N-CHIME state (object), as depicted in Fig. 11.5, consistent with such design? Explain.

11.9. Read the paper by Nievergelt and Weydert (1980). Is the locality–purpose–actions format of the explanations available in N-CHIME (as outlined in Section 11.7) adequate for answering the questions that are likely to be on a user's mind? Would you add any other parts to the format?

11.10. Read the paper by MacLean *et al.* (1989). Is the illustrative design decision rationale (listed, in abbreviated form, in Section 11.7) consistent with what the authors advocate about recordings of such rationales? How can it be improved?

SPECIAL-PURPOSE DESIGNS

The design definitions and methods that were presented in Part III are general-purpose in nature. That is, the designer is expected to select whatever combination of design principles (i.e., goals) is to be pursued and then to utilize the methodology as appropriate. A substantial variety of user-oriented design principles were profiled and numerous other principles can be formulated. Depending on which one(s) the designer chooses, a special set of design techniques and tools may become necessary. Accordingly, this part describes two special-purpose designs. Their main foci are on rendering the interface *network-oriented* (Chapter 12) and *adaptive* to the user (Chapter 13). The chapters illustrate how a particular design principle, especially one that is predominant, invokes special models and refinements within the design methodology, to ensure that the indicated goal(s) is(are) achieved.

NETWORK-ORIENTED DESIGN

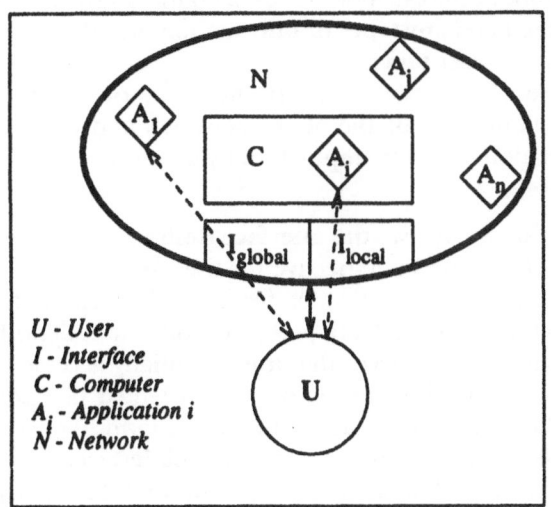

U - User
I - Interface
C - Computer
A_i - Application i
N - Network

12.1. Overview

Most HCI designs have focused on a user interacting with an application that is resident in a single computer system. Indeed, Chapters 9 through 11 took this approach. Whether or not the target computer is actually a node in a larger system, namely, a network of computers, is often treated as secondary if not altogether irrelevant. After all, as long as the user can somehow log into a remotely located computer and then be treated as if it were local, the network environment seems unimportant.

The view adopted in this chapter is that we should deliberately design the interface to relate to and take advantage of network context when applicable (Treu et al., 1989). The design principle of rendering the interface "network-oriented" (P29, Table 9.1) is the dominant goal. A corollary principle is for the interface to be context-providing (P13), specifically to include network-oriented context. As a result, the network should also be more "usable" and "sociable" (Taulbee et al., 1975) as well as

265

more "visualizable" (Treu, 1975b, 1990). Actually, "network" is used here to connote several different types of multicomponent patterns:

- A network of interconnected computers
- A network of computer applications and resources, spanning one or more computers
- A network of people (computer users) wanting to interact or collaborate with each other (e.g., in CSCW)
- A network of information nodes containing any data types (e.g., in hypertext) and any types of information, whether or not related to the current user task
- A network arrangement at the interface of different data types (representing any of the above networks and network nodes) for presentation to and manipulation by the user (e.g., in a multimedia interface)

To accommodate the above, the interface designer must create and reinforce a network-oriented perspective for the user.

First, in Section 12.2, motivation for network-oriented design is given. Then, several relevant models are presented. Section 12.3 profiles different kinds of information resources that are potentially accessible to the user, including those that reinforce the network-oriented perspective. Section 12.4 relates the network interface to the well-known hypertext and multimedia models. Section 12.5 describes a multilevel context model that distinguishes various layers of task-specific and task-peripheral interaction. The model can influence the organization of both the visible interface and the functionality of the supportive system behind it.

A prototype implementation is outlined in Section 12.6. It emphasizes the network-based collection and presentation of task-peripheral information. Finally, the chapter concludes with a description of a task-based cognitive model for user–network interaction.

12.2. Motivation

Present-day users are increasingly likely to have a PC or WS connected via one or more computer networks (e.g., Tanenbaum, 1988; Metcalfe and Boggs, 1976) to a variety of information systems and information types. The mental model that a user acquires and employs at an interface is very important, as discussed in Chapter 3. But, especially in the network-oriented situation, it is extremely dependent on what the designer conceives and implements.

The designer's conceptual model of a network-oriented user interface should be purposely extended to reinforce and enrich the user's mental model of both interface and network. Each individual user should be provided with information not only about a particular task, but also about any task-peripheral resources, activities, and events that might be of interest. These distinctions are drawn in Section 12.3. Further, the composite networkwide system should be user-accessible, at the visible interface, in a facilitated and logically organized manner.

Figure 12.1 indicates the general dichotomy. T_1 through T_n are used to denote the range (or set) of all possible types of information-creating, -storing, -seeking, -notifying, and -observing tasks across all information systems and applications in a particular network. The figure implies concern not only about a user's interaction local to an application or task, such as T_i. The interface must also encompass those information resources that are global in nature or situated in the surroundings. For this view of a networkwide information system, a global perspective, or "Networkanschauung" (Treu, 1988b), is required.

An analogy between human–computer interaction and human–human conversation may be useful, although it is not desirable to have all aspects of the latter emulated in the former (e.g., Nickerson, 1977). Certain characteristics such as "shared situational context" are relevant. Consider a person involved in a social or business gathering of a variety of people. Some of them may be very interesting; others not at all. Some may be very important and possibly necessary contacts; others may be irrelevant or useless. While conversing with a particular individual (i.e., accessing a specific information resource), the person in question may also attend (although to a lesser degree) to other stimuli that occur in the visible and

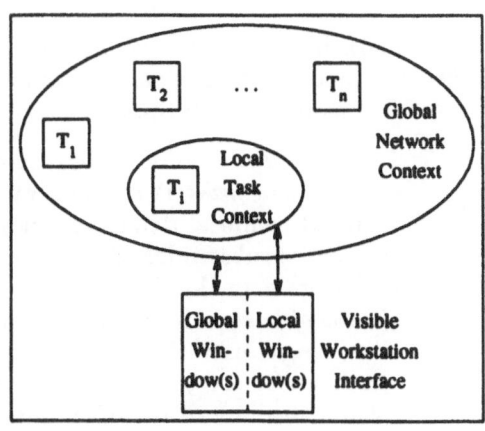

FIGURE 12.1. Local within global network context. [This figure and Figs. 12.2 through 12.6 are reprinted from *Information Systems*, Vol. 14, Treu *et al.*, "A Network-Wide Information System: Multi-Level Context for the User at the Workstation Interface," pp. 393–406, 1989, with kind permission from Pergamon Press Ltd., Heading-ton Hill Hall, Oxford OX3 0BW, UK.]

audible environment. In addition, he/she may wish to be informed (perhaps by the host) of other noteworthy events or opportunities (e.g., an important executive has just arrived, or a certain person is now standing alone and hence is available for conversation). This situation is analogous to a human user faced with a computer-based network of resources. Users need support for a more global perspective than what comes with attention to a single application-specific task in traditional interface design.

Such a perspective is not only intended for an individual user, as if in isolation. A user may want to cooperate or collaborate (e.g., in the sense of CSCW) with other users who have similar perspectives. All members of the group can then share both global context as well as the task-specific context. This relates to the features that have been suggested for face-to-face groupware (Elwart-Keys *et al.*, 1990), including the "What You See Is What I See" paradigm.

Capitalizing on the mind's natural capabilities, e.g., in spatial referencing, parallel information channels, association-based memory, and with suitable support, guidance, and reinforcement from the system, it is possible to utilize rich information resources much more effectively. Help from the system can be deliberately designed into the interface, if the designer's conceptual model includes the necessary levels and types of supportive, contextual information. We must not only provide what is minimally required by or local to the currently executed computer-aided task; we must ensure that the user, subject to his/her preferences and capabilities, is given well-structured access to all types of useful, network-based information.

12.3. Networkwide Resources Model

Remarkable advances have been made in the availability of increasingly voluminous, complex, and diverse information resources. A five-component model of such resources is outlined as follows:

1. *Controlling Entity:* The resources may be directly accessible in a *human-determined* (H) manner, by persons knowledgeable in the required technical details, or they may be contained within the confines of substantial *software* (S) packages, thereby shielding the user from many low-level details.

2. *Number of Users:* The resources may be intended for the independent, single user (1U), although other similar users may have simultaneous access, or they may be designed for the collective, collaborative use of multiple users (mU).

3. *Number of Computers:* The body of information may be situated in a single computer (1C) or network node, or it may be stratified or distributed among a number of interconnected computers (nC).
4. *Usage Interest:* The user's or user group's interest in accessing any such information resources may be very *task-specific* (TS) and thereby clearly defined and delimited, or it may be *task-peripheral* (TP), not necessarily related to the user's primary purpose.
5. *Usage Mode:* The mode of access may be *disjoint* (DISJ) in that the user interacts with a selected subsystem without any deliberate, interface-supported coordination or connection with any other subsystem. On the other hand, a mode may involve some kind of *connected* or *conjunctive* (CONJ) access among the different subsystems as well as a sense of *continuity* (for the user) on the interface display, with regard to how to move (mentally) among the variously displayed types of information and how to relate them to each other.

This five-component profile enables general categorization of existing information systems:

1. User-directed information creation, manipulation, and search systems {H; 1U; 1C; TS; DISJ}, including the traditional file systems, editors, etc., that an individual, skilled user can utilize on a selected computer
2. Software-packaged information updating, search, and retrieval systems, including:
   a. Individual (single-node) systems {S; 1U; 1C; TS; DISJ}, such as the well-known DBMS and bibliographic IS & R systems
   b. Distributed (multinode) systems {S; 1U; nC; TS; DISJ}, such as distributed DBMS and hypertext systems
   c. Coordinated systems {S; 1U; nC; TS; CONJ}, involving various software mechanisms for logically connecting selected information resources, to facilitate user access for task-specific purposes
3. Group-oriented information interchange systems {S; mU; 1C or nC; TS; DISJ}, including: CSCW systems and electronic mail systems
4. User-directed, network-oriented information systems {H; 1U; nC; TS or TP; DISJ}: these are the networkwide versions of category 1 above, requiring a user's detailed technical knowledge of how to access (e.g., rlogin to) different nodes and utilize their different file systems, editors, etc., as well as to check on network activity using any available network management tools.

As stated earlier, most attention has been paid to designing the DISJ and TS information systems that the user must call on separately. Although some research on the CONJ and TS category (2c above) has been carried out, little has been done to provide software-packaged (S) coordination of TS systems, either with each other or with TP systems. Ever-increasing numbers of network users are faced with this combination. Coherent, continuous, and manageable methods must be designed to support them.

The main focus of this chapter is on the composite, networkwide information system characterized by the {S; 1U; nC; TS and TP; CONJ} profile. The design and implementation of an illustrative prototype system are described in Section 12.6. The TP side of the TS + TP dichotomy is emphasized.

12.4. Hypertext and Multimedia Models

The term "hypertext," (also "hypermedia") has become very popular in recent years (e.g., Conklin, 1987; Halasz, 1988), although it was already used and pursued a quarter of a century ago (as discussed in Chapter 1). It denotes any approach to organizing and accessing information such that

1. The data are stored in a network of nodes.
2. The nodes are variously interconnected by links.
3. The nodes can contain any data types, including text, programs (source code), graphics, video, audio, etc.

This organization is then intended to be searched, manipulated, and viewed interactively. The concept of hypertext was recognized years ago. Starting with Bush's (1945) memex ideas and through innovative system designs by investigators like Engelbart and English (1968), in their hierarchical file system (NLS), the importance of imposing networks of association links on sets of different information items was demonstrated.

Because any types of data are allowable in the nodes of a hypertext system, and since the users should be able to access and obtain outputs from all of them, the interface must obviously be capable of presenting the different data types in effective ways. This promotes increasing attention to *multimedia* interface designs (e.g., Hodges and Sasnett, 1992). Several exercises at the end of this chapter relate to this topic.

Hypertext can apply to the local, task-specific interaction (Fig. 12.1) with an information system containing a variety of logically interconnected types of information through which the user must navigate (e.g.,

Utting and Yankelovich, 1989; Rein and Ellis, 1991; Nielsen, 1990). Second, at a hierarchically higher level, each network node can itself contain a separate information system (e.g., a DBMS), and the user's application may require access to the logical composite of several such systems. Both interpretations are "consistent" with the definition of hypertext in its broadest sense. Such *hypertext-consistent* applications require that the interface be designed to be supportive of whatever particular patterns are involved.

But first, beyond the task-specific focus, other kinds of useful information in the network environment can be produced. These constitute the "complement" of the local (hypertextlike) task domain (Fig. 12.1) and may include information that is:

- Temporary in terms of life span or usefulness and hence in duration of storage
- A result of real-time monitoring, measurement, and analysis of various network activities and events
- Supportive or peripheral to the primary application or task being carried out, as opposed to being an integral part of it
- Descriptive of other available applications, totally unrelated to the current work, including necessary instructions and guidelines for utilizing them

Such information can be termed *hypertext-complementary*, and it may itself be structured in a hypertext-consistent way (Exercise 12.5). The information may be user-requested or it may be automatically provided by processes designed to be active in various network nodes. The range of different information resources is treated as if it were a collection of uniformly accessible objects.

The patterns should affect the design of the visual layout and its multimedia capabilities. Because of the complexity of a network-oriented, hypertextlike information system, *logically layered or partitioned display organization* is desirable. For a user, trying to cope with an assortment of information types, the visible, multimedia interface must be very carefully organized. The layout should be predictable and nonoverwhelming. The natural mental capabilities and inclinations of the user should be reinforced, e.g., through concepts like "cognitive layouts" of the screen (Norman *et al.*, 1986). A general, multilevel context model is described in the next section.

Furthermore, the display organization must support *continuity in layer transitions*. This relates to the desired concept of "visual momentum" as the user's mind transitions across window boundaries (Woods, 1984). To present a well-organized composite, even within limitations of display size and capability, the system must try to facilitate contiguous, continuous mental movement between nodes and from one layer or partition (e.g., task-specific) to another one (e.g., task-peripheral). In doing so, it is important to minimize disruptions or total replacements of one display mode/ medium with another. This point relates to the mental effort imposed on users by having to make transitions between different interface structures during an interactive session (Treu, 1994).

12.5. Multilevel Context Model

In this chapter, we identified several different types of networks: (1) networks of computers, (2) networks of applications/tasks, (3) networks of users (e.g., in CSCW), (4) networks of different data types (e.g., nodes in hypertext), and (5) networks of different output media to represent any/all of the above networks and nodes within them. The last of these, combined with the TS + TP dichotomy, prompts us to organize the visible user interface in some manner. One way is to use a layered organization.

To impose a layered structure on a composite, networkwide information system, the layers must be properly defined. We do so in terms of levels of context, relating to one of the basic interface structures (Treu, 1992). Other patterns are possible, especially if necessitated by physical constraints of the (multimedia) interface (Exercise 12.8).

The meaning of interaction context was given by Definition 6.11. For network-oriented design, context is equivalent to the information environment, which in some sense surrounds the primary task a user is currently trying to accomplish within the network of computer-based resources. That environment consists of the universe of facts, patterns, relationships, conditions, activities, directions, circumstances, and backgrounds—all pertaining to the primary task of the user, although to greatly varying degrees or extents.

But more exact definitions of the contextual layers are needed. Just as a user's mental model should have order and directionality to it, interface context should be structured meaningfully and in correspondence to expectations of the user's mind. It is then more likely to have favorable influence on the user's mental model and performance.

A very high-level model is the local–global dichotomy depicted in Fig. 12.2. The interface modules and the visible regions of the screen simply separate the task-specific (local) layer from the context-providing (global) layer. The distinction is consistent with Fig. 12.1. But it really needs refinement to make it more realistic and useful.

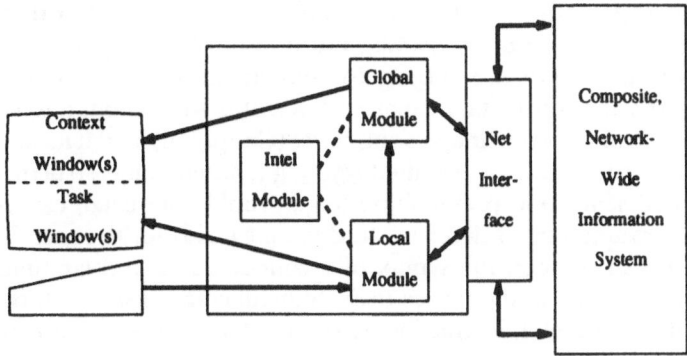

FIGURE 12.2. A user's information-gathering workstation.

12.5.1. Task-Specific (Local) Context

A four-level model is shown in Fig. 12.3. The lowest two levels, *task-inherent* and *task-supportive*, and part of the third, *task-enhancing*, are considered to be *task-specific* or *local* to the task. The remainder of the third level, *task-enhancing*, plus Level 4, *task-peripheral*, are said to be *global* to the task. *Local* context is information relevant to the user's current task. It does not imply that execution of the task is taking place in the local workstation. It may be executed in any network node. Furthermore, the selected task may only be one among many that can be performed in the network environment. Given the necessary global context, the user may want to switch to some other task or, in some cases, perform two or more tasks in parallel.

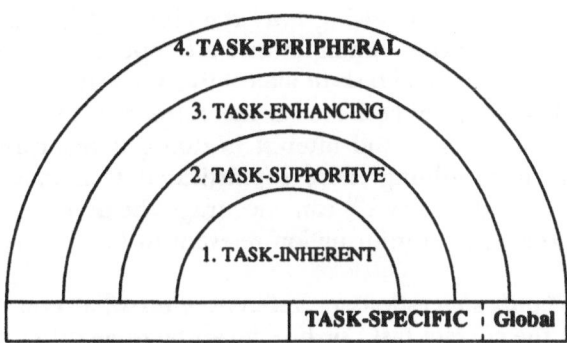

FIGURE 12.3. Four-level interface context model.

The task model is primarily relevant to the fifth level of the layered structure of HCI design (Fig. 4.2), but it also relies on lower levels. The layers of the model are subject to refinement into sublevels. This is particularly true of the task-inherent layer. It is wide enough to subsume different interaction techniques and styles (Chapter 6), and it itself exhibits a kind of context. The terminology (e.g., mnemonic), structure (e.g., logical ordering), and presentation (e.g., graphic or visual) can produce special prompts, cues, inferences, and memory aids for the user. This is a basic form of context; the syntax of a concise command language gives cues on semantics to the novice user (Shneiderman, 1983). On the other hand, if the Level 1 interaction is oriented to manipulation of visual objects, the inherent cues are at a higher, more conceptual and semantic (as opposed to syntactic) level.

The second form of task-specific context is directly supportive or immediately surrounding the task. Included are various forms of help and explanation, whether explicitly requested by the user or automatically (perhaps adaptively) produced by the system. The focus of such assistance can be on individual commands, task plans (or paths), error conditions, and other objects or events. Adaptively provided help (Chapter 13) is relevant here. Separation of the task-supportive level from Level 1 is justified by the following criterion: a knowledgeable user should be able to complete a task within the task-inherent level alone, i.e., without information from the task-supportive level. However, a learning or less experienced user may find Level 2 context not only desirable but essential.

Levels 1 and 2, combined, still amount to a limited-perspective view of a user communicating with a resource (e.g., a DBMS, an operating system, a text editor) located somewhere in the network. For all practical purposes, as far as the user's mental model of that user-network interface is concerned, the rest of the network resources might as well not be there. This motivates the inclusion of task enhancement features, suggested by Level 3 in Fig. 12.3. The task-enhancing level remains largely task-specific, although it may also provide stimuli for user attempts at other relevant tasks or at performing the same task in alternative ways. It also remains task-supportive. However, unlike Level 2, the support is less direct. It is to enhance the user's ability and interest in doing things differently, with more insight, and utilizing more sophisticated techniques. Again, an adaptive interface (Chapter 13) can encourage the user in that direction.

Among the types of information relevant to Level 3 are:

1. *Procedural:* suggestions or references on what else can be done (with the current task) or how it can be done differently or more effectively; examples can be provided to the user.

2. *Resources:* suggestions or references on which relevant information resources (both computer-based and human) are available (for the current task) and how they can be accessed or contacted.

3. *Presentation:* orderly, compacted or abstracted portrayals, using visual, graphic, and other techniques, of the changing status and ultimate results of the execution of the current task in the network environment, especially if that task has distributed aspects to it, such as in hypertext (involving two or more network nodes and resources).

The criteria for separating task-supportive context from task-enhancing context are different than those for the lowest two layers. Task-enhancing context is more likely to be of interest to the user who is actively advancing his/her knowledge of the network and who wants to progress beyond the minimal understanding of how a task can be carried out (Levels 1 and 2).

12.5.2. Task-Peripheral (Global) Context

Finally, the highest, *task-peripheral* level of the model supplies context that is independent of, or peripheral to, the task. As stated earlier, the task-enhancing context of Level 3 might give the user ideas on trying other things, aborting a task, or focusing on other objectives. But, analogous to the person talking with someone else in a crowd (Section 12.2), there may be activities and events, unrelated to the current conversation, about which the individual may want or need to be informed. In part, it pertains to giving the user (group) awareness of who is "around," what is going on, etc. (Dourish and Bly, 1992).

To foster that kind of networkwide view in the user's mental model, interprocess communication mechanisms must be implemented to enable systematic, user-specific gathering and presentation of the collectible, measurable, and reportable information the user may want to see, whether or not it has anything to do with the current task. Care and discretion must be exercised to distinguish between public or specifically authorized information and information that is private or confidential. The potential categories of information are:

1. *Network-oriented,* including: network (communication) load and status, availability of information resources and other network facilities, gateways (to other networks)

2. *System-oriented,* including: system (cpu) load, availability of files, peripherals, job status, and other administrative information

3. *Users and user groups,* including: electronic mail arrival, list of current users, cooperative work events (e.g., a co-author has finished editing a file)

4. *Other activities and events*, not included among the above, for which programs to collect and analyze the data can be written. These are very user-specific and allow for a great deal of flexibility and expansion.

The first three categories are implementable by tying mostly into existing facilities and command structures within the network-oriented systems. The fourth category provides for custom-made capabilities for gathering any collectible (and appropriately authorized) information, as long as the necessary procedures/processes can be created and then situated at suitable collection points. Some of the task-peripheral information may still have a bearing on the current task, although only indirectly or by inference. On the other hand, much of the information may have no relationship to the task at all. This distinction suggests a further division of the task-peripheral layer, into *task-related* and *task-independent* sublevels (not shown in Fig. 12.3).

An information system application (e.g., DBMS, IS&R, hypertext) is an example of task-specific work by a user at Levels 1 through 3. The hypertextlike complement thereof is the supplementary or task-surrounding information of Level 4. The primary emphasis in the prototype described below is on Level 4. That level is desirable for users who are capable of attending to and learning about other activities and information resources in the network, beyond those that are tied to the primary task.

12.6. A Context-Providing Prototype

A prototype system for gathering global context information (Treu *et al.*, 1989) was implemented by Paul Mullins with the help of Joel Adams. It used an ethernet style LAN consisting of SUN workstations and a VAX 11/780. All communication between processes was via virtual circuits (stream sockets) in the INTERNET domain. Each of the host machines was running a UNIX operating system. Modularity was maintained so the code could be used for either a workstation (with additional interface code) or on a multiuser host (VAX or SUN).

Figure 12.4 shows the interprocess communication scheme employed. Notice the general correspondence to Fig. 12.2. The dashed lines represent transient connections established via virtual circuits. One workstation is shown gathering information from a network of hosts. The workstation host can itself be a network host. Commands are run and controlled by a child process of one of the processes. Although not shown, the I/O devices

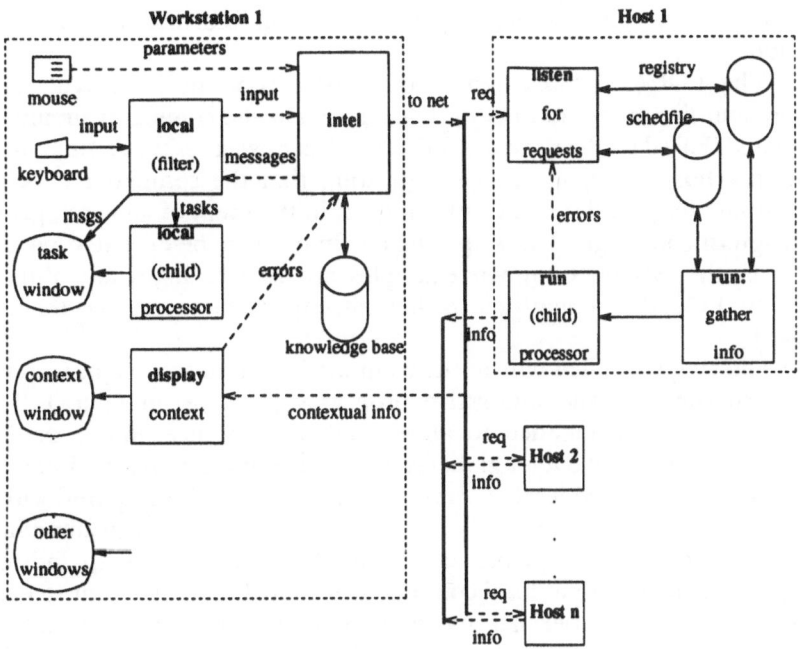

FIGURE 12.4. Interprocess communication.

of the workstation interact normally with the Suntools environment, as suggested by *other windows*.

Each host must be able to accept a request for information, gather it, and return it to the source of the request. The host may disseminate information autonomously or respond to explicit requests. Further, each host can vary its degree of cooperation (perhaps for security reasons) by restricting the types of requests it responds to or by not participating at all.

Two main processes provide service. A LISTEN process accepts requests for a particular host. A RUN process handles the gathering and dissemination of information. There is also a third process which may be invoked remotely to restart one process each of LISTEN and RUN. The LISTEN process waits for requests directed at a well-known network address. Each such request is parsed before sending an acknowledgment to its source.

Every user has an associated set of local processes forming the interface. It includes: a LOCAL process that filters commands and controls task-specific execution in a *task* window; an intelligent process, intel, which relieves the user of unnecessary specification; a DISPLAY process that formats and outputs the highest-level contextual information in a *context* window.

The LOCAL process reads commands from the keyboard. Each command line is sent to intel to determine how the command should be handled. Based on the response, LOCAL either executes the command on the task host, prints a message indicating that the command is being scheduled for global context gathering, or, in the event of an error, prints a diagnostic message. A task-specific command may be executed on any host in the system. Common examples are remote login and remote editing. LOCAL also manages the help facility when accessed via the keyboard.

Filtering is applied only at the command level, not to the interaction between the user and interactive programs (such as an editor). The filtering action is intended to allow intel to recognize and/or modify commands to be sent out for global context gathering. At present, intel can only provide a limited level of service. Each command is compared with a list of preidentified commands for possible errors or special handling. Intel may also trigger global execution of a command as an indirect response to a user-input local command. A global request is sent to each host in which the user has indicated interest, for remote execution. Repeated failure to respond causes intel to attempt to start new service processes on the offending host, providing a type of system reset capability.

The DISPLAY process (Fig. 12.4) simply waits for contextual information from remote, or local, sources. The information is accompanied by a type indicator which determines the format of the output. DISPLAY formats the data appropriately and sends it to a context window. It is also possible to receive an error indication from a remote source. Whenever an error is received, DISPLAY sends a similar indication to intel for appropriate action.

Local (task-specific) execution of commands provides access to all standard UNIX facilities, including other hosts, except the shell (command interpreter) itself. Each command is executed as a child process in a new shell. Other details on the interface software are available (Treu *et al.*, 1989).

12.6.1. Activating the Interface

The prototype enables an individual user to collect networkwide, task-peripheral information and to display it using a layered screen organization. The kinds of information that can be gathered are those pertaining to status and availability of network-based resources (computers, software, databases, jobs, and also users), as outlined in Section 12.5.

Requests for such global information can be *initiated* in any of the following modes:

- By the *User*:
    1. *Explicitly* authorized *during session start-up*, by adding to the user's stored profile of such requests in each network-based host. This results in prespecified or preprogrammed requests for execution at periodic (or other) intervals.
    2. *Explicitly* entered commands *during real-time interaction*. Such commands must be uniquely prefixed to designate global execution.
- By any *Network Host*: based on its stored profile of such requests, as authorized by each individual user (above).
- By the *User's Workstation*: based on parsing of the user's task-specific commands by the intelligent (intel) module. If it decides that certain task-peripheral information would be useful to the user at a point in time, it issues the global command(s) on its own. To accomplish this option, a knowledge base about user preferences, capabilities, and interests must be utilized in conjunction with appropriate expert system technology. Such capability is described in Chapter 13 but was not implemented for this project.
- By a *System/Network Administrator*: when some global information is to be broadcast to all or to some group of network users. The workstation can accept such information and present it to the user in the task-peripheral pattern of windows.

The first three, above-implied "requests" for global information must be one of: (1) literal commands (e.g., for UNIX) and associated parameters, that can be executed on the target network host, (2) literal commands that can be translated by the local workstation into commands known to and executable on a particular network host, or (3) user-created "commands," that is, identifiers and associated parameters for specially designed, programmed procedures, already stored and executable in a network host. The actual code for such procedures is only transmitted once, during the initial start-up phase.

12.6.2. Interface Layout and Features

An approximation to the model of Fig. 12.3 was used for the prototype. Several of the features indicated below were implemented; others were not but can be. The semicircular layer boundaries can each have variable radii, so that the user can expand or contract them (or have intel do it adaptively) in correspondence to current user activity and display area requirements. The different layers could be distinguished (e.g., with different colors, labels) and change in size but should always remain in fixed relative order. This requirement is consistent with the user's natural inclination to remember and find information by position.

Within existing limits of available display area, each layer can contain as many or as few windows as appropriate. User focus and activity should orchestrate which ones, in which layer(s), should be enlarged and which ones might be scaled down, perhaps to icon size, or totally removed. Explicit sunbeam-like connections between related windows across respective layers can be helpful. It can reinforce the desired mental association and continuity between a window in one layer and a related window in another.

A simplified version based on the above features is shown in Fig. 12.5. It reduces the layering to the task-specific and task-peripheral dichotomy. Where known relationships between local and global windows exist, explicit association links can be displayed. While this layout is somewhat more practical, it still is not convenient for any reasonable mapping into commonly used workstation display areas. We, therefore, took the semicircular arrangement (two upper quadrants) of Fig. 12.5 and cut it symmetrically in half. The result is the "left upper quadrant" shown in Fig. 12.6. The user can interact with the system using either the menu-based technique or the command line (keyboard) technique.

All output from global command execution is displayed in context windows. The form of output is determined by an encoded *type* value, which is passed along with each command. The amount of output must be reduced to bare essentials, while still providing the required contextual information. Often the output is more appropriately displayed as the

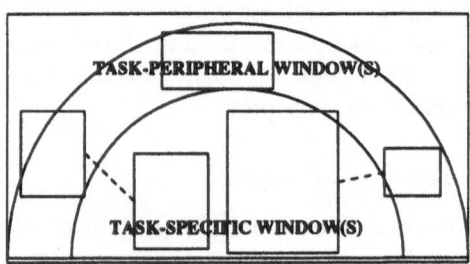

FIGURE 12.5. Dichotomous screen layout.

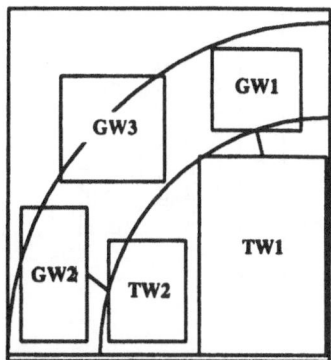

FIGURE 12.6. Condensed (left upper quadrant) layout.

different between current execution and the previous. We used a system utility (diff) to provide this function. Various improvements (such as graphical output of information, pop-up windows when required, creation of icons to indicate availability of more detailed output, and hierarchically structured output) can be added.

Consistent with the model (Fig. 12.6), the context windows are physically separated from the interactive task windows. Some forms of contextual information deserve the prompt attention of the user. This information may be of a system nature (equipment on/off line) or more personal (an important background job just completed). In either case, the user's attention can be drawn to the context window using a visual or audio cue. Depending on display type, some output is visually highlighted and/or sounds the terminal bell. These options are generally chosen by the user but may happen by default according to the specific command, or the user's stored profile.

12.6.3. Illustration of Use

To illustrate how the system works, a time step-oriented protocol can be used. It is depicted by the combination of Tables 12.1 and 12.2. The example was prepared by Paul Mullins. The columns of Table 12.1 refer to the five, labeled windows in Fig. 12.6. For the example, the task-specific window TW1 is associated with the task-related, global window GW1. Likewise, windows TW2 and GW2 are associated. Lastly, the fifth window, namely, GW3, is task-independent.

Table 12.1 displays what a particular user is doing in one or two task windows and what contextual information is provided in one, two, or three

TABLE 12.1
Multiwindow Workstation Protocol[a]

Time	Task 1 (TW1)	Global1 (GW1)	Task2 (TW2)	Global2 (GW2)	General (GW3)
1	Primary task window (shell emulation)	TW1-related context messages go here			Context messages: initial display of load, time and calendar messages
2	rlogin to syst2				D: load on syst2
3	g: monitor coauthors	coauthor: Jones on syst2 current DB state:			D: load & time
4	Invoke author tool on database (DB)	DB.C locked by Jones			...
5	Edit file DB.A	Mullins: lock DB.A			...
6	(editing)	D: DB accesses & coauthors			Mail on syst1 from Treu
7	(pause)	Jones: unlock DB.C	Secondary task: invoke mailtool	TW2-related context info (mail) goes here	D: load & time
8		D: DB accesses & coauthors	Read mail (about a conference in progress) from Treu	Mail from Jones	D: load & time
9		Jones: lock DB.B	Read the message from Jones. Exit the mailtool	...	D: mail info, load & time

10		**D:** DB accesses & coauthors	Invoke on-line conference tool	**D:** conferees & documents available *Mullins: joins*	⋯
11	(continued editing of DB.A)	*Jones: unlock DB.B*	(monitor)	*Jones: quits; doc2.8 available*	⋯
12		*Warning: Lock conflict on DB.A by Jones*	Scan document doc2.8; converse with conferees	**D:** conference info	⋯
13	Complete editing of file DB.A	*Jones: quit authoring; Mullins: unlock DB.A*	(monitor)	⋯	
14	Exit author tool	*Mullins: quit authoring*	⋯	⋯	⋯
15	Invoke the mailtool; send a note to Jones	**D:** mail info	⋯	⋯	⋯
16	Exit mailtool	**D:** coauthors	⋯	**D:** mail info	
17	**g:** stop monitoring coauthors		⋯	*Warning: meeting in 15 minutes!!*	
18	Exit conf tool	*Mullins quits*	Exit conf tool		
19	Delete window TW2	GW2 deleted also	Delete window TW2	**D:** load & time	⋯

ᵃModified from *Information Systems*, Vol. 14, Treu et al., "A Network-Wide Information System: Multi-Level Context for the User at the Workstation Interface," pp. 393–406, 1989, with kind permission from Pergamon Press Ltd., Headington Hill Hall, Oxford OX3, OBW, UK.

TABLE 12.2
Protocol for Context Gathering[a]

Time	Reaction	Autonomous
1	Start-up procedure. Accept broadcasts from netload, syst1-load, and mail monitor. Start time & calendar monitors (agents)	Begin net-load broadcasts, syst-load broadcasts, users on systems, and mail monitors (if required) **B:** *Mullins on syst1*
2	Accept syst2-load messages	Begin syst2-load broadcasts
3	Start user process to watch for login or logout of coauthors (use login broadcasts)	
4	Begin monitoring access to DB files— accept broadcasts about DB	
5		**B:** *Mullins: lock on DB.A*
6		**B:** *mail on syst1 for Mullins, from Treu*
7	Send mail-related information to GW2	**B:** *Jones unlocks DB.C*
8		**B:** *mail on syst1 for Mullins, from Jones*
9	Send mail-related information to GW3	**B:** *Jones: lock on DB.B*
10	Request broadcasts on conferees and related documents	Broadcast names of conferees & documents **B:** *joined conference: Mullins*
11		**B:** *left conference: Jones* **B:** *Smith: document doc2.8 available* **B:** *Jones: unlock DB.B*
12		**B:** *Warning: Jones: attempt to lock DB.A*
13		**B:** *Jones: quit author tool* **B:** *Mullins: unlocks DB.A*
14	Stop monitoring DB access	**B:** *Mullins: quit author tool*
15	Send mail-related information to GW1	
16	Send mail-related information to GW3	**B:** *Mullins: sent mail to Jones*
17	Abort processes watching for coauthors	**B:** *Calendar: you have a meeting in 15 minutes*
18	Stop monitoring conference	**B:** *Mullins: left conference*
19	Redirect all GW2 info to GW3	

[a] Modified from *Information Systems*, Vol. 14, Treu *et al.*, "A Network-Wide Information System: Multi-Level Context for the User at the Workstation Interface," pp. 393–406, 1989, with kind permission from Pergamon Press Ltd., Headington Hill Hall, Oxford 0X3, 0BW, UK.

of the global windows. Table 12.2, on the other hand, shows the corresponding behavior of the global context-gathering software. In Column 1, it lists the system's immediate reactions to user actions that either involve *explicit* commands (preceded by g:) or that contain *implied* requests for contextual information. Examples are indicated at time Steps 3 and 4, respectively. Column 2 of Table 12.2 shows the system's actions taken autonomously, based on initial (start-up) authorization or the stored user profile as well as on any standing (task-duration) requests resulting from current user activity.

Italics in the two tables indicate specific messages transmitted and displayed. General messages are identified by the preceding **B:**, when sent out or broadcast (in Table 12.2), and by the preceding **D:**, when displayed in a window of Table 12.1.

At start-up time (0), the system is assumed to have been invoked, creating only windows TW1, GW1, and GW3, along with any associated processes. The context gathering system is also started at this time, if it is not already running. Collected information can be either user-specific or of common interest (to any user with access to this software), such as network load. But the individual user can choose not to accept broadcast information. In the example, the user does not receive broadcasts of all names of other users logged in. Instead, that information is used as input to a customized routine looking for a particular set of users (the co-authors).

The user in the example is generally interested in database editing work, as a co-author, along with attending to mail and conferencing information. As a result, as the user moves into a parallel (two-task) mode at Step 7, a separate task window (TW2) as well as the associated global window (GW2) are opened. Later on, at Step 19, they are again closed.

The protocol illustrates the system in a relatively limited manner. It does not demonstrate the creation and display of more complicated types of global information, based on user-specific, custom-made processes (or programmed procedures) executing in various network nodes. An example would be a standing current awareness request, processed against daily updated retrieval systems or statistical reports, based on a user's topical interest profile. In addition, the tables do not exhibit the potential power of adaptive actions taken by a more intelligent (intel) module in the interface (Chapter 13); nor do they show how the more complex and voluminous outputs of contextual information could be displayed using graphical and multimedia interaction techniques (Chapter 6).

12.6.4. Observations

In Section 12.3, a networkwide information resources model was characterized. The following profile applies to the prototype system we implemented: {S; 1U; nC; TS and TP; CONJ}. That is, it is a networkwide (nC), software-packaged (S) information system that composes both task-specific (TS) and task-peripheral (TP) information resources in a conjunctive (CONJ), visually coordinated, and spatially structured layout at the workstation interface.

The primary design principles pursued are to render the interface network-oriented (P29) and context-providing (P13). Some of the design features selected (e.g., interaction techniques) are well-known and have been used in numerous individual information systems. The prototype is different because it (1) integrates the features into a network-oriented composite, (2) encompasses both task-specific and task-peripheral information resources in a coordinated manner, and (3) assists the user actively (through network agents and/or the intel module) to collect relevant task-peripheral information. Although the user has the option of issuing explicit global requests while working in task-specific mode, he/she can instead rely on the autonomous, preprogrammed context gathering by the network-based software. Except in moving visually from one window to another in a logical pattern, the user does not have to make a total switch from a task-specific subsystem to an independent, global subsystem. They are coordinated and displayed in parallel on a layered interface surface.

The prototype was only intended to serve as a research vehicle. This means that its operational efficiency has not as yet been of major concern. The system can produce a substantial overhead in a network, especially if every user has a personal copy of the software installed. One approach to alleviating that difficulty is to provide more types of global information, which might be of common interest to many users, through centralized servers in the network. The prototype does include that kind of centralized resource sharing, as is implied by the messages that can be broadcast to any interested users.

A number of extensions and improvements are indicated. Much more functionality can be built into the intel module. Also, we can envision the distribution of emissary expert systems to selected nodes in the network. They could collect only user-specific information (i.e., according to a particular user's U-factors) and be controlled by a managing expert system in that user's workstation.

Also, much more research is necessary on how to present information of different types and volumes in more meaningful and concise forms. This is a potentially rich area of application of novel techniques in visual information processing, organization, and presentation. The prototype as implemented was not intended to illustrate full multimedia interface capabilities. However, these should ultimately be part of a system of the type represented.

12.7. Network Tasks: A Cognitive Model

This chapter has dichotomized the task-specific and task-peripheral aspects of network-oriented interface design and, then, paid primary attention to the task-peripheral side. But much can be said about the task-specific side as well, that is, about the need for clear and consistent definition of all tasks to be carried out by users in network environments.

The need to consider a user's ability to conceptualize or visualize what is available and what is going on in a single computer also extends to the network interface. The designer should help the user to construct an appropriate mental model and then reinforce that model by making the necessary functionality available in the network and visible at the network interface. An example is the model of Fig. 12.7. It uses a tool kit as a metaphor.

To utilize such a model, especially in the context of a decentralized network involving a heterogeneous assortment of hardware and software, the interface (I) should support the user's (U) interaction with any network-based application domain (A) with a clearly defined set of available tasks. Most important here is the design principle of consistency (P12, Table 9.1). Regardless of how a task is actually implemented using the software and hardware of a particular interface, its high-level definition and functions should be consistent throughout the network. Whatever tools are involved in performing the task, they should enable the same kinds of manipulations or operations wherever they are applicable. Hence, they should also be uniformly available (P42) and clear in terminology needed to invoke them (P7).

A substantial hierarchy of network-oriented tasks has been developed and evaluated (Mullins, 1990; Mullins and Treu, 1993). This was done in correspondence to the components of a special-purpose cognitive model developed for a user information processing system. It resulted in 89 basic tasks being represented by leaf nodes in the task hierarchy. Although there are a number of similarities to the task actions that are listed in Table 4.2,

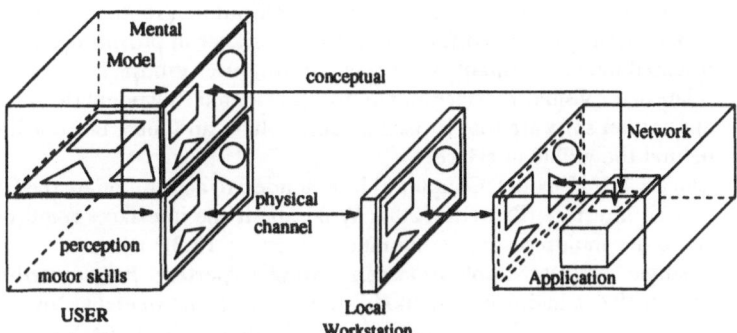

FIGURE 12.7. Tool-based consistency model. [Reprinted from Mullins and Treu (1993) with permission of Butterworth-Heinemann, Ltd.]

the network-oriented taxonomy is very structured and much more extensive. Hence, it is also too lengthy to be included here. A prototype interface (NUIS) was implemented (Mullins, 1990) to illustrate a selected subset of the tasks.

The main purpose of this brief discussion is to advocate that designers of network-oriented interfaces extend the task analysis defined in Chapter 4 to include the special considerations related to the network environment. Definitions of tasks that are clear, consistent, and uniform, while transcending different systems and application domains, will tend to avoid user confusion and thereby facilitate the user's job.

Exercises

12.1. The networkwide resources model described in Section 12.3 is a special refinement of the three-entity model ($U–I–A$) emphasized throughout this book. For each of the five components, identify which one (or more) of the three major entities is being "refined" or qualified, and how.

12.2. With reference to Exercise 12.1, the resources model can be interpreted as involving:
   (a) One *or* more users, wanting access to
   (b) One *or* more applications/tasks, resident in
   (c) One *or* more computers
   and the user(s) should be able to gain such access via *one* composite, user–network interface design. How many possible combinations of single/multiple resources are there (assuming two choices for each above-indicated resource)? Given the outline of "existing information systems" in Section 12.3, which of those combinations is/are represented? Which ones are not? Do we have a need for the latter types of systems?

12.3. CSCW is listed as an application in Table 4.1. With regard to the resources model of Section 12.3, it can be viewed as involving application software that enables a group of users to have coordinated access to the software resources resident in one or more computers. Hence, it is like superimposing a network of users on a network of computers (Taulbee *et al.*, 1975). What are the principal difficulties for the designer in providing a network-oriented interface suitable for a collaborating user group? Do they mainly relate to the visible interface and its group-oriented functionalities, or to the application software that is resident somewhere and must be coordinated behind the visible interface?

12.4. Can the UIMS model (Chapter 8) be extended to accommodate the CSCW type of interface (Exercise 12.3)? What about the interfaces required for any other multiresource combination (Exercise 12.2)? Discuss.

12.5. A single-computer application can involve hypertext. But, according to Section 12.4, a high-level multinode application can be viewed as "hypertext-consistent," while the task-peripheral information is "hypertext-complementary" as well as hypertext-consistent. All of that terminology may be quite confusing. Try to clarify it by the use of graphs, G_L, G_H, and G_P

which are initially disconnected but then become subgraphs of a composite, hypertextlike space. Suppose G_L represents the graph for an ordinary hypertext application. Then, at a higher level, it becomes a subgraph (representing only a single, logical node) in a graph, G_H, which encompasses a number of hypertext and other applications in its interconnected set of nodes. Finally, graph G_P represents the hypertextlike nodes containing peripheral (or contextual) information of interest to users. The nodes of G_P are variously connected to (selected) nodes of either G_L or G_H, or both, depending on time-based or other types of associations. Draw an example of the above kind of composite graph, labeling its nodes and arcs to illustrate the components and relationships that could be involved.

12.6. With reference to Exercise 12.5, do you see any similarity between your answer and Fig. 11.5? Explain.

12.7. With reference to Exercise 12.5, if the information designed for the user is to support access to, and navigation through, such a large, composite, hypertextlike space, it must not only be well-organized but also accommodate effective and efficient multimedia outputs. How does the internal organization and identification of different types of data located at different nodes in the composite space affect the interface design that is required, in terms of needed capabilities for processing multimedia outputs? (Note: Think in terms of visible, multimedia display arrangement and capacity, and how these must relate to the information types to be processed for simultaneous output.)

12.8. Instead of the four-level model of Fig. 12.3, which is based on surrounding layers of context, what other patterns in interface arrangement might be reasonable, especially when multimedia interface regions and screens are involved? Why?

12.9. A multimedia interface may be indicated by any application involving two or more very different data types. It is especially logical for any network-oriented, hypertext-based application, because, by definition, the latter seems to require multimedia outputs. In either case, does a multimedia interface for an application involving each of (a) numeric data, (b) graphical objects, and (c) speech, necessarily demand that corresponding interaction techniques (Chapter 6) be available simultaneously? Explain.

12.10. Can the four-level context model of Fig. 12.3 be mapped into (a) Fig. 4.2 and (b) Fig. 4.3? If so, how? If not, why not?

12.11. With reference to Fig. 12.4, what (in general terms) would be the minimal changes required in the supportive software to enable it to serve not only the single user's network perspective but also the multiuser (group) wanting to carry out CSCW? Select an example of group work and discuss it within the "TS and TP" dichotomy of Fig. 12.3.

12.12. Suppose you had at least five different CRT displays or other (multimedia) devices to accommodate the five windows of the example layout of Fig. 12.6. How would you arrange them (a) to be consistent with the pattern of Figs. 12.3 and 12.5, and (b) in whatever pattern you prefer? Why, in each case? Discuss with reference to an application you select.

ADAPTIVE DESIGN

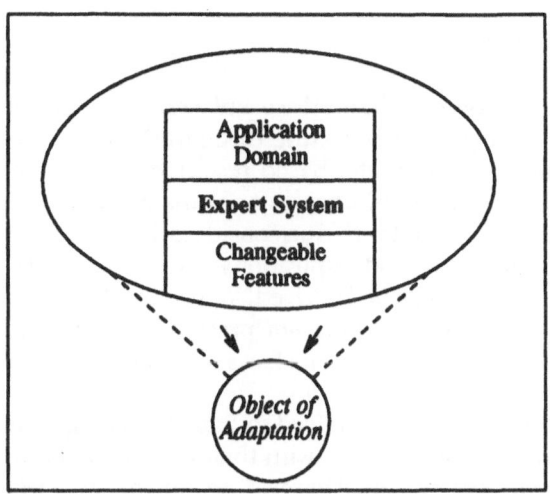

13.1. Overview

Two of the user-oriented design principles (P3 and P4) identified in Table 9.1 deserve special attention. The adjectives used for them are "adaptable" and "adaptive." They represent two different kinds of adaptation. The adaptive version is of primary interest in this chapter, although both kinds are defined.

The importance of designing interfaces to adapt to human users has been recognized (e.g., Sullivan and Tyler, 1991; Schneider-Hufschmidt *et al.*, 1993). Motivation for such design is discussed in Section 13.2. Then, four different models are used to characterize it. First, it is pointed out that adaptation can go in either direction, benefiting either the system or the user. Section 13.3, therefore, presents a general model of that symmetry, along with describing the essential components of the user-oriented version of an adaptive interface. Another model is developed in Section 13.4. It is knowledge-based and leads to portrayal of a rule-based expert system. The third model is an extension of the function-based view that was introduced in earlier chapters. It is given in Section 13.5.

The fourth model, discussed in Section 13.6, is condition-based. It represents the major ingredients for justifying and carrying out any adaptive design. That model is utilized to outline two prototype designs, in Sections 13.7 and 13.8. Finally, some observations about the results are made in Section 13.9.

13.2. Motivation

Modern, computer-enhanced workplaces must not only provide the means of presenting and integrating through the user interface a potentially large variety of computer-based resources; even more significantly, they must do so for an ever-increasing population and diversity of users. Such users must be treated with due consideration, taking their individual differences, limitations, and aspirations into account. If possible, the interface should somehow be "derived" (e.g., Good *et al.*, 1984) from the characteristics of users. We must not present either excessively sophisticated or overly simple-minded interfaces and expect the users to learn to use and enjoy them.

Careful interface design can lead to staged learning by users (Mozeico, 1982; Treu, 1985), in accordance with their current abilities and interests, as recognized by the system. However, to do this and to accommodate other user differences, we need adaptation. What is it? Dictionary definitions include:

Definition 13.1. **Adaptation**: adjustment to different circumstances or conditions; the condition of being altered for a different use; a change in structure, form, or habits to fit different conditions; suitableness.

Evidently, the word "adapt" is synonymous with words like "adjust," "change," and "being altered"—all to give a better fit or become more suitable . But who or what is to adapt to what or whom? Our primary objective is of course to benefit the user. To that end, we need to design an interface that either can be changed upon request or that changes itself automatically.

Definition 13.2. **Adaptable interface**: an interface that is designed to enable the user (or a representative) to modify its appearance and/or behavior, based on explicitly entered information or instructions for doing so.

Definition 13.3. **Adaptive interface**: an interface that is designed to make changes automatically in its appearance and/or behavior, based on knowledge (about the user and the system) that is stored, collected, updated, and analyzed dynamically.

In other words, the two major alternatives for user-oriented adaptation are: (1) letting the user (or someone acting on the user's behalf) *direct* the changes explicitly, by requesting specific changes and/or supplying personal information, e.g., about user preferences, to invoke changes, and (2) enabling the system to solicit, detect, analyze, modify, and remember the characteristics of the user, and then to make dynamic changes to that user model. The latter alternative requires knowledge bases and expert systems technology. The differences between these two kinds of interfaces have been understood and discussed for some time (e.g., Hayes *et al.*, 1981; Fischer, 1993). As stated before, our attention in this chapter is restricted mostly to the adaptive variety.

Early influence on adaptation in HCI came from the interface system structure proposed by Hayes *et al.* (1981), the intelligent monitor function defined by Edmonds (1981, 1982), and the "soft facade" concept of Innocent (1982). Croft (1984) discussed adaptation as the system's ability to act appropriately in a given context, e.g., by making only those tools available that are currently relevant and by changing their functionality according to user preferences. Researchers typically have taken one or the other version, or a composite of the two types, to define an interface that somehow adapts to the user. Trumbly (1991) outlined a variety of relevant "triggering mechanisms" and distinguished them from AI-based techniques for adaptation.

One example of an "adaptable" interface was created in the early 1980s (Bournique, 1981; Bournique and Treu, 1985). Two more recent projects focused primarily on "adaptive" designs (Tyler, 1986; Tyler and Treu, 1986, 1989; Sanderson, 1991; Sanderson and Treu, 1993). Prototypes from the latter two are outlined in Sections 13.7 and 13.8.

13.3. Symmetric Model

Figure 13.1 shows a symmetric model of an adaptive user interface system (Tyler and Treu, 1986). The fundamental situation is dichotomous. The user and the user-visible interface features and devices are packaged into the left (the USER) module of the communicating pair. Likewise, the right (the SYSTEM) module consists of the resources available in the system or network. Then either of the following two modes can apply:

1. The SYSTEM must be *adapted* for the benefit of the USER; the USER is the object of adaptation or the *adaptee*, or
2. The USER must be *adapted* or must do the adapting to conform to the design of the SYSTEM; in this case, the SYSTEM is the object of adaptation or the *adaptee*.

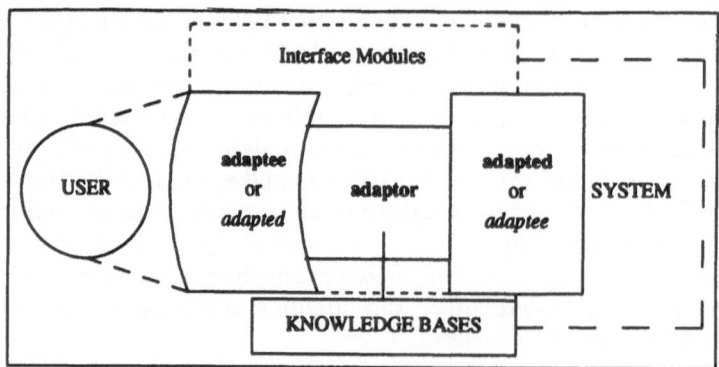

FIGURE 13.1. Symmetric adaptation model. [This figure and Fig. 13.6 are reprinted from Tyler and Treu (1986) with permission of ACM Press.]

The USER module is purposely defined to include not only the user but also the user-visible interface features and devices. The latter must serve as a kind of surrogate representation for the user. When the user is the adaptee and is being served effectively, it is assumed that a one-to-one correspondence exists between what the user wants or needs and what the interface features are actually providing. Likewise, when the user is the adapted, the surrogate is the concrete medium through which the user gives evidence of adapting to what the system requires. In either case, the surrogate may only encompass a subset of the features that the user wants to have adapted or to which the user could be required to adapt. But, in any particular interface design, it is obviously necessary to focus on those interface characteristics that are in fact modifiable under system control. Other features that might be important to users, but that are either not available or changeable in a given interface, can only be considered as goals for interface redesign.

The third major component of the model is the *adaptor*. In order to implement an adaptive interface system, the tools and techniques from artificial intelligence must be utilized to transform or modify the adapted resources for more suitable use at the adaptee interface. To accomplish this, a variety of supportive knowledge bases must be developed. The types of required knowledge depend on which of the interface features (or variables) are to be subject to modification. These are considered further in the model of the next section.

A cautionary note with regard to the adaptor agent in the model of Fig. 13.1. A carefully thought-out philosophy on who/what is in charge of the adaptive interface system must be established and instantiated. Even a totally unsophisticated computer user should not be unknowingly subjected to and manipulated by an intelligent interface. Rules of discretion and confidentiality must be adhered to. While the system may be designed to observe, guide, correct, encourage, and even challenge the user, the latter must always retain the right to override what the system wants or does. Appropriate safeguards are absolutely essential.

Although we are obviously more interested in treating the user as the adaptee, the symmetric portrayal of Fig. 13.1 has a certain aesthetic appeal. Furthermore, the option of having the computer in that privileged role reflects what really happened for many years, often by default. Until relatively recently, nearly all systems forced users to adapt to the idiosyncratic and cryptic designs of computers. Increasingly user-oriented designs have made things somewhat easier for users. However, we have a long way to go to advance the user-oriented adaptive approach.

13.4. Knowledge-Based Model

The term "knowledge" has been defined (Definition 7.2). Human beings and, because of advancements made in artificial intelligence (AI), computers can learn to "know" very many different "objects." For purposes of providing the computer with knowledge, a large variety of knowledge types have been recognized (Buchanan and Shortliffe, 1984), including the following: algorithmic, procedural, structural, hierarchical, factual, symbolic, domain-specific, inexact, judgmental, heuristic, common sense, default, temporal, support, pedagogical, strategy, and meta-level knowledge. The last of these refers to knowledge about knowledge. A number of the terms are interrelated, if not synonymous. The list is not exhaustive. Most of the terms are reasonably self-explanatory, at least at a superficial level. Some of them are utilized below.

AI researchers concentrate on subsets of the above, depending on the kind of application or expert system they with to pursue. They then analyze and represent the pertinent knowledge in great detail. According to Rolston (1988), an expert system is dependent on knowledge as follows:

Definition 13.4. **Expert system:** computer software that can solve complicated problems that would otherwise require extensive human expertise; computer software that simulates the human reasoning process, or a human expert, by applying specific knowledge and inferences.

An expert system (ES), then, is characterized as being dependent on domain-specific knowledge, rather than understanding of generic expert behavior. Furthermore, there are certain components of knowledge that are particularly important to an expert's ability to perform (Rolston, 1988):

1. *Factual:* statements that relate to some element of truth about the subject domain; they generally express a static "state of being" associated with an object, rather than its more dynamic activities.
2. *Procedural:* well-defined instructions pertaining to sequences of events or relations; they describe dynamic actions and decision-making logic relative to parts of the domain.
3. *Heuristic:* rules of thumb suggesting how to proceed when the well-defined procedural knowledge is not available.

The last of these tends to distinguish expert systems from traditional (non-AI) software. Besides the above-mentioned forms of knowledge, an expert must have a global view and be able to "put it all together." That is, a *general conceptual model* and an *overall scheme* for solving a problem are required.

13.4.1. Representational Schemes

Having identified the types of knowledge prominent in ESs, it becomes important to consider how to represent such knowledge. The representation of any object was already given a generic meaning, in Definition 7.3. But now, the object of representation is the knowledge that pertains to a specific domain (Jackson, 1986; Rolston, 1988).

Definition 13.5. **Knowledge representation:** a systematic way of organizing and describing what an expert knows about a domain; a model of expert knowledge that encompasses the structure for describing elements of knowledge and the interpretive process required to use the knowledge described.

Schemes for representing knowledge can be categorized roughly as being either

* *Declarative:* with emphasis on static facts, along with limited information on how the facts can be used, or
* *Procedural:* with emphasis on the form of dynamic rules that describe procedures for using the knowledge, with little of it stored directly as facts.

Practical knowledge representation may stress one of these over the other, but both are variously required in any realistic expert system. The relevant controversy among AI researchers has been discussed extensively in the literature (e.g., Buchanan and Shortliffe, 1984). We do not recount it here.

The declarative category focuses on the use of simple statements of truth, or assertions, about the domain. Formal logic can then be employed. *First-order predicate logic*, with its four major components (an alphabet, a formal language, basic statements called axioms, and a set of inference rules), is in wide use. Schemes for knowledge representation that are less formal than symbolic logic have also been developed. Included are (Rolston, 1988):

- *Semantic network:* using nodes and links of a network to provide a graphical representation of the (binary) relations between the objects of a domain.
- *Frame:* a series of slots in which attributes (characteristics and expectations) about objects in a domain are stored; emphasis is on providing default values in the slots, in order to use them as representative of the object's properties.
- *Script:* specialization of the frame, in that the expectations now are stored in terms of sequences of events likely to occur in a given situation.

These "structured objects" (Jackson, 1986) are representational schemes whose fundamental building blocks are analogous to the nodes and arcs of graph theory or the slots and fillers of record structures (Nilsson, 1982).

One further scheme is that of the *production system.* It is the most commonly used scheme for ESs and is based on:

1. A memory used to keep track of the *current state* of the domain-specific universe
2. A set of *production rules*, or condition–action (IF–THEN) pairs
3. An *interpreter* that repeatedly checks out the current state and, as appropriate, initiates the called-for actions, by executing the applicable production rules

The three above-characterized types of formalisms, namely, predicate logic, structured objects, and production systems, are called "pattern-directed inference systems" (Waterman and Hayes-Roth, 1978). They are the most popular among ES designers and their respective pros and cons have been discussed (and debated) extensively (Jackson, 1986). Each system must include the following: (1) modules that can be activated or triggered by arriving or monitored data; (2) data structures that can be accessed and changed dynamically by an active module; and (3) an interpreter that can control the module selection and activation in some regular (cyclic) pattern. Modularity is important in accommodating these ingredients. This fact will be evident in the prototype examples presented later.

13.4.2. ES Applications and Users

ES applications have in the past been considered mainly in the following general categories of work (Hayes-Roth *et al.*, 1983): interpretation, prediction, diagnosis, design, planning, monitoring, debugging, repair, instruction, and control. Each of these applications typically focuses on carrying out a certain task, or combination of tasks, by means of an ES, as if some "universal" or "composite" human expert were doing the work. For example, diagnosis of a system malfunction emphasizes only how an expert, based on available knowledge about the system (including a human patient's body), might reach a conclusion on what is causing the problem and, then, what might be done about it. Until recently, relatively little attention was paid to how a user of such an ES, who may or may not be an expert in the domain of interest, might effectively interact with and complement the ES. Further, we need ESs that can negotiate, enhance, regulate, and utilize the composite knowledge of the user *and* the applications domain (or the ES representing it) in order to take advantage of both of those intelligent entities. The interface between user and computer-based application is itself a multifaceted domain for ES design and development.

13.4.3. User-Oriented Knowledge Model

Following is a descriptive, knowledge-based model of an expert system intended to serve the interactive user. The types of knowledge are categorized as pertaining to the:

- Applications domain (*A*-factors)
  - *M*: Methodology required
  - *L*: Language tools and techniques
- Computer interface (*I*-factors)
  - *I*: Intermediary tools and techniques
- User (*U*-factors)
  - *U*: Domain-specific user

The indicated categories of factors are consistent with those described in Part II. Given the above, we can distinguish various types of knowledge using the following terminology:

$K_U(M)$ = User knowledge about M
$K_U(L)$ = User knowledge about L
$K_U(I)$ = User knowledge about I
$K_U(M, L, I)$ = User knowledge about all three

In addition, if we set $T=M+L+I$, we can consider

K_T = Total domain-dependent (i.e., domain-specific plus domain-supportive) knowledge

Now, if we let

K_U = Domain-dependent plus domain-independent user knowledge

we can characterize a user according to the set relations of Fig. 13.2.

For the very knowledgeable user (Fig. 13.2a), it would seem that an ES, designed to supply some of the requisite knowledge about the domain, is really not needed. However, such a user may want it to be available nevertheless. For the somewhat knowledgeable user (Fig. 13.2b), the situation is different. We should design an ES that can minimally accommodate the domain-dependent knowledge that the user does not know, namely:

$$K_T - (K_U \cap K_T) \qquad (13.1)$$

Again, the user may in fact want to take advantage of more than this minimum level of ES knowledge.

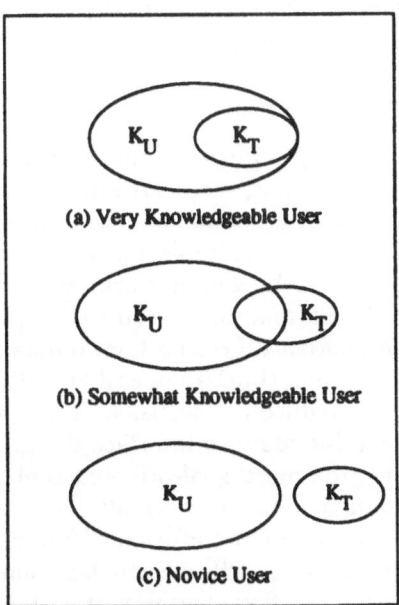

(a) Very Knowledgeable User

(b) Somewhat Knowledgeable User

(c) Novice User

FIGURE 13.2. Major user categories.

Third, the novice user (Fig. 13.2c) is going to need a lot of help. In fact, the ES should be able to handle all of K_T. Let us label it $K_{ES}(T)$, the ES knowledge of the domain. But to complicate things further, one more category of knowledge must be added:

$$K_{ES}(U) = \text{Expert system knowledge about the user}$$

This knowledge is potentially sensitive in nature and must be determined on a very selective and user-authorized basis.

As a result of the above-characterized model of user + system knowledge, the ES must in general possess some suitably specified combination of the following:

$$K_{ES} = K_{ES}(T) + K_{ES}(U) \qquad (13.2)$$

Then, as the ES learns more and more about the user's current level of knowledge and also performance (through real-time observations, inferences, and knowledge base updating), it should perform its role of adapting the system to the user.

Needless to say, it is difficult to ascertain how much a user really knows about a particular domain. However, as portrayed below, we can start with selected knowledge elements and make some simplifying assumptions (e.g., about user level of experience). Then, the ES should be able to improve or fine-tune its knowledge and performance over time.

13.4.4. Rule-Based ES Distinctions

The use of rule-based production systems has become very prevalent in real-life (industrial, business, medical) kinds of applications. Such a system can be prepared to accommodate both factual and procedural knowledge, as required of an ES. Typical production systems do *forward chaining*, that is, they match the data in working memory against the left side of each IF–THEN rule and then execute the right-hand side. This is also called *data-directed inference*, because known data drive the inferences from left to right in the rules (Buchanan and Shortliffe, 1984). The rules then chain together to deduce a conclusion. The forward chaining approach is quite suitable for adaptive interface design.

Backward chaining, the more goal-oriented control strategy, is really not necessary. A production system normally does not support it. As a result, the ES turns out to be more efficient. However, some goal-driven effects can be achieved using well-selected task statements in working memory (Rolston, 1988). The first condition of each rule can be a test for the currently applicable task or subtask. This type of structuring, or "layering," of the production rules according to current context or locality is illustrated later.

13.4.5. Knowledge Base Partitioning

Figure 13.3. portrays the high-level organization of a modular interface system. It is a generic version of Fig. 10.7. The ES is assumed to have knowledge about each system module (M, L, and I) as well as about the user (U). It may distinguish the user's knowledge of each of the modules.

With the assumption that the ES has a knowledge base representing each type of knowledge (K) indicated among the conditions, the general format of a rule in the production system is:

IF condition ($K(M)$) AND condition ($K_U(M)$) THEN ES_action

That is, if some aspect of the application-specific methodology is currently being invoked or relevant (to what the user is trying to do), and the user's knowledge of that aspect is known to meet a certain condition or threshold, then the ES will take the appropriate action.

Analogously, such a rule can apply to the other modules (Fig. 13.3) or a subset combination of them. So, for example, the rule format can be:

IF condition ($K(L,M)$) AND condition ($K_U(L,M)$) THEN ES_action

where a combined situation or status is of interest, involving aspects of the details of language as well as higher-level methodology.

The above-suggested partitioning implies that the rules can consequently be organized into modular groupings. This feature is important and has been found to be very helpful. It tends to make the stored production rules more efficiently accessible and manipulable.

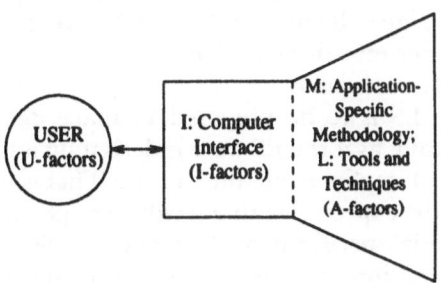

FIGURE 13.3. Knowledge domain modules.

13.4.6. Contextual Structures

Such modular organization suggests one means for categorizing the production rules and hence creating a more manageable knowledge base for a production system. Other meaningful structures can be added. In particular, assuming that the design principle (P13) of "providing context" is specified for a design, suitable structures must be determined to support context (Definition 6.11), thereby identifying the locality of adaptive action. Contextual structures can be superimposed on the production rules of an ES. They help by triggering information that will support the user both (1) to better understand the current state, and (2) to decide where to go next in order to complete a task. As a result, the format of the above-indicated rule, using ES knowledge about both user and domain, is extended as follows:

IF condition $(K(M))$ AND condition $(K_U(M))$ AND context()

THEN ES_action

That is, the ES action would only be triggered if, in addition to the other two conditions, the user's current work (or state or focus) is within the appropriate context.

13.5. Decision Function: Update

In Chapter 9, the high-level functional interpretation of the decision-making process for interface design was updated as follows:

$$\text{FEATURES}_n \leftarrow$$

$$D_{\text{criteria},n} (\text{KNOWLEDGE}_{\text{designer}}, \text{FACTORS}_n, \text{PRINCIPLES}_n) \quad (13.3)$$

The variables in this mapping were defined by Eqs. (9.2), (9.3), and (9.4), and the decision criteria were also discussed. Emphasis was of course on the human designer being the "expert," having all of the required knowledge to render effective decisions.

Now we are interested in having an ES take over the role of the human designer. But the ES is to be prepared to make decisions to alter the interface dynamically, as if the ES were redesigning it in real time. Notice that Function (13.3) implies a one-time result. That is, a design feature is determined with the expectation that it will be implemented and retained according to its initial specification. Variability in a feature is normally not a part of traditional interface design, except in the sense of providing different selectable options (e.g., input devices). However, for adapting the interface to different users or to changing user needs, the features must be dynamically variable. Function (13.3) must be reinterpreted and modified. For its independent variables, we must do the following:

1. The set of principles must include P4; the interface is to be "adaptive" to the user.
2. The sets of A-factors, I-factors, and any other factors must all provide the necessary support to enable the application software and the computer (interface) to generate different versions, values, or ranges of options for any FEATURE deemed significant to the user.
3. The U-factors now become truly variable; their values must be dynamically changed in the knowledge base representing the user model, thereby affecting the ES determination (decision-making) and instantiation of currently desirable feature options.

Instead of arriving at a relatively static set of features with Function (13.3), as is done in nonadaptive HCI design, the designer of an adaptive interface must focus on the following:

- The dependent variable, $FEATURES_n$, must be specified as a range or set of permissible values or options, within/among which the interface can switch dynamically.
- The criteria employed in the decision-making process must be suitably extended and rendered conditional.

These extensions mean that the designer makes it possible for the interface to dynamically select among a number of permissible feature versions, in reaction to changes observed among the U-factors. The general logic of the conditional changes is:

$$\text{If } \{u_i\} \rightarrow \{u'_i\} \text{ then } F_n \rightarrow F'_n \qquad (13.4)$$

In other words, if the set of U-factors changes adequately, or significantly enough, a previous version or value of a design feature, F_n, is changed to a different version or value, F'_n. Such a transformation assumes that the various relevant design factors remain supportive and that the change is consistent with the criteria for adaptive design.

Notice that the above implies, in effect, that the decision-supporting criteria discussed in Chapter 9 are formalized by the designer and embedded in production rules usable by an ES.

If the above-indicated conditions are all met, the functional representation of an adaptive, dynamically changing design becomes:

$$FEATURES_N \leftarrow D_{ES,n} (K(FACTORS_n), K(context), K(prod\_rules) \qquad (13.5)$$

This mapping portrays how the designer has basically created the ability in the interface to *redesign* itself dynamically. The independent variables identified are different from those of Function (13.3). The designer's knowledge is omitted because it now is contained in the ES, to the extent feasible and appropriate. The design principles are already reflected in the allowable range of options. Hence, they also need not be repeated. Instead, the independent variables that are used by the ES to determine a feature are:

1. The *knowledge bases*, denoted collectively by K, which encompass the changing U-factors (some subset of $\{u_i\}$) and whatever information must be available about the application domain (A-factors) and also the computer interface environment (I-factors).
2. *Structural support pattern*, denoted by K(context), which is dynamically superimposed on the interaction to determine the locality and granularity of any adaptive changes that are decided and then instantiated; this knowledge can be interpreted as being subsumed by the knowledge of A-factors and also I-factors.
3. The set(s) of production rules, denoted by K(prod_rules), which are to be utilized by the ES to make decisions and invoke the changes.

The last of these requires the kinds of IF–THEN (or cause-and-effect) clauses implied by Statement (13.4) and discussed in Section 13.4. These can be grouped and also composed into compound clauses. They represent how different features can be triggered when changes in the user model occur. Such conditional statements are directly usable in productions, as is illustrated by the prototype interfaces described later.

13.6. Condition-Based Model

The designer of an adaptive interface is confronted by a myriad of decisions on why, where, when, and how to provide for adaptation. The task of HCI design is thereby complicated considerably beyond the normal task of creating nonadaptive interfaces. Further, much room exists for differences in design emphases, approaches, styles, and overall design philosophy. It is not correct to talk about adaptive interface design as if it were some kind of singular or homogeneous result to be achieved. Too many variables are involved; too many different versions of adaptation are possible.

Accordingly, to enable a designer to clearly organize, select, specify, and describe an adaptive interface design, a descriptive, condition-based model has been developed (Sanderson and Treu, 1993). It can be used to prompt a designer to consider the most significant conditions to be met in order to achieve a successful design. A condition is taken to mean "something upon which something else depends," i.e., adaptation cannot be designed effectively without being able to satisfy the stipulated conditions properly. Figure 13.4 gives an overview. These conditions must be distinguished from the "criteria" for adapting and also from the "rule conditions" of the expert system (Section 13.4), which are used in actually making adaptation decisions. Each condition listed in Fig. 13.4 is discussed in the following subsections. But first there is one fundamental condition that seems to be prerequisite: the availability of supportive structure.

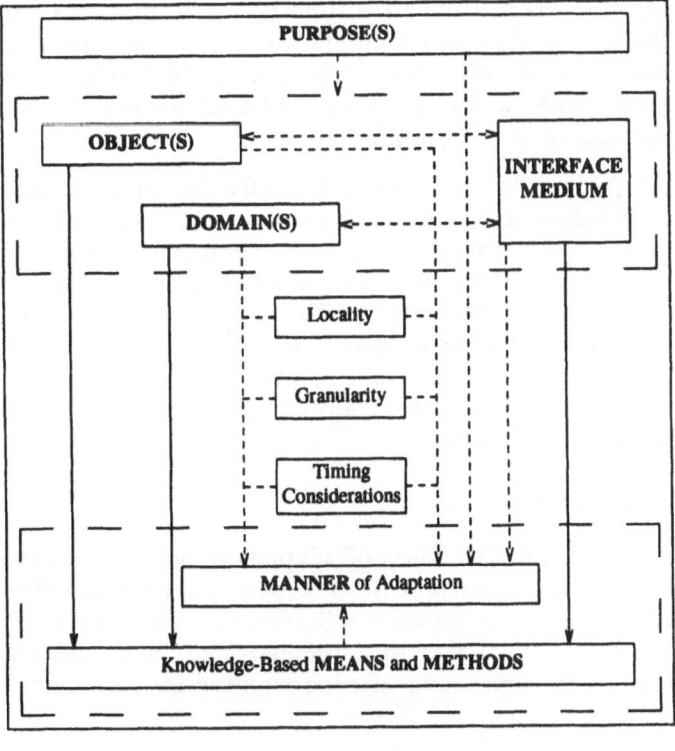

Legend:
⟶ Knowledge Representation
--⇢ Design Influence or Effect

FIGURE 13.4. Framework of adaptation conditions. [This figure and Figs. 13.7 through 13.9 are reprinted from Sanderson and Treu (1993) with permission of North-Holland Elsevier.]

13.6.1. Supportive Structure

Structure is a theme of this book. It is inherent to the methodologies for nonadaptive designs (Chapters 10 and 11); it is also important to adaptive interfaces. Besides having relevance to methodology, structures are representative of the user, the computer, and the application (Treu, 1992). Structure dependency is especially significant for:

1. Users who are novices in an application area, trying to learn more about it and improve their skills in using it, *or* who perhaps are individuals without any expectation of (or aspiration to) becoming experts; in either case, the users are in need of, and likely to be receptive to, being carefully guided or directed in the use of the interface system and the application domain.

2. Applications that are "structurable," that is, that are conducive to having organizational paradigms superimposed, in a manner that enables the designer to provide the user with assistance (at various levels and in various localities) and goal-oriented guidance (e.g., accordance to task plans.)

Thus, the perspective on adaptive interface design presented here is significantly influenced by wanting to serve users who have need for structure-contingent, adaptive support, in conjunction with structurable applications. To take advantage of supportive structures, the designer must know the conditions under which adaptation is to take place. It is necessary to understand in advance the answers to questions like: why adapt? to whom? where? when? how? and with what? The answers establish a meaningful framework for adaptive interface design, which is used in the following subsections.

13.6.2. Object of Adaptation

Adapt to whom? The object of adaptation, not to be confused with adaptation objective or purpose (next section), is the intended beneficiary of adaptive behavior. In the model of Section 13.3, the term "adaptee" was used. As with any HCI design, the target user must be identified and then be represented through the knowledge required in the decision-making process.

13.6.3. Purpose of Adaptation

Why adapt? Indeed, there may be good reasons not to have the system adapt dynamically to the user. For example, experienced users working in very familiar application domains may wish to have direct, explicit control over system functionality and initiate shortcuts on their own, subject to whatever limits (in being "adaptable") the system imposes. This is somewhat analogous to an automobile driver who insists on being able to change gears, using a manual transmission. On the other hand, for the novice user an automatic transmission is a very desirable option.

Actually, the above only asks *whether* to adapt. Once it is determined that adaptation is really needed or desired, the more detailed purpose(s) must be prescribed. They can be couched within the design principles, or goals, to which the interface is to adhere. For example, if a stated principle in HCI design is to cause the interface to be "facilitative" of the user's interaction with the system, then any adaptation decisions should be consistent with that goal. That is, depending on the needs of a particular user to whom the interface is to adapt, the adaptation behavior should be facilitative, such as by helping the user to complete tasks more quickly or with less knowledge and effort.

13.6.4. Adaptation Domain

Knowing who is to benefit from adaptation does not yet identify what is to be adapted within the environment of a computer system. In other words, where or in which domain(s) does the adaptation take effect? Several potential domains are subject to being dynamically utilized and/or changed for the benefit of the user. Corresponding knowledge modules characterized in Section 13.4 (see Fig. 13.3) are indicated in parentheses:

1. The way the chosen application software appears to work, at a low (command-specific) level of interaction with the user $(K(L))$
2. The way the chosen application is to be carried out by the user, in terms of high-level methodology and task plans $(K(M))$
3. The way the interface software/hardware appear(s) to work in terms of functional capabilities and options $(K(I))$, not necessarily dependent on the application
4. The way the interface appears to work in terms of guiding, directing, and explaining objects and tasks to a user at a high level of interaction with the application $K(I,M)$

For Prototype A (Section 13.7), Domains 1, 2, and 4 became involved; in Prototype B (Section 13.8), focus was on Domains 2, 3, and 4. But it can be extended to encompass Domain 1 also.

As shown in Fig. 13.4, the objects of adaptation, namely, the users, and the adaptation domains are necessarily associated with the interface medium. Knowledge about each of them (the U, M, L, and I modules) must be representable in conjunction with the ES that is to make the adaptation decisions. This is suggested by the solid, downward arrows in Fig. 13.4.

13.6.5. Locality and Granularity

As also shown in the figure, identifying the application domain that is subject to being changed is not enough. The designer must analyze and structure the domain to meet the conditions of

- *Locality*: exactly where, in which states in the user–domain inter- action should changes be made or assistance be provided?
- *Granularity*: at what level of generality (e.g., high-level, goal- oriented decisions) or specificity (e.g., low-level commands) within a locality should changes be made or assistance be provided?

The adaptation domain and the locality and granularity within it pertain to the question: adapt where? One more related condition deals with *when* to adapt, under what circumstances, or the timing for making changes.

13.6.6. Timing for Adaptation

If a user, while interacting with a particular application domain, encounters a particular locality and level of granularity, the interface can be designed to trigger a form of adaptation at that time. This represents one kind of timing. But other kinds exist. For example, the timing can be triggered by current circumstances, such as how well the user seems to be prepared for performing the task at hand, as reflected by the stored user model (which may just have changed); or some real-time consideration about the critical nature of the application, the completion of which has become more urgent today (than it was yesterday). This means that adaptation does not necessarily take place consistently, in a particular context (e.g., locality, granularity); it may instead be affected by circum- stances involving other factors including how well the user seems to be doing. The user is, after all, the object of adaptation.

Hence, some conditions for designing an adaptive interface, as they are depicted in Fig. 13.4, contribute directly to the criteria for making adaptation decisions. Consistent with the definition of a design criterion (Definition 9.6), an adaptation criterion is a rule or standard for deciding when and where to adapt. This is symbolized within Function (13.5). That is, when the current context (locality, granularity) and circumstances (various knowledge-based timing considerations) meet the requirements for an adaptive action, that action is invoked and a changed feature results or special assistance is provided.

13.6.7. Manner of Adapting

Adapt how? In what ways? After determining why, when, where, and for whom to adapt, the really difficult task arises: selecting the ways or forms of adaptation that are possible and useful. These are of course dependent on answers to the previous questions. As indicated by the dashed arrows in Fig. 13.4, the purpose, object, interface, and domain conditions collectively influence the manner of adaptation. The manner is also contingent on available means and methods designed to carry out the adaptation.

Adaptation actions and the resulting ranges of values and options for changed features must be clearly defined. Again, this is implied symbolically by Function (13.5). For example, under certain conditions, two or more alternative forms of assistance might be available. Or, in certain localities or states of interaction, a complex decision point might be bypassed because the current knowledge about the user suggests that it is advisable to do so.

13.6.8. Means and Methods

Finally, the different available ways or forms of adaptation must be implementable. That is, the designer must decide: with what?

As discussed in Section 13.4, the means and methods can generally be based on

1. Knowledge modules that represent each of the adaptation object (U), domain (A), and interface medium (I), and
2. Rule-based ES techniques that utilize those knowledge bases, according to stipulated conditions and contexts, and then invoke changes or provide special assistance.

These are among the independent variables of Function (13.5). Resulting changes are either visible to the user in the interface, and/or applied to the knowledge bases themselves, thereby affecting future adaptation decisions. Accordingly, the designer of an adaptive interface must carefully formulate condition–action rules for an ES and then incorporate the latter within the architecture of the interface system. All of this must be done with the hope of meeting the purpose(s) for adaptation that were originally prescribed.

The above-outlined, condition-based model is used in the next two sections to present two different prototypes. However, the conditions are discussed in a different order. Some are considered collectively. For each of Sections 13.7 and 13.8, the conditions are discussed in the following order: object and domain (in introductory paragraph), purpose and manner, supportive structures, means and methods (separated into the ES, knowledge bases, and illustrative rules), and interface software. In addition, the subsections on illustrative rules implicitly convey how each prototype deals with the conditions of locality, granularity, and other timing considerations for taking adaptive action, when combined with supportive structures.

13.7.   Prototype Example A

The first prototype, named SAUCI, was part of the Ph.D. dissertation research of Sherman Tyler (1986). It involved the design of an adaptive interface for users wanting to carry out tasks in a UNIX-based system. Emphasis was on using most of the basic UNIX commands for purposes of accomplishing two tasks: (1) document preparation and (2) programming.

13.7.1.   Purpose and Manner

Besides making the interface adaptive (P4), the design principles applied in this project were, broadly stated, to render the interface more *learnable* and more *usable*. These are identified as P26 and P44 in Table 9.1. The two goals were pursued by providing the user with *context* (P13) in ways supportive of learning and usability. That context was restricted to the domain of interest. Thus, the overriding goal was to create adaptive, task-specific context (Tyler and Treu, 1989).

But what were the actual adaptive results experienced by the users? What manner of adaptation was contained in the task-specific context? The answer is intimately tied to the interaction "phases" through which the user must transition in order to complete a chosen task. The phases are components of the supportive structures discussed in the next section. To summarize, the manner of adaptation involved (1) command-specific prompting, error checking, and advice and (2) task-oriented direction and guidance.

13.7.2.   Supportive Structures

User interaction with the target system was organized into a series of "interaction events" defined by Fig. 13.5 (Tyler and Treu, 1989). The model of an interaction event is related to what was previously proposed by Benbasat and Wand (1984). It is basically a flowchart identifying the user input and directing it into one of several possible phases. In each phase, the adaptive interface takes whatever action is called for and produces output accordingly.

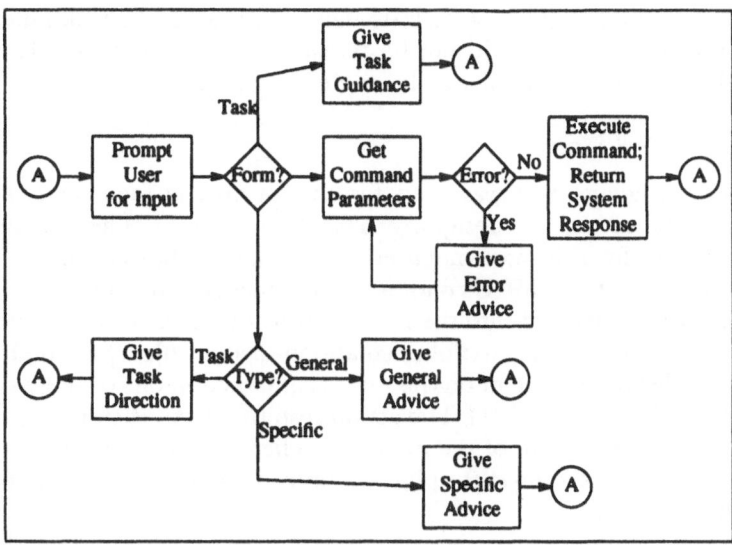

FIGURE 13.5. The interaction event. [Reprinted from Tyler and Treu (1989) with permission of Academic Press.]

The phases are briefly outlined as follows:

1. *Prompting* the user for commands or other inputs
2. *Collecting parameters*, as required for any user-selected command
3. *Error checking and advice*, to help with correcting errors in commands as well as various local and global errors
4. *Command-related advice*, both (a) general in nature, to indicate purpose, arguments, and operation of each command, and (b) specific, in enabling the user to enter an exploratory mode to test the validity of command arguments in the interface locally
5. *Task direction*, providing textual information on the steps or the path required toward completing a high-level task on the target system
6. *Task guidance*, leading the user in a step-by-step manner toward the task goal

The sequence of invoking the above phases is context-dependent, and subject to what the user requests and the errors he/she commits. Also, some of the phases (or corresponding phase windows) can be active (or appear) in parallel on the screen. The display regions are organized accordingly.

Besides the structure implied by the sequencing of phases via various paths in an interaction event flowchart, the interface must also have structural knowledge of the task domain. Otherwise, the task guidance and direction phases would not be possible. This type of knowledge is included among the knowledge bases described below.

13.7.3. Expert System

The language that was used for this prototype (namely, LOOPS) includes the means for designing sets of production rules for an ES. However, that formalism was not used. It was found to be too cumbersome. Instead, the INTERLISP-D conditional statements were employed. They can be easily translated into the LOOPS-provided formalism, if desired. The ES, then, is designed to utilize condition–action rules. The conditions of each rule are dependent on the values contained in one or more of the knowledge bases (see below). The action resulting from each rule is to set or change some feature of the interface. These rules are, in turn, organized into sets according to the phase of user–system interaction (outlined earlier).

13.7.4. Knowledge Bases

Four different knowledge bases were defined and implemented for the SAUCI prototype.

User Model. Information about the user consisted of two categories:

1. *Solicited* from the user directly; this included asking about and recording the *experience level* with each of two different operating systems (UNIX and VMS), and *user group membership*, e.g., whether the user was a computer science student or a systems programmer.
2. *Monitored* information collected dynamically; this varied with the target application; the purpose was to gauge user performance and status.

Over 35 variables constituted the user model. These included: command usage, requests for task guidance and other help, specific errors (in commands used), and general measures of each of response, help, and error rates.

High-Level Task Model. This knowledge base contained the interface's information about how a selected task can be carried out on the target system. It is high-level information, permitting the interface to guide the user through the required steps and providing enough context for the user to know where he/she is and how things are going. This information is critical to achieve task-orientation in the interface. The representation of a high-level task is by means of a hierarchy of objects, each corresponding to a step along the task plan.

Figure 13.6 shows the hierarchy for the document preparation task.
Target Commands. This knowledge base describes in declarative form
the functionality of the target system. It represents every command as a
separate object. The objects then provide the information for

1. Constructing the primary interface to the target system, by dynamically building menus of target system commands
2. Enabling decisions, in conjunction with the user model, on which
   commands and command arguments are appropriate for a particular user
3. Supplying textual descriptions about each command

Because this knowledge base represents the application that can be
carried out on the target system via the commands defined, it contributes
to separation of the interface from the application.

File and Domain Relations. The final knowledge base encodes the
information on the main objects of the target system, namely, the files in
the implemented prototype, and on their types and interrelationships,
with regard to high-level tasks known to the interface. This information
helps to provide context to the user about the current state of the file
system and the files used in executing a task. It is also used to detect global
errors, such as in attempting to edit an object file or to compile a file when
the corresponding object file already exists.

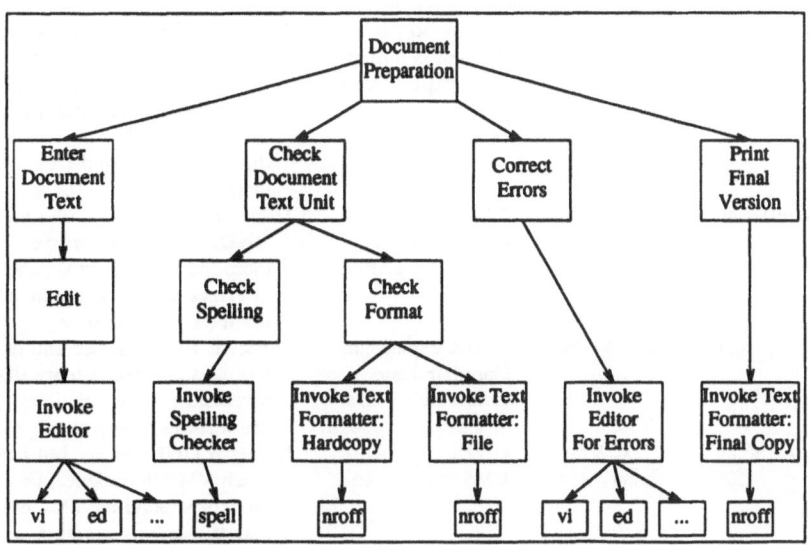

FIGURE 13.6. High-level task plan for document preparation.

13.7.5. Illustrative Rules

One of the phases of interaction is the prompt phase (see Fig. 13.5). It puts the interface in a state of readiness to receive input from the user, indicating what action is desired on the target system. It is concerned with the layout of the screen. Usually, a window or menu is set up through which the user can select a command for execution. The commands are organized into submenus depending on what functions they are designed to support.

The prompt phase can be tailored to the user in a number of ways. The corresponding rule set is activated before the screen features of this phase are composed. The rules set includes various parameters to control adaptation to the user. They are illustrated in Table 13.1.

Another interaction phase is that of giving general advice. This advice relates to the purpose, arguments, and operation of a command. It is generated as a series of segments of text displayed for the user in a special window on the left side of the screen. Each such window has a heading indicating its contents. The text for each command is obtained from the

TABLE 13.1
ES Rules for Prompt Phase[a]

Parameter	Possible values	Knowledge used	Logic of example rule
MenuItem Inclusion	Include, Omit	Command use Type of command User experience on UNIX	If command is used mostly by experts, and the user is a UNIX novice who has used the command less than the threshold number of times, then omit command from menu.
MenuForm	Terse, Verbose	UNIX experience Command use Command errors	If user is very experienced on UNIX and has not made more than threshold number of errors using the command, use terse menu entries.
PromptForm	Terse, Verbose	UNIX experience Command use Command errors	If user is UNIX novice and has not used command more than threshold number of times, use verbose prompts.
Annotation	UNIX, VMS, none	UNIX experience VMS experience	If user is UNIX novice but has much VMS experience, then give corresponding VMS commands as menu annotations.

[a]Reprinted from Tyler and Treu (1989) with permission of Academic Press.

object representing it. There is also an associated menu so that information that the interface has decided not to display can still be selected for examination by the user. The dimensions of variability underlying this phase are indicated by the Possible Values column of Table 13.2. A rule set is exercised prior to appearance of this phase's output, to determine how the tailoring to the user will occur. Potential results are indicated in the table.

Similarly, each of the other interaction phases of SAUCI (Fig. 13.5) is tailored to the user based on corresponding ES rules (Tyler, 1986).

13.7.6. Interface Software Architecture

The prototype architecture is highly object-oriented. In addition, it incorporates an ES in which a set of rules is used to determine current interface appearance and behavior. Those rules, in turn, rely on the information in the several knowledge bases for making decisions about the interface.

The prototype was built on a Xerox 1108 "LISP machine," which served as the intelligent interface connected to a UNIX system running on a VAX-11/780. The interface-controlling software was written in the LOOPS language, a special-purpose language growing out of the INTER-LISP-D dialect of LISP (Bobrow and Stefik, 1983). The hardware provided the necessary memory capacity to contain the large knowledge bases and the substantial rule sets. The processing power was sufficient to execute the rules and modify the interface while still not unduly slowing the user's ability to interact with the target system. In addition, the bit-mapped graphics, multiple windowing, menuing, and mouse interaction capabilities facilitated rapid prototyping of the interface as designed.

Besides being significantly hinged on ES rules, the interface software is very much organized in an object-oriented manner. Almost everything, ranging from individual commands to the knowledge bases, is defined as an object or a set of objects, that is, a package of variables and methods. The prototype implementation of SAUCI can, therefore, best be characterized as a combination of the rule-based and object-oriented paradigms.

13.8. Prototype Example B

The second prototype, named N-CHIME, was part of the Ph.D. dissertation research of Peter Sanderson (1991). It involves the system already described in the case study of Chapters 10 and 11. The objects of adaptation were to be users interested in carrying out the tasks of modeling and simulating different kinds of systems.

TABLE 13.2
ES Rules for General Advice Phase[a]

Parameter	Possible values	Knowledge used	Logic of example rule
PurposeForm	Terse, Verbose	UNIX experience Command help Command errors	If user is moderate in UNIX experience but has not asked for help on the command before, then use verbose explanation of purpose of command.
OperationForm	Terse, Verbose	Command help	If user has received advice on command before, give only brief explanation of arguments and operation of command.
Example	NoviceExample, ExpertExample, none	UNIX experience Command use Command help	If user is UNIX expert but has neither asked for help nor used the command more than threshold number of times, then provide expert-level example.
Warnings	GeneralMessage, SpecificPast-Errors, none	UNIX experience Past local errors on command	If user has made any local errors on the command in recent past, then print out a warning about these.
DirectEntry	Mention, Details, none	Group membership UNIX experience Number of sessions Command use	If user is C.S. student, then mention how the command can be entered directly.
VMS Command	Include, Exclude	UNIX experience VMS experience	If user is UNIX novice but VMS expert, then include differences between command and equivalent VMS command.
Implementation	Include, Exclude	Group membership Command help	If user is system programmer and has not asked for help before, then tell user about implementation of command.
Uses	Include, Exclude	UNIX experience Command use Command help	If user is UNIX novice and command use and command help are less than thresholds, then include description of command uses.

[a]Reprinted from Tyler and Treu (1989) with permission of Academic Press.

13.8.1. Purpose and Manner

This prototype actually supports elements of both adaptive and adaptable interface designs. The manner of adapting to users was dictated by the three other design principles specified for the N-CHIME design (Section 10.6). The interface was to (1) facilitate, (2) provide context, and (3) not constrain (i.e., not preclude user learning) during interaction. These are the principles P20, P13, and P41 listed in Table 9.1.

How then is it adaptive to users? At present it basically does the following:

1. Provide high-level guidance to enable a user to reach a declared goal
2. Bypass certain decision points, thereby shortening the number of steps required to complete a task
3. Tailor the forms of output as well as the alternative input techniques to the current needs and preferences of the user
4. Produce explanations pertaining to the current high-level state and its associated lower-level objects

If we relate the above to the different categories of features [symbolized by Eq. (9.3)] that are subject to being changed in the interface, the third action involves the feature of interaction technique (Chapter 6). The first two actions pertain to features evident through representational models and structures (Chapter 7) that are superimposed on the interaction. The fourth action represents context-based enhancement, through explanatory support, for the components of the other three.

In addition to above-identified adaptive actions, the prototype is "adaptable" in certain ways. It maintains an easily accessible user profile of preferences that can be modified explicitly, when invoked by the user. The system will then change its appearance and behavior accordingly (Sanderson, 1991).

Finally, the interface adapts or prepares for adaptation behind the scene, by

5. Accumulating evidence about user behavior and performance
6. Updating the user model (knowledge base) whenever changes in the stored variables occur, thereby affecting future adaptation decisions relating to the four actions listed above

13.8.2. Supportive Structures

Detailed analysis of the modeling and simulation domain led to creation of a user-visible state scenario graph (Treu *et al.*, 1991). This directed graph consists of high-level states or nodes (H-nodes) and transitions (arcs) between them, as shown in Fig. 11.1. A sequence of such state transitions constitutes a scenario (or path) through the graph. Each H-node, in turn, provides context for lower-level support nodes, including special nodes that reflect the ES rules designed to trigger adaptation actions whenever specified conditions are satisfied. The user can, therefore, follow high-level paths of H-nodes, with adaptive support provided whenever invoked, in order to reach his/her objectives within the application domain.

To illustrate, a subgraph extracted from the user state scenario graph (Fig. 11.1) is displayed in Fig. 13.7. The high-level states (H0 through H4) and scenarios running through them (S1 through S5) are labeled for referencing from the text. Note that the state labels are *not* in direct correspondence to those of Fig. 11.1. The state scenarios or task plans are again predefined paths through the graph. They serve to guide the user toward achieving specified goals.

13.8.3. Expert System

The means and methods for making and carrying out N-CHIME adaptation decisions are provided by a rule-based ES. It is diagrammed in Fig. 13.8. The type of ES chosen for N-CHIME is of the *control* variety (Hayes-Roth *et al.*, 1983), because it generally addresses the problem of interpreting, predicting, repairing, and monitoring system behaviors. Like the ES in Prototype A, it is also a rule-based production system (Sanderson and Treu, 1991).

The ES was embedded in the interface so that it can act on the user's behalf efficiently and without the user necessarily being aware of its activities. Most information it needs is contained in a knowledge model of the individual user.

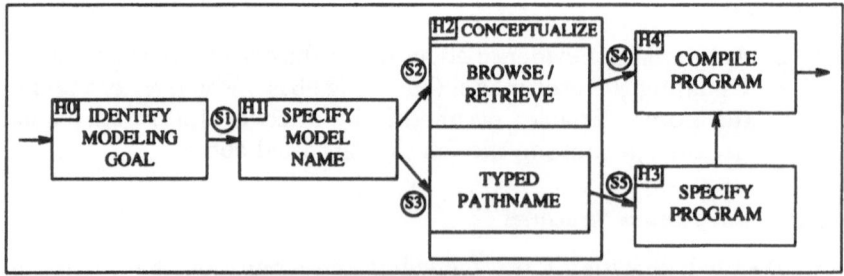

FIGURE 13.7. Subgraph of user state scenario graph.

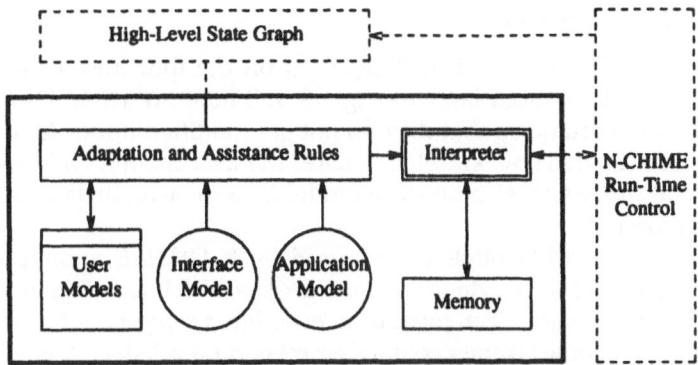

FIGURE 13.8. Expert system model for N-CHIME.

N-CHIME's ES includes modular partitioning of production rules for computational efficiency and use of individual user models in working memory. The high-level state scenario graph, although external to the ES, helps determine which production rules are evaluated. Each modular set of production rules is associated with a high-level interaction state, or a context. That fact is confirmed by the top layer of Fig. 13.9.

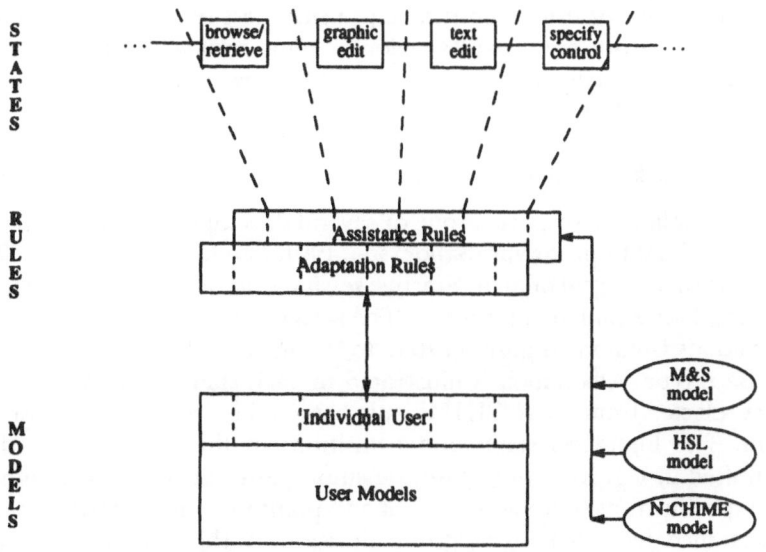

FIGURE 13.9. Knowledge base representation model.

13.8.4. Knowledge Bases

The ES of Prototype B is dependent on the four knowledge bases identified in the bottom layer of Fig. 13.9. There are three knowledge models that are static, in that they do not get modified under ES control. The fourth is a dynamic knowledge base, the user model. Only the user model and the N-CHIME interface model (I) were actually implemented for the prototype.

The three static models can be used by N-CHIME to support the assistance feature. Once their contents are specified, they remain intact during interactive use. Each piece of knowledge is represented by a frame that is linked to other frames containing related knowledge. A network of frames constitutes each model.

The user model is distinguished from the other knowledge sources in that it is dynamic in nature and is utilized by the production rules to control the adaptive capability of N-CHIME. The model uses a combination of techniques for acquiring its values. Like Prototype A, it uses both solicited and monitored information about the user. When a user accesses N-CHIME for the first time, he/she engages in a short question-and-answer session to determine experience and knowledge in certain areas. Once these initial values are obtained, the model is updated by the ES. In addition, the user may specify preferences and modify certain user model parameters using special software tools.

Among the variables maintained about each user: command selection, frequency of using and time lapse since last usage of a tool, recent command history, and past behavior in same context, including errors committed and help requests made. These are reflected by the rules descriptions below.

13.8.5. Illustrative Rules

The following scenario is one of several developed for demonstration of the N-CHIME prototype (Sanderson, 1991; Sanderson and Treu, 1993). Assume that the goal of an interactive session is for a novice user to run an existing HSL simulation program. The scenario follows the user as he/she transitions from one high-level state to the next. The states are shown in boldface type. Adaptation is illustrated in each state through annotated rules selected from the N-CHIME rule base and presented in English-like form. The high-level states and transitions in this scenario are those identified in Fig. 13.7, with state transition paths labeled S1 through S5. The specific transition that occurs at any point in an interactive session is determined by either an adaption decision or the operation the user selects.

1. **Session Login.** Each user has an individual I.D. Until the user is identified, no adaptation can occur. The user model contains the fact that this user is an N-CHIME novice.
2. **Identify Modeling Goal** (H0). Several goals are predefined and are found in the *goals* menu. Goal selection activates the corresponding task plan, which defines an idealized path through the high-level state graph. The only adaptation at this point concerns the appearance of the visible interface, which may vary depending on previously specified user preferences. Selecting the goal *run stored model* results in a state transition along Path S1 to State H1.
3. **Specify Model Name** (H1). The first step is to specify the name of the HSL program. Two means are available: a browse/retrieval tool or a dialog box into which the name is typed. Sample adaptation rules for this state are:

   IF   user is Novice AND goal is RunStoredModel
   THEN   message "Browser is invoked automatically"; invoke BrowserTool;
   IF   user is Apprentice AND goal is RunStoredModel
   THEN   message "Unless you know the pathname, use the Browser"

   Since the conditions of the first rule are met, it is fired and its actions are carried out. In this case, N-CHIME automatically selects the means for name specification. This is an example of *decision bypassing*. The rationale is that use of the browse/retrieval tool, which allows selection from a list of HSL programs, is easier for the novice than is the use of the dialog box. The novice is automatically transitioned along Path S2 to State H2. The apprentice user (next higher expertise level above novice) in a similar situation is able to select the file specification method, but is given *advice* regarding that decision. The apprentice who chooses to use the dialog box will also be transitioned to State H2, but via Path S3.

   Notice that three components of the knowledge representation scheme are involved in adaptive decision-making. The high-level state determines which set of rules to evaluate. The rules themselves determine under what conditions adaptation occurs and what form it takes, and the user model provides information utilized in rule conditions.
4. **Conceptualize** (H2). Once the novice has selected an HSL program using the browse/retrieval tool, N-CHIME effects the transition to this new high-level state. Several new operations are now available, including the ability to edit the textual version of the program. Sample adaptation rules for this state are:

> IF   user is Novice AND goal is RunStoredModel
> THEN   message "Compiler is invoked automatically";
>   invoke CompileTool;
> IF   user is Apprentice AND goal is RunStoredModel
> THEN   message "Based on your goal, Compile is the best
>   choice";
> IF   CheckStateExpertise(Conceptualize)
> THEN   SetStateExpertise(Conceptualize)

The first two rules demonstrate the same types of adaptation as those in the previous state. The next logical step toward the novice's goal is to compile the selected HSL program. That choice is made by the system. The novice is thereby transitioned along Path S4 to State H4. The apprentice user is advised to select *Compile* but is free to choose. Other choices available include those to invoke the text editor tool or the graphic editor tool.

The third rule checks the user's history in using this high-level state. That history is stored in the user model. If it indicates that the user's state-specific expertise rating should be updated (i.e., CheckStateExpertise returns *true*), then that will occur. This rating reflects only the user's experience in this high-level state and must be distinguished from the N-CHIME expertise rating, which appears in the rule conditions of this example.

5. **Compile Program** (H4). The novice user was transitioned here by N-CHIME as a consequence of the previous automatic action and successful compilation. Adaptation in this state for the novice running a stored HSL model takes the same form as before; the decision to run the program is made for the user. Thus, once the user specified the HSL program in Step 3, all subsequent decisions were made by N-CHIME based on the stated session goal.

6. **Specify Program** (H3). Suppose the N-CHIME apprentice elected in Step 4 to invoke the text editor, and after its use he/she was transitioned here via path S5. Following is one of the rules defined for this state.

> IF   user is Apprentice AND goal is RunStoredModel AND
>   previous selection was TextualEdit
> THEN   message "Use of the Text Editor was inconsistent with
>   your goal"

This rule applies to a very specific situation. An apprentice user, who has stated *run stored model* as the session goal, decided, once the stored model was retrieved, to invoke the text editor. Since the action most consistent with the stated goal would have been to compile it instead, N-CHIME provides *feedback* concerning that decision.

13.8.6. Interface Software Architecture

Prototype B was implemented in C++ (Stroustrup, 1986). The hardware platform was an NCR PC 916, running under NCR DOS. Two design approaches, one general and one specific to user interface design, were applied to N-CHIME. First, it used *object-oriented* design. The software system is viewed as focusing on objects rather than on processes (Booch, 1991). Second, it utilizes an extended UIMS model. Both were described in Chapter 8.

The object-oriented specification technique is based on nodes as descriptors of N-CHIME components. The abstract interface model consists of a network of these nodes. Besides the nodes for high-level states (H-nodes), it contains lower-level nodes (L-nodes) and tool objects, as described in Chapter 11. Other node types include the rules to control adaptation (R-nodes) and nodes for the supportive knowledge (K-nodes). The latter two, along with the H-nodes, are especially relevant to the expert system. These correspond to the state, rule, and model components, respectively, of the knowledge representation models depicted in Fig. 13.9.

The interface system design also includes two special object types, the *help object* and the *user model*. Both are refinements of the K-node. Any object in the N-CHIME design may have a help object attached to it. The help object contains information about the associated object, which can be presented to the user upon request. The user model contains the interface system's description of the current user, which is crucial for rendering adaptation decisions as described earlier. Its attributes fall into three general categories: global, state-specific, and operation-specific. Each global attribute is a single variable representing either a preference or an expertise rating (novice, apprentice, expert). State-specific expertise consists of a rating of N-CHIME expertise for each high-level state. Each rating is calculated based on state- and operation-specific monitored values, which are collected upon state transition or operation selection.

The N-CHIME interface specification itself consists of networks of objects created from the different object classes. These networks are complex; the H-node network alone is similar in structure and complexity to the user state scenario graph (Fig. 11.1). Every high-level interaction state can be represented as a mapping from a subnetwork of nodes to objects visible on the screen (Sanderson, 1991). A notable feature of the interface specification method developed for N-CHIME is that this mapping can be carried out in a straightforward manner. It is accomplished by associating node classes with widget classes. A widget is an object which can be displayed on the display screen, as indicated in Chapter 8. At runtime, a widget is bound to a node so that the results of widget manipulations by the user can be communicated to the node, and changes to nodes can be reflected on the visible interface.

13.9.   Observations on Results

The evaluation methods for Prototypes A and B are summarized in the companion book (Treu, 1994). Results generally indicate improvements due to the adaptive design, especially in numbers of errors committed but also in the times taken to complete tasks. However, there were also some negative indicators. For example, some users expressed reservations about an adaptive interface seemingly taking away the feeling of being in charge. Indeed, a lot of room exists for differences in opinion on adaptive interface design. Yet, evidence suggests that its potential is great. At the same time, the designer's task is extremely complex. Although we have implemented only selected forms of adaptation, substantial amounts of time and effort were required. Much more research and development are necessary to advance the methodology for adaptive interface design and to gain wider acceptance of such interfaces.

Exercises

13.1. With reference to the symmetric adaptation model of Fig. 13.1, an important point is made in the text about ensuring that the user is informed and retains control over what happens at the interface, regardless of whether he/she is the adapted or the adaptee. Identify any safety mechanisms that can be built into the interface to support this requirement. Is it realistic for a user to always know what an (intelligent) interface is doing, presumably for the user's benefit? Discuss the pros and cons.

13.2. With reference to the knowledge-based model discussed in Section 13.4, the representation of knowledge in terms of its structural bases has been covered extensively (Treu, 1992). What interface structures are reflected by (a) the knowledge-based model itself, and (b) the ES upon which the model becomes dependent? Explain.

13.3. For each of (a) factual, (b) procedural, and (c) heuristic knowledge, give an example of an HCI-oriented production rule. Relate your examples to an application domain of your choosing.

13.4. Describe how the partitioning of knowledge, e.g., according to Figs. 13.3

and 13.9, is likely to render the ES performance in the interface system more efficient.

13.5. Function (13.5) basically implies that the interface designer, as the expert, has relegated further responsibility for changing (or dynamically "re-designing") the interface to an ES. What does that suggest about the role played by the HCI design expert in providing for an intelligent interface, as compared with the roles played by domain experts in the design of ESs in other application areas, such as medical diagnosis? In what ways are the roles (a) similar and (b) different? What are the respective advantages and disadvantages, especially with regard to designing ESs that are reliable and effective?

13.6. The condition-based model of Section 13.6 suggests that the designer must be able to meet all of the conditions (Fig. 13.4), or answer the questions they imply, in order to carry out a successful adaptive design. Is there a particular order, or sequence of steps, which the designer should follow toward meeting all of the conditions? If so, outline it. If there are alternatives, describe them and explain why they exist.

13.7. With regard to Prototype A, which interface structures (Treu, 1992) are reflected by its design? Would it be possible (a) to change or replace those structures, or (b) to do without them altogether, and still retain the intended adaptive capabilities for the domain of interest? Discuss.

13.8. Repeat Exercise 13.7 for Prototype B.

13.9. Find a description of another adaptive interface design (different from those discussed in the text) in one of the resources cited. Try to select a design that involves a well-structured application domain. Present it in terms of the condition-based model of Section 13.6, in a manner similar to (but more abbreviated than) what is done for each of the two prototypes.

13.10. Repeat Exercise 13.9, but do so by trying to find an adaptive design that involves an application domain that is not as "structurable" as M&S (or as the application you chose for Exercise 13.9).

BIBLIOGRAPHY

ACKERMANN, D., AND TAUBER, M. J. (eds.), 1990, *Mental Models and Human–Computer Interaction 1*, North-Holland, Amsterdam.

ALLEN, R. B., 1982, Cognitive factors in human interaction with computers, *Behav. Inf. Technol.* 1(3):257–278.

ANDERSON, J. R., 1985, *Cognitive Psychology and Its Implications*, 2nd ed., Freeman, San Francisco.

ARNETT, K.P., AND TRUMBLY, J., 1991, Performance relationship considerations for user interface design, in *Human Factors in Information Systems: An Organization Perspective* (J. M. Carey, ed.), Ablex, Norwood, N.J., pp. 105–116.

ASH, S. E., HAY, J., AND DIAMOND, R. M., 1960, Perceptual organization in serial rote-learning, *Am. J. Psychol.* 73:194–198.

BACH, M. J., 1986, *The Design of the UNIX Operating System*, Prentice–Hall, Englewood Cliffs, N.J.

BAECKER, R., 1980, Towards an effective characterization of graphical interaction, in *Methodology of Interaction* (R. A. Guedj, P. J. W. ten Hagen, F. R. A. Hopgood, H. A. Tucker, and D. A. Duce, eds.), North-Holland, Amsterdam, pp. 127–147.

BAECKER, R. M., AND BUXTON, W. A. S. (eds.), 1987, *Readings in Human–Computer Interaction—A Multidisciplinary Approach*, Morgan Kaufmann Publishers, San Mateo, Calif.

BANKS, J., AND CARSON, J. S., 1985, Process-interaction simulation languages, *Simulation* 44(5):225–235.

BARFIELD, L., 1993, *The User Interface: Concepts & Design*, Addison–Wesley, Reading, Mass.

BELLOTTI, V., 1993, Integrating theoretician's and practitioners' perspectives with design rationale, *Human Factors in Computing Systems*, INTERCHI'93 *Conference Proceedings*, ACM, pp. 101–106.

BENBASAT, I., AND TODD, P., 1993, An experimental investigation of interface design alternatives: Icon vs. text and direct manipulation vs. menus, *Int. J. Man Mach. Stud.* 38:369–402.

BENBASAT, I., AND WAND, Y., 1984, A structured approach to designing human–computer dialogues, *Int. J. Man Mach. Stud.* 21:105–126.

BENNETT, J. L., 1972, The user interface in interactive systems, in *Annual Review of Information Science and Technology* (C. Cuadra, ed.), 7:159–196.

BENNETT, J. L., 1977, User-oriented graphics systems for decision support in unstructured tasks, in *User-Oriented Design of Interactive Graphics Systems* (S. Treu, ed.), ACM Press, New York, pp. 3–11.

BENNETT, J. L., 1986, Observations on meeting usability goals for software products, *Behav. Inf. Technol.* 5:183–193.

BIERMAN, A. W., FINEMAN, L., AND HEIDLAGE, J. F., 1992, A voice- and touch-driven natural language editor and its performance, *Int. J. Man Mach. Stud.* 37:1–21.

BLANKENBERGER, S., AND HAHN, K., 1991, Effects of icon design on human–computer interaction, *Int. J. Man Mach. Stud.* 35:363–377.

BLY, S. A., AND ROSENBERG, J. K., 1986, A comparison of tiled and overlapping windows, *Human Factors in Computing Systems*, CHI'86 *Conference Proceedings*, ACM, pp. 101–106.

BOBROW, D. G., AND STEFIK, M., 1983, *The LOOPS Manual*, Xerox Corp.

BØDKER, S., 1991, *Through the Interface—A Human Activity Approach to User Interface Design*, Lawrence Erlbaum Associates, Hillsdale, N.J.

327

328

BOOCH, G., 1991, *Object Oriented Design With Applications*, Benjamin/Cummings, Menlo Park, Calif.

BOOTH, P., 1989, *An Introduction to Human–Computer Interaction*, Lawrence Erlbaum Associates, Hillsdale, N.J.

BOURNIQUE, R., 1981, User-Oriented Features and Language-Based Agents—A Study of Graphical Interaction Language Specification, Ph.D. dissertation, Department of Computer Science, University of Pittsburgh, Pittsburgh, Pa.

BOURNIQUE, R., AND TREU, S., 1985, Specification and generation of variable, personalized graphical interfaces, *Int. J. Man Mach. Stud.* **22**:663–684.

BROWN, C. M., 1988, *Human–Computer Interface Design Guidelines*, Ablex, Norwood, N.J.

BUCHANAN, B. G., AND SHORTLIFFE, E. H. (eds.), 1984, *Rule-Based Expert Systems*, Addison–Wesley, Reading, Mass.

BUDDE, R., KAUTZ, K., KUHLENKAMP, K., AND ZUELLIGHOVEN, H., 1992, *Prototyping: An Approach to Evolutionary System Development*, Springer-Verlag, Berlin.

BUSH, V., 1945, As we may think, *Atlantic Monthly* **176**:101–108.

BUXTON, W., LAMB, M. R., SHERMAN, D., AND SMITH, K. C., 1983, Towards a comprehensive user interface management system, *Comput. Graphics* **17**(3):35–42.

CALLAHAN, J., HOPKINS, D., WEISER, M., AND SHNEIDERMAN, B., 1988, An empirical comparison of pie vs. linear menus, *Human Factors in Computing Systems, CHI'88 Conference Proceedings*, ACM, pp. 95–100.

CARBONELL, J. R., ELKIND, J. I., AND NICKERSON, R. S., 1968, On the psychological importance of time in a time sharing system, *Hum. Factors* **10**(2):135–142.

CARD, S. K., MORAN, T. P., AND NEWELL, A., 1980a, Computer text editing: An information processing analysis of a routine cognitive skill, *Cognit. Psychol.* **12**:32–74.

CARD, S. K., MORAN, T. P., AND NEWELL, A., 1980b, The keystroke model for user performance time with interactive systems, *Commun. ACM* **23**(7):396–410.

CARD, S. K., MORAN, T. P., AND NEWELL, A., 1983, *The Psychology of Human–Computer Interaction*, Lawrence Erlbaum Associates, Hillsdale, N.J.

CARD, S. K., MACKINLAY, J. D., AND ROBERTSON, G. G., 1990, The design space of input devices, *Human Factors in Computing Systems, CHI'90 Conference Proceedings*, pp. 117–124.

CARENINI, G., AND MOORE, J. D., 1993, Generating explanations in context, *Proceedings of the 1993 International Workshop on Intelligent User Interfaces*, Orlando, Fla., pp. 175–182.

CAREY, J. M. (ed.), 1991, *Human Factors in Information Systems: An Organization Perspective*, Ablex, Norwood, N.J.

CARROLL, J. M., 1984, Minimalist training, *Datamation*, Nov. 1, pp. 125–136.

CARROLL, J. M. (ed.), 1987, *Interfacing Thought: Cognitive Aspects of Human–Computer Interaction*, MIT Press, Cambridge, Mass.

CARROLL, J. M., AND THOMAS, J. C., 1982, Metaphor and the cognitive representation of computing systems, *IEEE Trans. Syst. Man Cybern.* **12**(2):107–116.

CARTER, J. A., JR., 1991, Combining task analysis with software engineering in a methodology for designing interactive systems, in *Taking Software Design Seriously—Practical Techniques for Human–Computer Interaction Design* (J. Karat, ed.), Academic Press, New York, pp. 209–234.

CARTER, J. A., LUKEY, J. M., AND SCHWEIGHARDT, M. F., 1991, The action-modifier-object-attribute (AMOA) classification of user-oriented functions, *Int. J. Man Mach. Stud.* **34**:1–22.

CHADWICK, M., AND HANNAH, J. A., 1986, *Expert Systems for Personal Computers*, Sigma Press, Washington, D.C.

CHANG, S. K., 1987, Visual languages: A tutorial and survey, *IEEE Software* pp. 29–39.

CHANG, S. K., ICHIKAWA, T., AND LIGOMENIDES, P. A. (eds.), 1986, *Visual Languages*, Plenum Press, New York.

CHI, U. H., 1985, Formal specification of user interfaces: A comparison and evaluation of four axiomatic approaches, *IEEE Trans. Software Eng.* **SE-11**(8):671–685.

CHIANESE, A., CORDELLA, L. P., DESANTO, M., AND VENTO, M., 1992, Classifying character shapes, in *Visual Form Analysis and Recognition* (C. Arcelli, L. P. Cordella, and G. S. diBaja, eds.), Plenum Press, New York, pp. 155–164.

CLEMENT, D., 1984, The role of documentation in human–computer interaction, in *Human–Computer Interaction* (G. Salvendy, ed.), North-Holland Elsevier, Amsterdam, pp. 203–206.

COHEN, D. I. A., 1986, *Introduction to Computer Theory*, Wiley, New York.

COHEN, M., AND LUDWIG, L. F., 1991, Multidimensional audio window management, *Int. J. Man Mach. Stud.* **34**:319–336.

COHILL, L. F., 1984, A taxonomy of user–computer interface functions, in *Human–Computer Interaction, Vol. 1* (G. Salvendy, ed.), North-Holland Elsevier, Amsterdam, pp. 125–128.

CONKLIN, J., 1987, Hypertext: An introduction and survey, *IEEE Comput.* **20**(9):17–41.

CROFT, W. B., 1984, The role of context and adaptation in user interfaces, *Int. J. Man Mach. Stud.* **21**:283–292.

CUSHMAN, W. H., OJHA, P. S., AND DANIELS, C. M., 1990, Usable OCR: What are the minimum performance requirements? *Human Factors in Computing Systems, CHI'90 Conference Proceedings*, ACM, pp. 145–151.

DAGWELL, R., AND WEBER, R., 1983, System designers' user models: A comparative study and methodological critique, *Commun. ACM* **26**:987–997.

DAYTON, T., 1991, Cultivated eclecticism as the normative approach to design, in *Taking Software Design Seriously—Practical Techniques for Human–Computer Interaction Design* (J. Karat, ed.), Academic Press, New York, pp. 21–44.

DE BAAR, D. J. M. J., FOLEY, J. D., AND MULLET, K. F., 1992, Coupling application design and user interface design, *Human Factors in Computing Systems, CHI'92 Conference Proceedings*, ACM, pp. 259–266.

DEGREENE, K. B., 1991, Emergent complexity and person–machine systems, *Int. J. Man Mach. Stud.* **35**:219–234.

DOURISH, P., AND BLY, S., 1992, Portholes: Supporting awareness in a distributed work group, *Human Factors in Computing Systems, CHI'92 Conference Proceedings*, ACM, pp. 541–547.

DRAPER, S. W., AND NORMAN, D. A., 1985, Software engineering for user interfaces, *IEEE Trans. Software Eng.* **SE-11**(3):252–258.

DRURY, C. G., PARAMORE, B., VanCOTT, H. P., GREY, S. M., AND CORLETT, E. M., 1987, Task analysis, in *Handbook of Human Factors* (G. Salvendy, ed.), Wiley, New York, p. 370.

DUFFY, T. M., PALMER, J. E., AND MEHLENBERGER, B., 1993, *Online Help: Design and Evaluation*, Ablex, Norwood, N.J.

DURHAM, I., LAMB, D., AND SAXE, J., 1983, Spelling correction in user interfaces, *Commun. ACM* **26**(10):764–773.

EBERTS, R. E., AND BITTIANDA, K. P., 1993, Preferred mental models for direct manipulation and command-based interfaces, *Int. J. Man Mach. Stud.* **38**:769–785.

EDMONDS, E. A., 1981, Adaptive man–computer interfaces, in *Computing Skills and the User Interface* (Coombs and Alty, eds.), Academic Press, New York.

EDMONDS, E. A., 1982, The man–computer interface: A note on concepts and design, *Int. J. Man Mach. Stud.* **16**:231–236.

ELWART-KEYS, M., HALONEN, D., HORTON, M., KASS, R., AND SCOTT, P., 1990, User interface requirements for face to face groupware, *Human Factors in Computing Systems, CHI'90 Conference Proceedings*, ACM, pp. 295–301.

ENGELBART, D. C., 1963, A conceptual framework for augmentation of man's intellect, in *Vistas in Information Handling, Vol. 1* (Howerton and Weeks, eds.), Spartan Books, Washington, D.C., pp. 1–29.

ENGELBART, D. C., AND ENGLISH, W. K., 1968, A research center for augmenting human intellect, *Proceedings of Fall Joint Computer Conference*, AFIPS, Montvale Press, Montvale, N.J., pp. 395–410.

ERO, J., AND VAN LIERE, R., 1988, User interface management systems, in *Advances in Computer Graphics III* (M. M. de Ruiter, ed.), Springer-Verlag, Berlin, pp. 99–131.

FAIRLEY, R., 1985, *Software Engineering Concepts*, McGraw–Hill, New York.

FALZON, P. (ed.), 1990, *Cognitive Ergonomics: Understanding, Learning, and Designing Human–Computer Interaction*, Academic Press, New York.

FIRTH, C., AND THOMAS, R. C., 1991, The use of command language grammar in a design tool, *Int. J. Man Mach. Stud.* **34**:479–496.

FISCHER, G., 1993, Shared knowledge in cooperative problem-solving systems—Integrating adaptive and adaptable components, in *Adaptive User Interfaces: Principles and Practice* (M. Schneider-Hufschmidt, T. Kuehme, and U. Malinowski, eds.), North-Holland Elsevier, Amsterdam, pp. 49–68.

FISHER, R. B., 1989, *From Surfaces to Objects: Computer Vision and Three Dimensional Analysis*, Wiley, New York.

FISHMAN, G. S., 1978, *Principles of Discrete Event Simulation*, Wiley, New York.

FOLEY, J. D., 1979, The structure of interactive command languages, in *Methodology of Interaction* (R. A. Guedj, P. J. W. ten Hagen, F. R. A. Hopgood, H. A. Tucker, and D. A. Duce, eds.), North-Holland, Amsterdam, pp. 227–234.

FOLEY, J. D., 1987, Interfaces for advanced computing, *Sci. Am.* **257**(4):126–135.

FOLEY, J. D., AND WALLACE, V. L., 1974, The art of natural graphic man–machine conversation, *Proc. IEEE*, Special Issue on Computer Graphics **62**(4):462–471.

FOLEY, J. D., WALLACE, V. L., AND CHAN, P., 1984, The human factors of computer graphics interaction techniques, *IEEE Comput. Graphics* **4**(1):13–48.

FOLEY, J. D., GIBBS, C., KIM, W. C., AND KOVACEVIC, S., 1988, A knowledge-based user interface management system, in *Human Factors in Computing Systems, CHI'88 Conference Proceedings*, ACM, pp. 67–72.

FOLEY, J. D., VAN DAM, A., FEINER, S. K., AND HUGHES, J. F., 1990, *Computer Graphics—Principles and Practice*, 2nd ed., Addison–Wesley, Reading, Mass.

FUNKE, D. J., NEAL, J. G., AND PAUL, R. D., 1993, An approach to intelligent automated window management, *Int. J. Man Mach. Stud.* **38**:949–983.

GAINES, B., 1981, The technology of interaction-dialogue programming rules, *Int. J. Man Mach. Stud.* **14**:133–150.

GAINES, B. R., AND SHAW, M. L. G., 1983, Dialog engineering, *Designing for Human–Computer Communication*, Academic Press, New York, pp. 23–53.

GAINES, B. R., AND SHAW, M. L. G., 1986, From timesharing to the sixth generation: The development of human–computer interaction, Part I, *Int. J. Man Mach. Stud.* **24**:1–27.

GAIT, J., 1985, An aspect of aesthetics in human–computer communications: Pretty windows, *IEEE Trans. Software Eng.* **SE-11**:714–717.

GASEN, J. B., AND AIKEN, P., 1993, Report on the CHI'92 Workshop on Lessons Learned from Teaching HCI: Challenges, innovations and visions, *SIGCHI Bull.* **25**:5–7.

GAVER, W. W., 1993, Synthesizing auditory icons, *Human Factors in Computing Systems, INTERCHI'93 Conference Proceedings*, ACM, pp. 228–235.

GAVER, W., MORAN, T., LOEVSTRAND, L., DOURISH, P., CARTER, K., AND BUXTON, W., 1992, Realizing a video environment: EuroPARC's RAVE system, *Human Factors in Computing Systems, CHI'92 Conference Proceedings*, ACM, pp. 27–35.

GENTNER, D., AND STEVENS, A. L. (eds.), 1983, *Mental Models*, Lawrence Erlbaum Associates, Hillsdale, N.J.

GIESKENS, D. F., AND FOLEY, J. D., 1992, Controlling user interface objects through pre- and postconditions, *Human Factors in Computing Systems, CHI'92 Conference Proceedings*, ACM, pp. 189–194.

GITTINS, D., 1986a, Icon-based human–computer interaction, *Int. J. Man Mach. Stud.* **24**:519–543.

GITTINS, D., 1986b, *Query Language Systems*, Arnold, London.

GOETTLER, H., 1992, Diagram editors = graphs + attributes + graph grammars, *Int. J. Man Mach. Stud.* **37**:481–502.

GOLDBERG, A., AND ROBSON, D., 1983, *Smalltalk-80 The Language and its Implementation*, Addison–Wesley, Reading, Mass.

GOLDBERG, D., AND RICHARDSON, G., 1993, Touch-typing with a stylus, *Human Factors in Computing Systems, INTERCHI'93 Conference Proceedings*, ACM, pp. 80–87.

GOOD, M. D., WHITESIDE, J. A., WIXON, D. R., AND JONES, S. J., 1984, Building a user-derived interface, *Commun. ACM* **27**(10):1032–1043.

GOODFELLOW, M. J., 1986, WHIM, the window handler and input manager, *IEEE Comput. Graphics Appl.* **6**(5):46–52.

GORDON, G., 1978, *System Simulation*, 2nd ed., Prentice–Hall, Englewood Cliffs, N.J.

GOULD, J. D., AND LEWIS, C., 1985, Designing for usability: Key principles and what designers think, *Commun. ACM* **28**(3):300–311.

GRAY, W. D., JOHN, B. E., AND ATWOOD, M. E., 1992, The precis of project Ernestine or an overview of a validation of GOMS, *Human Factors in Computing Systems, CHI'92 Conference Proceedings*, ACM, pp. 307–312.

GREEN, M., 1981, A methodology for the specification of graphical user interfaces, *Comput. Graphics* **15**(3):99–108.

GREEN, M., 1985, The University of Alberta User Interface Management System, *Proceedings of SIG-GRAPH '85*, pp. 205–213.

GREIF, I., 1988, *Computer-Supported Cooperative Work: A Book of Readings*, Morgan Kaufman, San Mateo, Calif.

GRUDIN, J., 1989, The case against user interface consistency, *Commun. ACM* **32**:1164–1173.

GRUDIN, J., 1992, Consistency, standards, and formal approaches to interface development and evaluation, *Trans. Inf. Syst.* **10**:103–111.

GUEST, S. P., 1982, The use of software tools for dialogue design, *Int. J. Man Mach. Stud.* **16**(3):263–285.

GUGERTY, L., 1993, The use of analytical models in human–computer–interface design, *Int. J. Man Mach. Stud.* **38**:625–660.

GUILLEMETTE, R. A., 1991, The usability criterion for designing information systems: A conspectus, in *Human Factors in Information Systems: An Organization Perspective* (J. M. Carey, ed.), Ablex, Norwood, N.J., pp. 65–87.

GUINDON, R. (ed.), 1988, *Cognitive Science and Its Applications for Human–Computer Interaction*, Lawrence Erlbaum Associates, Hillsdale, N.J.

GUYNES, J. L., 1988, Impact of system response time on state anxiety, *Commun. ACM* **31**(3):342.

HALASZ, F., 1988, Reflections on notecards: Seven issues for the next generation of hypermedia systems, *Commun. ACM* **31**(7):836–851.

HANAU, P., AND LENOROVITZ, D., 1980, Prototyping and simulation tools for user/computer dialogue design, *Comput. Graphics* **14**(3):271–278.

HANUSA, H., 1983, Tools and techniques for the monitoring of interactive graphics dialogues, *Int. J. Man Mach. Stud.* **19**:163–180.

HARMON, P., MAUS, R., AND MORRISSEY, W., 1988, *Expert Systems: Tools and Applications*, Wiley, New York.

HARRISON, M. D., AND MONK, A. F. (eds.), 1986, *People and Computers: Designing for Usability*, Proceedings of Second Conference of the British Computer Society Human Computer Interaction Specialist Group, University of York, 23–26 September, 1986, Cambridge University Press, London.

HARRISON, M., AND THIMBLEBY, H. (eds.), 1990, *Formal Methods in Human–Computer Interaction*, Cambridge University Press, London.

HARTSON, H. R., SIOCHI, A. C., AND HIX, D., 1990, The UAN: User-oriented representation for direct manipulation interface design, *ACM Trans. Inf. Syst.* **8**:181–203.

HAUPTMANN, A. G., AND McAVINNEY, P., 1993, Gestures with speech for graphic manipulation, *Int. J. Man Mach. Stud.* **38**:231–249.

HAYES, P. J., AND REDDY, D. R., 1983, Steps toward graceful interaction in spoken and written man–machine communication, *Int. J. Man Mach. Stud.* **19**:231–284.

HAYES, P., BALL, E., AND REDDY, R., 1981, Breaking the man–machine communication barrier, *Computer* pp. 19–30.

HAYES-ROTH, F., WATERMAN, D. A., AND LENAT, D. B. (eds.), 1983, *Building Expert Systems*, Addison–Wesley, Reading, Mass.

HEBB, D. O., 1949, *The Organization of Behavior*, Wiley, New York.

HERBSLEB, J. D., AND KUWANA, E., 1993, Preserving knowledge in design projects: What designers need to know, *Human Factors in Computing Systems, INTERCHI'93 Conference Proceedings*, ACM, pp. 7–14.

HILL, R., 1986, Supporting concurrency, communication, and synchronization in human–computer interaction—the Sassafras UIMS, *ACM Trans. Graphics* **5**(3):179–210.

HODGES, M. E., AND SASNETT, R. M., 1992, *Multimedia Computing: Case Studies from MIT Project Athena*, Addison–Wesley, Reading, Mass.

HOPGOOD, F. R. A., DUCE, D., FIELDING, E., ROBINSON, K., AND WILLIAMS, A. (eds.), 1986, *Methodology of Window Management*, Springer-Verlag, Berlin.

HOROWITZ, E., 1983, *Fundamentals of Programming Languages*, Computer Science Press, Washington, D.C.

HOUDE, S., 1992, Iterative design of an interface for easy 3-D direct manipulation, *Human Factors in Computing Systems, CHI'92 Conference Proceedings*, ACM, pp. 135–142.

HOUGHTON, R. C., JR., 1984, Online help systems: A conspectus, *Commun. ACM* **27**(2): 126–133.

HUNT, E. B., 1962, Memory and concept learning, in *Concept Learning*, Wiley, New York.

HURLEY, W. D., 1993, A process model for interactive systems, *J. Syst. Integration* **3**(3/4): 251–271.

HUTCHINS, E. L., HOLLAN, J. D., AND NORMAN, D. A., 1986, Direct manipulation interfaces, in *User Centered System Design: New Perspectives on Human–Computer Interaction* (D. A. Norman and S. W. Draper, eds.), Lawrence Erlbaum Associates, Hillsdale, N.J., pp. 87–124.

INNOCENT, P. R., 1982, Towards self-adaptive interface systems, *Int. J. Man Mach. Stud.* **16**:287–299.

JACKSON, P., 1986, *Introduction to Expert Systems*, Addison–Wesley, Reading, Mass.

JACOB, R. J. K., 1985, A state transition diagram language for visual programming, *IEEE Comput.* **18**(8):51–59.

JACOB, R. J. K., 1990, What you look at is what you get: Eye movement-based interaction techniques, *Human Factors in Computing Systems, CHI'90 Conference Proceedings*, ACM, pp. 11–18.

JACOB, R. J. K., AND SIBERT, L. E., 1992, The perceptual structure of multidimensional input device selection, *Human Factors in Computing Systems, CHI'92 Conference Proceedings*, ACM, pp. 211–218.

JAMES, M. G., 1991, PRODUSER: PROcess for Developing USER interfaces, in *Taking Software Design Seriously—Practical Techniques for Human–Computer Interaction Design* (J. Karat, ed.), Academic Press, New York, pp. 235–255.

JANSEN, H., NULLMEIER, E., AND ROEDIGER, K. H., 1985, Handsketching as a human factors aspect in graphical interaction, *Comput. Graphics* **9**(3):195–210.

JEFFRIES, R., AND ROSENBERG, J. K., 1987, Comparing a form-based and a language-based user interface for instructing a mail program, *Proceedings of CHI + GI 1987 Conference*, ACM, Toronto, pp. 261–266.

JOHN, B. E., AND VERA, A. H., 1992, A GOMS analysis of a graphic, machine-paced, highly interactive task, *Human Factors in Computing Systems, CHI'92 Conference Proceedings*, ACM, pp. 251–258.

JOHNSON, J., 1992, Selectors: Going beyond user–interface widgets, *Human Factors in Computing Systems, CHI'92 Conference Proceedings*, ACM, pp. 273–279.

JONES, M. K., 1989, *Human–Computer Interaction: A Design Guide*, Educational Technology Pubs, Englewood Cliffs, N.J.

KACMAR, C. J., 1991, An experimental comparison of text and icon menu formats, in *Human Factors in Information Systems: An Organization Perspective* (J. M. Carey, ed.), Ablex, Norwood, N.J., pp. 27–41.

KARAT, J. (ed.), 1991, *Taking Software Design Seriously—Practical Techniques for Human–Computer Interaction Design*, Academic Press, New York.

KARAT, J., AND BENNETT, J. L., 1991, Using scenarios in design meetings—A case study example, in *Taking Software Design Seriously—Practical Techniques for Human–Computer Interaction Design* (J. Karat, ed.), Academic Press, New York, pp. 63–94.

KIERAS, D., 1993, Diagrammatic displays for engineered systems: Effects of human performance in interacting with malfunctioning systems, *Int. J. Man Mach. Stud.* **36**: 861–895.

KIM, J., AND LERCH, F. J., 1992, Towards a model of cognitive processing in logical design: Comparing object-oriented and traditional functional decomposition software methodologies, *Human Factors in Computing Systems, CHI'92 Conference Proceedings*, ACM, pp. 489–498.

KLINGER, A. (ed.), 1991, *Human–Machine Interactive Systems*, Plenum Press, New York.

KOBSA, A., AND WAHLSTER, W. (eds.), 1989, *User Models in Dialog Systems*, Springer-Verlag, Berlin.

KOFFLER, R. P., 1986, Classifying users: A hard look at some controversial issues, *SIGCHI Bull.* **18**:75–83.

KRILOFF, H. Z., 1977, Human factor considerations for interactive display systems, in *User-Oriented Design of Interactive Graphics Systems* (S. Treu, ed.), ACM Press, New York, pp. 45–52.

KUBRICK, S. (dir.), 1968, *2001: A Space Odyssey*.

LANSDALE, M. W., SIMPSON, M., AND STROUD, T. R. J., 1990, A comparison of words and icons as cue enrichers in an information retrieval task, *Behav. Inf. Technol.* **9**:111–131.

LARKIN, J. H., AND SIMON, H. A., 1987, Why a diagram is (sometimes) worth ten thousand words, *Cognitive Sci.* **11**:65–99.

LAW, A. M., AND KELTON, W. D., 1991, *Simulation Modeling and Analysis*, McGraw–Hill, New York.

LEDGARD, H., WHITESIDE, J. A., SINGER, A., AND SEYMOUR, W., 1980, The natural language of interactive systems, *Commun. ACM* **23**(10):556–563.

LEWIS, T. G., AND SMITH, B. J., 1979, *Computer Principles of Modeling and Simulation*, Houghton Mifflin, Boston.

LICKLIDER, J. C. R., 1960, Man–computer symbiosis, *IRE Trans. Hum. Factors Electron.* 4–11.

LICKLIDER, J. C. R., 1968, Man–computer communication, *Annu. Rev. Inf. Sci. Technol.* **3**: 201–240.

LINDQUIST, T. E., 1985, Assessing the usability of human–computer interfaces, *IEEE Software* pp. 74–82.

LISKOV, B., AND GUTTAG, J., 1986, *Abstraction and Specification in Program Development*, MIT Press and McGraw–Hill, Cambridge, Mass., and New York.

LOEWGREN, J., AND NORDQVIST, T., 1992, Knowledge-based evaluation as design support for graphical user interfaces, *Human Factors in Computing Systems, CHI'92 Conference Proceedings*, ACM, pp.181–188.

LONG, J., 1989, Cognitive ergonomics and human–computer interaction: An introduction, in *Cognitive Ergonomics and Human–Computer Interaction* (J. Long and A. Whitefield, eds.), Cambridge University Press, London,pp. 4–34.

LONG, J., AND WHITEFIELD, A. (eds.), 1989, *Cognitive Ergonomics and Human–Computer Interaction*, Cambridge University Press, London.

MACGREGOR, J. N., 1992, A comparison of the effects of icons and descriptors in videotex menu retrieval, *Int. J. Man Mach. Stud.* **37**:767–777.

McGREW, J. F., 1991, Tools for task analysis: Graphs and matrices, in *Taking Software Design Seriously—Practical Techniques for Human–Computer Interaction Design* (J. Karat, ed.), Academic Press, New York, pp. 287–314.

MACLEAN, A., YOUNG, R. M., AND MORAN, T. P., 1989, Design rationale: The argument behind the artifact, in *Human Factors in Computing Systems, CHI'89 Conference Proceedings*, ACM, pp.247–252.

MANARIS, B. Z., AND DOMINICK, W. D., 1993, NALIGE: A user interface management system for the development of natural language interfaces, *Int. J. Man Mach. Stud.* **38**:891–921.

MARCUS, R. S., 1983, An experimental comparison of the effectiveness of computers and humans as search intermediaries, *J. Am. Soc. Inf. Sci.* **34**(6):381–404.

MARTIN, J., 1973, *Design of Man–Computer Dialogues*, Prentice–Hall, Englewood Cliffs, N.J.

MAYHEW, D., 1992, *Principles and Guidelines in Software User Interface Design*, Prentice–Hall, Englewood Cliffs, N.J.

MEADOW, C. T., 1970, *Man–Machine Communication*, Wiley–Interscience, New York.

METCALFE, R. M., AND BOGGS, D. R., 1976, ETHERNET: Distributed packet switching for local computer networks, *Commun. ACM* **19**(7):395–404.

MILLER, G. A., 1956, The magical number seven, plus or minus two: Some limits on our capacity for processing information, *Psychol. Rev.* **63**:81–97.

MILLER, R. B., 1968, Response time in man–computer conversational transactions, *Proceedings of Fall Joint Computer Conference*, AFIPS, Vol. 33, Part 1, Montvale Press, Montvale, N.J., pp. 267–277.

MILLER, R. B., 1977, The human task as reference for system interface design, in *User-Oriented Design of Interactive Graphics Systems* (S. Treu, ed.), ACM Press, New York, pp. 97–100.

MILLER-JACOBS, H. M., 1991, Rapid prototyping: An effective technique for system development, in *Taking Software Design Seriously—Practical Techniques for Human–Computer Interaction Design* (J. Karat, ed.), Academic Press, New York, pp. 273–286.

MONTAZEMI, A. R., 1991, The impact of experience on the design of user interface, *Int. J. Man Mach. Stud.* **34**:731–749.

MORAN, T. P., 1981, The command language grammar: A representation for the user interface of interactive computer systems, *Int. J. Man Mach. Stud.* **15**:3–50.

MOSIER, J. N., AND SMITH, S. L., 1986, Application of guidelines for designing user interface software, *Behav. Inf. Technol.* **5**(1):39–46.

MOZEICO, H., 1982, A human/computer interface to accommodate user learning stages, *Commun. ACM* **25**(2):100–104.

MULLINS, P., 1990, The Network User Interface Substrate (NUIS): A Task-Oriented Reference Model, Ph.D. dissertation, Department of Computer Science, University of Pittsburgh, Pittsburgh, Pa.

MULLINS, P., AND TREU, S., 1993, A task-based cognitive model for user–network interaction: Defining a task taxonomy to guide the interface designer, *Interact. Comput.* **5**(2): 139–166.

MUTER, P., AND MAYSON, C., 1986, The role of graphics in item selection from menus, *Behav. Inf. Technol.* **5**:89–95.

MYERS, B. A., 1988, A taxonomy of window manager user interfaces, *IEEE Comput. Graphics Appl.*, pp. 65–84.

MYERS, B. A., AND ROSSON, M.B., 1992, Survey on user interface programming, *Human Factors in Computing Systems, CHI'92 Conference Proceedings*, ACM, pp.195–202.

NAGY, G., 1982, Optical character recognition: Theory and practice, in *Handbook of Statistics II* (L. Kanal and P. R. Krishnaiah, eds.), North-Holland, Amsterdam, pp. 621–649.

NELSON, T. H., 1965, A file structure for the complex, the changing, and the indeterminate, *Proceedings of ACM National Conference*, ACM, pp. 84–100.

NEWMAN, W., AND SPROULL, R., 1979, *Principles of Interactive Computer Graphics*, 2nd ed., McGraw–Hill, New York.

NICKERSON, R. S., 1977, On conversational interaction with computers, in *User-Oriented Design of Interactive Graphics Systems* (S. Treu, ed.), ACM Press, New York, pp. 101–113.

NICKERSON, R. S., 1986, *Using Computers: Human Factors in Computer Systems*, MIT Press, Cambridge, Mass.

NICKERSON, R. S., ELKIND, J. I., AND CARBONELL, J. R., 1968, Human factors and the design of time sharing computer systems, *Hum. Factors* **10**(2):127–134.

NIELSEN, J., 1990, The art of navigating through hypertext, *Commun. ACM* **33**(3):296–310.

NIEVERGELT, J., AND WEYDERT, J., 1980, Sites, modes, and trails: Telling the user of an interactive system where he is, what he can do, and how to get places, in *Methodology of Interaction* (R. A. Guedj, P. J. W., ten Hagen, F. R. A. Hopgood, H. A. Tucker, and D. A. Duce, eds.), North-Holland, Amsterdam, pp. 327–338.

NILSSON, N. J., 1982, *Principles of Artificial Intelligence*, Springer-Verlag, Berlin.

NORMAN, D. A., 1983, Some observations on mental models, in *Mental Models* (D. Gentner and L. A. Stevens, eds.), Lawrence Erlbaum Associates, Hillsdale, N.J., pp. 7–14.

NORMAN, D. A., 1988, *The Psychology of Everyday Things*, Basic Books, New York.

NORMAN, D. A., AND DRAPER, S. W. (eds.), 1986, *User Centered System Design: New Perspectives in Human–Computer Interaction*, Lawrence Erlbaum Associates, Hillsdale, N.J.

NORMAN, K. L., WELDON, L. J., AND SHNEIDERMAN, B., 1986, Cognitive layouts of windows and multiple screens for user interfaces, *Int. J. Man Mach. Stud.* **25**:229–248.

O'BRIEN, S. M., 1993, Knowledge-based systems in speech recognition: A survey, *Int. J. Man Mach. Stud.* **38**(1):71–95.

OLSEN, D., 1992, *User Interface Management Systems: Models and Algorithms*, Morgan Kaufman, San Mateo, Calif.

OLSEN, D. R., AND DEMPSEY, E. P., 1983, SYNGRAPH: A graphical user interface generator, *Comput. Graphics* 17(3):43–50.

OOPSLA, 1992, Conference on Object-Oriented Programming Systems, Languages, and Applications (A. Paepcke, ed.), 22 Oct. 1992, Vancouver, B.C.

PAAP, K. P., 1988, Design of menus, in *Handbook of Human–Computer Interaction* (M. Helander, ed.), Elsevier, Amsterdam, pp. 205–235.

PAYNE, S. J., AND GREEN, T. R. G., 1986, Task-action grammars: A model for the mental representation of task languages, *Hum. Comput. Interact.* 2(2):93–133.

PERLMAN, G., 1985, Making the right choices with menus, *Human–Computer Interaction— Interact '84*, North-Holland, Amsterdam, pp. 317–321.

PETERSON, J. L., AND SILBERSCHATZ, A., 1985, *Operating System Concepts*, 2nd ed., Addison–Wesley, Reading, Mass.

PFAFF, G. (eds), 1985, *User Interface Management Systems*, Springer-Verlag, Berlin.

PINSON, L. J., AND WIENER, R. S., 1988, *An Introduction to Object-Oriented Programming and Smalltalk*, Addison–Wesley, Reading, Mass.

PITTMAN, J. A., 1991, Recognizing handwritten text, *Human Factors in Computing Systems, CHI'91 Conference Proceedings*, ACM, pp. 271–275.

POLSON, P. G., 1988, The consequences of consistent and inconsistent user interfaces, in *Cognitive Science and Its Applications for Human–Computer Interaction* (R. Guindon, ed.), Lawrence Erlbaum Associates, Hillsdale, N.J., pp. 59–108.

PREECE, J. (ed.), 1993, *A Guide to Usability: Human Factors in Computing*, Addison–Wesley, Reading, Mass.

PRESSMAN, R. S., 1988, *Software Engineering: A Beginner's Guide*, McGraw–Hill, New York.

REIN, G. L., AND ELLIS, C. A., 1991, rIBIS: A real-time group hypertext system, *Int. J. Man Mach. Stud.* 34:349–367.

REISNER, P., 1981, Formal grammar and human factors design of an interactive graphics system, *IEEE Trans. Software Eng.* SE-7:229–240.

RICH, E., 1979, User modelling via stereotypes, *Cognit. Sci.* 3:329–354.

RICH, E., 1983, Users are individuals: Individualizing user models, *Int. J. Man Mach. Stud.* 18:199–214.

RICH, E., 1984, Natural-language interfaces, *IEEE Comput.* September 39–47.

ROGERS, Y., AND OBERNE, D. J., 1985, Some psychological attributes of potential computer command names, *Behav. Inf. Technol.* 4(4):349–365.

ROLSTON, D. W., 1988, *Principles of Artificial Intelligence and Expert System Development*, McGraw–Hill, New York.

ROSENTHAL, R., 1976, Network access techniques—A review, *Proceedings of 1976 NCC* pp. 495–500.

ROUFF, C., AND HOROWITZ, E., 1991, A system for specifying and rapidly prototyping user interfaces, in *Taking Software Design Seriously—Practical Techniques for Human–Computer Interaction Design* (J. Karat, ed.), Academic Press, New York, pp. 257–271.

ROZIN, R., AND TREU, S., 1991, A hybrid implementation of a process-oriented language for system simulation, *Software-Practice and Experience* 21(6):557–579.

RUBINSTEIN, R., AND HERSH, H. M., 1984, Design philosophy, in *The Human Factor: Designing Computer Systems for People*, Digital Press, Burlington, Mass., pp. 12–22.

RUMELHART, D. E., AND NORMAN, D. A., 1988, Representation in memory, in *Steven's Handbook of Experimental Psychology*, 2nd ed., Vol. 2 (Atkinson et al., eds.), Wiley, New York, pp. 511–587.

SACKMAN, H., 1968, Time-sharing versus batch processing: The experimental evidence, *Proceedings of Spring Joint Computer Conference* pp. 1–10.

SACKMAN, H., 1970, *Man–Computer Problem Solving: Experimental Evaluation of Time-Sharing and Batch Processing*, Auerbach Publishers, Princeton, N.J.

SANDERSON, D. P., 1991, Structured Design of an Adaptive Human–Computer Interface, Ph.D. dissertation, Department of Computer Science, University of Pittsburgh, Pittsburgh, Penn.

SANDERSON, D. P., AND TREU, S., 1991, Designing the intelligent component of a user interface for modeling and simulation, *Proceedings of the Artificial Intelligence and Simulation Conference*, New Orleans, April 1–5, pp. 47–52.

SANDERSON, D. P., AND TREU, S., 1993, Adaptive user interface design and its dependence on structure, in *Adaptive User Interfaces: Principles and Practice* (M. Schneider-Hufschmidt, T. Kuehme, and U. Malinowski, eds.), North-Holland Elsevier, Amsterdam, 1993.

SANDERSON, D. P., ROZIN, R., SHARMA, R., AND TREU, S., 1991. The hierarchical simulation language (HSL): A versatile tool for process-oriented simulation, *ACM Trans. Model. Simul.* 1(2):113–153.

SANTHANAM, R., AND WIEDENBECK, S., 1993, Neither novice nor expert: The discretionary user of software, *Int. J. Man Mach. Stud.* 38:201–229.

SCHEIFLER, R. W., AND GETTYS, J., 1986, The X window system, *ACM Trans. Graphics* 5(2): 79–109.

SCHIELE, F., AND GREEN, T., 1990, HCI formalisms and cognitive psychology: The case of task-action grammar, in *Formal Methods in Human–Computer Interaction* (M. Harrison and H. Thimbleby, eds.), Cambridge University Press, London, pp. 9–62.

SCHNEIDER-HUFSCHMIDT, M., KUEHME, T., AND MALINOWSKI, U. (eds.), 1993, *Adaptive User Interfaces: Principles and Practice*, North-Holland Elsevier, Amsterdam.

SCHULMAN, A., 1973, Recognition memory and the recall of spatial location, *Mem. Cognit.* 1:256–260.

SCHVANEVELDT, R., COOKE, N., DURVO, F., ONORATO, L., AND BAILEY, G., 1984, A taxonomy of human–computer interactions: Toward a modular interface, in *Human–Computer Interaction* (G. Salvendy, ed.), Elsevier, Amsterdam, pp. 121–124.

SCHWAB, E. C., AND NUSSBAUM, H. C., 1986a, *Pattern Recognition by Humans and Machines, Volume 1, Speech Perception*, Academic Press, New York.

SCHWAB, E. C., AND NUSSBAUM, H. C., 1986b, *Pattern Recognition by Humans and Machines, Volume 2, Visual Perception*, Academic Press, New York.

SCOTT, M. L., AND YAP, S.-K., 1988, A grammar-based approach to the automatic generation of user–interface dialogues, *Human Factors in Computing Systems, CHI'88 Conference Proceedings*, ACM, pp. 73–78.

SEARS, A., AND SHNEIDERMAN, B., 1991, High precision touchscreens: Design strategies and comparisons with a mouse, *Int. J. Man Mach. Stud.* 34:593–613.

SHACKEL, B. (ed.), 1981, *Man–Computer Interaction: Human Factors Aspects of Computers & People*, NATO Advanced Studies Series E, Applied Sciences-No. 44, Sijthoff and Noordhoff, Winchester, Mass.

SHACKEL, B., 1985, Ergonomics in information technology in Europe—A review, *Behav. Inf. Technol.* 4(4):263–287.

SHACKEL, B., 1987, Human factors of input and output devices, in *Techniques for Computer Graphics* (Rogers and Earnshaw, eds.), Springer-Verlag, Berlin.

SHEEHAN, J. J., AND SOSNA, M. (eds.), 1991, *The Boundaries of Humanity—Humans, Animals, Machines*, University of California Press, Berkeley.

SHEPHERD, M. A., AND WATTERS, C., 1985, A common interface for accessing document retrieval systems and DBMS for retrieval of bibliographic data, *Inf. Process. Manage.* 21(2):127–138.

SHNEIDERMAN, B., 1980, *Software Psychology: Human Factors in Computer and Information Systems*, Winthrop Publishers, Cambridge, Mass.

SHNEIDERMAN, B., 1982, The future of interactive systems and the emergence of direct manipulation, *Behav. Inf. Technol.* 1(3):237–256.

SHNEIDERMAN, B., 1983, Direct manipulation: A step beyond programming languages, *Computer* 57–69.

SHNEIDERMAN, B., 1992, *Designing the User Interface—Strategies for Effective Human Computer Interaction*, 2nd ed., Addison–Wesley, Reading, Mass.

SIBERT, J. L., HURLEY, W. D., AND BLESER, T. W., 1988, Design and implementation of an object-oriented user interface management system, in *Advances in Human–Computer Interaction*, Vol. II (H. R. Hartson and D. Hix, eds.), Ablex Publishing, Norwood, N.J., pp. 175–213.

SIMES, D. K., AND SIRSKY, P. A., 1985, Human factors: An exploration of the psychology of human–computer dialogues, in *Advances in Human–Computer Interaction*, Vol. I (H. R. Hartson, ed.), Ablex Publishing, Norwood, N.J., pp. 49–103.

SMITH, D., IRBY, C., KIMBALL, R., VERPLANK, W., AND HARSLEM, E., 1982, Designing the star user interface, *Byte* 7(4):242–282.

SMITH, M. J., 1984, Human factors issues in VDT use: Environmental and workstation design considerations, *IEEE Comput. Graphics Appl.* 4(11):56–63.

SMITH, S. L., 1986, Standards versus guidelines for designing user interface software, *Behav. Inf. Technol.* 5(1):47–61.

SOMBERG, B. L., 1987, A comparison of rule-based and positionally constant arrangements of computer menu items, *Proceedings of CHI + GI 1987 Conference*, ACM, Toronto, pp. 255–260.

SONDHEIMER, N. K., AND RELLES, N., 1982, Human factors and user assistance in interactive computing systems: An introduction, *IEEE Trans. Syst. Man Cybern.* 12(2): 102–107.

SPARCK-JONES, K., 1989, Realism about user modeling, in *User Models in Dialog Systems* (A. Kobsa and W. Wahlster, eds.), Springer-Verlag, Berlin, pp. 343–363.

SPENCE, R. H., 1985, *Computer Usability Testing and Evaluation*, Prentice–Hall, Englewood Cliffs, N.J.

STAGGERS, N., AND NORCIO, A. F., 1993, Mental models: Concepts for human–computer interaction research, *Int. J. Man Mach. Stud.* 38:587–605.

STASKO, J., BADRE, A., AND LEWIS, C., 1993, Do algorithm animations assist learning? An empirical study and analysis, *Human Factors in Computing Systems, INTERCHI'93 Conference Proceedings*, ACM, pp.61–66.

STIFELMAN, L. J., ARONS, B., SCHMANDT, C., AND HULTEEN, E. A., 1993, VoiceNotes: A speech interface for a hand-held voice notetaker, *Human Factors in Computing Systems, INTERCHI'93 Conference Proceedings*, ACM, pp.179–186.

STROUSTRUP, B., 1986, *The C++ Programming Language*, Addison–Wesley, Reading, Mass.

SULLIVAN, J. W., AND TYLER, S. W. (eds.), 1991, *Intelligent User Interfaces*, ACM Press, Frontier Series, Addison–Wesley, Reading, Mass.

SUTCLIFFE, A. G., AND McDERMOTT, M., 1991, Integrating methods of human–computer interface design with structured system development, *Int. J. Man Mach. Stud.* 34: 631–655.

SUTHERLAND, I. E., 1963, Sketchpad: A man–machine graphical communication system, *AFIPS Conf. Proc.* 23:329–346.

SWARTOUT, W., AND BALZER, R., 1982, On the inevitable intertwining of specification and implementation, *Commun. ACM* 25(7):438–440.

TANENBAUM, A. S., 1988, *Computer Networks*, 2nd ed., Prentice–Hall, Englewood Cliffs, N.J.

TAUBER, M. J., 1988, On mental models and the user interface, in *Working with Computers* (T. R. G. Green et al., eds.), Academic Press, New York.

TAULBEE, O. E., TREU, S., AND NEHNEVAJSA, J., 1975, User orientation in networking, *Proceedings of National Computer Conference* pp. 637–644.

TE'ENI, D., 1990, Direct manipulation as a source of cognitive feedback: A human–computer experiment with judgment task, *Int. J. Man Mach. Stud.* 33:453–466.

TETZLAFF, L., AND SCHWARTZ, D. R., 1991, The use of guidelines in interface design, *Human Factors in Computing Systems, CHI'92 Conference Proceedings*, ACM, pp.329–333.

THIMBLEBY, H., 1990, *User Interface Design*, ACM Press, New York.

THOMAS, J. C., AND GOULD, J. D., 1975, A psychological study of query by example, *AFIPS Conf. Proc.* 44:439–445.

THORELL, L. G., AND SMITH, W. J., 1990, *Using Computer Color Effectively: An Illustrated Reference*, Prentice–Hall, Englewood Cliffs, N.J.

TREU, S., 1971, A conceptual framework for the searcher–system interface, in: *Interactive Bibliographic Search: The User/Computer Interface* (D. Walker, ed.), AFIPS Press, Montvale, N.J., pp. 53–66.

TREU, S., 1972, *A Computer Terminal Network for Transparent Stimulation of the User of an On-Line Retrieval System*, National Bureau of Standards, TN 732.

338 BIBLIOGRAPHY

TREU, S., 1975a, Interactive command language design based on required mental work, *Int. J. Man Mach. Stud.* **7**:135–149.

TREU, S., 1975b, On-line student debate: An experiment in communication using computer networks, *Int. J. Comput. Inf. Sci.* **4**(1):39–51.

TREU, S. (ed.), 1977, *User-Oriented Design of Interactive Graphics Systems*, Based on ACM/SIGGRAPH Workshop, October, 1986, Pittsburgh, ACM.

TREU, S., 1982, Uniformity in user–computer interaction languages: A compromise solution, *Int. J. Man Mach. Stud.* **16**:183–210.

TREU, S., 1985, Adaptive staging and advancement of user–computer interaction skills in office environments, *SIGOA Bull.* **6**(1,2):27–32.

TREU, S., 1988a, Designing a 'cognizant interface' between the user and the simulation software, *Simulation* **51**(6):227–234.

TREU, S., 1988b, Networkanschauung and complex information systems: Different viewpoints for usage, management, and research, *Int. J. Policy Inf.* **12**(1):27–38.

TREU, S., 1989, Recognition of logical interface structures to enhance human–computer interaction, *Int. J. Pattern Recognition Artif. Intell.* **3**(2):217–236.

TREU, S., 1990, 'Conceptual distance' and interface-supported visualization of information objects and patterns, *J. Visual Languages Comput.* **1**(4):369–388.

TREU, S., 1992, Interface structures: Conceptual, logical, and physical patterns applicable to human–computer interaction, *Int. J. Man Mach. Stud.* **37**:565–593.

TREU, S., 1994, *User Interface Evaluation: A Structured Approach*, Plenum Press, New York.

TREU, S., MULLINS, P., AND ADAMS, J., 1989, A network-wide information system: Multi-level context for the user at the workstation interface, *Inf. Syst.* **14**(5):393–406.

TREU, S., SANDERSON, D. P., ROZIN, R., AND SHARMA, R., 1990, Design process and decision rationale models for the N-CHIME interface system, *SIGCHI Bull.* **22**(1):73–79.

TREU, S., SANDERSON, D. P., ROZIN, R., AND SHARMA, R., 1991, High-level, three-pronged design methodology for the N-CHIME interface system software, *Inf. Software Technol.* **33**:306–320.

TRUMBLY, J. E., 1991, Adaptive user interface: The evolutionary mechanism in *Human Factors in Information Systems: An Organization Perspective* (J. M. Carey, ed.), Ablex, Norwood, N.J., pp. 17–25.

TRUMBLY, J. E., ARNETT, K. P., AND MARTIN, M. P., 1993, Performance effect of matching computer interface characteristics and user skill level, *Int. J. Man Mach. Stud.* **38**:713–724.

TUFTE, E., 1990, *The Visual Display of Quantitative Information*, Graphics Press, Washington, D.C.

TULLIS, T. S., 1983, The formatting of alphanumeric displays, *Hum. Factors* **25**(6):657–682.

TYLER, S., 1986, SAUCI: A Self-Adaptive User–Computer Interface, Ph.D. dissertation, Department of Computer Science, University of Pittsburgh, Pittsburgh, Pa.

TYLER, S. W., AND TREU, S., 1986, Adaptive interface design: A symmetric model and a knowledge-based implementation, *SIGOIS Bull.* **7**(2,3):53–60.

TYLER, S., AND TREU, S., 1989, An interface architecture to provide adaptive task-specific context for the user, *Int. J. Man Mach. Stud.* **30**(3):303–327.

ULICH, E., RAUTERBERG, M., MOLL, T., GREUTMANN, T., AND STROHM, O., 1991, Task orientation and user-oriented dialogue design, *Int. J. Hum. Comput. Interact.* **3**:117–144.

UTTING, K., AND YANKELOVICH, N., 1989, Context and orientation in hypermedia networks, *ACM Trans. Inf. Syst.* **7**(1):58–84.

VAN DER VEER, G. C., WIJK, R., AND FELT, M. A. M., 1990, Metaphors and metacommunication in the development of mental models, in *Cognitive Ergonomics: Understanding, Learning, and Designing Human–Computer Interaction* (P. Falzon, ed.), Academic Press, New York, pp. 133–149.

VASSILIOU, Y., AND JARKE, M., 1984, Query languages—A taxonomy, in *Human Factors and Interactive Computing Systems* (Y. Vassiliou, ed.), Ablex, Norwood, N.J., pp. 47–82.

VENOLIA, D., 1993, Facile 3D direct manipulation, *Human Factors in Computing Systems, INTERCHI'93 Conference Proceedings*, ACM, pp. 31–36.

WAERN, Y., 1987, Mental models in learning computerized tasks, in *Psychological Issues of*

Human–Computer Interaction in the Work Place (M. Frese, E. Ulich, and W. Dzida, eds.), Elsevier, Amsterdam, pp. 275–294.

WALKER, D. E. (ed.), 1971, *Interactive Bibliographic Search: The User/Computer Interface*, Proceedings of Workshop on "The User Interface for Interactive Search of Bibliographic Data Bases," Palo Alto, 14–15 January 1971, AFIPS Press, Montvale, N.J.

WALKER, N., SMELCER, J. B., AND NILSEN, E., 1991, Optimizing speed and accuracy of menu selection: A comparison of walking and pull-down menus, *Int. J. Man Mach. Stud.* **35**:871–890.

WASSERMAN, A. I., 1985, Extending state transition diagrams for the specification of human–computer interaction, *IEEE Trans. Software Eng.* **SE-11**(8):699–713.

WASSERMAN, A. I., PIRCHER, P. A., SHEWMAKE, D. T., AND KERSTEN, M. L., 1986, Developing interactive information systems with the user software engineering methodology, *IEEE Trans. Software Eng.* **SE-12**(2):326–345.

WATERMAN, D. A., AND HAYES-ROTH, F. (eds.), 1978, *Pattern-Directed Inference Systems*, Academic Press, New York.

WHITEFIELD, A., 1990, Human–computer interaction models and their roles in the design of interactive systems, in *Cognitive Ergonomics: Understanding, Learning, and Designing Human–Computer Interaction* (P. Falzon, ed.), Academic Press, New York, pp. 7–25.

WHITESIDE, J., BENNETT, J., AND HOLTZBLATT, K., 1988, Usability engineering: Our experience and evolution, in *Handbook of Human–Computer Interaction* (M. Helander, ed.), North-Holland, Amsterdam, pp. 791–817.

WIEDERHOLD, G., 1983, *Database Design*, McGraw–Hill, New York.

WILLIGES, R. C., 1987, The use of models in human–computer interface design, *Ergonomics* **30**:491–502.

WINOGRAD, T., AND FLORES, F., 1986, *Understanding Computers and Cognition: A New Foundation for Design*, Ablex, Norwood, N.J.

WONG, P. C. S., AND REID, E. R., 1982, FLAIR—A user interface dialog design tool, *Comput. Graphics* **16**(3):87–98.

WOODS, D. D., 1984, Visual momentum: A concept to improve the cognitive coupling of person and computer, *Int. J. Man Mach. Stud.* **21**:229–244.

WORLD BOOK DICTIONARY, THE, 1975, (C. L. Barnhart, editor-in-chief), Doubleday, New York.

WROBLEWSKI, D. A., 1991, The construction of human–computer interfaces considered a craft, in *Taking Software Design Seriously—Practical Techniques for Human–Computer Interaction Design* (J. Karat, ed.), Academic Press, New York, pp. 1–19.

ZHAO, R., 1993, Incremental recognition in gesture-based and syntax-directed diagram editors, *Human Factors in Computing Systems, INTERCHI'93 Conference Proceedings*, ACM, pp.95–100.

ZIEGLER, J. E., AND FAHNRICH, K. P., 1988, Direct manipulation, in *Handbook of Human–Computer Interaction* (M. Helander, ed.), North-Holland, Amsterdam, pp. 123–133.

ZLOOF, M. M., 1975, Query by example, *AFIPS Conf. Proc.* **44**:431–437.

INDEX